Hutchinson GCSE World History Factfinder

Arrow Books

Arrow Books Limited
20 Vauxhall Bridge Road
London SW1V 2SA

An imprint of the Random Century Group

London Melbourne Sydney Auckland
Johannesburg and agencies throughout
the world

First published in Great Britain in 1991

1 3 5 7 9 10 8 6 4 2

Set in Century Old Style

Phototypeset by Intype, London

ISBN 0 09 993530 9

Printed and bound in Great Britain by
Cox & Wyman Ltd, Reading, Berkshire

Consultant Editor
Robert Unwin BA, PhD, PhD

Project Editor
Penny Hext

Text Editors
Claire Jenkins
Denise Dresner
Rosamund Sales

Art Assistant
Terence Caven

Design
Edna A. Moore, Tek Art

Acknowledgements
The Mansell Collection
Popperfoto

A

abdication crisis the constitutional upheaval of the period 16 Nov – 10 Dec 1936, brought about by King Edward VIII's decision to marry Wallis Simpson, an American divorcee. The marriage of the 'Supreme Governor' of the Church of England to a divorced person was considered unsuitable and the king was finally forced to abdicate on 10 Dec when he left for voluntary exile in France. He was created Duke of Windsor, and married Mrs Simpson on 3 June 1937.

abstract art nonrepresentational art. Ornamental art without figurative representation occurs in most cultures. The modern abstract movement in sculpture and painting emerged in Europe and North America between 1910 and 1920. Two approaches produce different abstract styles: images that have been 'abstracted' from nature to the point where they no longer reflect a conventional reality, and nonobjective, or 'pure', art forms, supposedly without reference to reality.

Abyssinia former name of ◊Ethiopia.

Acheson Dean (Gooderham) 1893–1971. US politician; as undersecretary of state 1945–47 in ◊Truman's Democratic administration, he was associated with George C Marshall in preparing the ◊Marshall Plan, and succeeded him as secretary of state 1949–53.

Adenauer Konrad 1876–1967. German Christian Democrat politician, chancellor of West Germany 1949–63. With the French president de Gaulle he achieved the postwar reconciliation of France and Germany and strongly supported all measures designed to strengthen the Western bloc in Europe.

Adenauer was mayor of his native city of Cologne from 1917 until his imprisonment by Hitler in 1933 for opposition to the Nazi regime. After the war he headed the Christian Democratic Union and became chancellor.

Afghanistan mountainous, landlocked country in S central Asia, bounded N by the USSR, W by Iran, and S and E by Pakistan.

history Part of the Persian Empire in the ancient world, Afghanistan first became an independent emirate 1747. During the 19th century three Afghan Wars were fought to secure British interests in India and counter the growing Russian influence. Britain guaranteed Afghanistan's independence with the Treaty of Rawalpindi 1919, and helped General Nadir Shah to the throne in 1929. Although he attempted to modernize the country he was assassinated 1933 by Muslim extremists. His son, Mohammad Zahir Shah ruled 1933–73. During the 1950s, Lt-Gen Sardar Mohammad Daud Khan governed as prime minister and introduced a programme of social and economic modernization with Soviet aid. Opposition to his authoritarian rule forced Daud's resignation 1963; the king was made a constitutional monarch, but political parties were outlawed.

the republic After a famine 1972, General Daud Khan overthrew the monarchy in a Soviet-backed military coup 1973. The King fled to exile, and a republic was declared. Daud introduced moderate policies, built up support among minority ethnic groups, and reduced Afghanistan's dependence on the Soviet Union by drawing closer to the nonaligned and Middle East oil states (where many Afghans were employed). A new presidential constitution was adopted 1977, although undermined by fundamentalist Muslim insurgents funded by Libya, Iran, and Pakistan. In 1978 President Daud was assassinated in a military coup, and Nur Mohammad Taraki, the imprisoned leader of the radical Khalq (masses) faction of the banned PDPA, took charge as president of a revolutionary council. A one-party constitution was adopted, a Treaty of Friendship and Mutual Defence signed with the USSR, and major reforms introduced. Conservative Muslims opposed these initiatives, thousands of refugees fled to Iran and Pakistan, and there was an uprising in the Herat region. Taraki was replaced 1979 by foreign minister Hafizullah Amin.

Soviet invasion Internal unrest continued, and the USSR organized a further coup Dec 1979. Hafizullah Amin was executed and Babrak Karmal (1929–), the exiled leader of the gradualist Parcham (banner) faction of the PDPA, was installed as leader. The numbers of Soviet forces in Afghanistan grew to over 120,000 by 1985 as Muslim guerrilla resistance by the 'mujaheddin' ('holy warriors') continued. A war of attrition developed, with the USSR failing to gain control of rural areas.

Soviet withdrawal In May 1986 Karmal was replaced as PDPA leader by the Pushtun (Pathan) former secret police chief Dr Najibullah Ahmadzai (1947–), and several non-Communist politicians joined the new government. In Oct 1986, 8,000 Soviet troops were withdrawn as a goodwill gesture, and in Jan 1987 the Afghan government announced a six-month unilateral ceasefire. The Najibullah government extended the ceasefire, and in Nov 1987 a new multi-party Islamic constitution was ratified in an attempt to promote 'national reconciliation'. In Feb 1988 the USSR announced that it would withdraw its forces in a phased manner between May 1988 and Feb 1989, and in April 1988 the Afghan and Pakistan governments signed an agreement providing for non-interference in each others' internal affairs and the voluntary return of refugees, with the USA and the USSR acting as guarantors. On the completion of Soviet troop withdrawal in Feb 1989 a 'state of emergency' was imposed by the government. The guerrillas, whose commanders by now controlled a number of regions outside Kabul, demanded Najibullah's resignation. The civil war, in which since 1980 15,000 Soviet troops, 70,000 Afghan security force personnel, and more than a million Afghan civilians have died, and more than five million fled as refugees to Iran and Pakistan, thus continued. The ruling PDPA was renamed the Homeland Party (*Hezb-e Watan*) in June 1990, with President Najibullah being elected its chair.

African National Congress (ANC) multiracial nationalist organization formed in South Africa 1912 to extend the franchise to the whole population and end all racial discrimination there. Its president is Oliver Tambo, and vice president from 1990 Nelson ◊Mandela. Although originally nonviolent, the ANC was banned by the government from 1960 to Jan 1990, and in exile in Mozambique developed a military wing, ***Umkhonto we Sizwe***, which engaged in sabotage and guerrilla training. The armed struggle was suspended Aug 1990 when the organization's headquarters were moved to Johannesburg.

The ANC is supported by the Organization of African Unity as a movement aimed at introducing majority rule in South Africa. Former ANC leaders include Albert Luthuli and Solomon Plaatje. Several imprisoned leaders were released Oct 1989; Mandela in Feb 1990.

African nationalism political movement for the unification of Africa. African nationalism has its roots among the educated elite (mainly 'returned' Americans of African descent and freed slaves or their descendents) in W Africa in the 19th century. Christian Mission-educated, many challenged overseas mission control and founded independent churches. These were often involved in anti-colonial rebellions, for example in Natal 1906 and Nyasaland 1915. The Kitwala (Watchtower Movement) and Kimbanguist churches provided strong support for the nationalist cause in the 1950s. Early African political organizations included the Aborigines Rights Protection Society in the Gold Coast 1897, the ◊African National Congress in South Africa 1912, and the National Congress of West Africa 1920.

After World War I nationalists fostered moves for self determination. The ◊Fourteen Points encouraged such demands in Tunisia, and delegates to London 1919 from the Native National Congress in South Africa stressed the contribution to the war effort by the South African Native Labour Corps. Most nationalist groups functioned within the territorial boundaries of single colonies, for example the Tanganyika African Association and the Rhodesian Bantu Voters Association. One or two groups, including the National Congress of British West Africa, had wider pan-African visions. The first pan-African Congress was held in London 1900 and others followed after 1919.

Pan-African sentiment in Africa and the Americas was intensified with the Italian invasion of ◊Ethiopia in 1935. By 1939 African nationalist groups existed in nearly every territory of the continent. Africa's direct involvement in World War II, the weakening of the principal colonial powers, increasing anti-colonialism from America (see ◊Atlantic Charter), and Soviet criticism of imperialism inspired African nationalists.

Since 1958 pan-Africanism has become partially absorbed into wider Third World movements. In May 1963 it was decided to establish the Organization of African Unity (OAU).

Agadir Incident 1911 also known as the ***Second Moroccan Crisis*** international crisis provoked by Kaiser Wilhelm II of Germany. By sending the gunboat *Panther* to demand territorial concessions from the French, he hoped to drive a wedge into the Anglo-French ◊entente cordiale. In fact, German aggression during the second Moroccan crisis merely served to reinforce Anglo-French fears of Germany's intentions. The crisis gave rise to the term 'gunboat diplomacy'.

aggression in politics, an unprovoked attack

often involving an escalating series of threats aimed at intimidating an opponent. The actions of Nazi Germany, under Adolf Hitler in the 1930s, leading to World War II were considered to be aggressive. The invasion of Kuwait by Iraq in 1990 was condemned by the United Nations as an act of aggression.

agriculture the practice of farming, including the cultivation of the soil (for growing crops) and the raising of livestock. Mechanization made considerable progress in the US and Europe during the 19th century. After World War II, there was an explosive growth in the use of agricultural chemicals: herbicides, insecticides, fungicides, and fertilizers. In the 1960s there was development of high-yielding species in the ***green revolution*** of the Third World, and the industrialized countries began intensive farming of cattle, poultry, and pigs. From the 1970s there has been a movement – ***organic farming*** – towards more sophisticated natural methods without chemical sprays and fertilizers. In the 1980s, hybridization by genetic engineering methods and pest control by the use of chemicals with added animal secretions (pheromones) were developed.

overproduction The greater efficiency in agriculture achieved since the 19th century, coupled with post-World War II government subsidies for domestic production in the US and the European Community (EC), have led to the development of high stocks, nicknamed 'lakes' (wine, milk) and 'mountains' (butter, beef, grain). There is no simple solution to this problem, as any large-scale dumping onto the market displaces regular merchandise. Increasing concern about the starving and the cost of storage has led the US and the EC to develop measures for limiting production, such as letting arable land lie fallow to reduce grain crops. The US has had some success at selling surplus wheat to the USSR when the Soviet crop is poor, but the overall cost of bulk transport and the potential destabilization of other economies acts against the high producers exporting their excess on a regular basis to needy countries. Intensive farming methods also contribute to soil erosion and water pollution.

AIDS abbreviation for ***acquired immune deficiency syndrome***, the newest and gravest of sexually transmitted diseases or STDs. It is caused by the human immunodeficiency virus (HIV), now known to be a retrovirus, an organism first identified 1983. HIV is transmitted in body fluids, mainly blood and sexual secretions.

The HIV virus may have originated in Africa, where the total number of cases up to Oct 1988 was 19,141. In Africa, the prevalence of AIDS among high-risk groups such as prostitutes may approach 30%. Previous reports of up to 80% of certain populations being affected are thought to have been grossly exaggerated by inaccurate testing methods.

In Britain, 1,422 people had died of AIDS by Oct 1989, and between 30,000 and 50,000 people were thought to be carriers of the disease. A 1989 UK government survey estimated that 1.6% of all British males aged around 30 would die of AIDS-related diseases. In the USA one million are thought to be infected with the virus.

aircraft carrier oceangoing naval vessel with a broad, flat-topped deck for launching and landing military aircraft; an effort to provide a floating military base for warplanes too far from home for refuelling, repairing, reconnaissance, escorting, and various attack and defence operations. The first purpose-designed aircraft carrier was the British HMS *Hermes*, completed 1913. In World War II the most famous was HMS *Ark Royal*, completed 1938. HMS *Ark Royal* was repeatedly falsely claimed as sunk by the Axis powers, and was eventually torpedoed off Gibraltar, foundering in tow Nov 1941. After World War II the cost and vulnerability of such large vessels were thought to have outweighed their advantages. However, by 1980 the desire to have a means of destroying enemy aircraft beyond the range of a ship's own weapons, especially on convoy duty, led to a widespread revival of aircraft carriers of 20,000–30,000 tonnes.

air force a nation's fighting aircraft and the organization that maintains them.

history The emergence of the aeroplane at first brought only limited recognition of its potential value as a means of waging war. Like the balloon, used since the American Civil War, it was considered a way of extending the vision of ground forces. A unified air force was established in the UK 1918, Italy 1923, France 1928, Germany 1935 (after repudiating the arms limitations of the Versailles treaty), and the USA 1947 (it began as the Aeronautical Division of the Army Signal Corps in 1907, and evolved into the Army's Air Service Division by 1918; by 1926 it was the Air Corps and in World War II the Army Air Forces). The main specialized groupings formed during World War I – such as ***combat***, ***bombing*** (see ◊bomb), ***reconnaissance***, and ***transport*** – were adapted and modified in World War II; activity was extended, with self-contained tactical air forces to meet the needs of ground commanders in the main theatres of land operations and for the attack on and defence of shipping over narrow seas.

In 1945–60 the piston engine was superseded by the jet engine, which propelled its craft at supersonic speeds; extremely precise electronic guidance systems lessened the difference between missile and aircraft; and flights of unlimited duration became possible with air-to-air refuelling. The US Strategic Air Command's bombers can patrol 24 hours a day armed with thermonuclear weapons. It was formerly anticipated that the pilot might become obsolete, but the continuation of conventional warfare and the evolution of tactical nuclear weapons have led in the 1970s and 1980s to the development of advanced combat aircraft able to fly supersonically beneath an enemy's radar on strike and reconnaissance missions, as well as so-called stealth aircraft that cannot be detected by radar.

Alamein, El, Battles of in World War II, two decisive battles in the western desert, N Egypt. In the ***First Battle of El Alamein*** 1–27 Jul 1942 the British 8th Army under Auchinleck held the German and Italian forces under Field Marshal Rommel. In the ***Second Battle of El Alamein*** 23 Oct–4 Nov 1942, Field Marshal Montgomery defeated Rommel.

Åland Islands (Finnish ***Ahvenanmaa*** 'land of waters') group of some 6,000 islands in the Baltic Sea, at the southern extremity of the Gulf of Bothnia. Swedish until 1809, the islands came, (with Finland), under Russian control. In 1917, at the time of the Russian Revolution, the Swedes unsuccessfully tried to recover the islands. In 1921, the League of Nations ruled that the islands remain under Finnish sovereignty, be demilitarized, and granted autonomous status. Although the islands' assembly voted for union with Sweden 1945, the 1921 declaration remains valid.

Albania country in SE Europe, bounded W and SW by the Mediterranean sea, N and E by Yugoslavia, and SE by Greece.

history Albania was part of the ◊Ottoman empire from 1468. The country became independent 1912 and a republic 1925. In 1928 President Ahmed Beg Zogu was proclaimed King Zog. Overrun by Italy and Germany 1939–44, Albania became a republic with a communist government 1946 after a guerrilla struggle led by Enver Hoxha (1908–85).

the Hoxha experiment At first closely allied with Yugoslavia, Albania backed ◊Stalin in his 1948 dispute with ◊Tito and developed close links with the USSR 1949–55, entering ◊Comecon 1949. Hoxha imposed a Stalinist system with rural collectivization, industrial nationalization, central planning, and one-party control. Mosques and churches were closed in an effort to create the 'first atheist state'. Hoxha remained a committed Stalinist and, rejecting ◊Khrushchev's denunciations of the Stalin era, broke off diplomatic relations with the USSR 1961 and withdrew from Comecon. Albania also severed diplomatic relations with China 1978, after the post-Mao accommodation with the US, choosing isolation and neutrality. The 'Hoxha experiment' left Albania with the lowest per capita income in Europe. Since his death 1985, there have been policy adjustments and a widening of external economic contacts. In Feb 1988 Albania attended the conference of Balkan states for the first time since the 1930s.

reform A proposal for release of some political prisoners gave the first indication that the reforms spreading in E Europe were having an impact in Albania. Opposition to the regime began to mount during 1990. In early July unprecedented anti-government street demonstrations errupted in the capital of Tirana. Diplomatic relations with the Soviet Union, which had been broken off in 1961, were restored and embassies re-established. In Dec 1990 amid continuing protests in Tirana and economic collapse, the Communist Party leadership announced that, as part of a fundamental revision of the Stalinist constitution, the existence of opposition parties had finally been authorized and the ban on religion lifted. Five hardline Politburo members were dismissed. Albania held elections (by secret ballot) to the People's Assembly in Feb 1991.

Algeciras Conference an international conference held Jan–April 1906 when France, Germany, Britain, Russia, and Austria-Hungary, together with the USA, Spain, the Low Countries, Portugal, and Sweden, met to settle the question of Morocco. The conference was prompted by increased German demands in what had traditionally been seen as a French area of influence, but it resulted in a reassertion of Anglo-French friendship and the increased isolation of Germany.

Algiers, Battle of the bitter conflict in Algiers 1954–62 between the Algerian nationalist population and the French colonial army and French settlers. The conflict ended with Algerian independence 1962.

Allende (Gossens) Salvador 1908–1973. Chilean left-wing politician. Elected president 1970 as the candidate of the Popular Front alliance, Allende never succeeded in keeping the electoral alliance together in government. His failure to solve the country's economic problems or to deal with political subversion allowed the army, backed by the CIA, to stage the 1973 coup (led by General Pinochet) which brought about the death of Allende and many of his supporters.

Allies, the in World War I, the 23 countries allied against the Central Powers (Germany, Austria-Hungary, Turkey and Bulgaria), including France, Italy, Russia, the UK and Commonwealth, and, in the latter part of the war, the USA; and in World War II, the 49 countries allied against the ◊Axis powers (Germany, Italy and Japan), including France, the UK and Commonwealth, the USA, and the USSR.

Amethyst Incident UK–China episode arising when on 20 Apr 1949 a British frigate, HMS *Amethyst*, sailing on the Chang Jiang (Yangtse) River was fired on by communist Chinese forces. The ship was trapped for 14 weeks before breaking free and completing the journey to the sea. The temporary detention of this British vessel has been interpreted as an attempt by the Chinese to assert their sovereignty over what had been considered an international waterway.

Amin Dada Idi 1926– . Ugandan politician, president 1971–79. He led the coup that deposed Milton Obote 1971, expelled the Asian community 1972, and exercised a reign of terror over his people. He fled to Libya when insurgent Ugandan and Tanzanian troops invaded the country 1979.

Amnesty International human-rights organization established in the UK 1961 to campaign for the release of political prisoners worldwide. It has 700,000 members, and section offices in 43 countries. Amnesty International is politically unaligned. The organization was awarded the Nobel Peace Prize 1977.

Amritsar Massacre also called ***Jallianwallah Bagh massacre*** the killing of 379 Indians (and wounding of 1,200) in Amritsar (the site of a Sikh religious shrine) in the Punjab 1919. British troops under General Edward Dyer (1864–1927) opened fire without warning on a crowd of some 10,000, assembled to protest against the arrest of two Indian National Congress leaders (see ◊Congress Party).

Dyer was subsequently censured and resigned his commission, but gained popular support in the UK for his action, both by mention in the House of Lords and by private subscriptions totalling £926,000. The favourable treatment Dyer received spurred Mahatma ◊Gandhi to a policy of active noncooperation with the British.

anarchism (Greek *anarkhos* 'without ruler') political belief that society should have no government, laws, police, or other authority, but should be a free association of all its members. It does not mean 'without order'; most theories of anarchism imply an order of a very strict and symmetrical kind, but they maintain that such order can be achieved by cooperation. Anarchism must not be confused with nihilism (a purely negative and destructive activity directed against society); anarchism is essentially a pacifist movement.

From the 1960s there were outbreaks of politically motivated violence popularly identified with anarchism; in the UK, the bombings and shootings carried out by the Angry Brigade 1968–71, and in the 1980s actions directed towards peace and animal-rights issues, and to demonstrate against large financial and business corporations.

ANC abbreviation for ◊***African National Congress***, South African nationalist organization.

Angola country in SW Africa, bounded to the west by the Atlantic ocean, to the N and NE by Zaïre, to the E by Zambia, and to the S by Namibia.

history Angola became a Portuguese colony in 1491 and an Overseas Territory of Portugal in 1951. In 1956 a movement for complete independence was established, the MPLA, based originally in the Congo. This was followed by the formation of two other nationalist movements, the National Front for the Liberation of Angola (FNLA), and the National Union for the Total Independence of Angola (UNITA). War for independence from Portugal broke out in 1961, involving all the factions, with MPLA supported by socialist and communist states, UNITA helped by the Western powers and FNLA backed by the 'non-left' power groups of southern Africa.

the republic Three months of civil war followed the granting of full independence in 1975, with MPLA and UNITA the main contestants and foreign mercenaries and South African forces helping FNLA. By 1975 MPLA, with the help of mainly Cuban forces, controlled most of the country and had established the People's Republic of Angola in Luanda. Agostinho Neto, the MPLA leader, became its first president. FNLA and UNITA had, in the meantime, proclaimed their own People's Democratic Republic of Angola, based in Nova Lisboa, renamed Huambo. President Neto died in 1979 and was succeeded by José Eduardo dos Santos, who maintained Neto's links with the Soviet bloc.

the Lusaka Agreement UNITA guerrillas, supported by South Africa, continued to operate and in 1980–81 South African forces raided Angola to attack bases of the South-West Africa People's Organisation (SWAPO), who were fighting for Namibia's independence. Angola supported Namibia's claim but South Africa and the US called for the withdrawal of Cuban troops from Angola as a precondition for South Africa's departure from Namibia. In 1983 South Africa proposed a complete withdrawal of its forces if Angola could guarantee that the areas vacated would not be filled by Cuban or SWAPO units. In 1984 Angola accepted South Africa's proposals, and a settlement was made (the Lusaka Agreement), whereby a Joint Monitoring Commission (JMC) was set up to oversee South Africa's withdrawal. In 1985 South Africa announced that this was complete and the mandate for the JMC was ended. In 1986 relations between the two countries deteriorated when further South African raids into Angola occurred. UNITA also continued to receive South African support. Despite the securing of a peace treaty with South Africa and Cuba in 1988, guerrilla activity by the UNITA rebels began again in 1989. In July 1990 rebel forces announced their willingness to sign a peace treaty and in Oct President dos Santos promised a return to multi-party politics.

Anschluss (German 'union') the annexation of Austria with Germany, accomplished by the German chancellor Adolf Hitler 12 Mar 1938.

Anti-Comintern Pact (Anti-Communist Pact) agreement signed between Germany and Japan 25 Nov 1936, opposing communism as a menace to peace and order. The pact was signed by Italy 1937 and by Hungary, Spain, and the Japanese puppet state of Manchukuo in 1939. While directed against the USSR, the agreement also had the effect of giving international recognition to Japanese rule in Manchuria.

anticommunism fierce antagonism towards communism, linked particularly with right-wing politician Joseph ◊McCarthy's activities in the USA during the 1950s. He made numerous unsubstantiated claims that the State Department had been infiltrated by Communist activity, thus triggering a wave of anti-communist hysteria. He did not succeed in identifying any Communists employed by the government.

anti-Semitism literally, prejudice against Semitic people (see Semite), but in practice it has meant prejudice or discrimination against, and persecution of, the Jews as an ethnic group. Anti-Semitism was a tenet of Hitler's Germany, and in the Holocaust of 1933–45 about 6 million Jews died in concentration camps and in local extermination ◊pogroms, such as the siege of the Warsaw ghetto. In the USSR and the Eastern bloc, as well as in Islamic nations, anti-Semitism exists and is promulgated by neofascist groups. It is a form of ◊racism.

Late 18th- and early 19th-century liberal thought improved the position of Jews in European society (in the Austro-Hungarian Empire they were allowed to own land)—for example, after the French Revolution the 'rights of man' were extended to French Jews 1790 until 19th-century nationalism and the rise of unscientific theories of race instigated new resentments. Anti-Semitism became strong in Austria, France, and Germany, and from 1881 pogroms in Poland and Russia caused refugees to flee to the USA, where freedom of religion was enshrined in the constitution, to the UK, and to other European countries as well as Palestine (see ◊Zionism). In the 20th century, fascism and the Nazi Party's application of racial theories led to organized persecution and genocide. After World War II, the creation of Israel 1948 provoked Palestinian anti-Zionism, backed by the Arab world. Anti-Semitism is still fostered by extreme right-wing groups, such as the National Front in the UK and France, the Neo-Nazis in the US and Germany, and the Palestine Liberation Organization in the Arab nations.

ANZAC acronym from the initials of the ***Australian and New Zealand Army Corps***, applied in general to all troops of both countries serving in World War I and to some extent those in World War II.

apartheid (Afrikaans 'apartness') the racial-segregation policy of the government of South Africa, which was legislated 1948, when the Afrikaner National Party gained power. Non-whites (Bantu, coloured or mixed, or Indian) do not share full rights of citizenship with the 4.5 million whites (for example, the 23 million black people cannot vote in parliamentary elections), and many public facilities and institutions were until 1990 and, in some cases, remain restricted to the use of one ethnic group only; the establishment of ◊Black National States is another manifestation of apartheid.

The term 'apartheid' was coined in the late 1930s by the South African Bureau for Racial Affairs (Sabra), which called for a policy of 'separate development' of ethnic groups.

Internally, organizations opposed to apartheid (such as the African National Congress and the United Democratic Front) were banned, and leading campaigners for its abolition, like Steve Biko, have been killed, or, like Archbishop Tutu, harassed. Anger at the policy has sparked off many uprisings, from ◊Sharpeville 1960 and Soweto 1976 to the Crossroads squatter camps 1986. There are anti-apartheid movements in many countries. In 1961 South Africa was forced to withdraw from the Commonwealth because of apartheid; during the 1960s and 1970s there were

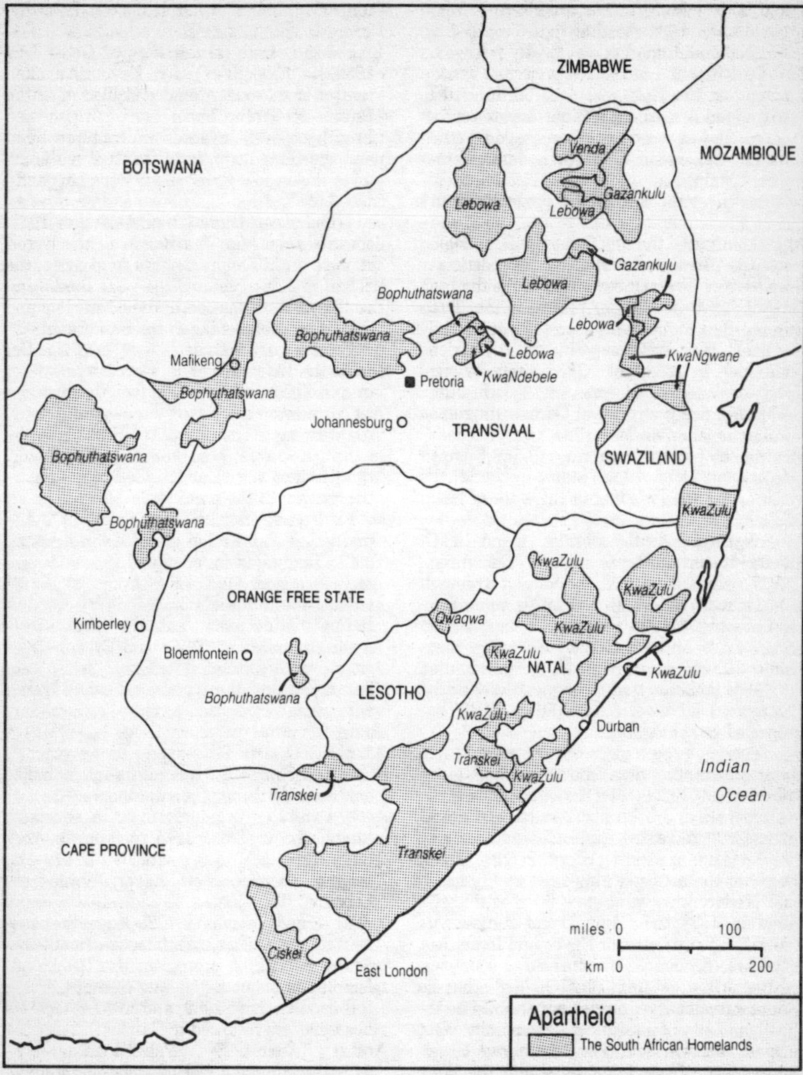

calls for international ◊sanctions, especially boycotts of sporting and cultural links; and in the 1980s advocates of sanctions extended them into trade and finance. The South African government's reaction to internal and international pressure was twofold: it abolished some of the more hated apartheid laws (the ban on interracial marriages was lifted 1985 and the pass laws, which restricted the movement of nonwhites, were repealed 1986); and it sought to replace the term 'apartheid' with 'plural democracy'. Under states of emergency 1985 and 1986 it used force to quell internal opposition, and from 1986 there was an official ban on the reporting of it in the media. In Oct 1989 President F W de Klerk permitted anti-apartheid demonstrations; the Separate Amenities Act was abolished 1990 and a new constitution promised. In 1990 Nelson Mandela, a leading figure in the African National Congress was finally released.

Apollo project US space project to land a person on the Moon, achieved 20 July 1969, when Neil Armstrong was the first to set foot there. He was accompanied on the Moon's surface by Col Edwin E Aldrin Jr; Michael Collins remained at the orbiting command controls. The total cost of the programme was over $24 billion.

appeasement the conciliatory policy adopted by the British government, in particular under Neville Chamberlain, towards the Nazi and Fascist dictators in Europe in the 1930s in an effort to maintain peace. It was strongly opposed by Winston Churchill, but the ◊Munich Agreement 1938 was almost universally hailed as its justification. Appeasement ended when Germany occupied Bohemia–Moravia Mar 1939.

Arab-Israeli Wars a series of wars between Israel and various Arab states in the Middle East since the founding of the state of Israel 1948.

background Arab opposition to an Israeli state began after the Balfour Declaration 1917, which supported the idea of a Jewish national homeland. In the 1920s there were anti-Zionist riots in Palestine, then governed by the UK under a League of Nations mandate. In 1936 an Arab revolt led to a British royal commission that recommended partition (approved by the United Nations 1947, but rejected by the Arabs).

Tension in the Middle East remained high, and the conflict was sharpened and given East–West overtones by Soviet adoption of the Arab cause and US support for Israel. Several wars only increased the confusion over who had a claim to what territory. Particularly in view of the area's strategic sensitivity as an oil producer, pressure grew for a settlement, and in 1978 the Camp David Agreements brought peace between Egypt and Israel, but this was denounced by other Arab countries. Israel withdrew from Sinai 1979–82, but no final agreement on Jerusalem and the establishment of a Palestinian state on the West Bank was reached. The continuing Israeli occupation of the Gaza Strip and the West Bank in the face of a determined uprising (intifada) by the residents of these areas has seemingly hardened attitudes on both sides.

First Arab-Israeli War 14 Oct 1948–13 Jan/24 Mar 1949. As soon as the independent state of Israel had been proclaimed by the Jews in Palestine, it was invaded by combined Arab forces. The Israelis defeated them and went on to annex territory until they controlled 75% of what had been Palestine under British mandate.

Second Arab-Israeli War 29 Oct–4 Nov 1956, the ***Suez War***. After Egypt had taken control of the Suez Canal and blockaded the Straits of Tiran, Israel, with British and French support, invaded and captured Sinai and the Gaza Strip, from which it withdrew under heavy US pressure after the entry of a UN force.

Third Arab-Israeli War 5–10 Jun 1967, the ***Six Day War***. It resulted in the Israeli capture of the Golan Heights from Syria; the E half of Jerusalem and the West Bank from Jordan; and, in the south, the Gaza Strip and Sinai Peninsula as far as the Suez Canal.

Fourth Arab-Israeli War 2–22/24 Oct 1973, the 'October War' or ***Yom Kippur War***, so called because the Israeli forces were taken by surprise on the Day of Atonement. It started with the recrossing of the Suez Canal by Egyptian forces who made initial gains, though there was some later loss of ground by the Syrians in the north.

Fifth Arab-Israeli War From 1978 the presence of Palestinian guerrillas in Lebanon led to Arab raids on Israel and Israeli retaliatory incursions, but on 6 Jun 1982 Israel launched a full-scale invasion. By 14 Jun Beirut was encircled, and ◊Palestine Liberation Organization (PLO) and Syrian forces were evacuated (mainly to Syria) 21–31 Aug, but in Feb 1985 there was a unilateral Israeli withdrawal from the country without any gain for losses incurred. Israel maintains a 'security zone' in S Lebanon and supports the South Lebanese Army militia as a buffer against Palestinian guerrilla incursions.

Arab League organization of Arab states established in Cairo 1945 to promote Arab unity, especially in opposition to Israel. The original members were Egypt, Syria, Iraq, Lebanon, Transjordan (Jordan 1949), Saudi Arabia, and Yemen. In 1979 Egypt was suspended and the league's headquarters transferred to Tunis in protest against the Egypt-Israeli peace, but Egypt was readmitted as a full member May 1989, and in Mar 1990 its headquarters returned to Cairo.

Arafat Yasser 1929– . Palestinian nationalist politician, cofounder of al-Fatah 1956 and president of the ◊Palestine Liberation Organization (PLO) from 1969. In the 1970s his activities in pursuit of an independent homeland for Palestinians made him a prominent figure in world politics, but in the 1980s the growth of factions within the PLO effectively reduced his power. He was forced to evacuate Lebanon 1983, but remained leader of most of the PLO.

In 1985 he agreed with Talal ibn Hussein to recognize the existence of Israel if territory seized since 1967 was restored. The peace initiative foundered 1986, but improved 1988. In 1990 he persuaded the PLO to formally recognize the state of Israel.

armistice a cessation from arms while awaiting a peace settlement. 'The Armistice' refers specifically to the end of World War I between Germany and the Allies on 11 Nov 1918. On 22 June 1940 French representatives signed an armistice with Germany in the same railway carriage at Compiègne as in 1918. No armistice was signed with either Germany or Japan in 1945; both nations surrendered and there was no provision for the suspension of fighting. The Korean armistice signed at Panmunjom on 27 July 1953 terminated the Korean War 1950–1953.

Armistice Day anniversary of the armistice signed 11 Nov 1918, ending World War I. In the UK it is commemorated on the same day as Remembrance Sunday.

Arnhem, Battle of in World War II, airborne operation by the Allies, 17–26 Sept 1944, to secure a bridgehead over the river Rhine, thereby opening the way for a thrust towards the Ruhr valley in Germany and a possible early end to the war. It was only partly successful, with 7,600 casualties. Arnhem is a city in the Netherlands, on the Rhine SE of Utrecht.

ASEAN acronym for ◊***Association of South East Asian Nations***.

Asquith Herbert Henry, 1st Earl of Oxford and Asquith 1852–1928. British Liberal politician, prime minister 1908–16. As chancellor of the Exchequer he introduced old-age pensions 1908. He limited the powers of the House of Lords and attempted to give Ireland Home Rule.

Asquith was born in Yorkshire. Elected member of Parliament 1886, he was home secretary in Gladstone's 1892–95 government. He was chancellor of the Exchequer 1905–08 and succeeded Campbell-Bannerman as prime minister. Forcing through the radical budget of his chancellor ◊Lloyd George led him into two elections 1910, which resulted in the Parliament Act 1911, limiting the right of the Lords to veto legislation. His endeavours to pass the Home Rule for Ireland Bill led to the Curragh 'Mutiny' and incipient civil war. Unity was re-established by the outbreak of World War I in 1914, and a coalition government was formed May 1915. However, his attitude of 'wait and see' was not adapted to all-out war, and in Dec 1916 he was replaced by Lloyd George. In 1918 the Liberal election defeat led to the eclipse of the party. Created 1st Earl of Oxford and Asquith 1925.

Association of South East Asian Nations (ASEAN) regional alliance formed in Bangkok 1967; it took over the nonmilitary role of the Southeast Asia Treaty Organization 1975. Its members are Indonesia, Malaysia, the Philippines, Singapore, Thailand, and (from 1984) Brunei; its headquarters are in Jakarta, Indonesia.

Atatürk Kemal. Name assumed 1934 by Mustafa Kemal Pasha 1881–1938. ('Father of the Turks'). Turkish politician and general, first president of Turkey from 1923. After World War I he established a provisional rebel government and in 1921–22 the Turkish armies under his leadership expelled the Greeks who were occupying Turkey. He was the founder of the modern republic, which he ruled as virtual dictator, with a policy of consistent and radical westernization.

Kemal, born in Thessaloniki, was banished 1904 for joining a revolutionary society. Later he was pardoned and promoted in the army, and was largely responsible for the successful defence of the Dardanelles against the British 1915. In 1918, after Turkey had been defeated, he was sent into Anatolia to implement the demobilization of the Turkish forces in accordance with the armistice terms, but instead he established a provisional government opposed to that of Constantinople (under Allied control), and in 1921 led the Turkish armies against the Greeks, who had occupied a large part of Anatolia. He checked them at the Battle of the Sakaria, 23 Aug–13 Sept 1921, for which he was granted the title of Ghazi (the Victorious), and within a year had expelled the Greeks from Turkish soil. War with the British was averted by his diplomacy, and Turkey in Europe passed under Kemal's control. On 29 Oct 1923, Turkey was proclaimed a republic with Kemal as first president.

Atlantic, Battle of the the German campaign during World War I to prevent merchant shipping from delivering food supplies from the USA to the Allies, especially the UK. By 1917, some 875,000 tons of shipping had been lost. The odds were only turned by the belated use of naval ***convoys*** and ***depth charges*** to deter submarine attack.

Notable action included the British defeat at ***Coronel*** off Chile on 1 Nov 1914, the subsequent British success at the ***Falkland Islands*** on 8 Dec 1914, and the battle at ***Jutland*** on 31 May 1916, which effectively neutralized the German surface fleet for the rest of the war.

Atlantic, Battle of the continuous battle

fought in the Atlantic Ocean throughout World War II (1939–45), by the sea and air forces of the Allies and Germany, to control the supply routes to Britain. The number of U-boats destroyed by the Allies during the war was nearly 800. At least 2,200 convoys of 75,000 merchant ships crossed the Atlantic, protected by US naval forces. Before the US entry into the war 1941, destroyers were suplied to the British under the Lend-Lease Act 1941.

The battle opened on the first night of the war, when on 4 Sept 1939 the ocean liner *Athenia*, sailing from Glasgow to New York, was torpedoed by a German submarine off the Irish coast. Germany tried U-boats, surface-raiders, indiscriminate mine-laying, and aircraft, but every method was successfully countered. The U-boats were the greatest menace, especially after the destruction of the German battleship *Bismarck* by British forces on 27 May 1941.

Atlantic Charter declaration issued 1941 during World War II by the British prime minister Churchill and the US president Roosevelt after meetings Aug 1941. It stressed their countries' good intentions and war aims and was largely a propaganda exercise to demonstrate public solidarity between the Allies.

The Atlantic Charter stated that Britain and the USA sought no territorial gains; desired no territorial changes not acceptable to the peoples concerned; respected the rights of all peoples to choose their own form of government; wished to see self-government restored to the occupied countries; would promote access by all states to trade and raw materials; desired international collaboration for the raising of economic standards; hoped to see a peace affording security to all nations, enabling them to cross the seas without hindrance; and proposed the disarmament of the aggressor states as a preliminary step to general disarmament. This charter was incorporated by reference into the Declaration of the United Nations 1941.

atom bomb bomb deriving its explosive force from nuclear fission (see ◊nuclear energy) as a result of a neutron chain reaction, developed in the 1940s in the USA into a usable weapon.

Research began in the UK 1940 and was transferred to the USA after its entry into World War II the following year. Known as the ***Manhattan Project***, the work was carried out under the direction of the US physicist J Robert Oppenheimer at Los Alamos, New Mexico. After one test explosion, two atom bombs were dropped on the Japanese cities of Hiroshima (6 Aug 1945) and Nagasaki (9 Aug 1945), each nominally equal to 200,000 tonnes of TNT. The USSR first detonated an atom bomb in 1949 and the UK in 1952.

The test site used by the UK was in the Monte Bello Islands off Australia. The development of the hydrogen bomb in the 1950s rendered the early atom bomb obsolete. See ◊nuclear warfare.

Attlee Clement (Richard), 1st Earl 1883–1967. British Labour politician. Leader of the Labour party from 1935, he served in the wartime coalition government from 1940, becoming deputy prime minister from 1942. As prime minister 1945–51 he introduced a sweeping programme of nationalization and a whole new system of social services.

Attlee was educated at Oxford and practised at the Bar 1906–09. Social work in London's East End and cooperation in poor-law reform led him to become a socialist; he joined the Fabian Society and the Independent Labour Party 1908. He became lecturer in social science at the London School of Economics 1913. After service in World War I he was mayor of Stepney, E London, 1919–20; Labour member of Parliament for Limehouse 1922–50 and for W Walthamstow 1950–55. In the first and second Labour governments he was under-secretary for war 1924 and chancellor of the Duchy of Lancaster and postmaster general 1929–31. In 1935 he became leader of the opposition. In the coalition government during World War II he was Lord Privy Seal 1940–42, dominions secretary 1942–43, and Lord President of the Council 1943–45, as well as deputy prime minister from 1942. In July 1945 he became prime minister after a Labour landslide in the general election. The government was returned to power with a much reduced majority 1950 and was defeated 1951. In 1955 he accepted an earldom on retirement as leader of the opposition. He was also awarded the Order of Merit.

Auschwitz (Polish ***Oswiecim***) town near Kraków in Poland, the site of a notorious ◊concentration camp used by the Nazis in World War II to exterminate Jews and other political and social minorities, as part of the 'final solution'. Each of the four gas chambers could hold 6,000 people.

Australia country occupying the smallest continent in the world, situated S of Indonesia, between the Pacific and Indian oceans.

history Australia's native inhabitants, the Aborigines, arrived in Australia at least 40,000 years ago, according to present evidence. A wave of European immigration began 1770, when Captain James Cook claimed New South Wales as a British colony. In the 1890s the depression produced the

Labor Party and an increase in trade union activity, which has proved such a feature of Australian politics ever since. State powers waned following the creation of the Commonwealth 1901. Australia played an important role in both World Wars, and after World War II it embarked on a fresh period of expansion, with new mineral finds playing a large part in economic growth. Since 1945 Australia has strengthened its ties with India and other SE Asian countries; since Britain's entry into the EC 1973, and under the Labour government, which came to power 1972, there was a growth of nationalism. After heading a Liberal-Country party government for 17 years, Robert Menzies resigned 1966 and was succeeded by Harold Holt, who died shortly after. In 1968 John Gorton became prime minister but lost a vote of confidence in the House and was succeeded by a Liberal-Country Party coalition under William McMahon 1971. At the end of 1972, the Australian Labor Party took office, led by Gough Whitlam. The 1974 general election gave the Labor Party a fresh mandate to govern despite having a reduced majority in the House.

the 1975 constitutional crisis In 1975 the Senate blocked the government's financial legislation and, with Whitlam unwilling to resign, the governor general took the unprecedented step of dismissing him and his cabinet and inviting Malcolm Fraser to form a Liberal-Country party coalition caretaker administration. In the 1977 general election the coalition was returned with a reduced majority that was further reduced 1980.

the Hawke era In the 1983 general election the coalition was eventually defeated and the Australian Labor Party, now under Bob Hawke, again took office. Hawke called together employers and unions to agree to a wage and price policy and to deal with unemployment. In 1984 he called a general election 15 months early and was returned with a reduced majority. Hawke has placed even greater emphasis than his predecessors on links with SE Asia and has imposed trading sanctions against South Africa as a means of influencing the dismantling of apartheid. In the 1987 general election, Labor marginally increased its majority in the House but did not have an overall majority in the Senate, where the balance was held by the Australian Democrats. The 1990 election was won by Labor, led by Bob Hawke, with a reduced majority in the House of Representatives. The Australian Democrats maintain the balance of power in the senate.

Austria landlocked country in central Europe, bounded by Hungary to the E, Yugoslavia to the SE, Italy to the SW, Switzerland to the W, West Germany to the NW, and Czechoslovakia to the NE.

history In 1848 the mixed nationalities within the Austrian empire flared into a rebellion, which was soon crushed. In 1867 Franz Joseph established the dual monarchy of Austria-Hungary. The treaty of Berlin 1878 gave Austria the administration of Bosnia and Herzegovina in the Balkans, though they remained nominally Turkish until Austria annexed them 1908. World War I began 1914 with an Austrian attack on Serbia. Austria-Hungary collapsed 1918, after which Austria comprised only Vienna and its immediately surrounding provinces. A precarious republic was proclaimed, and in 1938 Austria was incorporated into the German Reich under Hitler. Austria returned to its 1920 constitution 1945, with a provisional government led by Dr Karl Renner. The Allies divided the country into four zones, occupied by the USSR, the USA, Britain, and France. The first postwar elections resulted in an SPO-OVP coalition government. The country was occupied until independence was formally recognized 1955.

the sixties The first post-war non-coalition government was formed 1966 when the OVP came to power with Josef Klaus as chancellor. In 1970 the SPO formed a minority government under Dr Bruno Kreisky and increased its majority in the 1971 and 1975 general elections. In 1978 the government was nearly defeated over proposals to install the first nuclear power plant. The plan was abandoned, but nuclear energy remained a controversial issue. In 1983 the SPO lost its majority. Kreisky resigned, refusing to join a coalition. Dr Fred Sinowatz, the new SPO chairman, formed an SPO-FPO coalition government.

the Waldheim controversy In 1985 a controversy arose with the announcement that Dr Kurt Waldheim, former UN secretary-general, was to be a presidential candidate. Despite allegations of his having been a Nazi officer in Yugoslavia, Waldheim eventually became president 1986, leading to diplomatic isolation by many countries. Later that year Sinowatz resigned as chancellor for 'personal reasons' and was succeeded by Franz Vranitzky. Vranitzky formed a 'grand coalition' of the SPO and the OVP, and remained as chancellor with the OVP leader, Dr Alois Mock, as vice-chancellor. Sinowatz denounced the coalition as a betrayal of socialist principles and resigned as chairman of the SPO. In March 1989 Austria announced that it intended to seek membership of the European Community. In the Oct 1990 general election the Socialists won a clear lead over other parties and Vranitzky began another term as prime minister.

Austro-Hungarian empire the Dual Monarchy established by the Habsburg Franz Joseph 1867 between his empire of Austria and his kingdom of Hungary (including territory that became Czechoslovakia as well as parts of Poland, the Ukraine, Romania, Yugoslavia and Italy.) In 1910 it had an area of 261,239 sq km/100,838 sq mi with a population of 51 million. It collapsed autumn 1918 with the end of World War I. Only two king-emperors ruled: Franz Joseph 1867–1916 and Charles 1916–18.

autocracy a form of government in which one person holds absolute power. The autocrat has uncontrolled and undisputed authority. Russian government under the Tsars was an autocracy extending from the mid-16th century to the early 20th century.

Axis the alliance of Nazi Germany and Fascist Italy before and during World War II. The ***Rome–Berlin Axis*** was formed 1936, when Italy was being threatened with sanctions because of its invasion of Ethiopia (Abyssinia). It became a full military and political alliance May 1939. A 10-year alliance between Germany, Italy, and Japan (***Rome–Berlin–Tokyo Axis***) was signed Sept 1940 and was subsequently joined by Hungary, Bulgaria, Romania, and the puppet states of Slovakia and Croatia. The Axis collapsed with the fall of Mussolini and the surrender of Italy 1943, followed by Germany and Japan 1945.

Ayub Khan 1907–1974. Pakistani soldier, and president 1958–69. He served in the Burma Campaign 1942–45, and was commander in chief of the Pakistan army 1951. In 1958 martial law was proclaimed in Pakistan and Ayub Khan assumed power after a bloodless army coup. He won the presidential elections in 1960 and 1965. He established a stable economy and achieved limited land reforms. His militaristic form of government was unpopular, particularly with the Bengalis. In 1968 student riots resulted from imprisonment of the opposition. He resigned after widespread opposition and civil disorder notably in Kashmir.

B

Baader-Meinhof gang popular name for the West German guerrilla group the *Rote Armee Fraktion* ('Red Army Faction'), active from 1968 against what it perceived as US imperialism. Its two leaders were Andreas Baader and Ulrike Meinhof who died in prison under mysterious circumstances.

Ba'ath Party socialist party aiming at the extended union of all Arab countries, active in Iraq and Syria. Founded 1943 by Michael Affaq and Salah al-Din al-Bitar.

Baird John Logie 1888–1946. Scottish electrical engineer who pioneered television. In 1925 he gave the first public demonstration of television and in 1926 pioneered fibre optics, radar (in advance of Robert Watson-Watt), and 'noctovision', a system for seeing at night by using infrared rays. He also developed video recording on both wax records and magnetic steel discs (1926–27), colour TV (1925–28), 3-D colour TV (1925–46), and transatlantic TV (1928).

balance of power in politics, the theory that the best way of ensuring international order is to have power so distributed among states that no single state is able to achieve a dominant position. The term, which may also refer more simply to the actual distribution of power, is one of the most enduring concepts in international relations. Since the development of nuclear weapons, it has been asserted that the balance of power has been replaced by a ***balance of terror***.

Baldwin Stanley, 1st Earl Baldwin of Bewdley 1867–1947. British Conservative politician, prime minister 1923–24, 1924–29, and 1935–37; he weathered the general strike 1926, secured complete adult suffrage 1928, and handled the ◊abdication crisis of Edward VIII 1936, but failed to prepare Britain for World War II.

Born in Bewdley, Worcestershire, the son of an iron and steel magnate, in 1908 he was elected Unionist member of Parliament for Bewdley, and in 1916 he became parliamentary private secretary to Andrew Bonar Law. He was financial secretary to the Treasury 1917–21, and then appointed to the presidency of the Board of Trade. In 1919 he gave the Treasury £150,000 (for cancellation of the war loan), representing about 20% of his fortune. He was a leader in the disruption of David Lloyd George's coalition 1922, and, as chancellor under Bonar Law, achieved a settlement of war debts with the USA.

As prime minister 1923–24 and again 1924–29, Baldwin passed the Trades Disputes Act of 1927 after the general strike, granted widows' and orphans' pensions, and complete adult suffrage 1928. He joined the national government of Ramsay MacDonald 1931 as Lord President of the Council. His third premiership 1935–37, was later much criticized for his failures to resist popular desire for an accommodation with the dictators Hitler and Mussolini, and to rearm more effectively. Created 1st Earl Baldwin of Bewdley 1937.

Balfour Arthur James, 1st Earl of Balfour 1848–1930. British Conservative politician, prime minister 1902–05 and foreign secretary 1916–19, when he issued the ***Balfour Declaration*** 1917 and was involved in peace negotiations after World War I, signing the Treaty of Versailles.

Son of a Scottish landowner, Balfour was elected a Conservative member of Parliament in 1874. In Lord Salisbury's ministry he was secretary for Ireland 1887, and for his ruthless vigour was called 'Bloody Balfour' by Irish nationalists. In 1891 and again in 1895 he became First Lord of the Treasury and leader of the Commons, and in 1902 he succeeded Salisbury as prime minister. His Education Act 1902 established a national system of secondary education. His cabinet was divided over Joseph Chamberlain's tariff-reform proposals, and in the 1905 elections suffered a crushing defeat.

Balfour retired from the party leadership in 1911. In 1915 he joined the Asquith coalition as First Lord of the Admiralty. As foreign secretary 1916–19 he issued the Balfour Declaration in favour of a national home in Palestine for the Jews. He was Lord President of the Council 1919–22 and 1925–29. Created 1st Earl of Balfour 1922.

Balkan Wars two wars 1912–13 and 1913 (preceding World War I) which resulted in the

The Balkans after the Congress of Berlin 1878–1913

1889 year state became independent

expulsion by the Balkan states of Ottoman Turkey from Europe, except for a small area around Istanbul.

The ***First Balkan War***, 1912, of Bulgaria, Serbia, Greece, and Montenegro against Turkey, forced the Turks to ask for an armistice, but the London-held peace negotiations broke down when the Turks, while agreeing to surrender all Turkey-in-Europe W of the city of Edirne (formerly Adrianople), refused to give up the city itself. In Feb 1913 hostilities were resumed. Edirne fell on 26 Mar and on 30 May, by the Treaty of London, Turkey retained in Europe only a small piece of E Thrace and the Gallipoli peninsula.

The ***Second Balkan War***, June–July 1913, took place when Bulgaria attacked Greece and Serbia, which were joined by Romania. Bulgaria was defeated, and Turkey secured from that country the cession of Edirne.

Baltic States collective name for the former independent states of Estonia, Latvia, and Lithuania, from 1940 republics within the USSR, but contemplating secession in 1990.

Banda Hastings Kamuzu 1902– . Malawi politican, president from 1966. He led his country's independence movement and was prime minister of Nyasaland (the former name of Malawi) from 1963. He became Malawi's first president in 1966 and in 1971 was named president for life; his rule has been authoritarian.

Bandaranaike Sirimavo (born Ratwatte) 1916–
. Sri Lankan politician, who succeeded her

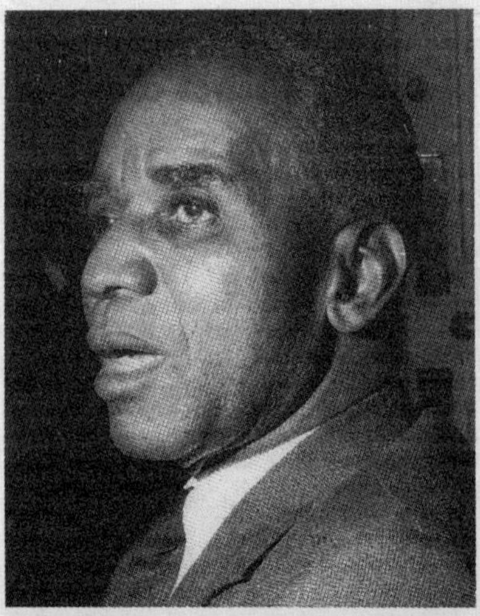

Banda *Hastings Banda, first president of Malawi.*

husband Solomon Bandaranaike to become the world's first female prime minister 1960–65 and 1970–77, but was expelled from parliament 1980 for abuse of her powers while in office. She was largely responsible for the new constitution 1972.

Bandaranaike Solomon West Ridgeway Dias 1899–1959. Sri Lankan nationalist politician. In 1951 he founded the Sri Lanka Freedom party and in 1956 became prime minister, pledged to a socialist programme and a neutral foreign policy. He failed to satisfy extremists and was assassinated by a Buddhist monk.

Bandung Conference the first conference 1955 of the Afro-Asian nations, proclaiming anticolonialism and neutrality between East and West.

Bangladesh country in S Asia, surrounded on three sides by India and bounded to the south by the Bay of Bengal.

history For history before 1947 see ◊India; for history 1947–1971 see ◊Pakistan. Contemporary Bangladesh formerly comprised E Bengal province and Sylhet district of Assam in British India. Predominantly Muslim, it was formed into the eastern province of Pakistan when India was partitioned 1947. Substantially different in culture, language, and geography from the western provinces of Pakistan 1,000 miles away and with a larger population, it resented the political and military dominance exerted by W Pakistan during the 1950s and 1960s. A movement for political autonomy grew after 1954 under the Awami League headed by Sheik Mujibur Rahman.

the republic In Pakistan's first general elections 1970 the Awami League gained an overwhelming victory in E Pakistan and an overall majority in the all-Pakistan National Assembly. Talks on redrawing the constitution broke down, leading to E Pakistan's secession and the establishment of a Bangladesh ('Bengal Nation') government in exile in Calcutta (India) 1971. Civil war resulted in the flight of 10 million E Pakistani refugees to India, administrative breakdown, famine, and cholera. The W Pakistani forces in E Pakistan surrendered 1971 after India intervened on the secessionists' side. A republic of Bangladesh was proclaimed and rapidly gained international recognition 1972. Sheik Mujibur Rahman became prime minister 1972 under a secular, parliamentary constitution. He introduced a Socialist economic programme of nationalization but became intolerant of opposition, establishing a one-party presidential system Jan 1975. In Aug 1975 Sheik Mujibur was assassinated. A further military coup Nov 1975 established as president and chief martial law administrator the non-political chief justice Abu Sadat Mohammed Sayem. In 1976, Major-General Zia ur-Rahman (1936–81) became chief martial law administrator. Becoming president 1977, he adopted an Islamic constitution, approved by a national referendum in May. In June he won a 4:1 majority in a direct presidential election. A civilian government was installed, and martial law and the state of emergency were lifted 1979. The administration was undermined, however, by charges of corruption and by a guerrilla movement in Chittagong 1980. On 30 May 1981 Zia was assassinated in an attempted coup, and interim power was assumed by Vice-President Justice Abdus Sattar.

Ershad's administration With disorder increasing, the civilian administration was overthrown March 1982 by a coup led by Lt Gen Mohammad Hussain Ershad (1930–). Martial law was re-imposed, and political activity banned. The economy improved and in 1983 a broad opposition coalition, the Movement for the Restoration of Democracy, was formed. In Jan 1986 the ban on political activity was removed, and parliamentary elections were held in May. The Awami League agreed to participate in these elections, but the Bangladesh National Party and many other opposition parties boycotted them. With a campaign marked by violence, widespread abstentions, and claims of ballot-rigging, Ershad was re-elected president in Oct 1986, and in Nov 1986 martial law was lifted. During 1987 the Awami League, led by Sheika Hasina Wazed (the daughter of Sheik Mujibur Rahman), and the Bangladesh National Party, led by Begum Khalida Zia, campaigned against the Ershad government, demanding the president's resignation and free elections. In the wake of a wave of violent strikes and demonstrations, Ershad proclaimed a state of emergency in Nov 1987. Parliament was dissolved and fresh elections called in March 1988. A combination of ballot-rigging and an opposition boycott resulted in the ruling *Jatiya Dal* gaining a sweeping victory. The state of emergency was lifted April 1988. A bill passed by parliament June 1988 making Islam the state religion.

monsoon flooding In Sept 1988 Bangladesh received the heaviest monsoon rains in 70 years; in the resulting floods several thousand people died and 30 million became homeless. In March 1989 the *Jatiya Sangsad* approved legislation devolving power to directly elected, substantially autonomous councils in three Chittagong Hill Tract districts in SE Bangladesh, which had been devastated by a 14-year tribal insurgency led by the *Shanti Bahini* 'Peace Force' organization. In June 1989, constitutional amendments were also passed restricting the president to two elected five-year terms and creating the post of elected vice president.

On 4 Dec 1990, following a protracted opposition-led campaign for the government's removal, with mass protests Ershad resigned as president. The state of emergency was lifted, parliament dissolved, and Ershad replaced by Shahabuddin Ahmed, the country's chief justice, who agreed to serve as an interim executive president pending the holding of free multi-party elections within three months.

Bantustan (or ***homeland***) name until 1978 for the ◊Black National States in the Republic of South Africa.

Barbarossa, operation German code name for the plans to invade the USSR during World War II in 1941.

Basque a member of a people who occupy the autonomous Basque region (created 1980) of NE Spain and the adjoining French *département* of Pyrénées-Atlantiques. During the Spanish Civil War 1936–39 they were on the Republican side and were defeated by Franco. The Basque separatist movement ETA (*Euskadi ta Azkatasuna*, 'Basque Nation and Liberty') and the French organization *Enbata* ('Ocean Wind') have engaged in guerrilla activity from 1968 in an unsuccessful attempt to secure a united Basque state.

Batista Fulgencio 1901–1973. Cuban dictator 1933–44 and 1952–59, whose authoritarian methods enabled him to jail his opponents and amass a large personal fortune. He was overthrown by rebel forces led by Fidel ◊Castro 1959.

Bay of Pigs inlet on the S coast of Cuba about 145 km/90 mi SW of Havana, the site of an unsuccessful invasion attempt by 1,500 US-sponsored Cuban exiles 17–20 Apr 1961; 1,173 were taken prisoner.

The creation of this anti-revolutionary force by the CIA had been authorized by the Eisenhower administration, and the project was executed under that of J F Kennedy. In 1962 most of the Cuban prisoners were ransomed for $53 million in food and medicine. The incident served to strengthen Cuba's links with the USSR.

BBC abbreviation for ◊***British Broadcasting Corporation***.

Beaverbrook (William) Max(well) Aitken, 1st Baron Beaverbrook 1879–1964. British newspaper proprietor and politician, born in Canada. He bought a majority interest in the *Daily Express* 1919, founded the *Sunday Express* 1921, and bought the London *Evening Standard* 1929. He served in David Lloyd George's World War I cabinet and Winston Churchill's World War II cabinet.

Between the wars he used his newspapers, in particular the *Daily Express*, to campaign for empire and free trade and against Prime Minister Baldwin. Created 1st Baron Beaverbrook 1917.

Begin Menachem 1913– . Israeli politician, born in Poland. He was a leader of the extremist Irgun Zvai Leumi organization in Palestine from 1942; was prime minister of Israel 1977–83, as head of the right-wing Likud party; and in 1978 shared a Nobel Peace Prize with President Sadat of Egypt for work on the ◊Camp David Agreements for a Middle East peace settlement.

Belgian Congo a former territory in central Africa lying in the vast basin of the Congo (Zaïre) river, established under Leopold II as a personal possession. The European powers recognized the Congo Free State at the Berlin Conference 1885. In 1908, following international protests about atrocities, Leopold handed the Congo over to Belgium as a colony. Despite the rich mineral resources (notably copper and uranium) at Katanga, the Congo remained underdeveloped. In 1959, riots in the capital, Leopoldville, incited African national feeling, and a conference in Brussels in Jan 1960 decided on independence. The Democratic Republic of the Congo was established 30 June 1960 under President Kasavubu. The sudden independence resulted in chaos. Local politicians, for example, were dependent on tribal rather than national support and there was a strong reaction from companies. The Congolese national army mutinied and the United Nations urged the use of force to prevent civil war. The USSR waged a campaign against the UN secretary general and called for the restoration of an independent Congo. A major focus of hostilities centred on the attempts of Katanga to secede. The 'Congo Problem' remained a concern for the United Nations until 1964–65 when Kasavubu was deposed and a stable, if ruthless regime was established under General Mobutu. In Oct 1971 the Congo Republic and river were renamed ◊Zaïre.

Belgium country in N Europe, bounded to the NW by the North Sea, to the SW by France, to the E by Luxembourg and West Germany, and to the NE by the Netherlands.

government The constitution dates from 1831 and was most recently revised 1971. The prime minister and cabinet are drawn from and answerable to the legislature, which exercises considerable control over the executive.

The legislature consists of a senate and a chamber of representatives elected by universal suffrage.

history Although Prussia had been a party to the treaty 1839 recognizing Belgium's permanent neutrality, Germany invaded Belgium 1914 and occupied a large part of it until 1918. Again in 1940 Belgium was overrun by Germany, to whom Leopold III surrendered. His government escaped to London, and Belgium had a strong resistance movement. After Belgium's liberation by the Allies 1944–45 the king's surrender caused acute controversy, ended only by his abdication 1951 in favour of his son Baudouin. Since 1945 Belgium has been a major force for international cooperation in Europe, being a founding member of the Benelux Economic Union, the Council of Europe, and the EC. Belgium's main problems stem from the division between French- and Dutch-speaking members of the population, aggravated by the polarization between the predominantly Conservative Flanders in the N, and the mainly Socialist French-speaking Wallonia in the S. About 55% of the population speak Dutch, 44% French, and the remainder German.

decentralization From 1971–73, attempts to close the linguistic and social divisions included the transfer of greater power to the regions, the inclusion of German-speaking members in the cabinet, and linguistic parity in the government. In 1974 separate regional councils and ministerial committees were established. In 1977 a coalition government, headed by Leo Tindemans (CVP) proposed the creation of a federal Belgium, based on Flanders, Wallonia, and Brussels, but the proposals were not adopted, and in 1978 Tindemans resigned. He was succeeded by Wilfried Martens, heading another coalition. In 1980 the language conflict developed into open violence, and it was eventually agreed that Flanders and Wallonia should be administered by separate regional assemblies, with powers to spend up to 10% of the national budget on cultural facilities, health, roads, and urban projects. Brussels was to be governed by a three-member executive. Such was the political instability that by 1980 Martens had formed no less than four coalition governments. In 1981 a new coalition, led by Mark Eyskens (CVP), lasted less than a year, and Martens again returned to power. In 1981–82 economic difficulties resulted in a series of public sector strikes, and in 1983 linguistic divisions again threatened the government. Between 1983 and 1985 there was much debate about the siting of US cruise missiles in Belgium before a majority vote in parliament allowed their installation. The 1985 elections led to Martens forming another coalition. The 1987 general election produced no decisive result and Martens formed a new five-party coalition government that broke up March 1987, when the king asked Martens to form a new caretaker government pending a general election and the adoption of a new constitution, devolving more power to the regions. In 1988, Martens formed a new coalition government, following a general election.

Ben Bella Ahmed 1916– . Algerian leader of the National Liberation Front (FLN) from 1952; prime minister of independent Algeria 1962–65, when he was overthrown by Algerian politician Houari Boumédienne and detained until 1980. He founded a new party, Mouvement pour la Démocratie en Algérie, in 1985. In 1990 he returned to Algeria.

Benelux customs union of ***Be***lgium, the ***Ne***therlands, and ***Lux***embourg (agreed 1944, fully effective 1960); precursor of the European Community.

Beneš Eduard 1884–1948. Czechoslovak politician. He worked with Thomas Masaryk towards Czechoslovak nationalism from 1918 and was foreign minister and representative at the League of Nations. He was president of the republic from 1935 until forced to resign by the Germans; he headed a government in exile in London during World War II. He returned home as president 1945 but resigned again after the Communist coup 1948.

Ben-Gurion David. Adopted name of David Gruen 1886–1973. Israeli statesman and socialist politician, one of the founders of the state of Israel, the country's first prime minister 1948–53, and again 1955–63.

He was born in Poland, and went to Palestine in 1906 to farm. He was a leader of the Zionist movement, and as defence minister he presided over the development of Israel's armed forces into one of the strongest armies in the Middle East.

Berlin blockade the Soviet blockade of Berlin June 1948–May 1949. It ultimately resulted in the division of Berlin, and consequently Germany, into two separate administrative units. East and West Germany officially reunited as one country Oct 1990, and Berlin became the capital of a unified Germany once more with East and West Berlin reunited as the 16th Land (state) of the Federal Republic.

After World War II, Berlin was divided into four sectors – British, US, French, and Soviet – and until 1948 was under quadripartite government by the Allies. In June 1948, the USSR withdrew from the combined board and blockaded the city in response to the introduction of a new currency in West Germany. The Allies flew in food supplies (the Berlin Airlift). The blockade was lifted in May 1949, but the airlift continued until Sept. The Soviets created a separate municipal government in their sector; and in Oct 1949 East Berlin was proclaimed capital of East Germany. The other three sectors, in West Germany became a Land of the Federal Republic of Germany in May 1949.

Berlin Olympics Olympic Games held in Berlin in 1936. Adolf Hitler and the Nazi party attempted to use the occasion for propaganda purposes and to demonstrate German physical prowess.

Berlin Wall the dividing barrier between East and West Berlin 1961–89, erected by East Germany to keep its citizens in. Escapers from East to West were shot on sight.

Beginning 13 Aug 1961, the East German security forces sealed off all but 12 of the 80 crossing points to West Berlin with a barbed wire barrier. It was reinforced with concrete by the Russians to prevent the escape of unwilling inhabitants of East Berlin to the rival political and economic system of West Berlin. The interconnecting link between East and West Berlin was ***Checkpoint Charlie***, where both sides exchanged captured spies. On 9 Nov 1989 the East German government opened its borders to try to halt the mass exodus of its citizens to the West via other Eastern bloc countries, and the wall was gradually dismantled.

Bernadotte Count Folke 1895–1948. Swedish diplomat and president of the Swedish Red Cross. In 1945 he conveyed the Nazi commander Himmler's offer of capitulation to the British and US governments, and in 1948 was United Nations mediator in Palestine, where he was assassinated by Stern Gang guerrillas (Israeli terrorists).

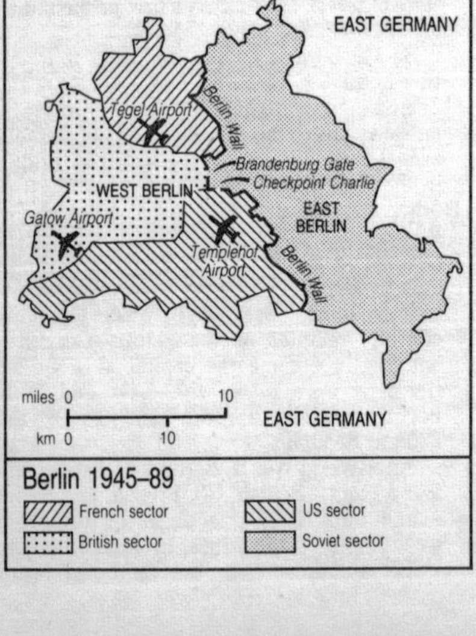

Berlin 1945–89

Bevan Aneurin 1897–1960. British Labour politician. Son of a Welsh miner, and himself a miner at 13, he became member of Parliament for Ebbw Vale 1929–60. As minister of health 1945–51, he inaugurated the National Health Service (NHS); he was minister of labour Jan–Apr 1951, when he resigned (with Harold Wilson) on the introduction of NHS charges and led a Bevanite faction against the government. He became chief labour spokesman on foreign affairs 1956, and deputy leader of the labour party 1959.

Beveridge Report, the popular name for a parliamentary report on *Social Insurance and Allied Services*, also known as the *Report on Social Security* written by British economist William Beveridge 1942 which formed the basis for the social reform legislation of the Labour Government of 1945–50. The report identified five 'giants': illness, ignorance, disease, squalor, and want. It proposed a scheme of social insurance from 'the cradle to the grave', and recommended a national health service, social insurance and assistance, family allowances and full-employment policies. It formed the basis of the welfare state in Britain.

Bevin Ernest 1881–1951. British Labour politician. Chief creator of the Transport and General Workers' Union, he was its general secretary 1921–40, when he entered the war cabinet as minister of labour and National Service. He organized the 'Bevin boys', chosen by ballot to work in the coal mines as war service, and was foreign secretary in the Labour government 1945–51.

Bhutto Benazir 1953– . Pakistani politician, leader of the Pakistan People's Party (PPP) from 1984 (in exile until 1986), and prime minister of Pakistan 1988–90. She was the first female leader of a Muslim state.

Benazir Bhutto was educated at Harvard and Oxford universities. She returned to Pakistan 1977 but was placed under house arrest after General Zia ul Haq seized power from her father, Prime Minister Zulfiqar Ali Bhutto. On her release she moved to the UK and became, with her mother Nusrat (1934–), the joint leader in exile of the opposition PPP. When martial law had been lifted, she returned to Pakistan Apr 1986 to launch a campaign for open elections. In her first year in office she struck an uneasy balance with

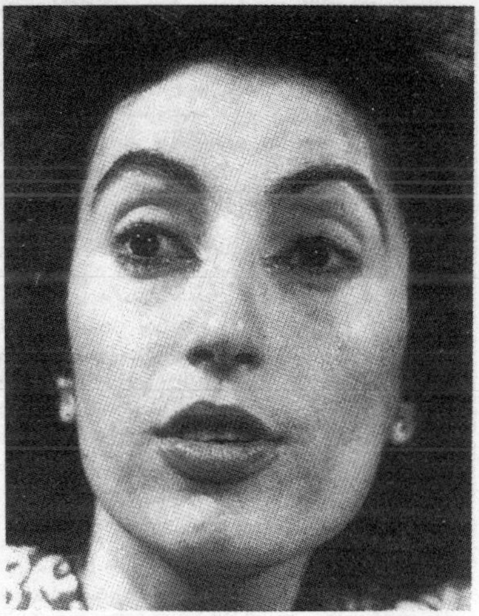

***Bhutto** Benazir Bhutto at a press conference in Islamabad, 31 Dec 1988.*

the military establishment and improved Pakistan's relations with India. She led her country back into the Commonwealth 1989.

In Aug 1990, she was removed from office by presidential decree, and a caretaker government installed. Charges of corruption and abuse of power were levelled, and her party was defeated in the subsequent general election.

Bhutto Zulfikar Ali 1928–1979. Pakistani politician, president 1971–73; prime minister from 1973 until the 1977 military coup led by General Zia ul Haq. In 1978 he was sentenced to death for conspiring to murder a political opponent and was hanged the following year.

Biafra, Republic of African state proclaimed in 1967 when fears that Nigerian central government was increasingly in the hands of the rival Hausa tribe led the predominantly Ibo Eastern Region of Nigeria to secede under Lt Col Odumegwu Ojukwu. On the proclamation of Biafra, civil war ensued with the rest of the federation. In a bitterly fought campaign federal forces confined the Biafrans to a shrinking area of the interior by 1968, and by 1970 Biafra ceased to exist.

Biko Steve (Stephen) 1946–1977. South African civil rights leader. An active opponent of ◊apartheid, he was arrested in Sept 1977; he died in detention six days later. Since his death in the custody of South African police he has been a symbol of the anti-apartheid movement.

He founded the South African Students Organization (SASO) in 1968 and was cofounder in 1972 of the Black People's Convention, also called the Black Consciousness movement, a radical association of South African students that aimed to develop black pride. His death while still in the hands of the police caused much controversy.

birth control another name for ◊family planning.

black English term first used in 1625 to describe West Africans, now used to refer to Africans south of the Sahara and to people of African descent living outside Africa. In the UK and some other countries (but not in North America) the term is sometimes also used for people originally from the Indian subcontinent, for Australian Aborigines, and peoples of Melanesia.

The term 'black', at one time considered offensive by many people, was first adopted by militants in the USA in the mid-1960s to emphasize ethnic pride; they rejected the terms 'coloured' and 'Negro' as euphemistic. 'Black' has since become the preferred term in the USA and largely in the UK. Currently, some US blacks prefer the term 'Afro-American' or 'African American'.

history Black Africans were first brought to the West Indies in large numbers as slaves by the Spanish in the early 16th century, and to the North American mainland in the early 17th century. They were brought to South America by both the Spanish and Portuguese from the 16th century. African blacks were also taken to Europe to work as slaves and servants. The Emancipation Proclamation 1863 of President Abraham Lincoln officially freed the slaves (about 4 million), but it could not be enforced until the period after the American Civil War 1861–65 in the period known as Reconstruction. Freed slaves were often resented by poor whites as economic competitors, and vigilante groups in the South, such as the ◊Ku Klux Klan were formed to intimidate them. In addition, although freed slaves had full US citizenship under the 14th Amendment to the Constitution, and were thus entitled to vote, they were often disenfranchised in practice by state and local literacy tests and poll taxes.

'separate but equal' A 'separate but equal' policy was established when the US Supreme Court ruled 1896 (*Plessy* vs *Ferguson*) that segregation was legal if equal facilities were provided for blacks and whites. The ruling was overturned 1954 (*Brown* vs *Board of Education*) with the Supreme Court decision outlawing segregation in state schools. This led to a historic confrontation in Little Rock,

Arkansas, 1957 when Governor Orval Faubus attempted to prevent black students from entering Central High School, and President Eisenhower sent federal troops to enforce their right to attend. Another landmark in the blacks' struggle for civil rights was the Montgomery bus boycott in Alabama 1955, which first brought Martin Luther ◊King Jr to national attention.

civil-rights movement In the early 1960s the civil-rights movement had gained impetus, largely under the leadership of King, who in 1957 had founded the Southern Christian Leadership Conference (SCLC), a coalition group advocating nonviolence. Moderate groups such as the National Association for the Advancement of Colored People (NAACP) had been active since early in the century; for the first time they were joined in large numbers by whites, in particular students, as in the historic march converging on Washington DC 1963 from all over the USA. At about this time, impatient with the lack of results gained through moderation, the militant ◊Black Power movements began to emerge, such as the Black Panther Party founded 1966, and black separatist groups such as the Black Muslims gained support. Increasing pressure led to the passage of federal legislation, the Civil Rights acts of 1964 and 1968, and the Voting Rights Act of 1965, under President Johnson; they guaranteed equal rights under the law and prohibited discrimination in public facilities, schools, employment and voting. However, in the 1980s, despite some advances, legislation, and affirmative action (positive discrimination), blacks, who comprise some 12% of the US population, continued to suffer discrimination and inequality of opportunities in practice in such areas as education, employment and housing. Despite these obstacles, blacks have made positive contributions in the arts, the sciences, and politics.

Unlike the USA, England did not have a history of slavery at home; Britain outlawed the slave trade 1807 and abolished slavery in the British Empire 1833. In the UK only a tiny proportion of the population was black until after World War II, when immigration from Commonwealth countries increased. Legislation such as the Race Relations Act 1976 specifically outlawed discrimination on grounds of race and emphasized the official policy of equality of opportunity in all areas, and the Commission for Racial Equality was established 1977 to work towards eliminating discrimination; nevertheless, there is still considerable evidence of ◊racism in British society as a whole. The Swann Report on education 1985 emphasized that Britain was a multicultural society, and suggested various ways in which teachers could ensure that black children were able to reach their full potential. Black people are now beginning to take their place in public life in the UK; the election of Diane Abbott (1953–) as Britain's first black woman member of Parliament 1987 was an example.

Black and Tans nickname of a special auxiliary force of the Royal Irish constabulary employed by the British in 1920–21 to combat the Sinn Féiners (Irish nationalists) in Ireland; the name derives from the colours of the uniforms, khaki with black hats and belts.

black nationalism a movement towards black separatism in the USA during the 1960s see ◊Black Power.

Black National State area in the Republic of South Africa set aside for development towards self-government by black Africans in accordance with ◊apartheid. Before 1980 these areas were known as black homelands or ***bantustans***. They make up less than 14% of the country and tend to be in arid areas (though some have mineral wealth), and may be in scattered blocks. Those that have so far achieved nominal independence are Transkei 1976, Bophuthatswana 1977, Venda 1979, and Ciskei 1981. They are not recognized outside South Africa because of their racial basis. 11 million blacks live permanently in the country's white-designated areas.

Black Power movement towards black separatism in the USA during the 1960s, embodied in the ***Black Panther Party*** founded 1966 by Huey Newton and Bobby Seale. Its declared aim was the establishment of a separate black state in the USA established by a black plebiscite under the aegis of the United Nations. Following a National Black Political Convention in 1972, a National Black Assembly was established to exercise pressure on the Democratic and Republican parties.

The Black Power concept arose when existing ◊civil rights organizations such as the National Association for Advancement of Colored People and the Southern Christian Leadership Conference were perceived to be ineffective in producing major change in the status of black people. Stokely Carmichael then advocated the exploitation of political and economic power and abandonment of nonviolence, with a move towards the type of separatism first developed by the Black Muslims. Leaders such as Martin Luther King rejected this approach, but the Black Panther Party (so named because the panther, though not generally aggressive, will fight to the death under attack) adopted it fully and, for a time, achieved nationwide influence.

Black Thursday day of the Wall Street stock market crash 29 Oct 1929, which precipitated the ◊Depression in the US and throughout the world.

Blitzkrieg (German 'lightning war') a swift military campaign, as used by Germany at the beginning of World War II 1939–41. The abbreviation ***Blitz*** was applied to the German air raids on London 1940–41.

blockade the cutting-off of a place by hostile forces by land, sea or air so as to prevent any movement to or fro, in order to compel a surrender without attack. For example, during World War I Germany attempted to blockade Britain with intensive submarine warfare, and Britain attempted to blockade Germany. In 1948 the Russians blockaded the land routes into West Berlin but the Americans and British organized an airlift of essential supplies. The blockade was lifted in May 1949. In 1990 a United Nations resolution implemented a blockade in an unsuccessful attempt to force Iraq, under the leadership of President Saddam Hussein, to withdraw from the invaded territory of Kuwait.

No nation has the right to declare a blockade unless it has the power to enforce it, according to international law. The Declaration of London 1909 laid down that a blockade must not be extended beyond the coasts and ports belonging to or occupied by an enemy.

Boer War the second of the South African Wars 1889–1902; war between the Dutch settlers in South Africa and the British.

Bolshevik (from Russian *bolshinstvo*, 'a majority') member of the majority of the Russian Social Democratic Party who split from the Mensheviks 1903. The Bolsheviks, under ◊Lenin, advocated the destruction of capitalist political and economic institutions, and the setting-up of a socialist state with power in the hands of the workers. The Bolsheviks set the ◊Russian Revolution 1917 in motion. The Bolsheviks changed their name to the Russian Communist Party 1918.

bomb a container filled with explosive or chemical material and generally used in warfare. There are also incendiary bombs and nuclear bombs and missiles (see ◊nuclear warfare). Any object designed to cause damage by explosion can be called a bomb (car bombs, letter bombs). Initially dropped from aeroplanes (from World War I), bombs were in World War II also launched by rocket (V1, V2). The 1960s saw the development of missiles that could be launched from aircraft, land sites, or submarines. In the 1970s laser guidance systems were developed to hit small targets with accuracy.

Aerial bombing started in World War I (1914–18) when the German air force carried out 103 raids on Britain, dropping 269 tonnes of bombs. In World War II (1939–45) nearly twice this tonnage was dropped on London in a single night, and at the peak of the Allied air offensive against Germany, more than ten times this tonnage was regularly dropped in successive nights on one target. Raids in which nearly 1,000 heavy bombers participated were frequent. In 1939 bombs were commonly about 115 kg/250 lb and 230 kg/500 lb, but by the end of the war the ten-tonner was being produced.

The fission or ◊***atom bomb*** was developed in the 1940s and the USA exploded three during World War II: first a test explosion on 16 Jul 1945, at Alamogordo, New Mexico, USA, then on 6 Aug the first to be used in actual warfare was dropped over ◊Hiroshima and three days later another over Nagasaki, Japan. The fusion or hydrogen bomb was developed in the 1950s, and by the 1960s intercontinental 100-megatonne nuclear warheads could be produced (5,000 times more powerful than those of World War II).

Bonner Yelena 1923– . Soviet human-rights campaigner. Disillusioned by the Soviet invasion of Czechoslovakia 1968, she resigned from the Communist Party after marrying her second husband, Andrei ◊Sakharov, in 1971, and became active in the dissident movement.

Botha P(ieter) W(illem) 1916– . South African politician. Prime minister from 1978, he initiated a modification of ◊apartheid, which later slowed in the face of Afrikaner (Boer) opposition. In 1984 he became the first executive state president. In 1989 he unwillingly resigned both party leadership and presidency after suffering a stroke, and was succeeded by F W de Klerk.

Boxer member of the *I ho ch'üan* ('Righteous Harmonious Fists'), an antiforeign society of Chinese nationalists. The ***Boxer Rebellion*** or ***Uprising*** 1900, was instigated by the Dowager Empress Tzu Hsi (1834–1908). European and US diplomats in Beijing were beseiged, and thousands of Chinese Christian converts and missionaries were murdered. An international punitive force was dispatched, Beijing was captured 14 Aug 1900, and China agreed to pay a large indemnity.

Brandt Willy. Adopted name of Karl Herbert Frahm 1913– . West German socialist politician, federal chancellor (premier) 1969–74. He played a key role in the remoulding of the Social Democratic Party (SPD) as a moderate socialist force (leader 1964–87). As mayor of

West Berlin 1957–66, Brandt became internationally known during the Berlin Wall crisis 1961. He received the Nobel Peace Prize 1971.

Brandt, born in Lübeck, changed his name when he fled to Norway 1933 and became active in the anti-Nazi resistance. He returned 1945 and entered the Bundestag (federal parliament) 1949. In the 'grand coalition' 1966–69 he served as foreign minister and introduced ***Ostpolitik***, a policy of reconciliation between East and West Europe, which was continued when he became federal chancellor 1969, and culminated in the 1972 signing of the Basic Treaty with East Germany.

He resigned from the chancellorship 1974 following the discovery that a close aide, Günther Guillaume, had been an East German spy. Brandt continued to wield considerable influence in the SPD, in particular over the party's new radical left wing. He chaired the Brandt Commission on Third World problems 1977–83 and was a member of the European Parliament 1979–83.

Brest-Litovsk, Treaty of bilateral treaty signed 3 Mar 1918 between Russia and Germany, Austria-Hungary, and their allies. Under it, Russia agreed to recognize the independence of Georgia, Ukraine, Poland and the Baltic States, and pay heavy compensation. Under the Nov 1918 Armistice that ended World War I, it was annulled.

Bretton Woods Conference the United Nations Monetary and Financial Conference held 1944 in Bretton Woods, New Hampshire, USA to discuss post-war international payments problems. The agreements reached on financial assistance and measures to stabilize exchange rates led to the creation of the International Bank for Reconstruction and Development in 1945 and the International Monetary Fund.

Brezhnev Leonid Ilyich 1906–1982. Soviet leader. A protégé of Stalin and Khrushchev, he came to power (after he and ◊Kosygin forced Khrushchev to resign) as general secretary of the Soviet Communist Party (CPSU) 1964–82 and was president 1977–82. Domestically he was conservative; abroad the USSR was established as a military and political superpower during the Brezhnev era, extending its influence in Africa and Asia.

Brezhnev, born in the Ukraine, joined the CPSU in the 1920s. In 1938 he was made head of propaganda by the new Ukrainian party chief Khrushchev and ascended in the local party hierarchy. After World War II he caught the attention of the CPSU leader Stalin, who inducted Brezhnev into the secretariat and Politburo 1952. Brezhnev was removed from

Brezhnev *Soviet leader Leonid Brezhnev. Appointed Secretary-General of the Communist Party in 1964 and President in 1977, he held both offices until his death.*

these posts after Stalin's death 1953, but returned 1956 with Khrushchev's patronage. In 1960, as criticism of Khrushchev mounted, Brezhnev was moved to the ceremonial post of state president and began to criticize Khrushchev's policies.

Brezhnev stepped down as president 1963 and returned to the Politburo and secretariat. He was elected CPSU general secretary 1964, when Khrushchev was ousted, and gradually came to dominate the conservative and consensual coalition. In 1977 he regained the additional title of state president under the new constitution. He suffered an illness (thought to have been a stroke or heart attack) Mar–Apr 1976 that was believed to have affected his thought and speech so severely that he was not able to make decisions. These were made by his entourage, for example committing the troops to Afghanistan to prop up the government. Within the USSR, economic difficulties mounted; the Brezhnev era was a period of caution and stagnation, although outwardly imperialist. His leadership was denounced during Gorbachev's administration.

Britain, Battle of World War II air battle between German and UK air forces over Britain lasting from 10 July to 31 Oct 1940.

At the outset the Germans had the advantage because they had seized airfields in the Netherlands, Belgium, and France, which were basically safe from attack and from which SE England was within easy range. On 1 Aug 1940 the Luftwaffe had about 4,500 aircraft of all kinds, compared to about 3,000 for the RAF. The Battle of Britain had been intended as a preliminary to the German invasion plan *Seelöwe* (Sea Lion), which Hitler indefinitely postponed 17 Sept and abandoned 10 Oct, choosing instead to invade the USSR.

The Battle of Britain has been divided into five phases: 10 July–7 Aug, the preliminary phase; 8–23 Aug, attack on coastal targets; 24 Aug–6 Sept, attack on Fighter Command airfields; 7–30 Sept, daylight attack on London, chiefly by heavy bombers; and 1–31 Oct, daylight attack on London, chiefly by fighter-bombers. The main battle was between some 600 Hurricanes and Spitfires and the Luftwaffe's 800 Messerschmidt 109s and 1,000 bombers (Dornier 17s, Heinkel 111s, and Junkers 88s). Losses Aug–Sept were, for the RAF: 832 fighters totally destroyed; for the Luftwaffe: 668 fighters and some 700 bombers and other aircraft.

British Broadcasting Corporation (BBC) in the UK, the state-owned broadcasting network. It operates television and national and local radio stations, and is financed solely by the sale of television viewing licences. It is not allowed to carry advertisements, but overseas radio broadcasts (World Service) have a government subsidy.

The BBC was converted from a private company (established 1922) to a public body under royal charter 1927. Under the Charter, news programmes were required to be politically impartial. The first Director-General 1922–1938 was John Reith.

British Empire the various territories all over the world conquered or colonized by Britain from about 1600, most now independent or ruled by other powers; the British Empire was at its largest at the end of World War I, with over 25% of the world's population and area. The ◊Commonwealth is composed of former and remaining territories of the British Empire.

broadcasting the transmission of sound and vision programmes by radio and television. Broadcasting may be organized under complete state control, as in the USSR, or private enterprise, as in the USA, or may operate under a compromise system, as in Britain, where there is a television and radio service

British Empire

current name	*colonial names and history*	*colonized*	*independent*
India	British E India Co. 18th cent.–1858	18th cent.	1947
Pakistan	British E India Co. 18th cent.–1858	18th cent.	1947
Sri Lanka	Portuguese, Dutch 1602–1796; Ceylon 1802–1972	16th cent.	1948
Ghana	Gold Coast	1618	1957
Nigeria		1861	1960
Cyprus	Turkish to 1878, then British rule	1878	1960
Sierra Leone	British protectorate	1788	1961
Tanzania	German E Africa to 1921; British mandate from League of Nations/UN as Tanganyika	19th cent.	1961
Jamaica	Spanish to 1655	17th cent.	1962
Trinidad & Tobago	Spanish 1532–1797; British 1797–1962	1532	1962
Uganda	British protectorate	1894	1962
Kenya	British colony from 1920	1895	1963
Malaysia	British interests from 1786; Federation of Malaya 1957–63	1874	1963
Malawi	British protectorate of Nyasaland 1907–53; Federation of Rhodesia & Nyasaland 1953–64	1891	1964
Malta	French 1798–1814	1798	1964
Zambia	N Rhodesia—British protectorate; Federation of Rhodesia & Nyasaland 1953–64	1924	1964
The Gambia		1888	1965
Singapore	Federation of Malaya 1963–65	1858	1965
Guyana	Dutch to 1796; British Guiana 1796–1966	1620	1966
Botswana	Bechuanaland—British protectorate	1885	1966
Lesotho	Basutoland	1868	1966
Bangladesh	British E India Co. 18th cent.–1858; British India 1858–1947; E Pakistan 1947–71	18th cent.	1971
Zimbabwe	S Rhodesia from 1923; UDI under Ian Smith 1965–79	1895	1980

controlled by the state-regulated ◊British Broadcasting Corporation (BBC) and also the commercial Independent Television Commission (known as the Independent Broadcasting Authority before 1991).

In the USA, broadcasting is only limited by the issue of licences from the Federal Communications Commission to competing commercial companies; in Britain, the BBC is a centralized body appointed by the state and responsible to Parliament, but with policy and programme content not controlled by the state; in Japan, which ranks next to the USA in the number of television sets owned, there is a semigovernmental radio and television broadcasting corporation (NHK) and numerous private television companies.

Television broadcasting entered a new era with the introduction of high-powered communications satellites in the 1980s. The signals broadcast by these satellites are sufficiently strong to be picked up by a small dish ariel located, for example, on the roof of a house. Direct broadcast by satellite thus became a feasible alternative to land-based television services.

Brownshirts the SA (*Sturmabteilung*), or Storm Troops, the private army of the German Nazi party who derived their name from the colour of their uniform.

Bulgaria country in SE Europe, bounded N by Romania, W by Yugoslavia, S by Greece, SW by Turkey, and E by the Black Sea.

history Bulgaria formed part of the ◊Ottoman empire for almost 500 years, becoming an independent kingdom in 1908. Bulgaria allied itself with Germany during World War I. From 1919 a government of the leftist Agrarian Party introduced land reforms, but was overthrown in 1923 by a fascist coup. A monarchical-fascist dictatorship was established 1934 under King Boris III. During World War II Bulgaria again allied itself with Germany, and was occupied in 1944 by the USSR. In 1946 the monarchy was abolished, and a republic was proclaimed under a communist-leaning alliance, the Fatherland Front, led by Georgi Dimitrov (1882–1949). Bulgaria reverted largely to its 1919 frontiers.

the republic The new republic adopted a Soviet-style constitution in 1947, with nationalized industries and cooperative farming introduced. Vulko Chervenkov, became the dominant political figure 1950–54, introducing a Stalinist regime. He was succeeded by the more moderate Todor Zhivkov, under whom Bulgaria became one of the Soviet Union's most loyal satellites.

reform During the 1980s the country faced mounting economic problems. During 1985–89, under the promptings of the Soviet leader ◊Gorbachev, a haphazard series of administrative and economic reforms was instituted. In Nov 1989, influenced by the democratization movements sweeping other East European countries and backed by the Army and the USSR, the foreign secretary, Petar Mladenov ousted Zhivkov in a skilful committee coup, becoming leader of the BCP and president of the state council. He rapidly promoted genuine political pluralism. In Dec 1989 legislation was passed to allow the formation of free opposition parties and trade unions; political prisoners were freed; the secret police was abolished; and free elections were promised for 1990. In Feb 1990 Alexander Lilov, a reformer, was elected party chief, and Andrey Loukanov became prime minister. A special commission was established to investigate allegations of nepotism and high-level embezzlement of state funds under Zhivkov. Zhivkov was placed under house arrest, and later imprisoned, pending trial on charges of corruption and abuse of power. In Feb 1990 a government decree re-legalized private farming and in April 1990 a phased lifting of price controls commenced, as part of a drive towards a market economy.

Bulgaria's relations with neighbouring Turkey deteriorated during 1989, following the flight of 310,000 ethnic Turks from Bulgaria to Turkey after violent government suppression of their protests at the programme of 'Bulgarianization' (forcing them to adopt Slavic names and resettle elsewhere). The Mladenov government officially abandoned the forced assimilation programme Dec 1989, thus provoking demonstrations by anti-Turk nationalists but encouraging the return of more than 100,000 refugees. Petar Mladenov resigned as president July 1990. In Nov 1990, following mass demonstrations in the capital of Sofia, a general strike, and a boycott of parliament by opposition deputies, the reform-communist government of Andrei Lukanov resigned. He was replaced in Dec 1990 by a non-party politician, Dimitar Popov, who headed a caretaker government pending fresh elections and the drafting of a new constitution 1991.

Burma former name (to 1989) of ◊Myanmar.

Burma War war 1942–45 during which Burma (now ◊Myanmar) was occupied by Japan.

Bush George 1924– . The 41st president of the USA from 1989, a Republican. He was director of the Central Intelligence Agency (CIA) 1976–81 and US vice president 1981–89. Evidence came to light in 1987 linking him with the ◊Irangate scandal. His responses as

Bush *US president from 1989, George Bush.*

president to the Soviet leader Gorbachev's diplomatic initiatives were initially criticized as inadequate, but sending US troops to depose his former ally, General Noriega of Panama, proved a popular move at home. In 1990 he sent a large army to Saudi Arabia after Iraq's annexation of Kuwait, and successfully expelled the Iraqis from Kuwait following the United Nations' 'Desert Storm' operation 15 Jan–28 Feb 1991.

Bush, son of a Connecticut senator, moved to Texas in 1948 to build up an oil-drilling company. A congressman 1967–70, he was appointed US ambassador to the United Nations (1971–73) and Republican national chair (1973–74) by President Nixon. During the Ford administration, Bush was a special envoy to China 1974–75. During his time as head of the CIA he is alleged to have supported the cocaine-trafficking General Noriega of Panama as a US ally. Panama was also used as a channel for the secret supply of arms to Iran and the Nicaraguan Contra guerrillas, of which Bush, then vice president, claimed to have been unaware. In the trial of Oliver ◊North, evidence emerged that Bush had visited the president of Honduras in 1985 and offered him extra US aid in exchange for help to the Contras. When, in Dec 1989, Noriega proved uncontrollable, Bush sent an invasion force to Panama and set up a puppet government; Noriega was sent to the USA to stand trial.

Butler Richard Austen ('Rab'), Baron Butler 1902–1982. British Conservative politician. As minister of education 1941–45, he was responsible for the Education Act 1944; he was chancellor of the Exchequer 1951–55, Lord Privy Seal 1955–59, and foreign minister 1963–64. As a candidate for the premiership, he was defeated by Harold Macmillan in 1957 (under whom he was home secretary 1957–62), and by Douglas-Home in 1963. Created Baron Butler 1965.

C

Callaghan (Leonard) James, Baron Callaghan 1912– . British Labour politician. As chancellor of the Exchequer 1964–67, he introduced corporation and capital-gains taxes, and resigned following devaluation. He was home secretary 1967–70 and prime minister 1976–79 in a period of increasing economic stress.

As foreign secretary 1974, Callaghan renegotiated Britain's membership of the European Community. In 1976 he succeeded Harold Wilson as prime minister and in 1977 entered into a pact with the Liberals to maintain his government in office. Strikes in the so called 'winter of dicontent' 1978–79 led to his defeat May 1979. Created Baron Callaghan 1987.

Cambodia country in SE Asia, bordered N and NW by Thailand, N by Laos, E and SE by Vietnam, and SW by the South China Sea.

history Cambodia was occupied by the Khmer empire from the 6th–15th centuries. The region, subject to attacks by the neighbouring Vietnamese and Thai, became a French protectorate in 1863. A nationalist movement began in the 1930s, and in 1940–41 anti-French feeling was fuelled when the French agreed to Japanese demands for bases in Cambodia, and allowed Thailand to annex Cambodian territory. During World War II Cambodia was occupied by Japan. France regained control of the country in 1946, but it achieved semi-autonomy within the French Union in 1949 and full independence in 1953. Prince Norodom Sihanouk (1922–), elected king in 1941, abdicated in favour of his parents and became prime minister as leader of the Popular Socialist Community in 1955. In 1960, when his father died, he became head of state.

Khmer republic Sihanouk remained neutral during the ◊Vietnam War and was overthrown by a right-wing revolt led by pro-USA Lt-Gen Lon Nol in 1970. Lon Nol first became prime minister 1971–72 and then president 1972–75 of the Khmer Republic. His regime was opposed by the exiled Sihanouk and by the communist Khmer Rouge (backed by N Vietnam and China) who merged to form the National United Front of Cambodia. A civil war developed and despite substantial military aid from the USA during its early stages, Lon Nol's government fell in 1975. The country was renamed Kampuchea, with Sihanouk as head of state.

Khmer Rouge regime The Khmer Rouge proceeded ruthlessly to introduce an extreme communist programme, forcing urban groups into rural areas, which led to over 2,500,000 deaths from famine, disease and maltreatment. In 1976 a new constitution removed Sihanouk from power, appointed Khieu Samphan (the former deputy prime minister) president and placed the Communist Party of Kampuchea, led by Pol Pot, in control. The Khmer Rouge developed close links with China and fell out with its former sponsors Vietnam and the Soviet Union. In a Vietnamese invasion of Kampuchea launched in 1978, Pol Pot was overthrown and a pro-Vietnamese puppet government was set up under Heng Samrin, head of the newly formed Kampuchean National United Front for National Salvation. The defeated regime kept up guerrilla resistance under Pol Pot, causing over 300,000 Kampuchean refugees to flee to Thailand in 1979.

resistance movement In 1982 the resistance movement broadened with the formation in Kuala Lumpur (Malaysia) of an anti-Vietnamese coalition and Democratic Kampuchea government-in-exile with Sihanouk as president. The coalition received sympathetic support from ◊ASEAN countries and China. However, its 60,000 troops were outnumbered by the 170,000 Vietnamese who supported the Heng Samrin government. With the resistance coalition's base camps being overrun in 1985, a military victory appeared unlikely. From 1982 the USA aided the KPNLF and the Sihanoukist National Army (ANS) – allies of the Khmer Rouge – with millions of dollars in 'humanitarian' aid and secret 'nonlethal' military aid.

political settlement Hopes of a political settlement were improved by the retirement of the reviled Pol Pot as Khmer Rouge military leader in 1985 and by the appointment of the reformist Hun Sen as prime minister. In spring 1989, following talks with the resistance coalition, the Phnom Penh government agreed to a package of constitutional reforms, including the adoption of Buddhism as the state religion and a change of name to the ideologically neutral State of Cambodia. Withdrawal of the Vietnamese army was completed Sept 1989. However, the United Nations continued to refuse recognition of the Hun Sen government and the civil war intensified, with the Khmer Rouge making advances in the western provinces, capturing the border town of Pailin Oct 1989. The Phnom Penh government was left with an army of 40,000, backed by a 100,000-strong militia, against the resistance coalition's 45,000 guerrillas, half of whom belonged to the Khmer Rouge. In Nov 1990 the five permanent members of the UN Security Council, including the USA, USSR, and China, agreed on the final draft of a Cambodian peace settlement, which provided for an immediate ceasefire and the formation of of an interim administration under UN auspices. The Phnom Penh government dismissed it, objecting to the establishment of a UN administration within the country. However, it is intended that the Paris international conference on Cambodia be reconvened as the preliminary to the signing of a final accord.

Campaign for Nuclear Disarmament (CND) nonparty-political British organization advocating the abolition of nuclear weapons worldwide: CND seeks unilateral British initiatives to help start the multilateral process and end the arms race.

The movement was launched by the philosopher Bertrand Russell and Canon John Collins in 1958. It grew out of the demonstration held outside the government's Atomic Weapons Research Establishment at Aldermaston, Berkshire, at Easter 1956. It held annual marches from Aldermaston to London 1959–63, after the initial march in 1958 which was routed from London to Aldermaston. From 1970 CND has also opposed nuclear power.

Camp David Agreements two framework agreements signed at Camp David, Maryland, USA, in 1978 by the Israeli prime minister Begin and Egyptian president Sadat, under the guidance of US president Carter, covering an Egypt–Israel peace treaty and phased withdrawal of Israel from Sinai, which was completed in 1982, and an overall Middle East settlement including the election by the West Bank and Gaza Strip Palestinians of a 'self-governing authority'. The latter issue stalled over questions of who should represent the Palestinians and what form the self-governing body should take.

Canada country occupying the N part of the North American continent, bounded to the S by the USA, to the N by the Arctic Ocean.

history English and French colonies developed from the 17th century with growing antagonism. In 1791 Canada was divided into English-speaking Upper Canada and French-speaking Lower Canada (Ontario and Québec). The two were united as Canada Province 1841–67, when the self-governing Dominion of Canada was founded by the British North America Act 1867.

Trudeau's era The Canadian Liberal politician Pierre Trudeau was federal prime minister 1968–84 (apart from 1979–80). Trudeau maintained Canada's defensive alliance with the USA but aimed to widen its world influence. Faced with the problems of Québec's French Canadian separatist movement he set about creating the 'just society' and in his later years of office was concerned with 'patriation', or the extent to which the British parliament should determine Canada's constitution. The position was resolved with the passing of the Canada Act 1982, which gave Canada power to amend its constitution and added a charter of rights and freedoms. This represented Canada's complete independence, though it remains a member of the Commonwealth.

changing direction The years after 1984 under the premiership of Brian Mulroney of the Progressive Conservatives were marked by an international realignment with less emphasis on links with Asia, Africa, and Latin America, and a closer trading relaltionship with the USA and more cooperation with Europe; and by constitutional negotiations between the federal and provincial governments.

capitalism economic system in which the principal means of production, distribution, and exchange are in private (individual or corporate) hands and competitively operated for profit. For Karl Marx capitalism was a system in which there were two principal classes of producers, the capitalists, and the labourers who exchanged their labour for wages.

World War I, the Russian Revolution, the Depression of the 1930s, and World War II were interpreted by Marxists as stages towards the collapse of capitalism. After World War II many industrial countries moved towards a ***mixed economy*** which combined the private enterprise of capitalism and a degree of state monopoly, as in nationalized industries. In the 1970s and early 1980s the world economic crises led to Marxist and Communist hopes that capitalism was in its final decline. However, the events of 1989 onwards suggested that the communist systems of central and eastern Europe were in terminal decay, rather than the mixed economies and capitalist systems of western Europe, the US, and Japan.

car small, driver-guided, passenger-carrying motor vehicle; originally the automated version of the horse-drawn carriage. Most are four-wheeled and have water-cooled, piston-type internal-combustion engines fuelled by petrol or diesel.

Although a Frenchman, Jean Etienne Lenoir, patented the first internal combustion engine (gas driven) in 1860, and an Austrian, Siegfried Marcus, built a vehicle which was shown at the Vienna Exhibition (1873), two Germans, Gottleib Daimler and Karl Benz are generally regarded as the inventors of the motorcar. In 1885 Daimler and Benz built and ran the first petrol-driven motorcar. The pattern for the modern motorcar was set by Panhard in 1890 (front radiator, engine under bonnet, sliding-pinion gearbox, wooden ladder-chassis) and Mercédès 1901 (honeycomb radiator, in-line four-cylinder engine, gate-change gearbox, pressed-steel chassis).

In Britain, cars were still considered to be light locomotives, and since the Red Flag Act 1865, had theoretically required someone to walk in front with a red flag (by night, a lantern). The period 1905–06 inaugurated a world motorcar boom continuing to the present day. After World War I popular motoring began with the era of cheap, light (baby) cars made by Citroën, Peugeot, and Renault (France); Austin 7, Morris, Clyno, and Swift (England); Fiat (Italy); Volkswagon (Germany); and the cheap though bigger Ford, Chevrolet, and Dodge in USA. From the 1950s a creative resurgence produced in practical form automatic transmission for small cars, rubber suspension, transverse engine mounting, self-levelling ride, disc brakes, and safer wet-weather tyres. The drive against pollution from the 1960s and the fuel crisis from the 1970s led to experiments with steam cars (cumbersome), diesel engines (slow and heavy, though economical), solar-powered cars, and hybrid cars using both electricity (in town centres) and petrol (on the open road).

In Britain, the Ministry of Transport was established 1919, roads were improved, and various laws and safety precautions imposed to govern the use of cars. A driver must possess a licence, a road tax is imposed, and the law also insists on insurance for third-party risks.

carrier warfare naval warfare involving ◊aircraft carriers. Carrier warfare was conducted during World War II in the battle of the Coral Sea May 1942, which stopped the Japanese advance in the South Pacific, and in the battle of Midway Islands June 1942, which weakened the Japanese navy through the loss of four aircraft carriers.

Carter Jimmy (James Earl) 1924– . The 39th president of the USA 1977–81, a Democrat. In 1976 he narrowly wrested the presidency from Gerald Ford. Features of his presidency were the return of the Panama Canal Zone to Panama, the ◊Camp David Agreements for peace in the Middle East, and the Iranian seizure of US embassy hostages. He was defeated by Ronald Reagan 1980.

Casement Roger David 1864–1916. Irish nationalist. While in the British consular service, he exposed the ruthless exploitation of the people of the Belgian Congo and Peru, for which he was knighted in 1911 (degraded 1916). He was hanged for treason by the British for his part in the Irish republican ◊Easter Rising.

Castro (Ruz) Fidel 1927– . Cuban Communist politician, prime minister 1959–76 and president from 1976. He led two unsuccessful coups against the right-wing Batista regime and led the revolution that overthrew the dictator 1959. From 1979 he was also president of the nonaligned movement, although promoting the line of the USSR, which subsidized his regime.

The Castro regime introduced a centrally planned economy based on the production for export of sugar, tobacco, and nickel. Aid for development has been provided by the USSR

Castro (Ruz) *Cuban revolutionary and premier Fidel Castro.*

while Cuba joined ◊Comecon in 1972. By nationalizing US-owned businesses in 1960 Castro gained the enmity of the USA, which came to a head in the ◊Cuban missile crisis of 1962. His regime became socialist and he espoused Marxism-Leninism until, in 1974, he rejected Marx's formula 'from each according to his ability and to each according to his need' and decreed that each Cuban should 'receive according to his work'.

Cat and Mouse Act popular name for the *Prisoners, Temporary Discharge for Health, Act* 1913; an attempt by the UK Liberal government under Herbert Asquith to reduce embarrassment caused by the incarceration of ◊suffragettes accused of violent offences against property.

When they embarked on hunger strikes, prison authorities introduced forced feeding, which proved humiliating and sometimes dangerous to the women. Following a public outcry, the hunger strikers were released on a licence that could be revoked without further trial. The government was accused of playing cat to suffragette mice by its adoption of powers of release and rearrest.

Ceauşescu Nicolae 1918–1989. Romanian politician, leader of the Romanian Communist Party (RCP), in power 1965–89. He pursued a policy line independent of and critical of the USSR. He appointed family members, including his wife ***Elena Ceauşescu***, to senior state and party posts, and governed in an increasingly repressive manner, zealously implementing schemes that impoverished the nation. The Ceauşescus were overthrown in a bloody revolutionary coup Dec 1989 and executed on Christmas Day 1989.

censorship the suppression by authority of material considered immoral, heretical, subversive, libellous, damaging to state security, or otherwise offensive. It is generally more stringent under totalitarian or strongly religious regimes and in wartime.

The British government uses the D-notice (censorship of matters relating to national security) and the Official Secrets Act to protect itself. Laws relating to obscenity, libel, and blasphemy act as a form of censorship. The media exercise a degree of self-censorship, for example in the British Board of Film Classification, run by the film industry. There is a similar body, popularly called the Hays Office (after its first president, 1922–45, Will H Hays), in the USA.

The libel laws in Britain are more rigid than in France or the USA, for example. Censorship of plays in the UK by the Lord Chamberlain (under the Theatres Act 1843, a continuation of the Licensing Act 1737) ended in 1968. In July 1989 the Soviet government announced the removal of import restrictions on all banned authors, the only remaining constraints being on material calling for the violent overthrow of the state and on pornography. In Oct 1989 a Japanese court upheld the censorship by the education ministry of history textbooks depicting Japanese atrocities during the invasion of China in the 1930s.

Central Intelligence Agency (CIA) US intelligence organization established 1947. It has actively intervened overseas, generally to undermine left-wing regimes or to protect US financial interests; for example, in the Congo (now Zaïre) and Nicaragua. William Webster became director 1987. From 1980 all covert activity by the CIA has by law to be reported to Congress, preferably beforehand, and must be authorized by the president.

Developed from the wartime Office of Strategic Services and set up by Congress, as part of the National Security Act, on the lines of the British Secret Service, the CIA was intended solely for use overseas in the Cold War. It was involved in, for example, the restoration of the Shah of Iran 1953, South Vietnam (during the Vietnam War), Chile (the coup against President Allende), and Cuba (the ◊Bay of Pigs). On the domestic front, it was illegally involved in the ◊Watergate political scandal and in the 1970s lost public confidence when US influence collapsed in Iran, Afghanistan, Nicaragua, Yemen, and elsewhere. Past directors include William Casey, Richard Helms, and George ◊Bush. Domestic intelligence functions are performed by the ◊Federal Bureau of Investigation.

Central Powers originally the signatories of the Triple Alliance 1882; Germany, Austria-Hungary, and Italy. During World War I, Italy remained neutral before joining the ◊Allies.

Chamberlain (Arthur) Neville 1869–1940. British Conservative politician, son of Joseph Chamberlain. He was prime minister 1937–40; his policy of appeasement towards the fascist dictators Mussolini and Hitler (with whom he concluded the ◊Munich Agreement 1938) failed to prevent the outbreak of World War II. He resigned 1940 following the defeat of the British forces in Norway.

Younger son of Joseph Chamberlain and half-brother of Austen Chamberlain, he was born in Birmingham, of which he was lord mayor in 1915. He was minister of health in 1923 and 1924–29 and worked at slum clearance. In 1931 he was chancellor of the Exchequer in the national government, and in 1937 succeeded Stanley Baldwin as prime

Chamberlain *British prime minister Neville Chamberlain waving the Munich Agreement that he negotiated with the Nazi dictator Hitler 1938.*

minister. Trying to close the old Anglo-Irish feud, he agreed to return to Eire those ports that had been occupied by the navy. He also attempted to appease the demands of the European dictators, particularly Mussolini. In 1938 he went to Munich and negotiated with Hitler the settlement of the Czechoslovak question. He was ecstatically received on his return, and claimed that the Munich Agreement brought 'peace in our time'. Within a year, however, Britain was at war with Germany.

Channel tunnel tunnel built beneath the English Channel, linking Britain with mainland Europe. It comprises twin rail tunnels, 50 km/31 mi long and 7.3 m/24 ft in diameter, located 40 m/130 ft beneath the seabed. Specially designed shuttle trains carrying cars and lorries will run between terminals at Folkestone, Kent, and Sangatte, W of Calais, France. It was begun 1986 and is scheduled to be operational 1993.

A channel tunnel is not a new idea. In the 1880s British financier and railway promoter Edward Watkin started boring a tunnel near Dover, abandoning it 1894 because of governmental opposition after driving some 1.6 km/1 mile out to sea. In 1973 Britain and France agreed to back a tunnel, but a year later Britain pulled out following a change of government. The estimated cost has continually been revised upwards and in 1989 was £6 billion. In 1990 the French and British tunnelling teams met underneath the Channel.

Chaplin *Comic film actor Charlie Chaplin.*

Chaplin Charlie (Charles Spencer) 1889–1977. English film actor-director. He made his reputation as a tramp with a smudge moustache, bowler hat, and twirling cane in silent comedies from the mid-1910s, including *The Rink* 1916, *The Kid* 1921, and *The Gold Rush* 1925. His work often contrasts buffoonery with pathos, and his later films combine dialogue with mime and music, as in *The Great Dictator* 1940, and *Limelight* 1952. He was one of cinema's most popular and greatest stars. He left the USA 1952 when accused of communist sympathies in the McCarthy era, and moved to Switzerland.

Cheka secret police operating in the USSR 1917–23. It originated from the tsarist Okhrana and became successively the OGPU (GPU) 1923–34, NKVD 1934–46, and MVD 1946–53, before its present form, the ◊KGB.

chemical warfare use in war of gaseous, liquid, or solid substances intended to have a toxic effect on humans, animals, or plants. Together with biological warfare, it was banned 1925 by the Geneva Convention, although this has not always been observed. In 1989, when the 149-nation Conference on Chemical Weapons unanimously voted to outlaw chemical weapons, the total US stockpile was estimated at 30,000 tonnes and the Soviet stockpile at 300,000 tonnes.

In a deal with the USA, the USSR offered

to eliminate its stocks; the USA is destroying its current stocks and replacing them with new 'binary' nerve-gas weapons. Some 20 nations currently hold chemical weapons, including Iraq, Iran, Israel, Syria, Libya, South Africa, and China.

There are several types of chemical weapons. ***Irritant gases*** may cause permanent injury or death. Examples include chlorine, phosgene (Cl_2CO), and mustard gas ($C_4H_8Cl_2S$), used in World War I (1914–18) and allegedly used by Soviet forces in Afghanistan, by Vietnamese forces in Laos, and by Iraq against Iran during their 1980–88 war. ***Tear gases***, such as CS gas, used in riot control, affect the lungs and eyes, causing temporary blindness. ***Nerve gases*** are organophosphorus compounds similar to insecticides, which are taken into the body through the skin and lungs and break down the action of the nervous system. Developed by the Germans for World War II, they were not used.

Chernobyl town in Ukraine, USSR, site of nuclear power station. In Apr 1986 a leak, caused by overheating, occurred in a non-pressurized boiling-water nuclear reactor. The resulting clouds of radioactive isotopes were traced as far away as Sweden; over 250 people were killed, and thousands of square miles contaminated. It has been calculated that the accident will be responsible for thousands of deaths from cancer in future years.

Chiang Kai-shek Pinyin *Jiang Jie Shi* 1887–1975. Chinese Nationalist Guomindang (Kuomintang) general and politician, president of China 1928–31 and 1943–49, and of Taiwan from 1949, where he set up a US-supported right-wing government on his expulsion from the mainland by the Communist forces. He was a commander in the civil war that lasted from the end of imperial rule 1911 to the Second Sino-Japanese War and beyond, having split with the Communist leader Mao Zedong 1927.

Chiang took part in the revolution of 1911 that overthrew the Qing dynasty of the Manchus, and on the death of the Nationalist Guomindang leader Sun Yat-sen was made commander in chief of the Nationalist armies in S China 1925. Collaboration with the communists, broken 1927, was resumed after the Xian incident 1936 when China needed to pool military strength, and Chiang nominally headed the struggle against the Japanese invaders of World War II, receiving the Japanese surrender 1945. The following year, civil war between the Nationalists and Communists erupted, and in Dec 1949 Chiang and his followers took refuge on the island of Taiwan, maintaining a large army in the hope of reclaiming the mainland. His authoritarian regime enjoyed US support until his death. His son, Chiang Ching-kuo, then became president.

Chile South American country, bounded N by Peru and Bolivia, E by Argentina, and S and W by the Pacific Ocean.

history Chile was colonized by Spanish settlers in the 16th century, although the indigenous Araucanian Indians continued to rebel until the late 19th century. Becoming independent from Spain 1818, Chile went to war with Peru and Bolivia 1879 and gained considerable territory from them. Most of the 20th century has been characterized by left- versus right-wing struggles. The Christian Democrats under Eduardo Frei held power 1964–70, followed by a left-wing coalition led by Dr Salvador ◊Allende, the first democratically elected Marxist head of state. He promised social justice by constitutional means and began nationalizing industries, including US-owned copper mines.

'authoritarian democracy' The ◊CIA saw Allende as a pro-Cuban communist and encouraged opposition to him. In 1973 the army, led by General Augusto Pinochet, overthrew the government. Allende was killed or, as the new regime claimed, committed suicide. Pinochet became president, and his opponents were tortured, imprisoned, or just 'disappeared'. In 1976 Pinochet proclaimed an 'authoritarian democracy' and in 1977 banned all political parties. His policies were 'endorsed' by a referendum 1978.

anti-government opposition In 1980 a 'transition to democracy' by 1989 was announced, but imprisonment and torture continued. By 1983 opposition to Pinochet had increased, with demands for a return to democratic government. He attempted to placate opposition by initiating public works. In 1984 an anti- government bombing campaign began, aimed mainly at electricity installations, resulting in a 90-day state of emergency, followed by a 90-day state of siege. In 1985, as opposition grew in the Catholic Church and the army as well as among the public, another state of emergency was declared, but the bombings and killings continued.

plural politics In Oct 1988 Pinochet's proposal to remain in office for another eight-year term was rejected in a plebiscite. Another plebiscite in Aug 1989 approved constitutional changes leading to a return to pluralist politics and in Dec the moderate PDC candidate, Patricio Aylwin Azocar, was elected president, his term of office beginning March 1990. Pinochet demanded the retention of his post as army commander in chief after his relinquishment of the presidency. In Jan 1990, the junta approved the disbanding of the secret police of the National Information Centre (CNI). In Sept 1990 a government commission was set up to investigate some 2,000 political executions 1973–78, 500 political murders 1978–90, and 700 disappearances. In the same month the former discredited politician, Salvador Allende, was officially recognized by being buried in a marked grave. In the same month President Aylwin censured General Pinochet for trying to return to active politics.

China country in SE Asia, bounded N by Mongolia; NW and NE by the USSR; SW by India and Nepál; S by Bhutan, Myanmar (Burma), Laos, and Vietnam; SE by the South China Sea; and E by the East China Sea, North Korea, and the USSR.

government China is divided into 21 provinces, 5 autonomous regions, and 3 municipalities (Beijing, Shanghai, and Tianjin), each having an elected local people's government with policy-making power in defined areas.

Ultimate authority resides in the single-chamber National People's Congress (NPC), indirectly elected through local people's congresses. The NPC also elects for a five-year term a State Central Military Commission (SCMC), leading members of the judiciary, the vice president, and the state president. Executive administration is effected by a prime minister and a cabinet. China's controlling force is the Chinese Communist Party (CCP).

history Imperial rule ended in 1911 with the formation of a republic in 1912. After several years of civil war the nationalist ◊Guomindang, led by ◊Chiang Kai-shek, was firmly installed in power in 1926, with Communist aid. In 1927 Chiang Kai-shek began a purge of the Communists, who began the 'Long March' (1934–36) to Shaanxi, which became their base. In 1931 Japan began its penetration of Manchuria and in 1937 began the second ◊Sino-Japanese War, during which both Communists and Nationalists fought Japan. Civil war resumed after the Japanese surrender in 1945, until in 1949, following their elimination of Nationalist resistance on the mainland, the Communists inaugurated the People's Republic of China. To begin with, the Communist regime concentrated on economic reconstruction. A centralized Soviet-style constitution was adopted in 1954, industries were nationalized, and central planning and moderate land reform introduced. The USSR provided economic aid, while China intervened in the ◊Korean War. Development during this period was based on material incentives and industrialization.

the Great Leap Forward From 1958, under state president and CCP chairman ◊Mao Zedong, China embarked on a major new policy, the ◊Great Leap Forward. This created large self-sufficient agricultural and industrial communes in an effort to achieve classless 'true communism'. The experiment proved unpopular and impossible to coordinate. Famine, combined with floods, led to the death of over 20 million people 1959–62. A breach in Sino-Soviet relations brought a withdrawal of Soviet technical advisers in 1960. The failure of the 'Great Leap' reduced Mao's influence 1962–65, and a successful 'recovery programme' was begun under President Liu Shaoqi. Private farming plots and markets were re-introduced, communes reduced in size, and income differentials and material incentives restored.

the Cultural Revolution Mao struck back against what he saw as a return to capitalism by launching the Great Proletarian Cultural Revolution (1966–69). During the campaign, Mao, supported by People's Liberation Army (PLA) chief Lin Biao and the Shanghai-based ◊'Gang of Four', encouraged student (Red Guard) demonstrations against party and government leaders. The chief targets were Liu Shaoqi, ◊Deng Xiaoping (head of the CCP secretariat) and Peng Zhen (Mayor of Beijing). All were forced out of office. The campaign grew anarchic during 1967, necessitating PLA intervention and the dispersal of Red Guards into the countryside to 'learn from the peasants'. Government institutions fell into abeyance during the Cultural Revolution, and new 'Three Part Revolutionary Committees', comprising Maoist party officials, trade unionists and PLA commanders, took over administration. By 1970, Mao sided with pragmatic Prime Minister ◊Zhou Enlai and began restoring order and a more balanced system. A number of 'ultra-leftists' were ousted in 1970, and in 1971 Lin Biao died after a failed coup. In 1972–73 Deng Xiaoping, finance minister Li Xiannian, and others, were rehabilitated, and a policy of détente towards the USA began. This reconstruction movement was climaxed by the summoning of the NPC in 1975 for the first time in 11 years to ratify a new constitution and approve an economic plan termed the 'Four Modernizations' – agriculture, industry, defence, and science and technology – that aimed at placing China on a par with the West by the year 2000.

Gang of Four The deaths of Zhou Enlai and Mao Zedong in 1976 unleashed a violent succession struggle between the leftist 'Gang of Four', led by Jiang Qing, and moderate 'rightists', grouped around vice-premier Deng

Xiaoping. Deng was forced into hiding by the 'Gang'; and Mao's moderate protegé ◊Hua Guofeng became CCP chair and head of government in 1976. Hua arrested the 'Gang' on charges of treason and held power 1976–78 as a stop-gap leader, continuing Zhou Enlai's modernization programme. His authority was progressively challenged, however, by Deng Xiaoping. By 1979, Deng had gained effective charge of the government, controlling a majority in the Politburo. State and judicial bodies began to meet again, and economic reforms were introduced. These involved the dismantling of the commune system, the introduction of direct farm incentives, and the encouragement of foreign investment. By June 1981 Deng's supremacy was assured when his protegés Hu Yaobang and ◊Zhao Ziyang became party chair and prime minister and the 'Gang of Four' were sentenced to life imprisonment. In 1982, Hua Guofeng and a number of senior colleagues were ousted from the Politburo, and the NPC adopted a definitive constitution, restoring the post of state president (abolished since 1975) and establishing a new civil rights code. The new administration was a collective leadership, of Hu Yaobang, Zhao Ziyang, and Deng Xiaoping. The triumvirate pursued a three-pronged policy aimed firstly at streamlining the party and state bureaucracies and promoting younger technocrats. Secondly, they sought to curb PLA influence by retiring senior commanders and reducing manpower. Thirdly, they gave priority to economic modernization by extending market incentives and local autonomy and by introducing a new 'open door' policy to encourage foreign trade and investment. These economic reforms met with substantial success in the agricultural sector (output more than doubled 1978–85) but had adverse side effects, widening regional and social income differentials and fuelling a wave of 'mass consumerism' that created balance of payments problems. Contact with the West brought demands for full-scale democratization in China. These calls led in 1986 to widespread student demonstrations, and party chief Hu Yaobang was dismissed in 1987 for failing to check the disturbances. Conservative forces sought to halt the changes and re-establish central party control, evidenced during 1987 by the launching of a campaign against 'bourgeois liberalization' (Western ideas).

pro-democracy movement Chen Yun, Peng Zhen, and Deng Xiaoping all retired from the Politburo in Oct 1987, and soon after Li Peng, the adopted son of Zhou Enlai, took over as prime minister, Zhao Ziyang having become CCP chair. With inflation spiralling, economic reform was halted in 1988 and an austerity budget introduced in 1989. This provoked urban unrest and, following Hu Yaobang's death April 1989, a student-led pro-democracy movement was launched in Beijing that rapidly spread to provincial cities with mass demonstrations. A brutal crackdown was launched against the demonstrators by Li Peng and President Yang Shangkun, with Deng Xiaoping's support. Martial law was proclaimed and in June 1989 more than 2,000 unarmed protesters were massacred in the capital's Tiananmen Square. A month later Zhao Ziyang, who had sought compromise with the demonstrators, was ousted as CCP chief and replaced by Jiang Zemin, the Shanghai party chief and new protegé of Deng Xiaoping. A crackdown on dissidents was launched, as the pendulum swung sharply away from reform towards conservatism.

foreign affairs In foreign affairs, China's 1960 rift with the USSR over policy differences became irrevocable in 1962 when Russia sided with India during a brief Sino-Indian border war. Relations with the USSR deteriorated further in 1969 after border clashes in the disputed Ussuri River region. China pursued ◊nonaligned strategy, projecting itself as the voice of Third World nations, although it achieved nuclear capability by 1964. During the early 1970s, concern with Soviet expansionism brought rapprochement with the USA, bringing China's entry to the UN (at ◊Taiwan's expense) in 1971 and culminating in the establishment of full Sino-American diplomatic relations in 1979. In recent years there has been a partial rapprochement with the USSR, culminating in Gorbachev's visit in May 1989. However, a new rift became evident in 1990, with the Chinese government denouncing the Soviet leader's 'revisionism'. Until the Tiananmen Square massacre in June 1989, relations with the West were warm during the Deng administration, with economic contacts broadening. In Dec 1989 President Bush sent a surprise mission to China, defending the contacts as an effort to prevent dangerous isolation of the Chinese and as a way to engage them in constructive peace proposals for Cambodia.

Chinese Revolution a series of major political upheavals in China 1911–49 that eventually led to Communist party rule and the establishment of the People's Republic of China. In 1912, a Nationalist revolt overthrew the imperial Manchu (or Ching) dynasty. Led by Sun Yat-sen 1923–25, and by Chiang Kai-shek 1925–49, the Nationalists, or Guomindang, were increasingly challenged by the growing Communist movement. The 10,000 km/6,000 mi ◊*Long March* to the NW by the Communists 1934–35 to escape from attacks by the Nationalist forces resulted in Mao Zedong's emergence as Communist leader. During World War II 1939–45, the various Chinese political groups pooled military resources against the Japanese invaders. After World War II, the conflict reignited into open civil war 1946–49, until the Nationalists were defeated at Nanking and forced to flee to Taiwan. Communist rule was established in the People's Republic of China under the leadership of Mao.

The Chinese revolution came about with the collapse of the Manchu (or Ching) dynasty, a result of increasing internal disorders, pressure from foreign governments, and the weakness of central government. A Nationalist revolt led to a provisional republican constitution being proclaimed and a government established in Beijing (Peking). Led by Sun Yat Sen and Chiang Kai- shek, the Nationalists were faced with the problems of restoring the authority of central government and meeting the challenges from militaristic factions and the growing Communist movement. After 1930, Chiang launched a series of attacks that encircled the communists in SE China and led to an attempt by communist army commander Chu Teh to break out. The resulting Long March to NW China from Oct 1934–Oct 1935 reduced the Communists' army from over 100,000 to little more than 8,000, mainly as a result of skirmishes with Chiang's forces and the severity of the conditions. During the march, a power struggle developed between Mao Zedong and Chang Kuo T'ao that eventually split the force. Mao's group finally based itself in Yen'an, where it remained throughout the war with the Japanese, forming an uneasy alliance with the Nationalists to expel the invaders. Mao's troops formed the basis of the Red Army that renewed the civil war against the nationalists 1946 and emerged victorious after defeating them at Nanking 1949. As a result, Communist rule was established in China under Mao's leadership.

Chou En-lai alternative transcription of ◊Zhou Enlai.

Churchill Winston (Leonard Spencer) 1874–1965. British Conservative politician. In Parliament from 1900, as a Liberal until 1923, he held a number of ministerial offices, including First Lord of the Admiralty 1911–15 and chancellor of the Exchequer 1924–29. Absent from the cabinet in the 1930s, he returned Sept 1939 to lead a coalition government 1940–45, negotiating with Allied leaders in World War II; he was again prime minister 1951–55. Nobel Prize for Literature 1953.

Churchill *British Conservative politician Winston Churchill, 1955.*

He was born at Blenheim Palace, the elder son of Lord Randolph Churchill. During the Boer War he was a war correspondent and made a dramatic escape from imprisonment in Pretoria. In 1900 he was elected Conservative member of Parliament for Oldham, but he disagreed with Chamberlain's tariff-reform policy and joined the Liberals. Asquith made him president of the Board of Trade 1908, where he introduced legislation for the establishment of labour exchanges. He became home secretary 1910.

In 1911 Asquith appointed him First Lord of the Admiralty. In 1915–16 he served in the trenches in France, but then resumed his parliamentary duties and was minister of munitions under Lloyd George 1917, when he was concerned with the development of the tank. After the armistice he was secretary for war 1918–21 and then as colonial secretary played a leading part in the establishment of the Irish Free State. During the postwar years he was active in support of the Whites (anti-Bolsheviks) in Russia. In 1922–24 Churchill was out of Parliament. He left the Liberals 1923, and was returned for Epping as a Conservative 1924. Baldwin made him chancellor of the Exchequer, and he brought about Britain's return to the gold standard and was prominent in the defeat of the General Strike of 1926. In 1929–39 he was out of office as he disagreed with the Conservatives on India, rearmament, and Chamberlain's policy of appeasement. On the first day of World War II he went back to his old post at the Admiralty. In May 1940 he was called to the premiership as head of an all-party administration and made a much quoted 'blood, tears, toil, and sweat' speech to the House of Commons. He had a close relationship with US president Roosevelt, and in Aug 1941 concluded the ◊Atlantic Charter with him. He travelled to Washington, Casablanca, Cairo, Moscow, and Tehran, meeting the other leaders of the Allied war effort. In Feb 1945 he met Stalin and Roosevelt in the Crimea and agreed on the final plans for victory. On 8 May he announced the unconditional surrender of Germany. On 23 May 1945 the coalition was dissolved, and Churchill formed a caretaker government drawn mainly from the Conservatives. Defeated in the general election in July, he became leader of the opposition until the election Oct 1951, in which he again became prime minister. In Apr 1955 he resigned.

CIA abbreviation for ◊***Central Intelligence Agency***.

cinema a 20th-century form of art and entertainment, consisting of 'moving pictures' in either black and white or colour, projected on to a screen.

film history The first moving pictures were shown in the 1890s. Thomas Edison persuaded James J Corbett (1866–1933), the world boxing champion 1892–97, to act a boxing match for a film. Lumière in France, Latham in the USA, R W Paul in England, and others were making moving pictures of actual events (for example, *The Derby* 1896, shown in London on the evening of the race), and of simple scenes such as a train coming into a station. D W Griffith, the US director, revolutionized film technique, introducing the close-up, the flashback, the fade-out, and the fade-in. His first epic was *The Birth of a Nation* 1915, and his second, *Intolerance*, with spectacular scenes in the Babylonian section, followed 1916.

artistic development Silent films were never completely silent, there was always a musical background, integral to the film, whether played by a solo pianist in a suburban cinema or a 100-piece orchestra in a big city theatre. The arrival of sound films (John Barrymore as *Don Juan* 1926 and Al Jolson as *The Jazz Singer* 1927), seen at first as having only novelty value, soon brought about a wider perspective and greater artistic possibilities through the combination of sight and sound.

early films Apart from story films, the industry produced newsreels of current events and 'documentaries' depicting factual life, of which the pioneers were the US film-maker Robert Flaherty (*Nanook of the North* 1920), and the Scot John Grierson (*Drifters* 1929). Animated cartoon films, which achieved their first success with Patrick Sullivan's *Felix the Cat* 1917, were later surpassed in popularity by Walt Disney's *Mickey Mouse* 1937 and the feature length *Snow White and the Seven Dwarfs* 1938 and others. During the 1930s classic dramas and screwball comedies were made; during the 1940s war films predominated; and during the 1950s *film noir* and Technicolour musicals competed with early television.

civil disobedience the deliberate breaking of laws considered unjust, a form of nonviolent direct action; the term was coined by the US writer Thoreau in an essay of that name 1849. It was advocated by Mahatma ◊Gandhi to prompt peaceful withdrawal of British power from India. Civil disobedience has since been employed by, for instance, the US civil-rights movement in the 1960s and the peace movement in the 1980s.

civil rights the rights of the individual citizen. In many countries they are specified (as in the Bill of Rights of the US constitution) and guaranteed by law to ensure equal treatment for all citizens. In the USA, the struggle to obtain civil rights for former slaves and their descendants, both through legislation and in practice, has been a major theme since the Civil War.

The ***civil rights movement*** is a general term for this aspect of US history. See ***history*** under ◊black.

Civil War, Russian a bitter conflict of nearly three years which followed Russian setbacks in World War I and the upheavals of the 1917 Revolution. In Dec 1917 counterrevolutionary armies, the 'Whites' began to organize resistance to the October Revolution of 1917. The Red Army (Bolsheviks), improvised by Leon Trotsky, opposed them and civil war resulted. Hostilities continued for nearly three years with the Bolsheviks being successful.

The war was fought in the regions of the Caucasus and Southern Russia; the Ukraine; the Baltic; Northern Russia; and Siberia. The Bolsheviks also had to fight against the armies of Latvia, Lithuania, Estonia and Finland. In N Russia the British and French landed troops at Murmansk in June 1918, seized Archangel, and set up a puppet government. They continued outbursts of fighting against the Bolsheviks until Oct 1919. In Siberia, Admiral Kolchak, with the assistance of a Czech legion (composed of prisoners of war) and of Japanese forces that had landed at Vladivostok, established a 'White' government at Omsk. Kolchak was captured and executed by the Bolsheviks in Nov 1922. While each of the 'White' armies was engaged in an isolated operation, the Soviet forces were waging a single war. Trotsky was an active agent for the Bolsheviks in all the crucial operations of the war. The Bolsheviks put down peasant risings in 1920 and a mutiny by sailors at Kronstadt in 1921. The Bolsheviks were far superior to the Whites in both organization and propaganda. The last foreign forces left in 1922 when the Japanese evacuated Vladivostok. The Soviet government was recognized by Britain in 1924, and by the USA in 1933.

Civil War, Spanish war 1936–39 precipitated by a military revolt led by General Franco against the Republican government. Inferior military capability led to the gradual defeat of the Republicans by 1939.

Franco's insurgents (Nationalists, who were supported by Fascist Italy and Nazi Germany) seized power in the south and northwest, but were suppressed in areas such as Madrid and Barcelona by the workers' militia. The loyalists (Republicans) were aided by the USSR and the volunteers of the International Brigade, which included several writers, among them George Orwell.

1937 Bilbao and the Basque country were bombed into submission by the Nationalists.
1938 Catalonia was cut off from the main Republican territory.
1939 Barcelona fell in Jan and Madrid in Apr, and Franco established a dictatorship.

Clemenceau Georges 1841–1929. French politician and journalist (prominent in the defence of Dreyfus). He was prime minister 1906–09 and 1917–20. After World War I he presided over the Peace Conference in Paris that drew up the Treaty of Versailles, but failed to secure for France the Rhine as a frontier.

Clemenceau was mayor of Montmartre, Paris, in the war of 1870, and in 1871 was elected a member of the National Assembly at Bordeaux. He was elected a deputy in 1876 after the formation of the Third Republic. An extreme radical, he soon earned the nickname of 'the Tiger' on account of his ferocious attacks on politicians whom he disliked. In 1893 he lost his seat and spent the next ten years in journalism. In 1902 he was elected senator for the Var, and was soon one of the most powerful politicians in France. When he became prime minister for the second time in 1917, he made the decisive appointment of Marshal Foch as supreme commander.

CND abbreviation for ◊*Campaign for Nuclear Disarmament*.

cold war hostilities short of armed conflict, consisting of tensions, threats, and subversive political activities describing the relations from about 1945–1990 between the USSR and Eastern Europe on one hand, and the USA and Western Europe on the other. The cold war was exacerbated by propaganda, covert activity by intelligence agencies, and economic sanctions; it intensified at times of conflict anywhere in the world. Arms reduction agreements between the USA and USSR in the late 1980s, and a diminution of Soviet influence in Eastern Europe, symbolized by the opening of the Berlin Wall 1989, led to a reassessment of positions and the 'war' officially ended in 1990.

1947 The term 'cold war' was first used by Bernard Baruch in a speech referring to the Truman Doctrine in April.
1950–53 The Korean War.
1956 The USSR intervened in Hungary to put down a revolution.
1962 The Cuban missile crisis.
1964–75 The USA participated in the Vietnam War.
1968 The USSR intervened in Czechoslovakia.
1972 SALT I accord on arms limitation signed by USA and USSR, beginning a thaw, or détente, in E–W relations.
1979 The USSR invaded Afghanistan.
1980–81 US support for the Solidarity movement in Poland. US president Reagan called the USSR an 'evil empire'.
1982 US covert and military intervention in Central America increases to aid antisocialist groups.
1983 US president Reagan proposed to militarize space (Star Wars).
1986 Soviet leader Gorbachev made a proposal for nuclear disarmament that was turned down by Reagan.
1988 Soviet and US leaders reach accord on medium-range nuclear missiles.
1989 Poland elects non-Communist government; Hungary declares itself a republic; East Germany opens borders to the West; Czechoslovakia lifts travel restrictions; revolution in Romania topples Communist dictatorship; Gorbachev renounces 'Brezhnev doctrine' of intervention and withdraws from Afghanistan.
1990 November – the formal end of the cold war.

collectivization the policy pursued by Stalin in the USSR after 1928 to reorganize agriculture by taking land into state or collective ownership. Much of this was achieved during the first two ◊Five Year Plans but only with much coercion and loss of life among the peasantry.

colonialism another name for ◊*imperialism*.

Comecon (*Council for Mutual Economic Assistance*, or CMEA) economic organization established 1949 and prompted by the ◊Marshall Plan, linking the USSR with Bulgaria, Czechoslovakia, Hungary, Poland, Romania, East Germany (from 1950), Mongolia (from 1962), Cuba (from 1972), and Vietnam (from 1978), with Yugoslavia as an associated member. Albania also belonged 1949–61.

The secretariat is based in Moscow and regular annual meetings are held in the member countries. Trade between member countries is hampered by the lack of a convertible currency, the transferable rouble being merely an accounting device. It was agreed in 1987 that official relations should be established with the European Community, and a free-market approach to trading was adopted 1990.

Cominform *Com*munist *Inform*ation Bureau 1947–56, established by the Soviet politician Andrei Zhdanov (1896–1948) to exchange information between European communist parties. Yugoslavia was expelled 1948.

commando member of a specially trained, highly mobile military unit. The term originated in S Africa, where it referred to Boer military reprisal raids against Africans in the nineteenth century and, in the South African Wars, against the British. Commando units have often carried out operations behind enemy lines.

In Britain, the first commando units were the British Combined Operations Command who raided enemy-occupied territory in World War II after the evacuation of Dunkirk 1940. Among the Commando raids were those on the Lofoten Islands (3–4 Mar 1941), Vaagsö, Norway (27 Dec 1941), St Nazaire (28 Mar 1942), and Dieppe (19 Aug 1942). In 1940 Commandos were sent to the Middle East. One of their most daring exploits was the raid Nov 1941 on Rommel's HQ in the desert. At the end of the war the army Commandos were disbanded, but the role was carried on by the Royal Marines.

Commandos were later active in other theatres of war, for example, in French N Africa, Sicily, and Italy, and went into action on D-Day, taking part in some of the hardest fighting in Normandy. In Nov 1944 Commandos took part in the capture of the island of Walcheren at the mouth of the Scheldt, and later distinguished themselves in the crossing of the Rhine. Commandos also fought in Burma (now Myanmar).

Common Agricultural Policy (CAP) system that allows the member countries of the ◊European Community (EC) jointly to organize and control agricultural production within their boundaries. The objectives of the CAP were outlined in the Treaty of Rome: to increase agricultural productivity, to provide a fair standard of living for farmers and their employees, to stabilize markets, and to assure the availability of supply at a price that was reasonable to the consumer.

The policy, applied to most types of agricultural product, was evolved and introduced 1962–67, and has since been amended to take account of changing conditions and the entry of additional member states. At the heart of the CAP is a price support system based on setting a target price for a commodity, imposing a levy on cheaper imports, and intervening to buy produce at a predetermined level to maintain the stability of the internal market. When the CAP was devised, the six member states were net importers of most essential agricultural products, and the intervention mechanism was aimed at smoothing out occasional surpluses caused by an unusually productive season. Since then, agricultural yields within the EC have increased greatly, so that surpluses of cereals and livestock during the 1980s put the CAP under intense financial and political strain, and led to mounting pressure for reform.

Common Market popular name for the ◊European Community (EC).

Commonwealth, the (British) voluntary association of 48 states that have been or still are ruled by Britain (see ◊British Empire). Independent states are full 'members of the Commonwealth', while dependent territories, such as colonies and protectorates, rank as 'Commonwealth countries'. Small self-governing countries, such as Nauru, may have special status. The Commonwealth survives more on tradition and sentiment than political or economic factors. Queen Elizabeth II is the formal head but not the ruler of member states. The Commonwealth secretariat, headed from Oct 1989 by Nigerian Emeka Anyaoko as secretary general, is based in London.

On 15 May 1917 Jan Smuts, representing South Africa in the imperial war cabinet of World War I, suggested that 'British commonwealth of nations' was the right title for the British Empire. The name was recognized in the Statute of Westminster 1931, but after World War II a growing sense of independent nationhood led to the simplification of the title to the Commonwealth.

Commonwealth Immigration Acts successive Acts which attempted to regulate the entry into the UK of British subjects from the Commonwealth. The Commonwealth Immigration Act, passed by the Conservative government in 1962 ruled that

Commonwealth immigrants entering Britain must have employment or be able to offer required skills.

In 1968, many Asians fleeing from Kenya claimed British citizenship and the Labour government extended the controls of the 1962 Act by the 1968 Commonwealth Act. The 1971 Act introduced by the Conservative government set up a single system of entry and ended the quota of employment vouchers. There were concessions for 'patrials' who were defined as those who held British citizenship by birth or who had parents or grandparents born in the UK, or who had lived in the UK for five years. Subsequent legislation (the 1983 Nationality Act and the 1988 Immigration Act) tightened admission controls.

commune a group of people or families living together, sharing resources and responsibilities.

In a communist country, the term refers to a communal division or settlement. In China, a policy of Mao Zedong involved the grouping of villages within districts (averaging 30,000 people) and thus, cooperatives were amalgamated into larger units, the communes. 1958 saw the establishment of peoples' communes (workers combines) with shared living quarters and shared meals. Communes organized workers brigades and were responsible for their own nurseries, schools, clinics and other facilities.

communications in mass media, a term often used to describe features and developments in the fields of telegraphy, the telephone, radio, cinema, television, communications satellites, microcomputers, and newspapers.

The earliest practicable ***telegraphic*** instrument, invented by William Cooke and Charles Wheatstone, was patented in 1837. Telegraph links were established between Britain and France in 1850 and the first transatlantic cable was laid in 1858.

The ***telephone*** was invented in 1876 by Alexander Graham Bell. In 1879 telephone exchanges were opened in London, Liverpool, and Manchester. In 1891 the first telephone cable was laid between England and France.

Guglielmo Marconi, an Italian pioneer of telegraphy, succeeded in transmitting a ***wireless*** signal across the Atlantic Ocean from Cornwall to Newfoundland in 1896.

The first ***photographic*** negative was produced by William Fox Talbot in 1839, and in the 1880s the 'box' camera was invented by US entrepreneur George Eastman.

In ***cinema*** the first 'moving pictures' were shown in public in Paris in 1895. The first successful feature film with sound was *The Jazz Singer* 1927.

The first working ***television*** system was demonstrated in London in 1926 by John Logie Baird. The first public television service in the world was started by the British Broadcasting Corporation (BBC) at Alexandra Palace in London 1936.

The first ◊***communications satellite*** Telstar, was launched in July 1962 to carry TV signals across the Atlantic Ocean. Other satellites followed, and are used by individual countries for internal communications, or for business or military use.

In the early 19th century Charles Babbage pioneered a very primitive form of ◊***computer***. By the early 20th century, simple automatic calculating machines were coming into use. The first electronic computers were made in the USA after World War II.

The first daily ***newspaper*** in the world, the *Daily Courant* appeared in 1702. In the later 19th and early 20th centuries, major technical changes in printing helped to reduce costs of newspaper production. In the late 1980s the production of newspapers was revolutionized with the introduction of more advanced technology and new printing methods.

communications satellite a relay station in space for sending telephone, television, telex, and other messages around the world. Messages are sent to and from the satellites via ground stations. Most communications satellites are in geostationary orbit, appearing to hang fixed over one point on the Earth's surface.

The first satellite to carry TV signals across the Atlantic Ocean was Telstar in July 1962. The world is now linked by a system of communications satellites called Intelsat. Other satellites are used by individual countries for internal communications, or for business or military use. A new generation of satellites, called ***direct broadcast satellites***, are powerful enough to transmit direct to small domestic aerials.

communism (French *commun* 'common, general') revolutionary socialism based on the theories of the political philosophers Marx and Engels, emphasizing common ownership of the means of production and a planned economy. The principle held is that each should work according to their capacity and receive according to their need. Politically, it seeks the overthrow of capitalism through a proletarian revolution. The first communist state was the USSR after the revolution of 1917. Revolutionary socialist parties and groups united to form communist parties in other countries (in the UK 1920). After World War

II, communism was enforced in those countries that came under Soviet occupation. China emerged after 1961 as a rival to the USSR in world communist leadership, and other countries attempted to adapt communism to their own needs. The late 1980s saw a movement for more individual freedoms in many communist countries, culminating in the abolition or overthrow of communist rule in some Eastern European countries, and further state repression in China.

Marx and Engels in the *Communist Manifesto* 1848 put forward the theory that human society, having passed through successive stages of slavery, feudalism, and capitalism, must advance to communism. This combines with a belief in economic determinism to form the central communist concept of ***dialectical materialism***. Marx believed that capitalism had become a barrier to progress and needed to be replaced by a ***dictatorship of the proletariat*** (working class), which would build a socialist society.

The Social Democratic parties formed in Europe in the second half of the 19th century professed to be Marxist, but gradually began to aim at reforms of capitalist society rather than at the radical social change envisaged by Marx. The Russian Social Democratic Labour Party, led by Lenin, remained Marxist, and after the Nov 1917 revolution changed its name to Communist Party to emphasize its difference from Social Democratic parties elsewhere. The communal basis of feudalism was still strong in Russia, and Lenin and Stalin were able to impose the communist system.
China's communist revolution was completed 1949 under Mao Zedong. Both China and the USSR took strong measures to maintain or establish their own types of 'orthodox' communism in countries on their borders (the USSR in Hungary and Czechoslovakia, and China in North Korea and Vietnam). In more remote areas (the USSR in the Arab world and Cuba, and China in Albania) and (both of them) in the newly emergent African countries, these orthodoxies were installed as the fount of doctrine and the source of technological aid. In 1956 the Soviet premier Khrushchev denounced ***Stalinism***, and there were uprisings in Hungary and Poland.

the 1960s During the late 1960s and the 1970s it was debated whether the state requires to be maintained as 'the dictatorship of the proletariat' once revolution on the economic front has been achieved, or whether it may then become the state of the entire people: Engels, Lenin, Khrushchev, and Liu Shaoqi held the latter view; Stalin and Mao the former. Many communist parties in capitalist countries, for example, Japan and the ***eurocommunism*** of France, Italy, and the major part of the British Communist Party, have since the 1960s or later rejected Soviet dominance.

the 1980s In the 1980s there was an expansion of political and economic freedom in Eastern Europe: the USSR remained a single-party state, but with a relaxation of strict party orthodoxy and a policy of *perestroika* ('restucturing'), while the other Warsaw Pact countries moved towards an end to communist rule and its replacement by free elections within more democratic political systems.

the Third World In the Third World, Libya has attempted to combine revolutionary socialism with Islam; the extreme communist Khmer Rouge devastated Cambodia (then called Kampuchea) 1975–78; Latin America suffers from the US. fear of communism in what it regards as its back yard, with the democratically elected Marxist regime in Chile violently overthrown 1973, and the socialist government of Nicaragua (until it fell 1990) involved in a prolonged civil war against US-backed guerrillas (Contras).

computer a programmable electronic device that processes data and performs calculations and other symbol manipulation tasks. There are three types: the ***digital computer***, which manipulates information coded as binary numbers, the ***analogue computer***, which works with continuously varying quantities, and the ***hybrid computer***, which has characteristics of both analogue and digital computers.

history Computers are only one of the many kinds of computing device. The first mechanical computer was conceived by Charles Babbage in 1835, but it never went beyond the design stage. In 1943, Thomas Flowers built Colossus, the first electronic computer. Working with him at the time was Alan Turing, a mathematician who seven years earlier had published a paper on the theory of computing machines that had a major impact on subsequent developments. John von Neumann's computer, EDVAC, built in 1949, was the first to use binary arithmetic and to store its operating instructions internally. This design still forms the basis of today's computers.

concentration camp a prison camp devised by the British during the Second Boer War in South Africa 1899 for the detention of Afrikaner women and children with the subsequent deaths of more than 20,000 people. A system of approximately 5,000 concentration camps was developed by the Nazis in Germany and occupied Europe (1933–45) to imprison political and ideological opponents after Hitler became chancellor Jan 1933. The most infamous extermination camps included Auschwitz, Belsen, Dachau, Maidanek, Sobibor, and Treblinka. The total number of people who died at the camps exceeded six million, and some inmates were subjected to medical experimentation before being killed.

Many camp officials and others responsible were tried after 1945 for war crimes, and executed or imprisoned. Foremost was Adolf Eichmann, the architect of the extermination system, who was tried and executed by the state of Israel in 1961.

Congress national legislature of the USA, consisting of the House of Representatives (435 members, apportioned to the states of the Union on the basis of population, and elected for two-year terms) and the Senate (100 senators, two for each state, elected for six years, one-third elected every two years). Both representatives and senators are elected by direct popular vote. Congress meets in Washington DC, in the Capitol. An Act of Congress is a bill passed by both houses.

The Congress of the United States met for the first time on 4 March 1789. It was preceded by the Congress of the Confederation representing the several states under the Articles of Confederation from 1781 to 1789.

Congress Party Indian political party, founded 1885 as the Indian National Congress. It led the movement to end British rule and was the governing party from independence 1947 until 1977, when Indira Gandhi lost the leadership she had held since 1966. Heading a splinter group, known as ***Congress (I)***, she achieved an overwhelming victory in the elections of 1980, and reduced the main Congress Party to a minority.

The ***Indian National Congress***, founded by the British colonialist Allan Hume (1829–1912) in 1885, was a moderate body until World War I when, under the leadership of Mahatma Gandhi, it began a campaign of non-violent non-cooperation with the British colonizers. It was declared illegal 1932–34, but was recognized as the paramount power in India at the granting of independence in 1947. Dominated in the early years of Indian independence by Nehru the party won the elections of 1952, 1957, and 1962. Under the leadership of Indira Gandhi from 1966, it went on to win the elections of 1967 and 1971, but was defeated for the first time in 1977.

conscription legislation for all able-bodied male citizens (and female in some countries, such as Israel) to serve with the armed forces. It originated in France 1792, and in the 19th and 20th centuries became the established practice in almost all European states. Modern conscription systems often permit alternative national service for conscientious objectors.

In Britain conscription was introduced for single men between 18 and 41 in Mar 1916 and for married men two months later, but was abolished after World War I. It was introduced for the first time in peace Apr 1939, when all men aged 20 became liable to six months' military training. The National Service Act, passed Sept 1939, made all men between 18 and 41 liable to military service, and in 1941 women also became liable to be called up for the women's services as an alternative to industrial service. Men on reaching the age of 18 continued to be called up until 1960.

conservatism approach to government favouring the maintenance of existing institutions and identified with a number of Western political parties, such as the British Conservative, German Christian Democratic, and Australian Liberal parties. It tends to be explicitly nondoctrinaire and pragmatic but generally emphasizes free-enterprise capitalism, minimal government intervention in the economy, rigid law and order, and the importance of national traditions.

Conservative Party UK political party, one of the two historic British parties (the Tories, and the Whigs); the name replaced ***Tory*** in general use from 1830 onwards. Traditionally the party of landed interests, it broadened its political base under Benjamin Disraeli's leadership in the 19th century. The present Conservative Party's free-market capitalism is supported by the world of finance and the management of industry.

The split of 1846 over Robert Peel's Corn Law policy led to 20 years out of office, or in office without power, until Disraeli 'educated' his party into accepting parliamentary and social change, extended the franchise to the artisan (winning considerable working-class support), launched imperial expansion, and established an alliance with industry and finance.

The Irish Home Rule issue of 1886 drove Radical Imperialists and old-fashioned Whigs into alliance with the Conservatives, so that the party had nearly 20 years of office, but fear that Joseph Chamberlain's protectionism would mean higher prices led to a Liberal landslide in 1906. The Conservative Party fought a rearguard action against the sweeping reforms that followed and only the outbreak of World War I averted a major crisis. During 1915–45, except briefly in 1924 and 1929–31, the Conservatives were continually in office, whether alone or as part of a coalition, largely thanks to the break-up of the traditional two-party system by the rise of Labour. Labour swept to power after World War II, but the Conservative Party formulated a new policy in their Industrial Charter of 1947, visualizing an economic and social system in which employers and employed, private enterprise and the state, work to mutual advantage. Antagonism to further nationalization and postwar austerity returned the Conservatives to power in 1951 with a small majority, and prosperity kept them in office throughout the 1950s and early 1960s. Narrowly defeated in 1964 under Alec Douglas-Home, the Conservative Party from 1965 elected its leaders, beginning with Edward Heath, who became prime minister 1970. The imposition of wage controls led to confrontation with the unions; when Heath sought a mandate Feb 1974, this resulted in a narrow defeat, repeated in a further election in Oct 1974. Margaret Thatcher replaced Heath, and under her leadership the Conservative Party returned to power in May 1979. Its economic policies increased the spending power of the majority, but also the gap between rich and poor; nationalized industries were sold off (see ◊privatization); military spending and close alliance with the USA were favoured, and the funding of local government was overhauled with the introduction of the poll tax. Margaret Thatcher was re-elected in 1983 and 1987, but resigned in Nov 1990. The Conservative government continued in office under John Major.

Contra member of a Central American right-wing guerrilla force attempting to overthrow the democratically elected Nicaraguan Sandinista government 1979–90. The Contras, many of them mercenaries or former members of the deposed Somoza's guard, have operated mainly from bases outside Nicaragua, mostly in Honduras, with covert US funding as revealed by the ◊Irangate hearings 1986–87. In 1989 US president Bush announced an agreement with Congress to provide $41 million in 'nonlethal' aid to the Contras until Feb 1990. The Sandinista government was defeated by the National Opposition Union, a US-backed coalition, in the Feb 1990 elections. In 1985 the Contra forces were estimated to number 15,000. In Aug 1989 Central American countries agreed to dismantle the Contra camps in Honduras.

convoy system grouping of ships to sail together under naval escort in wartime. In World War I (1914–18) navy escort vessels were at first used only to accompany troopships, but the convoy system was adopted for merchant shipping when the unrestricted German submarine campaign began 1917. In World War II (1939–45) it was widely used by the Allies to keep the Atlantic sea lanes open.

co-prosperity sphere a Japanese policy which provided the main strategy for government of E and SE Asia during the 1930s. The policy was developed to satisfy Japan's need for raw materials (such as oil, tin, and rubber) and new markets. Japan also tried to appeal to nationalist resentment against the colonial powers, to make the Pacific nations more amenable towards them. In practice the Japanese allowed the various Pacific nations little more freedom than they had enjoyed as colonies.

Coral Sea, Battle of the battle fought in World War II, May 7–8 1942; the US fleet prevented the Japanese from landing in SE New Guinea and thus threatening Australia.

Corfu incident an international crisis 27 Aug – 27 Sept 1923 which marked the first assertion of power in foreign affairs by the Italian Fascist government. In 1923 an international commission was determining the frontier between Greece and Albania. On 27 Aug 1923, its chief, Italian General Tellini was found (with four of his staff) murdered near the Albanian border, but on Greek territory. The Italian government under Benito Mussolini, backed by Italians, Fascist and anti-Fascist, sent an ultimatum to the Greek government demanding compensation, which was rejected. On 31 Aug Mussolini ordered the Italian bombardment and occupation of the Greek island of Corfu. The Greeks appealed to the League of Nations and, under pressure from Britain and France, Mussolini withdrew from Corfu on 27 Sept 1923. Greece had to accept most of the Italian demands, including the payment of a large indemnity.

Council of Europe body constituted 1949 at Strasbourg, France (still its headquarters) to secure 'a greater measure of unity between the European countries'. The widest association of European states, it has a ***Committee*** of foreign ministers, a ***Parliamentary Assembly*** (with members from national parliaments), and a ***European Commission*** investigating violations of human rights.

coup d'état or ***coup*** forcible takeover of the government of a country by elements from within that country, generally carried out by violent or illegal means. It differs from a revolution in typically being carried out by a small group (for example, of army officers or opposition politicians) to install its leader as head of government, rather than being a mass uprising by the people.

Early examples include the coup of 1799 in which Napoleon overthrew the Revolutionary

Directory and declared himself first consul of France, and the coup of 1851 in which Louis Napoleon (then president) dissolved the French national assembly and a year later declared himself emperor. Coups of more recent times include the overthrow of the socialist government of Chile in 1973 by a right-wing junta, and the military seizure of power in Fiji by Col Rabuka in Sept 1987.

credit in economics, means by which goods or services are obtained without immediate payment, usually by agreeing to pay interest. The three main forms are ***consumer credit*** (usually extended to individuals by retailers), ***bank credit*** (such as overdrafts or personal loans) and ***trade credit*** (common in the commercial world both within countries and internationally). Consumer credit is increasingly used to pay for goods. In the USA in 1989 it amounted to $711.8 billion, with about 18.5% of disposable income expended on hire purchase and credit card payments.

Cuba island in the Caribbean, the largest of the West Indies, off the south coast of Florida.

history From 1511 Cuba was a Spanish colony. It was ceded to the USA in 1898, at the end of the Spanish-American War. A republic was proclaimed in 1901, though the USA retained its naval base and asserted a right to intervene in internal affairs until 1934. In 1933 an army sergeant, Fulgencio Batista, seized and held power until he retired in 1944. In 1952 he regained power in a bloodless coup and began another period of rule that many Cubans found oppressive. In 1953 a young lawyer and son of a sugar planter, Dr Fidel Castro, tried to overthrow him but failed. He went into exile to prepare for another coup in 1956 but was again defeated. He fled to the hills with Dr Ernesto 'Che' Guevara and ten others to form a guerrilla force.

revolution In 1959 Castro's force of 5,000 men deposed Batista, to great popular acclaim. The 1940 constitution was suspended and replaced by a 'Fundamental Law', power being vested in a council of ministers with Castro as prime minister, his brother Raul as his deputy, and Che Guevara, reputedly, as the next in command. In 1960 the USA broke off diplomatic relations after all US businesses in Cuba were nationalized without compensation. In 1961 it went further, sponsoring a full-scale (but abortive) invasion, the ◊'Bay of Pigs' episode. In Dec of that year Castro proclaimed a communist state whose economy would develop along Marxist-Leninist lines.

Cuban Missile crisis In 1962 Cuba was expelled from the Organization of American States (OAS) which initiated a full political and economic blockade. Castro responded by tightening relations with the USSR that, in the same year, supplied missiles with atomic warheads for installation in Cuba. The ◊'Cuban missile crisis' brought the USA and USSR to the brink of nuclear war, but conflict was averted when the missiles were dismantled at the US president's insistence.

economic progress In 1965 Guevara left Cuba and was killed in Bolivia during an attempted uprising. Cuba's only political party later changed its name to the Cuban Communist Party (PCC). With Soviet help, Cuba made substantial economic and social progress 1965–72, in 1972 becoming a member of the Council for Mutual Economic Assistance (CMEA), a Moscow-based organization linking communist states. In 1976 a referendum approved a socialist constitution, and Fidel Castro and his brother were elected president and vice president. During the following five years Cuba played a larger role in world affairs, particularly in Africa, to the disquiet of the USA. Cuban troops played an important role in Angola, supporting the Luanda government against South African-backed rebels.

foreign policy Re-elected in 1981, Castro offered to discuss foreign policy with the USA but Cuba's support for Argentina, against Britain, cooled relations and drew it closer to other Latin American countries. Cuban support of leftist rebels seeking to overthrow the government of El Salvador caused continuing strains with the USA. Castro also reaffirmed his communist orthodoxy in the light of events in eastern Europe in 1989–90. The advent of ◊Gorbachev and the USSR's abandonment of its policy of supporting Third World revolutions led in 1989 to a curtailment of Cuba's foreign military interventions.

Cuban Missile Crisis a crisis in international relations in Oct 1962, when Soviet nuclear missiles had been installed in Cuba and President Kennedy compelled Khrushchev, by an ultimatum, to remove them. The US imposed a naval 'quarantine' around the island, and the two superpowers came closer to possible nuclear war than at any other time. Soviet inferiority in nuclear weapons forced a humiliating capitulation to Kennedy's demands. Some historians maintain that Kennedy's lack of resolve during the ◊Bay of Pigs operation gave Khruschev reason to believe that the US would not resist the introduction of Soviet missiles into Cuba. The drive by the USSR to match the US in nuclear weaponry dates from this event.

In Aug 1979 a lesser Cuban crisis occurred, when President Carter discovered a Soviet combat brigade on the island but failed to enforce its withdrawal.

Cultural Revolution a mass movement begun by Chinese Communist party chairman Mao Zedong 1966, directed against the upper middle class – bureaucrats, artists, and university intellectuals, who were killed, imprisoned, humiliated, or 'resettled'. Intended to 'purify' Chinese communism, it was also an attempt by Mao to renew his political and ideological pre-eminence inside China.

The 'revolution' was characterized by the violent activities of the semimilitary Red Guards, most of them students. Many established and learned people were humbled and eventually sent to work on the land, and the universities were closed 1966–70. Although the revolution was brought to an end in 1969, the resulting bureaucratic and economic chaos had many long-term effects.

curriculum in education, the range of subjects offered within an institution or course.

Until 1988, the only part of the school curriculum prescribed by law in the UK was religious education. Growing concern about the low proportion of 14- and 16-year-olds opting to study maths, science, and technology, with a markedly low take-up rate among girls, led to central government in the Education Reform Act 1988 introducing a compulsory National Curriculum, which applies to all children of school age (5–16) in state schools. There are three core subjects in the curriculum: English, maths, and science, and seven foundation subjects: technology, history, geography, music, art, physical education, and a foreign language.

Cyprus island in the Mediterranean Sea, off the S coast of Turkey.

history The strategic position of Cyprus has long made it a coveted territory and from earliest times it was colonised by a succession of peoples from the mainland. In the late 16th century it became part of the Turkish Ottoman Empire but became a British protectorate in 1878 and was annexed by Britain 1914. Rivalry between the Greek and Turkish speaking communities divided Cyprus; and in 1955 a guerrilla war against British rule was begun by Greek Cypriots, the majority of the population seeking 'enosis', or unification with Greece. After five years of conflict and negotiation Cyprus became independent of Britain, and for three years the Greeks and Turks shared power.

conflict However, in 1963 the Turks withdrew from power-sharing, and after armed conflict a United Nations peace-keeping force was set up to keep the Greeks and Turks apart. When hostilities broke out once more the Turkish Cypriots requested Turkey to send troops to the island and eventually established an independent government for what was called the 'Turkish Federated State of Cyprus'. The dispute between the communities remains unresolved but, because of its strategic importance in the Mediterranean, Cyprus remains a cause for concern among other countries.

Czechoslovakia landlocked country in E central Europe, bounded NE by Poland, E by the USSR, S by Hungary and Austria, W by West Germany, and NW by East Germany.

history Czechoslovakia came into existence as an independent republic 1918 after the break-up of the ◊Austro-Hungarian empire at the end of World War I. It consisted originally of the Bohemian crownlands (Bohemia, Moravia, and part of Silesia) and Slovakia, the area of Hungary inhabited by Slavonic peoples; to which was added as a trust part of Ruthenia when the Allies and Associated Powers recognized the new republic under the treaty of St Germain-en-Laye. Despite the problems of forging a nation from such a mixed group of people, Czechoslovakia made considerable political and economic progress until the troubled 1930s. It was the only E European state to retain a parliamentary democracy throughout the inter-war period, with five coalition governments, dominated by the Agrarian and National Socialist parties, with Thomas Masaryk serving as president. It also had a highly developed industrial sector.

Munich Agreement The rise to power of ◊Hitler in Germany brought a revival of opposition among the German-speaking population, and nationalism among the Magyar speakers. In addition, the Slovakian clerical party demanded autonomy for Slovakia. In 1938 the ◊Munich Agreement was made between Britain, France, Germany, and Italy, without consulting Czechoslovakia, and this took the Sudetenland from Czechoslovakia and gave it to Germany. Six months later Hitler occupied all Czechoslovakia. A government-in-exile was established in London under Eduard ◊Beneš until the liberation 1945 by Soviet and US troops. 2 million Sudeten Germans were expelled, and Czech Ruthenia was transferred to Ukraine, USSR. Elections 1946 gave the left a slight majority, and in Feb 1948 the Communists seized power. Beněs, who had been president since 1945, resigned. There was a Stalinist regime during the 1950s, under Presidents Klement Gottwald, Antonin Zapotocky, and Antonin Novotný.

Socialist Democratic Revolution Pressure from students and intellectuals brought about policy changes from 1965, and in 1968, following Novotný's replacement as CCP leader by Alexander ◊Dubček, a liberalization programme ('Socialist Democratic Revolution') began, promising the return of freedom of assembly, speech, and movement, and the imposition of restrictions on the secret police.

Prague Spring Despite assurances that Czechoslovakia would remain within the ◊Warsaw Pact, the USSR viewed these events with suspicion, and in Aug 1968 sent 600,000 troops from Warsaw Pact countries to restore the orthodox line. After the invasion a purge of liberals began in the CCP, with Dr Gustáv Husák (a Slovak Brezhnevite) replacing Dubček as CCP leader 1969 and Lubomír Štrougal (a Czech) becoming prime minister 1970. Svoboda remained as president until 1975 and negotiated the Soviet withdrawal. In 1968 a new constitution transformed unitary Czechoslovakia into a federal state. In 1973 an amnesty was extended to some of the 40,000 who had fled after the 1968 invasion, signalling a slackening of repression. In 1977, following the signature of a human rights manifesto ('Charter 77') by over 700 intellectuals and former party officials in response to the 1975 Helsinki Conference, a new crackdown commenced. The arrest of dissidents continued during the events of 1981 in ◊Poland. Czechoslovakia under Dr Husák emerged as a loyal ally of the USSR during the 1970s and early 1980s. However, following Mikhail ◊Gorbachev's accession to the Soviet leadership in 1985, pressure for economic and administrative reform mounted. In Dec Husák, while remaining president, was replaced as CCP leader by Miloš Jakeš (1923–), a Czech-born economist. Working with prime minister Ladislav Adamec, a reformist, he began to introduce a reform programme (*prestavba*, 'restructuring') on USSR's ◊perestroika model. However, his approach was cautious and dissident activity, which became increasingly widespread 1988–89, was suppressed.

protest movement Influenced by events elsewhere in E Europe, a series of initially student-led pro-democracy rallies were held in Prague's Wenceslas Square from 17 Nov 1989. Support for the protest movement rapidly increased following the security forces' brutal suppression of the early rallies. An umbrella opposition movement, Civic Forum, was swiftly formed under the leadership of playwright and Charter 77 activist Vaclav ◊Havel. With the protest movement continuing to grow, Jakeš resigned as CCP leader 24 Nov, and was replaced by Karel Urbanek, and the politburo was purged. Opposition parties, beginning with Civic Forum and its Slovak counterpart, Public Against Violence, were legalized. On 7 Dec Adamec resigned as prime minister and was replaced by Marion Calfa, who formed a coalition government in which key posts, including the foreign, financial, and labour ministries, were given to former dissidents. Calfa resigned from the CCP in Jan 1990, but remained premier. On 27 Dec the rehabilitated Dubček was sworn in as chair of the federal assembly, and on 29 Dec Havel became president of Czechoslovakia. The new reform government immediately extended an amnesty to 22,000 prisoners; secured agreements from the CCP that it would voluntarily give up its existing majorities in the federal and regional assemblies and state agencies; and promised multi-party elections for June 1990. It also announced plans for reducing the size of the armed forces, called on the USSR to pull out its 75,000 troops stationed in the country by the end of 1990, and applied for membership of the International Monetary Fund and World Bank. Vaclav Havel was re-elected, unopposed, as president for a further two years by the assembly on 5 July 1990.

D

Davison Emily 1872–1913. English militant suffragette, who died while trying to stop the king's horse at the Derby at Epsom (she was trampled by the horse). She was a teacher with degrees from Oxford and London universities. She joined the Women's Social and Political Union in 1906 and served several prison sentences for militant action such as stone throwing, setting fire to pillar boxes, and bombing Lloyd George's country house.

Dawes Charles Gates 1865–1951. US Republican politician. In 1923 he was appointed by the Allied Reparations Commission president of the committee that produced the ***Dawes Plan***, a $200 million loan that enabled Germany to pay enormous war debts after World War I. It reduced tensions temporarily in Europe but was superseded by the ◊Young Plan (which reduced the total reparations bill) 1929. Dawes was elected US vice president (under Calvin Coolidge) 1924, received the Nobel Peace Prize 1925, and was ambassador to Britain 1929–32.

Dayan Moshe 1915–1981. Israeli general and politician. As minister of defence 1967 and 1969–74, he was largely responsible for the victory over neighbouring Arab states in the 1967 Six Day War, but he was criticized for Israel's alleged unpreparedness in the 1973 October War and resigned along with Prime Minister Golda Meir. Foreign minister from 1977, Dayan resigned in 1979 in protest over the refusal of the Begin government to negotiate with the Palestinians.

D-day 6 June 1944, the day of the Allied invasion of Normandy under the command of General Eisenhower, with the aim of liberating Western Europe from German occupation. The Anglo-American invasion fleet landed on the Normandy beaches on the stretch of coast between the Orne River and St Marcouf. Artificial harbours known as 'Mulberries' were constructed and towed across the Channel so that equipment and armaments could be unloaded onto the beaches. After overcoming fierce resistance the allies broke through the German defences; Paris was liberated on 25 August, and Brussels on 2 September.

Davison *Militant suffragette Emily Davison, who was trampled on and killed by the king's horse at the Epsom Derby in 1913.*

decolonization the gradual achievement of independence by former colonies of the European imperial powers which began after World War I. The process of decolonization accelerated after World War II and the movement affected every continent, for example: India and Pakistan gained independence from Britain 1947; Algeria gained independence from France 1962.

de Gaulle Charles André Joseph Marie 1890–1970. French general and first president of the Fifth Republic 1959–69. He organized the Free French troops fighting the Nazis 1940–44, was head of the provisional French government 1944–46, and leader of his own Gaullist party.

Born in Lille, he graduated from Saint-Cyr 1911 and was severely wounded and captured by the Germans 1916. In June 1940 he refused to accept the new prime minister Henri Pétain's truce with the Germans and became leader of the Free French in England. In 1944 he entered Paris in triumph and was briefly head of the provisional government before resigning over the new constitution of the Fourth Republic 1946. In 1947 he founded the Rassemblement du Peuple Français, a non-party constitutional reform movement, then withdrew from politics in 1953. When national bankruptcy and civil war in Algeria loomed 1958, de Gaulle was called to form a government.

As premier he promulgated a constitution subordinating the legislature to the presidency and took office as president Dec 1958. Economic recovery followed, as well as Algerian independence after a bloody war. A nationalist, he opposed 'Anglo-Saxon' influence in Europe. Re-elected president 1965, he pursued a foreign policy that opposed British entry to the EEC, withdrew French forces from NATO 1966, and pursued the development of a French nuclear deterrent. He violently quelled student demonstrations May 1968 when they were joined by workers. The Gaullist party, reorganized as Union des Democrats pour la Cinquième République, won an overwhelming majority in the elections of the same year. In 1969 he resigned after the defeat of the government in a referendum on constitutional reform. He retired to the village of Colombey-les-Deux-Eglises in NE France.

De Klerk F(rederik) W(illem) 1936– . South African National Party politician, president from 1989. Trained as a lawyer, he entered the South African parliament in 1972. He served in the cabinets of B J Vorster and P W Botha 1978–89, and in Feb and Aug 1989 successively replaced Botha as National Party leader and state president. Projecting himself as a pragmatic conservative who sought gradual reform of the apartheid system, he won the Sept 1989 elections for his party, but with a reduced majority. In Feb 1990 he ended the ban on the ◊African National Congress opposition movement and released its effective leader, Nelson Mandela.

democracy (Greek *demos* 'the community', *kratos* 'sovereign power') government by the people, usually through elected representatives. In the modern world, democracy has developed from the American and French revolutions.

Representative parliamentary government existed in Iceland from the 10th century and in England from the 13th century, but the British working classes were excluded almost entirely from the vote until 1867, and women were admitted and property qualifications abolished only in 1918.

In ***direct democracy*** the whole people meets for the making of laws or the direction of executive officers, for example in Athens in the 5th century BC (and allegedly in modern Libya). Direct democracy today is represented mainly by the use of the referendum, as in the UK, Switzerland, and certain states of the USA.

Democratic Party one of the two main political parties of the USA. It tends to be the party of the working person, as opposed to the Republicans, the party of big business, but the divisions between the two are not clear cut. Its stronghold since the Civil War has traditionally been the Southern states, but conservative Southern Democrats were largely supportive of Republican president Reagan.

Democrats in UK politics, common name for the Social and Liberal Democrats.

Deng Xiaoping or ***Teng Hsiao-ping*** 1904– . Chinese political leader. A member of the Chinese Communist Party (CCP) from the 1920s, he took part in the ◊Long March 1934–36. He was in the Politburo from 1955 until ousted in the ◊Cultural Revolution 1966–69. Reinstated in the 1970s, he gradually took power and introduced a radical economic modernization programme. He retired from the Politburo in 1987 and from his last official position (as chair of State Military Commission) Mar 1990, but remained influential behind the scenes.

Deng, born in Sichuan province into a middle-class landlord family, joined the CCP as a student in Paris, where he adopted the name Xiaoping (Little Peace) 1925, and studied in Moscow 1926. After the Long March, he served as a political commissar to the People's Liberation Army during the civil war of

Deng Xiaoping *China's 'paramount ruler' Deng Xiaoping. In effective charge of the country throughout the 1980s, he promoted greater economic but not political liberalization.*

1937–49. He entered the CCP Politburo 1955 and headed the secretariat during the early 1960s, working closely with President Liu Shaoqi. During the Cultural Revolution Deng was dismissed as a 'capitalist roader' and sent to work in a tractor factory in Nanchang for 're-education'.

Deng was rehabilitated by his patron ◊Zhou Enlai 1973 and served as acting prime minister after Zhou's heart attack 1974. On Zhou's death Jan 1976 he was forced into hiding but returned to office as vice premier July 1977. By Dec 1978, although nominally a CCP vice chair, state vice premier, and Chief of Staff to the PLA, Deng was the controlling force in China. His policy of 'socialism with Chinese characteristics', misinterpreted in the West as a drift to capitalism, had success in rural areas. He helped to oust Hua Guofeng in favour of his protégés Hu Yaobang (later in turn ousted) and Zhao Ziyang. When Deng officially retired from his party and army posts, he claimed to have renounced political involvement. His reputation, both at home and in the West, was tarnished by his sanctioning of the army's massacre of more than 2,000 pro-democracy demonstrators in Tiananmen Square, Beijing, in June 1989. He retired shortly afterwards.

Depression a period of low output and investment, with high unemployment. Specifically, the term describes two periods of crisis in the world economies: 1873–96 and 1929–mid-1930s.

The term is most often used to refer to the world economic crisis precipitated by the ◊Wall Street crash of 29 Oct 1929 when millions of dollars were wiped off US share values in a matter of hours. This forced the closure of many US banks involved in stock speculation and led to the recall of US overseas investments. This loss of US credit had serious repercussions on the European economy, especially that of Germany, and led to a steep fall in the levels of international trade as countries attempted to protect their domestic economies. Although most European countries experienced a slow recovery during the mid-1930s, the main impetus for renewed economic growth was provided by rearmament programmes later in the decade.

détente (French) a reduction of political tension and the easing of strained relations between nations; for example, the ending of the Cold War 1989–90.

de Valera Eamon 1882–1975. Irish nationalist politician, prime minister of the Irish Free State/Eire/Republic of Ireland 1932–48, 1951–54, and 1957–59, and president 1959–73. Repeatedly imprisoned, he participated in the Easter Rising 1916 and was leader of the nationalist ◊Sinn Féin party 1917–26, when he formed the republican ◊Fianna Fáil party; he directed negotiations with Britain 1921 but refused to accept the partition of Ireland until 1937.

He was born in New York, the son of a Spanish father and an Irish mother, and sent to Ireland as a child, where he became a teacher of mathematics. He was sentenced to death for his part in the Easter Rising, but the sentence was commuted, and he was released under an amnesty 1917. In the same year he was elected member of Parliament for E Clare, and president of Sinn Féin. He was rearrested May 1918, but escaped to the USA 1919. He returned to Ireland 1920 and directed the struggle against the British government from a hiding place in Dublin. He authorized the negotiations of 1921, but refused to accept the ensuing treaty which divided Ireland into the Free State and the North.

Civil war followed. De Valera was arrested by the Free State government 1923, and spent a year in prison. He formed a new party, Fianna Fáil 1926, which secured a majority in 1932. De Valera became prime minister and foreign minister of the Free State, and at once abolished the oath of allegiance and suspended payment of the annuities due under the Land Purchase Acts. In 1938 he negotiated an agreement with Britain, under which all outstanding points were settled. Throughout World War II he maintained a strict neutrality, rejecting an offer by Winston Churchill 1940 to recognize the principle of a united Ireland in return for Eire's entry into the war. He resigned after his defeat at the 1948 elections but was again prime minister in the 1950s, and then president of the republic.

devaluation in economics, lowering of the official value of a currency against other currencies, so that exports become cheaper and imports more expensive. Used when a country is badly in deficit in its balance of trade, it results in the goods the country produces being cheaper abroad, so that the economy is stimulated by increased foreign demand.

The increased cost of imported food, raw materials, and manufactured goods as a consequence of devaluation may, however, stimulate an acceleration in inflation, especially when commodities are rising in price because of increased world demand. ***Revaluation*** is the opposite process.

Devaluations of important currencies upset the balance of the world's money markets and encourage speculation. Significant devaluations include that of the German mark in the 1920s and Britain's devaluation of sterling in the 1960s. To promote greater stability, many countries have allowed the value of their currencies to 'float', that is, to fluctuate in value.

development in the social sciences, the acquisition by a society of industrial techniques and technology; hence the common classification of the 'developed' nations of the First and Second Worlds and the poorer, 'developing' or 'underdeveloped' nations of the Third World. The assumption that development in the sense of industrialization was inherently good has been increasingly questioned since the 1960s.

dictatorship the term or office of an absolute ruler, overriding the constitution. Although dictatorships were common in Latin America during the 19th century, the only European example during this period was the rule of Napoleon III. The crises following World War I produced many dictatorships, including the regimes of Atatürk and Piłsudski (nationalist); Mussolini, Hitler, Primo de Rivera, Franco, and Salazar (all right-wing); and Stalin (Communist).

Dien Bien Phu, Battle of decisive battle in the ◊Indochina War at a French fortress in North Vietnam, near the Laotian border. French troops were besieged 13 Mar–7 May 1954 by the Communist Vietminh. The fall of Dien Bien Phu resulted in the end of French control of Indochina.

disarmament the reduction of a country's weapons of war. Most disarmament talks since World War II have been concerned with nuclear-arms verification, but biological, chemical, and conventional weapons have also come under discussion at the United Nations and in other forums. In the UK the Campaign for Nuclear Disarmament lobbies on this issue.

discrimination distinction made (social, economic, political, legal) between individuals or groups such that one has the power to treat the other unfavourably. ***Negative discrimination***, often based on stereotype, includes anti-Semitism, apartheid, caste, racism, sexism, and slavery. ***Positive discrimination***, or 'affirmative action', is sometimes practised in an attempt to counteract the effects of previous long-term discrimination. Minorities and, in some cases, majorities have been targets for discrimination.

National legislation in the UK includes the Race Relations Acts 1965 and 1976 and the Sex Discrimination Act of 1975.

dissident in one-party states, a person intellectually dissenting from the official line. Dissidents have been sent into exile, prison, labour camps, and mental institutions, or deprived of their jobs. In the USSR the number of imprisoned dissidents declined from more than 600 in 1986 to fewer than 100 in 1990, of whom the majority were ethnic nationalists. In China the number of prisoners of conscience increased after the 1989 Tiananmen Square massacre, and in South Africa, despite the release of Nelson Mandela in 1990, numerous political dissidents remained in jail.

In the USSR before the introduction of ◊glasnost, dissidents comprised communists who advocated a more democratic and humanitarian approach; religious proselytizers; Jews wishing to emigrate; and those who supported ethnic or national separatist movements within the USSR (among them Armenians, Lithuanians, Ukrainians, and Tatars). Their views were expressed through samizdat (clandestinely distributed writings) and sometimes published abroad. In the late 1980s Gorbachev lifted censorship, accepted a degree of political pluralism, and extended tolerance to religious believers. Almost 100,000 Jews were allowed to emigrate 1985–90. Some formerly persecuted dissidents, most prominently the physicist Andrei ◊Sakharov, emerged as supporters, albeit impatient, of the new reform programme.

dole popular name for unemployment benefit and unemployment assistance, the weekly payments to unemployed workers under the National Insurance Act. Modern unemployment benefits are based on the principles embodied in the National Insurance Act 1946.

domino theory idea popularized by US President Eisenhower in 1954 that if one country comes under communist rule, adjacent countries are likely to become communist as well. Initially used to justify US intervention in SE Asia, the domino theory has also been invoked in reference to Central America.

Dreadnought class of battleships built for the British navy after 1905 and far superior in speed and armaments to anything then afloat. It was first launched 18 February 1906, with armaments consisting entirely of big guns. The German Nassau class was begun in 1907, and by 1914, the USA, France, Japan and Austria- Hungary all had battleships of a similar class to the dreadnought. German plans to build similar craft led to the naval race that contributed to Anglo-German antagonism and the origins of World War I.

Dresden capital of the state of Saxony, Federal Republic of Germany, following the reunification of Germany in 1990; population (1990) 520,000. The city was bombed by the Allies on the night 13–14 Feb 1945, 15.5 sq km/6 sq mi of the inner town was destroyed, and deaths were estimated at 35,000–135,000.

Dubček Alexander 1921– . Czechoslovak politician, chair of the federal assembly from 1989. He was a member of the ◊resistance movement and after World War II became first secretary of the Communist Party 1967–69. He launched a liberalization campaign (called the ◊Prague Spring) that was opposed by the USSR and led to the Soviet invasion of Czechoslovakia in 1968. He was arrested by Soviet troops and expelled from the party 1970.

In 1989 he gave speeches at pro-democracy rallies, and in Dec, after the fall of the hard-line regime, he was elected speaker of the Czechoslovak parliament.

Dulles John Foster 1888–1959. US politician. Senior US adviser at the founding of the United Nations, he was largely responsible for drafting the Japanese peace treaty of 1951. As secretary of state 1952–59, he secured US intervention in support of South Vietnam following the expulsion of the French in 1954 and was critical of Britain in the Suez Crisis 1956.

Duma in Russia, before 1917, an elected assembly that met four times following the short-lived 1905 revolution. With progressive demands the government could not accept, the Duma was largely powerless. After the abdication of Nicholas II, the Duma directed the formation of a provisional government.

Dunkirk (French *Dunkerque*) seaport on the N coast of France, in Nord *département*, on the Strait of Dover. It was close to the front line during much of World War I, and in World War II, 337,131 Allied troops (including about 110,000 French) were evacuated 26 May–4 Jun 1940 from the beaches as German forces approached.

E

Eastern Front battlefront between Russia and Germany during World War I and World War II.

Easter Rising or ***Easter Rebellion*** a republican insurrection that began on Easter Monday, Apr 1916, in Dublin. It was inspired by the Irish Republican Brotherhood (IRB) in an unsuccessful attempt to overthrow British rule in Ireland. It was led by Patrick Pearce of the IRB and James Connolly of Sinn Féin.

Arms from Germany intended for the IRB were intercepted but the rising proceeded regardless with the seizure of the Post Office and other buildings in Dublin by 1,500 volunteers. The rebellion was crushed by the British Army within five days, both sides suffering major losses: 220 civilians, 64 rebels, and 134 members of the Crown Forces were killed during the uprising. Pearce, Connolly and about a dozen rebel leaders were subsequently executed in Kilmainham Jail. Others, including Eamon de Valera, were spared due to US public opinion, to be amnestied in June 1917.

East Pakistan a province of ◊Pakistan, now Bangladesh.

EC abbreviation for ◊***European Community***.

economic community or ***common market*** an organization of autonomous countries formed to promote trade. Examples include the Caribbean Community (Caricom) 1973, Central African Economic Community 1985, European Community (EC) 1957, and Latin American Economic System 1975.

ECSC abbreviation for ◊***European Coal and Steel Community***.

Eden (Robert) Anthony, 1st Earl of Avon 1897–1977. British Conservative politician, foreign secretary 1935–38, 1940–45, and 1951–55; prime minister 1955–57, when he resigned after the failure of the Anglo-French military intervention in the ◊Suez Crisis.

Upset by his prime minister's rejection of a peace plan secretly proposed by US president Franklin Roosevelt in Jan 1938, Eden resigned as foreign secretary in Feb 1938 in protest against Chamberlain's decision to open conversations with the Fascist dictator Mussolini. He was foreign secretary again in the wartime coalition formed Dec 1940 and in the Conservative government elected 1951. With the Soviets, he negotiated an interim peace in Vietnam 1954. In Apr 1955 he succeeded Winston Churchill as prime minister. His use of force in the Suez Crisis led to his resignation in Jan 1957, but he continued to maintain that his action was justified. Created Earl of Avon 1961.

education the process, beginning at birth, of developing intellectual capacity, manual skill, and social awareness, especially by instruction. In its more restricted sense, the term refers to the process of imparting literacy, numeracy, and a generally accepted body of knowledge.

1870 First Education Act created locally elected School Boards to set up dual system of voluntary and local Board Schools.

1880 Education Act made schooling for all children 5–10 compulsory.

1902 Board schools came under local education authorities (LEAs) control. They were authorized to develop existing elementary schools and to set up secondary or technical schools.

1918 Education Act raised school-leaving age to 14.

1944 (Butler) Education Act raised school-leaving age to 15 and provided free secondary schooling together with free meals and milk for all. The Board of Education became a Ministry of Education.

1951 Introduction of General Certificate of Education (Certificate of Secondary Education introduced 1965).

1963 Robbins Committee recommended massive expansion in university and newer polytechnic sector.

1964 First plans for comprehensive secondary education.

1969 Establishment of the Open University.

1973 School-leaving age raised to 16.

1976 Required all state secondary schools to become comprehensive.

1979 and 1980 Repealed the requirement of the 1976 Education Act and, in theory, increased parental involvement. LEAs were required to publish certain information about schools but were no longer required to provide meals and milk for pupils.

1986 Education Bill introduced sweeping changes to the administration of schools.

1987 Introduction of General Certificate of Secondary Education (GCSE) replacing GCE/CSE system.

1989 Introduction of a 'national ◊curriculum' for all schoolchildren, encompassing major subject areas. The powers of school governing bodies with the local management of schools (LMS) were increased.

Edward VII 1841–1910. King of Great Britain and Ireland from 1901. As Prince of Wales he was a prominent social figure, but his mother Queen Victoria considered him too frivolous to take part in political life. In 1860 he made the first tour of Canada and the USA ever undertaken by a British prince. He contributed to the ◊Entente Cordiale 1904 with France and the Anglo-Russian agreement 1907.

Edward VIII 1894–1972. King of Great Britain and Northern Ireland Jan–Dec 1936, when he renounced the throne to marry Wallis Warfield Simpson thus instigating the ◊abdication crisis. He was created Duke of Windsor and was governor of the Bahamas 1940–45, subsequently settling in France. Papers found 1987 revealed he offered to accept the presidency of a British socialist state.

EEC abbreviation for ***European Economic Community***; see ◊European Community.

EFTA acronym for ◊***European Free Trade Association***.

Egypt country in NE Africa, bounded N by the Mediterranean, E by the Suez Canal and Red Sea, S by Sudan, and W by Libya.

history Egypt was part of the Turkish ◊Ottoman Empire from 1517. After subduing a nationalist revolt 1881–82, Britain occupied Egypt, and the government was from then on mainly in the hands of British civilian agents who directed their efforts to the improvement of the Egyptian economy. On the outbreak of World War I 1914, nominal Turkish suzerainty was abolished, and the country was declared a British protectorate.

independence Postwar agitation by the nationalist Wafd party led to the granting of nominal independence 1922, under King Fuad I. He was succeeded by King Farouk 1936, and Britain agreed to recognize Egypt's full independence, announcing a phased withdrawal of its forces, except from the Suez Canal, Alexandria, and Port Said, where it had naval bases. The start of World War II delayed the British departure, as did the consequent campaign in Libya that ended in the defeat of the German and Italian forces that had threatened the Canal Zone.

republic In 1946 all British troops except the Suez Canal garrison were withdrawn. In the immediate postwar years a radical movement developed, calling for an end to the British presence and opposing Farouk for his extravagant life style and his failure to prevent the creation of Israel. This led, in 1952, to a bloodless coup by a group of army officers, led by Col Gamal ◊Nasser, who replaced Farouk with a military junta. The 1923 constitution was suspended, and all political parties banned. The following year Egypt declared itself a republic, with General Mohammad Neguib as president and prime minister. In 1954 Nasser became prime minister, and an agreement was signed for the withdrawal of British troops from the Canal Zone by 1956. After a dispute with Neguib, Nasser took over as head of state and embarked on a programme of social reform. He became a major force for the creation of Arab unity and a leader of the ◊nonaligned movement. In 1956 the presidency was strengthened by a new constitution, and Nasser was elected president, unopposed. Later that year, British forces were withdrawn, in accordance with the 1954 agreement.

Suez Crisis When the USA and Britain cancelled their offers of financial aid for the Aswan High Dam, Nasser responded by nationalizing the Suez Canal. In a contrived operation, Britain, France, and Israel invaded the Sinai Peninsula and two days later Egypt was attacked. US pressure brought a cease-fire and an Anglo-French withdrawal. The effect of the abortive Anglo-French operation was to push Egypt towards the USSR and to enhance Nasser's reputation in the Arab world.

Six Day War In 1967 Egypt led an attack on Israel that developed into the 'Six Day War', in which Israel defeated all its opponents, including Egypt. One result of the conflict was the blocking of the Suez Canal, which was not reopened until 1975. After Egypt's defeat, Nasser offered to resign but was persuaded to stay on. In 1969, aged 52, he died of a heart attack and was succeeded by Vice President Col Anwar ◊Sadat. In 1971 a new constitution was approved, and the title Arab Republic of Egypt adopted. Sadat continued Nasser's policy of promoting Arab unity, but proposals to create a federation of Egypt, Libya, and Syria again failed.

Yom Kippur War In 1973 an attempt was made to regain territory from Israel. After 18 days' fighting, US secretary of state Henry Kissinger arranged a cease-fire, resulting in

Israel's evacuation of parts of Sinai, with a UN buffer zone separating the rival armies. This US intervention strengthened ties between the two countries while relations with the USSR cooled.

Camp David agreements In 1977 Sadat went to Israel to address the Israeli parliament and plead for peace. Other Arab states were dismayed by this move, and diplomatic relations with Syria, Libya, Algeria, and the Yemen, as well as the Palestine Liberation Organisation (PLO), were severed and Egypt was expelled from the ◊Arab League 1979. Despite this opposition, Sadat pursued his peace initiative, and at the ◊Camp David talks in the USA, he and the Israeli prime minister, Menachem ◊Begin, signed two agreements. The first laid a framework for peace in the Middle East, and the second, a framework for a treaty between the two countries. In 1979 a treaty was signed and Israel began a phased withdrawal from Sinai. As a consequence, Egypt's isolation from the Arab world grew, and the economy suffered from the withdrawal of Saudi subsidies. US aid became vital to Egypt's survival, and links between the two governments steadily grew closer. In 1981 Sadat was assassinated by a group of Muslim fundamentalists and was succeeded by Lt-Gen Hosni ◊Mubarak, who had been vice president since 1975. President Mubarak continued the policies of Sadat, playing a growing role in the search for Middle East peace, and proposing a ten-point programme to bring about elections in the occupied territories. At home, problems with Muslim fundamentalists increased Mubarak's dependence on military support. In Oct 1987 President Mubarak was re-elected, by referendum, for a second term. Despite the success of the ruling party in the Dec 1990 general election, independents did well in many areas.

Eichmann (Karl) Adolf 1906–1962. Austrian Nazi. As an ◊SS official during Hitler's regime (1933–45), he was responsible for atrocities against Jews and others, including the implementation of genocide. He managed to escape at the fall of Germany 1945, but was discovered in Argentina 1960, abducted by Israeli agents, tried in Israel 1961 for ◊war crimes, and executed.

Einstein Albert 1879–1955. German-born US physicist, who formulated the theories of relativity, (concerning the nature of time and space), and worked on radiation physics and thermodynamics. In 1905 he published the special theory of relativity (in which he formulated the interrelationship between mass and energy), and in 1915 issued his general theory of relativity.

Originally a pacifist, Einstein wrote to President F D Roosevelt 1939, urging him to start a research programme into developing a nuclear bomb, before Nazi Germany did so; this letter initiated the US commitment to building the atomic bomb. After World War II, Einstein campaigned vigorously for nuclear disarmament, aware that his theory of relativity had contributed to the beginning of a nuclear age.

Eire Gaelic name for the Republic of ◊Ireland.

Eisenhower Dwight David ('Ike') 1890–1969. The 34th president of the USA 1953–60, a Republican. A general in World War II, he commanded the Allied forces in Italy 1943, then the Allied invasion of Europe, and from Oct 1944 all the Allied armies in the West. As president he promoted business interests at home and conducted the ◊Cold War abroad. His vice president was Richard Nixon.

Eisenhower was born in Texas. A graduate of West Point military academy in 1915, he served in a variety of staff and command posts before World War II. He became commander in chief of the US and British forces for the invasion of N Africa Nov 1942; commanded the Allied invasion of Sicily July 1943, and announced the surrender of Italy 8 Sept 1943. In Dec he became commander of the Allied Expeditionary Force. He served as president of Columbia University and chair of the joint chiefs of staff 1949–50. He resigned from the army 1952 to campaign for the presidency; he was elected and re-elected by a wide margin in 1956. A popular politician, Eisenhower held office during a period of domestic and international tension, with the growing civil rights movement at home and the Cold War dominating international politics, although the US was experiencing an era of postwar prosperity and growth.

Elizabeth II 1926– . Queen of Great Britain and Northern Ireland from 1952, the elder daughter of George VI. She married her third cousin, Philip, the Duke of Edinburgh, 1947. They have four children: Charles, Anne, Andrew, and Edward.

Princess Elizabeth Alexandra Mary was born in London 21 Apr 1926, educated privately, and assumed official duties at 16. During World War II she served in the Auxiliary Territorial Service, and by an amendment to the Regency Act she became a state counsellor on her 18th birthday. On the death of George VI she succeeded to the throne while in Kenya with her husband. She is the richest woman in the world, with an estimated wealth of £5.3 billion.

Enabling Act a legislative enactment enabling or empowering a person or corporation to take certain actions. Perhaps the best known example of an Enabling Law was that passed in Germany in March 1933 by the Reichstag and Reichsrat. It granted Adolf Hitler dictatorial powers until April 1937, and effectively terminated parliamentary government in Germany until 1950. The law firmly established the Nazi dictatorship by giving dictatorial powers to the government.

enosis (Greek 'union') the movement, developed from 1930, for the union of ◊Cyprus with Greece. The campaign (led by ◊EOKA and supported by Archbishop Makarios) intensified from the 1950s. In 1960, independence from Britain, without union, was granted. Increased demands for union led to its proclamation in 1974. As a result, Turkey invaded Cyprus, ostensibly to protect the Turkish community, and the island was effectively partitioned.

ENSA (*E*ntertainments *N*ational *S*ervice *A*ssociation) an organization formed 1938–39 to provide entertainment for British and Allied forces during World War II. Directed by Basil Dean (1888–1978) from headquarters in the Drury Lane Theatre, it provided a variety of entertainment throughout the UK and also in all war zones.

Entente Cordiale (French 'friendly understanding') the agreement reached by Britain and France 1904 recognizing British interests in Egypt and French interests in Morocco. It formed the basis for Anglo-French cooperation before the outbreak of World War I 1914.

EOKA (Greek ***Ethnikí Organósis Kipriakóu Agónos***/'National Organization of Cypriot Struggle') an underground organization formed by General George Grivas 1955 to fight for the independence of Cyprus from Britain and ultimately its union (*enosis*) with Greece. In 1971, 11 years after the independence of Cyprus, Grivas returned to the island to form EOKA B and to resume the fight for *enosis*, which had not been achieved by the Cypriot government.

equal opportunities the right to be employed or considered for employment without discrimination on the grounds of race, gender, physical or mental handicap.

In 1946 a Royal Commission in the UK favoured equal pay for women in Britain. The Equal Pay Act of 1970 guaranteed (in theory) equal pay for equal work. The Sex Discrimination Act 1975 made it illegal to discriminate between men and women in a number of areas (though there were some exceptions). In 1975 the Equal Opportunities Commission was founded, with the power to oversee the operation of both the Equal Pay Act and the Sex Discrimination Act. The Commission was able to examine allegations of discrimination and to take legal action if necessary.

Erhard Ludwig 1897–1977. West German Christian Democrat politician, chancellor of the Federal Republic 1963–66. The 'economic miracle' of West Germany's recovery after World War II is largely attributed to Erhard's policy of social free enterprise (German *Marktwirtschaft*), which he initiated during his period as federal economics minister 1949–63.

Eritrea province of N Ethiopia, area 117,600 sq km/45,394 sq mi. Eritrea was under Ethiopian influence until it fell to the Turks mid-16th century. It was an Italian colony 1889–1941, where it was the base for the Italian invasion of Ethiopia. It came under British administration 1941–52, when it became an autonomous part of Ethiopia. Since 1962, when it became a region, various secessionist movements have risen. During the civil war in the 1970s, guerrillas held most of Eritrea. The Ethiopian government, backed by Soviet and Cuban forces, recaptured most towns 1978. Resistance continued throughout the 1980s, aided by conservative Gulf states, and some cooperation with guerrillas in Tigray province.

Estonia constituent republic of the USSR from 1940, area 45,100 sq km/17,413 sq mi. Estonia was ceded to Russia by the Swedes in 1721. The workers' and soldiers' soviets took control Nov 1917, were overthrown by German troops Mar 1918, and were restored Nov 1918. They were overthrown with the help of the British navy May 1919, and Estonia was a democratic republic until overthrown by a fascist coup 1934. It was incorporated into the the USSR 1940. Nationalist dissent grew from 1980. In 1988 Estonia adopted its own constitution, with a power of veto on all Soviet legislation. The new constitution allowed private property and placed land and natural resources under Estonian control. In 1989 parliament passed a law replacing Russian with Estonian as the main language.

An Estonian popular front (*Rahvarinne*) was established in Oct 1988 to campaign for democratization, increased autonomy, and eventual independence, and held mass rallies. In Nov 1988 Estonia's Supreme Soviet (state assembly) voted to declare the republic 'sovereign' and thus autonomous in all matters except military and foreign affairs, although the Presidium of the USSR's Supreme Soviet rejected this as unconstitutional. In Nov 1989 Estonia's assembly denounced the 1940 incorporation of the republic into the USSR as 'forced annexation'. A multi-party system is effectively in place in the republic, embracing the Popular Front, Christian Democrats, Independence League, and the republican Communist Party, and coalition governments seemed set to be formed following the elections of Dec 1989.

Ethiopia country in E Africa, bounded NE by the Red Sea, E and SE by Somalia, S by Kenya, and W and NW by Sudan.

history Although it remained independent throughout the period of European colonization of Africa, Abyssinia suffered civil unrest and several invasions from the 16th century, and was eventually reunited 1889 under Menelik II, with Italian support. In 1896 Menelik put down an invasion by Italy, which claimed he had agreed to make the country an Italian protectorate, and annexed Ogaden in the southeast several provinces to the west.

Ethiopian Empire Ethiopia was dominated for over 50 years by Haile Selassie, who became regent 1916, king 1928, and emperor 1930. The country was occupied by Italy 1935–41, and Haile Selassie went into exile in Britain. Ogaden was returned to Somalia, which was also under Italian control. Haile Selassie returned from exile 1941 and ruled until 1974, when he was deposed by the armed forces after famine, high inflation, growing unemployment, and demands for greater democracy. His palace and estates were nationalized, parliament dissolved, and the constitution suspended.

secessionist movements General Teferi Benti, who had led the uprising and been made head of state, was killed 1977 by fellow officers and replaced by Col Mengistu Haile Mariam. The Ethiopian empire had been built up by Haile Selassie and Menelik, and annexed regions had made frequent attempts to secede. The 1975 revolution encouraged secessionist movements to increase their efforts, and the military government had to fight to keep Eritrea and Ogaden, where Somalian troops were assisting local guerrillas. The USSR, having adopted Ethiopia as a new ally, threatened to cut off aid to Somalia, and Cuban troops assisted Mengistu in ending the fighting there. Eritrea and its neighbour, Tigray, continued their struggle for independence.

famine Amid this confusion there was acute famine in the north, including Eritrea, when the rains failed for three successive seasons. In addition to a massive emergency aid programme from many Western nations, the Ethiopian government tried to alleviate the problem by resettling people from the north to the more fertile south. By 1986 more than 500,000 had been forcibly resettled. Meanwhile, the military regime had re-established normal relations with most of its neighbours, promising a return to civilian rule, and in 1986 publishing the draft of a new constitution. Tigray province was captured by Eritrean People's Liberation Front EPLF and Tigré People's Liberation Front TPLF Feb 1989, the first time the government had lost control of the entire province. In March 1989 the new constitution was adopted, ending 12 years of military rule and electing Col Mengistu Mariam as the country's first president. A coup against him in May 1989 was put down and the military high command subsequently purged. Following a mediation offer by the former US president Jimmy Carter, peace talks with the Eritrean rebels began in Aug 1989. At the same time, droughts in the north threatened another widespread famine.

Euratom acronym for ◊European Atomic Energy Commission, forming part of the ◊European Community organization.

Eurocommunism policy followed by communist parties in Western Europe to seek power within the framework of national political initiative rather than by revolutionary means. In addition, Eurocommunism has enabled these parties to free themselves from total reliance on the USSR.

European Atomic Energy Commission *(Euratom)* organization established by the second Treaty of Rome 1957, which seeks the cooperation of member states of the European Community in nuclear research and the rapid and large-scale development of non-military nuclear energy.

European Coal and Steel Community (ECSC) former organization established by the treaty of Paris 1951 (ratified 1952) as a single authority for the coal and steel industries of France, West Germany, Italy, Belgium, Holland, and Luxembourg, eliminating tariffs and other restrictions; in 1967 it became part of the European Community.

The ECSC arose out of the Schuman plan 1950, which proposed a union of the French and German coal and steel industries so as to make future war between the two countries impossible. The ECSC was, in effect, a prototype institution for the European Community itself. Subsequent members of the EC automatically became ECSC members also.

European Community (EC) political and economic alliance consisting of the European Coal and Steel Community (1952), European Economic Community (EEC, popularly called the Common Market, 1957), and the European Atomic Energy Commission (Euratom, 1957). The original six members – Belgium, France, West Germany, Italy, Luxembourg, and the

Netherlands – were joined by the UK, Denmark, and the Republic of Ireland 1974, Greece 1981, Spain and Portugal 1985. Its aims include the expansion of trade, reduction of competition, the abolition of restrictive trading practices, and the encouragement of free movement of capital and labour within the community.

From 1967 the EC has comprised the following institutions: the ***Commission*** of 13 members pledged to independence of national interests, who initiate Community action; the ***Council of Ministers***, which makes decisions on the Commission's proposals; the ◊***European Parliament***, directly elected from 1979, which is mainly a consultative body but can dismiss the Commission; and the ***European Court of Justice***, to safeguard interpretation of the Rome Treaties (1957) that established the Community.

In 1990 there were 320 million people in the EC countries. Almost 60% of the EC's budget is spent on supporting farmers (about 4 million people). The EC sheep policy cost over 1.7 billion in 1990, and 30 million tonnes of excess grain is exported every year at a subsidized price. Altogether it cost member countries' taxpayers almost 9 billion in 1989–90 to maintain the international competitiveness of the EC's overpriced produce under the ◊Common Agricultural Policy. In 1992 members will become one market with the free movement of goods and capital.

In 1963 and 1967 Britain's application for membership was blocked, largely by France under General de Gaulle.

European Free Trade Association (EFTA) an organization established 1960 and as of 1988 consisting of Austria, Finland, Iceland, Norway, Sweden, and Switzerland. There are no import duties between members. Of the original members, Britain and Denmark left (1972) to join the ◊European Community, as subsequently did Portugal (1985).

In 1973 the EC signed agreements with EFTA members, setting up a free-trade area of over 300 million consumers. Trade between the two groups amounts to over half of total EFTA trade.

European Parliament the parliament of the European Community, which meets in Strasbourg to comment on the legislative proposals of the Commission of the European Communities. Members are elected for a five-year term. The European Parliament has 518 seats, apportioned on the basis of population, of which the UK, France, West Germany, and Italy have 81 each, Spain 60, the Netherlands 25, Belgium, Greece, and Portugal 24 each, Denmark 16, the Republic of Ireland 15, and Luxembourg 6.

Originally merely consultative, the European Parliament became directly elected 1979, and assumed increased powers. Though still not a true legislative body, it can dismiss the whole Commission and reject the Community budget in its entirety. Full sittings are in Strasbourg; most committees meet in Brussels, and the seat of the secretariat is in Luxembourg. After the 1989 elections the Left (Socialist, Communist, and Green) held 260 seats and the Right (Christian Democrats, Liberals, European Democratic Group, European Right, European Democratic Alliance) held 242. Henry Plumb (UK) became president 1987.

evacuation the removal of civilian inhabitants from an area liable to aerial bombing or other hazards (or in the aftermath of an environmental disaster) to safer surroundings. The term is also applied to military evacuation, as occurred for example when Allied troops were evacuated from the beaches of ◊Dunkirk in 1940. Persons who have been evacuated are usually known as evacuees.

Large-scale evacuation took place during World War II in the UK when the government encouraged parents to send their children away from urban and industrial areas to places of greater safety.

F

fair deal the policy of social improvement advocated by Harry S Truman, President of the USA 1945–53. The 'Fair Deal' proposals, first mooted in 1945 after the end of World War II, aimed to extend the ◊New Deal on health insurance, housing development, and the laws to maintain farming prices. Although some of the proposals were passed – for example a Housing Act, a higher minimum wage, and wider social security benefits – the main proposals were blocked by a hostile Congress.

Falange Española (Spanish 'phalanx') former Spanish Fascist Party, founded 1933 by José Antonio de Rivera, son of the military ruler Miguel Primo de Rivera. It was closely modelled in programme and organization on the Italian fascists and on the Nazis. In 1937, when ◊Franco assumed leadership, it was declared the only legal party, and altered its name to Traditionalist Spanish Phalanx.

Falkland Islands British crown colony in the S Atlantic, area 12,173 sq km/4,700 sq mi; population (1986) 1,916. The governor (Gordon Jewkes from Oct 1985) is advised by an executive council, and a mainly elected legislative council.

The first British settlers arrived 1765; Spain bought out a French settlement 1766, and the British were ejected 1770–71, but British sovereignty was never ceded, and from 1833, when a few Argentines were expelled, British settlement was continuous. Argentina asserts its succession to the Spanish claim to the *Islas Malvinas*, but the inhabitants oppose cession. Occupied by Argentina April 1982, the islands were recaptured by British military forces in May–June of the same year.

family planning spacing or preventing the birth of children. Access to family-planning services is a significant factor in women's health as well as in limiting population growth.

English philosopher Jeremy Bentham put forward the idea of birth control 1797, but it was Francis Place, a Radical, who attempted to popularise it in the 19th century. In 1912, two articles by US feminist Margaret Sanger appeared in a New York socialist newspaper *The Call* advocating birth control as one means of female emancipation. In 1916, she opened a clinic in Brooklyn, and helped to found the American Birth Control League.

In the UK, family planning and birth control became acceptable partly through the efforts of Marie Stopes who opened a clinic in London in 1921. Other clinics subsequently opened in England were amalgamated to become the Family Planning Association 1930. Attitudes changed gradually from opposition to support: for example, in the 1930s the Family Planning Association in the UK ran clinics in hospitals and health centres; Sweden supported municipal clinics; while the USA set up some state public health programmes incorporating birth control. Internationally, in 1965, the United Nations Population Commission recommended the provision of technical assistance on birth control to member nations; while the World Health Organization instigated a programme of research.

The average number of pregnancies per woman is two in the industrialized countries, where 71% use family planning, as compared to six or seven pregnancies per woman in the Third World.

famine a severe shortage of food affecting a large number of people. Famines arise when one group in a society loses its opportunity to exchange its labour or possessions for food. Most Western famine-relief agencies, such as the International Red Cross, set out to supply food or to increase its local production, rather than becoming involved in local politics.

Famine was traditionally thought to result from some inadequacy in food supplies, from natural causes such as drought or earthquake, or from some failure in food distribution. Major famines include those of China 1920; Russia 1920–21, and 1932; and India 1964.

The ***food availability deficit*** (FAD) theory, was challenged in the 1980s. Crop failures do not inevitably lead to famine; nor is it always the case that adequate food supplies are not available nearby. For example, in 1990 the Ethiopian air force bombed grain depots in a rebel-held area.

Farouk 1920–1965. King of Egypt 1936–52. He succeeded his father Fuad I. In 1952 a coup headed by General Muhammed Neguib and

Col Gamal Nasser compelled him to abdicate, and his son Fuad II was temporarily proclaimed in his place.

fascism ideology that denies all rights to individuals in their relations with the state; specifically, the totalitarian nationalist movement founded in Italy 1919 by ◊Mussolini and followed by Hitler's Germany 1933.

Fascism was essentially a product of the economic and political crisis of the years after World War I. Units called *fasci di combattimento* (combat groups), from the Latin *fasces* were originally established to oppose communism. The fascist party, the *Partitio Nazionale Fascista*, controlled Italy 1922–43. Fascism protected the existing social order by forcible suppression of the working-class movement and by providing scapegoats for popular anger such as outsiders who lived within the state: Jews, foreigners or blacks; it also prepared the citizenry for the economic and psychological mobilization for war.

The term 'fascism' is also applied to similar organizations in other countries, such as the Spanish Falange and the British Union of Fascists under Oswald Mosley. Neofascist groups still exist in many W European countries and elsewhere.

Fatah, al- a Palestinian nationalist organization founded 1956 to bring about an independent state of Palestine. Also called the Palestine National Liberation Movement, it is the main component of the ◊Palestine Liberation Organization. Its leader is Yasser ◊Arafat.

FBI abbreviation for ◊***Federal Bureau of Investigation***, agency of the Department of Justice in the USA.

February Revolution (March in the Western calendar) the first of the two political uprisings of the ◊Russian revolution in 1917 that led to the overthrow of the tsar and the end of the ◊Romanov dynasty.

The immediate cause of the revolution was the inability of the tsardom to manage World War I. On 8 March strikes and bread riots broke out in Petrograd (formerly St Petersburg), where the troops later mutinied and joined the rioters. A provisional government was appointed by the ◊Duma (assembly) and Tsar Nicholas II abdicated on 15 March (27 Feb Julian calendar). The Petrograd Soviet of Workers, Peasants and Soldiers (formed originally during the Russian revolution of 1905) was revived by the Bolsheviks. The provisional government under Prince Lvov was opposed by the Petrograd Soviet, especially when Lenin returned from Switzerland in April. On 16–18 July the Bolsheviks made an unsuccessful attempt to seize power and Lenin was forced into hiding in Finland. The provisional government tried to continue the war, but was weakened by serious misunderstandings between the prime minister, Kerensky, and the commander in chief General Kornilov, who tried unsuccessfully to gain power in Sept 1917. Shortly afterwards the Bolsheviks seized power in the ◊October Revolution.

Federal Bureau of Investigation (FBI) agency of the US Department of Justice that investigates violations of federal law not specifically assigned to other agencies, being particularly concerned with internal security. The FBI was established 1908 and built up a position of powerful autonomy during the autocratic directorship of J Edgar Hoover 1924–72.

Field divisions are maintained in more than 60 US cities. The FBI's special agents are qualified in law, accounting, or auditing. In 1964 the agency was criticized by the Warren Commission concerning the assassination of President Kennedy, and in 1973 L Patrick Gray, the acting director, resigned when it was revealed that he had destroyed relevant material in the ◊Watergate investigation. Through the Freedom of Information Act it became known that the FBI had kept files on many eminent citizens and that Hoover had abused his power, for example in persecuting the civil-rights leader ◊Martin Luther King. Clarence M Kelley was director 1973–78, William Webster 1978–87, and Judge William Sessions from 1987.

Federal Reserve System ('Fed') US central banking system and note-issue authority, established 1913 to regulate the country's credit and monetary affairs. The Fed consists of the 12 federal reserve banks and their 25 branches and other facilities throughout the country; it is headed by a board of governors in Washington, appointed by the US president with Senate approval.

feminism an active belief in equal rights and opportunities for women; see ◊women's movement.

Fianna Fáil (Gaelic 'Soldiers of Destiny') Republic of Ireland political party, founded by the Irish nationalist Eamon de Valera 1926. It has been the governing party in the Republic of Ireland 1932–48, 1951–54, 1957–73, 1977–81, 1982, and 1987– . It aims to establish a united and completely independent all-Ireland republic.

fifth column a group within a country secretly aiding an enemy attacking from without. The term originated 1936 during the Spanish Civil War, when Gen Mola boasted that Franco supporters were attacking Madrid with four columns and that they had a 'fifth column' inside the city.

film, art of see ◊cinema.

final solution (to the Jewish question; German *Endlöosung der Judenfrage*) euphemism used by the Nazis to describe the extermination of Jews and other opponents of the regime during World War II. See ◊Holocaust.

Finland country in Scandinavia, bounded N by Norway, E by the USSR, S and W by the Baltic Sea, and NW by Sweden.

history In 1809, during the Napoleonic Wars, Finland was invaded and annexed by Russia; nationalist feeling grew, and the country proclaimed its independence during the 1917 Russian revolution. The Soviet regime initially tried to regain control but acknowledged Finland's independence 1920.

the 'Winter War' In 1939 the USSR's request for military bases in Finland was rejected, and the two countries were involved in the 'Winter War', which lasted for 15 weeks. Finland was defeated and forced to cede territory. In the hope of regaining it, in 1941 it joined Nazi Germany in attacking the USSR, but agreed to a separate armistice 1944. It was again forced to cede territory (12% of its total area) and agree to huge war reparations; in 1948 it signed the Finno-Soviet Pact of Friendship, Co-operation, and Mutual Assistance (the YYA Treaty). War reparations to the USSR were paid off in 1952 (amounting to 5% of the GDP 1945–48).

postwar treaties In 1955 Finland joined the UN and the Nordic Council (which includes Denmark, Iceland, Norway, and Sweden). The YYA Treaty was extended 1955, 1970, and 1983. Although the Treaty requires it to repel any attack on the USSR through Finnish territory by Germany or its allies, Finland has maintained a policy of strict neutrality. It signed a trade treaty with the EEC 1973 and a 15-year trade agreement with the USSR 1977. In 1989 it was admitted into the Council of Europe. Finnish politics have been characterized by instability in governments, (over 60 have been formed since independence), including many minority coalitions. The presidency, on the other hand, has been very stable, with only two presidents in over 30 years. Urho Kekkonen was elected president in 1956 and re-elected in 1962, 1968, and 1978. In 1981 he resigned from office due to ill health and Mauno Koivisto became president in Jan 1982; he was re-elected in 1988. The Social Democratic and Centre parties have dominated Finland's coalition politics for many years, but the 1987 general election resulted in the Social Democrats entering government in coalition with their archenemies, the Conservatives.

First World War another name for ◊World War I, 1914–18.

Five-Year Plan a long-term strategic plan for the development of a country's economy. Five-year plans were, from 1928, the basis of economic planning in the USSR, aimed particularly at developing heavy and light industry in a primarily agricultural country. They have since been adopted by many other countries.

flight or ***aviation*** air travel. People first took to the air in balloons and began powered flight in airships, but the history of flying, both for civilian and military use, is dominated by the aeroplane. The first planes were designed for gliding; the advent of the petrol engine saw the first powered flight by the Wright brothers 1903 in the USA. This inspired the development of aircraft throughout Europe. Biplanes were succeeded by monoplanes in the 1930s. The first jet plane was produced 1939, and after the end of World War II jetliners brought about continuous expansion in passenger air travel. In 1969 came the supersonic aircraft Concorde.

1903 First powered and controlled flight of a heavier-than-air machine by Orville Wright, at Kitty Hawk, North Carolina, USA.

1908 First powered flight in UK by Samuel Cody.

1909 Louis Blériot flew across the English Channel in 36 minutes.

1914–1918 World War I. Stimulated movements in increased speed and power.

1919 First flight across the Atlantic by Albert C Read, using a flying boat; first nonstop flight across the Atlantic by John William Alcock and Arthur Whitten Brown in 16 hours 27 minutes; first complete flight from Britain to Australia by Ross Smith and Keith Smith.

1923 Juan de la Cieva flew the first autogiro with a rotating wing.

1927 Charles Lindbergh made the first solo, nonstop flight across the Atlantic.

1928 First trans-Pacific flight, from San Francisco to Brisbane, by Charles Kinsford Smith and C T P Ulm.

1930 Frank Whittle patented the jet engine; Amy Johnson became the first woman to fly solo from England to Australia.

1937 The first fully pressurized aircraft, the Lockheed XC-35, came into service.

1939 Erich Warsitz flew the first jet aeroplane, in Germany; Igor Sikorsky designed the first helicopter, with a large main rotor and a smaller tail rotor.

1939–45 World War II. Developments included the Hawker Hurricane and Supermarine Spitfire fighters, and Avro Lancaster and Boeing Flying Fortress bombers.

1947 A rocket-powered plane, the Bell X-1, was the first aircraft to fly faster than the speed of sound.

1949 The de Havilland Comet, the first jet airliner, entered service; James Gallagher made the first nonstop round-the-world flight, in a Boeing Superfortress.

1953 The first vertical takeoff aircraft, the Rolls-Royce 'Flying Bedstead', was tested.

1968 The world's first supersonic airliner, the Russian TU-144, flew for the first time.

1970 The Boeing 747 jumbo jet entered service, carrying 500 passengers.

1976 A Lockheed SR-17A, piloted by Eldon W Joersz and George T Morgan, set the world air-speed record of 3,529.56 kmh/2,193.167 mph over Beale Air Force Base, California, USA. Anglo-French Concorde, which made a transatlantic crossing in under three hours, came into commercial service.

1979 First crossing of the English Channel by a human-powered aircraft, *Gossamer Albatross*, piloted by Bryan Allen.

1981 The solar-powered *Solar Challenger* flew across the English Channel, from Paris to Kent, taking 5 hours for the 262 km/162.8 mi journey.

1986 Dick Rutan and Jeana Yeager made the first nonstop flight around the world without refuelling, piloting *Voyager*, which completed the flight in 9 days 3 minutes 44 seconds.

1987 Richard Branson made the first transatlantic crossing by hot-air balloon.

1988 *Daedelus*, a human-powered craft piloted by Kanellos Kanellopoulos, flew 118 km/74 mi across the Aegean Sea.

Foch Ferdinand 1851–1929. Marshal of France during World War I. He was largely responsible for the Allied victory at the first battle of the ◊Marne Sept 1914, and commanded on the NW front Oct 1914–Sep 1916. He was appointed Commander in Chief of the Allied armies in the spring of 1918, and launched the Allied counter-offensive in July that brought about the negotiation of an armistice to end the war.

Ford Gerald R(udolph) 1913– . The 38th president of the USA 1974–77, a Republican. He was elected to the House of Representatives 1949, was nominated to the vice-presidency by Richard Nixon 1973, and in 1974, when Nixon resigned, Ford became president. He pardoned Nixon, and gave amnesty to those who had resisted the draft for the Vietnam War.

Ford was born in Omaha, Nebraska, was an All-American footballer at college, and graduated from Yale Law School. He was appointed vice president Dec 1973, at a time when Nixon's re-election campaign was already being investigated for 'dirty tricks', and became president the following Aug when the ◊Watergate scandal forced Nixon to resign. Ford's visit to Vladivostok 1974 resulted in agreement with the USSR on strategic arms limitation. He was defeated by Carter in the 1976 election by a narrow margin.

Ford Henry 1863–1947. US automobile manufacturer, who built his first car 1893 and founded the Ford Motor Company 1903. His Model T (1908–27) was the first car to be constructed solely by mass-production methods, and 15 million of these cars were made.

Fourteen Points the terms proposed by President Wilson of the USA in his address to Congress 8 Jan 1918, as a basis for the settlement of World War I. The creation of the League of Nations was one of the points.

Fourth Republic the French constitutional regime established 1944–46 and lasting until 4 Oct 1958. Its constitution created a figurehead president, a National Assembly and a weak second chamber. Despite some economic and industrial success it was weakened by political division causing a rapid succession of governments. The Fourth Republic collapsed with France in deep political turmoil, opening the way to Charles de Gaulle's Fifth Republic.

France country in W Europe, bounded NE by Belgium and West Germany, E by Switzerland and Italy, S by the Mediterranean, SW by Spain and Andorra, and W by the Atlantic Ocean.

government France has a two-chamber legislature and a 'shared executive' government. The legislature comprises a national assembly and a senate. France's executive is functionally divided between the president and prime minister. According to the constitution, however, ultimate control over policy making rests with the prime minister and council of ministers.

history A new constitution was framed and adopted for a Fourth Republic in Jan 1946. This provided for a weak executive and powerful national assembly that, being elected under a generous system of proportional representation, was to be divided between numerous small party groupings. With 26 impermanent governments being formed 1946–58, real power passed to the civil service, which engineered rapid economic reconstruction. Decolonization of French Indochina 1954, Morocco and Tunisia 1956 and entry into the EEC 1957 were also effected.

The Fourth Republic was overthrown in 1958 by a political and military crisis over Algerian independence (see ◊Algiers, Battle of), which threatened to lead to a French army revolt. De Gaulle was recalled from retirement to head a government of national unity and supervised the framing of the new Fifth Republic constitution.

the De Gaulle era De Gaulle, who became president in 1959, restored domestic stability and presided over the decolonization of Francophone Africa, including Algerian independence in 1962. Close economic links were maintained with former colonies. De Gaulle also initiated a new foreign policy, withdrawing France from military cooperation in ◊NATO in 1966 and developing an autonomous nuclear deterrent force. The de Gaulle era was one of economic growth and large scale rural-urban migration. Politically, however, there was tight censorship and strong centralization, and in 1967 the public reacted against de Gaulle's paternalism by voting the 'right coalition' a reduced majority.

the 1968 demonstrations A year later, in 1968, the nation was paralyzed by students' and workers' demonstrations which briefly threatened the government. De Gaulle called elections and won a landslide victory. In 1969, however, he was defeated in a referendum over proposed senate and local government reforms and resigned. De Gaulle's former prime minister, Georges Pompidou, was elected president and pursued Gaullist policies until his death in 1974. Pompidou's successor as president, Valéry Giscard d'Estaing, leader of the centre-right Independent Republicans, introduced domestic reforms and played a more active and co-operative role in the EEC. Giscard faced opposition, however, from his 'right coalition' partner, Jacques Chirac, who was prime minister 1974–76, and deteriorating international economic conditions. France performed better than many of its European competitors between 1974–81, with the president launching a major nuclear power programme to save on energy imports and, while Raymond Barre was prime minister (1976–81), a new liberal 'freer market' economic strategy. However, with 1.7 million unemployed, Giscard was defeated by the Socialist party leader, François ◊Mitterrand, in the 1981 presidential election.

the Left Coalition Mitterrand's victory was the first presidential success for the 'left coalition' during the Fifth Republic. The new administration, which included four Communist ministers, introduced a radical programme of social reform, decentralization, and nationalization, and passed a series of reflationary budgets aimed at reducing unemployment. Financial constraints, however, forced a switch towards a more conservative policy of 'rigueur' (austerity) in 1983. A U-turn in economic policy was completed in 1984 when prime minister Pierre Mauroy was replaced by Laurent Fabius, prompting the resignation of Communist members of the cabinet. Unemployment rose to over 2.5 million in 1985–86, increasing racial tension in urban areas. The extreme right-wing National Front, led by Jean-Marie Le Pen, benefited from this and gained seats in the March 1986 National Assembly elections. Mitterrand was obliged to appoint as prime minister the leader of the opposition, Jacques Chirac, who emerged as the dominant force in the 'shared executive'. Chirac introduced a radical 'new conservative' programme of denationalization, deregulation, and 'desocialization'. However, his reforms encountered serious opposition and Chirac was defeated by Mitterrand in the May 1988 presidential election. In the national assembly elections that followed in June 1988, the socialists emerged as the largest single political party. Mitterrand appointed Michel Rocard, a moderate social democrat, as prime minister.

the progressive programme Rocard implemented a progressive programme, aimed at protecting the underprivileged and improving the 'quality of life'. Between 1988 and 1990 France enjoyed a strong economic upturn and attention focused increasingly on 'quality of life', with the Green Party gaining 11% of the national vote in the European Parliament elections of June 1989. The extreme right National Front continued to do well in municipal elections.

In Sept 1990, after Iraqi violation of the French ambassador's residence in Kuwait, the French government despatched troops to Saudi Arabia, to form part of the Allied forces in the Gulf War 15 Jan–28 Feb 1991.

Franco Francisco (Paulino Hermenegildo Teódulo Bahamonde) 1892–1975. Spanish dictator from 1939. As a general, he led the insurgent Nationalists to victory in the Spanish ◊Civil War 1936–39, supported by Fascist Italy and Nazi Germany, and established a dictatorship. In 1942 Franco reinstated the Cortes (Spanish parliament), which in 1947 passed an act by which he became head of state for life.

Franco was born in Galicia, NW Spain. He entered the army 1910, served in Morocco 1920–26, and was appointed chief of staff 1935, but demoted to governor of the Canary Islands 1936. Dismissed from this post by the Popular Front (Republican) government, he plotted an uprising with German and Italian assistance, and on the outbreak of the Civil War organized the invasion of Spain by N

African troops and foreign legionaries. After the death of General Sanjurjo, he took command of the Nationalists, proclaiming himself *Caudillo* (leader) of Spain. The defeat of the Republic with the surrender of Madrid 1939 brought all Spain under his government. On the outbreak of World War II, in spite of Spain's official attitude of 'strictest neutrality', his pro-Axis sympathies led him to send aid, later withdrawn, to the German side.

At home, he curbed the growing power of the ◊Falange (the fascist party), and in later years slightly liberalized his regime. In 1969 he nominated Juan Carlos as his successor and future king of Spain. He relinquished the premiership 1973, but remained head of state until his death.

free trade an economic system where governments do not interfere in the movement of goods between states; there are thus no taxes on imports. In the modern economy, free trade tends to hold within economic groups such as the ◊European Community or the ◊Warsaw Pact, but not generally, despite such treaties as GATT (General Agreement on Tariffs and Trade) 1948 and subsequent agreements to reduce tariffs. The opposite of free trade is protectionism.

In the 1980s recession prompted by increased world oil prices and unemployment swung the pendulum back towards protectionism, which discourages foreign imports by heavy duties thus protecting home products. Within the European Community, a date of 1992 has been agreed for the abolition of all protectionist tariffs.

Franz Ferdinand or Francis Ferdinand 1863–1914. Archduke of Austria. He became heir to his uncle, Emperor Franz Joseph in 1884 but while visiting Sarajevo 28 June 1914, he and his wife were assassinated by Serbian nationalists. Austria used the episode to make unreasonable demands on Serbia that ultimately precipitated World War I.

Franz Joseph or Francis Joseph 1830–1916. Emperor of Austria-Hungary from 1848, when his uncle, Ferdinand I, abdicated. After the suppression of the 1848 revolution, Franz Joseph tried to establish an absolute monarchy but had to grant Austria a parliamentary constitution 1861 and Hungary equality with Austria 1867. He was defeated in the Italian War 1859 and the Prussian War 1866. In 1914 he made the assassination of his heir and nephew, Franz Ferdinand, the excuse for attacking Serbia, precipitating World War I.

Free French in World War II, movement formed by General Charles ◊de Gaulle in the UK June 1940, consisting of French soldiers who continued to fight against the Axis after the Franco-German armistice. They took the name ***Fighting France*** 1942 and served in many campaigns, among them General Leclerc's advance from Chad to Tripolitania 1942, the Syrian campaigns 1941, the campaigns in the Western Desert, the Italian campaign, the liberation of France, and the invasion of Germany. Their emblem was the Cross of Lorraine, a cross with two bars.

French Fourth Republic see ◊Fourth Republic.

French Third Republic see ◊Third Republic.

front-line states the black nations of southern Africa in the 'front line' of the struggle against the racist policies of South Africa: namely Mozambique, Tanzania, and Zambia. Botswana and Zimbabwe can also be included in this category.

During the 1970s the term was particularly associated with their respective presidents: Samora Machel, Julius Nyerere, and Kenneth Kaunda.

G

Gandhi *Indira Gandhi, Nehru's daughter, had a controversial political career, during which she was twice prime minister of India.*

Gaddafi alternative form of ◊Khaddhafi, Libyan leader.

Gagarin Yuri (Alexeyevich) 1934–1968. Soviet cosmonaut, who in 1961 became the first human in space aboard the spacecraft *Vostok 1*.

Gaitskell Hugh (Todd Naylor) 1906–1963. British Labour politician. In 1950 he became minister of economic affairs, and then chancellor of the Exchequer until Oct 1951. In 1955 he defeated Aneurin Bevan for the succession to Clement Attlee as party leader, and tried to reconcile internal differences on nationalization and disarmament. He was re-elected leader in 1960.

Gallipoli port in European Turkey, giving its name to the peninsula on which it stands. In World War I, at the instigation of Winston Churchill, an unsuccessful attempt was made Feb 1915–Jan 1916 by Allied troops to force their way through the Dardanelles and link up with Russia. The campaign was fought mainly by Australian and New Zealand (ANZAC – Australian and New Zealand Army Corps) forces, who suffered heavy losses. An estimated 36,000 Commonwealth troops died during the nine-month campaign.

Gandhi Indira (born Nehru) 1917–1984. Indian politician. Prime minister of India 1966–77 and 1980–84, and leader of the ◊Congress Party 1966–77 and subsequently of the Congress (I) party. She was assassinated 1984 by members of her Sikh bodyguard, resentful of her use of troops to clear malcontents from the Sikh temple at Amritsar.

Her father, Jawaharlat Nehru, was India's first prime minister. She married Feroze Gandhi in 1942 (died 1960, not related to Mahatma Gandhi) and had two sons, Sanjay Gandhi (1946–80), who died in an aeroplane crash, and Rajiv Gandhi (1944–1991). In 1975 the validity of her re-election to parliament was questioned, and she declared a state of emergency. During this time her son Sanjay was implementing a social and economic programme (including an unpopular family-planning policy) which led to her defeat in 1977, although he masterminded her return to power in 1980.

Gandhi Mohandas Karamchand (called ***Mahatma*** or 'Great Soul') 1869–1948. Indian Nationalist leader. A pacifist, he led the struggle for Indian independence from 1915. He was imprisoned several times by the British authorities and was influential in the Nationalist ◊Congress Party and in the independence negotiations 1947. He was assassinated by a Hindu nationalist in the violence that followed the partition of British India into India and Pakistan.

Gandhi studied law in London, later practising as a barrister. He settled in South Africa where until 1914 he led the Indian community in opposition to racial discrimination. Returning to India, he emerged as leader of the Indian National Congress. He organized hunger strikes and events of civil disobedience, and campaigned for social reform, including religious tolerance and an end to discrimination against the so-called untouchable caste. He proposed that Third World countries like India should develop their own village-based, non-capitalist system rather than pursuing Western-style industrialization. In 1947, following World War II, he played a significant role in negotiations for an autonomous Indian State.

Gang of Four chief members of the radical

faction that tried to seize power in China after the death of Mao Zedong 1976. It included his widow, Jiang Qing; the other members were Zhang Chunjao, Wang Hungwen, and Yao Wenyuan. The coup failed, and they were soon arrested.

In the UK the name was subsequently applied to four members of the Labour Party who in 1981 resigned to form the Social Democratic Party (SDP): Roy Jenkins, David Owen, Shirley Williams, and William Rodgers.

gangsterism organized crime, particularly in the USA. One result of the 18th Amendment (Prohibition) in 1919 was an increase in organized crime. The prohibition law was difficult to enforce; illicit liquor could be brought into the USA over the long land borders or coastline, and illegal distilleries were soon established. Bootlegging activities (importing or making illegal liquor) and 'speakeasies' (where alcohol could be illegally purchased) gave rise to rivalry which resulted in hired gangs of criminals (gangsters) and gun battles. Social unrest and a widening gap between rich and poor also created a climate in which crime flourished. One of the most notorious gangsters was Al Capone, who had his headquarters in Chicago. In 1933 the 21st Amendment was passed repealing Prohibition. This, and the actions of the Criminal Investigation Bureau (CIB) under J. Edgar Hoover limited the opportunities for the 'gangster' and contributed to some reduction in crime.

Gaulle Charles de. French politician, see Charles ◊de Gaulle.

Gaza Strip strip of Palestine under Israeli administration; capital Gaza; area 363 sq km/140 sq mi; population (1989) 645,000 of which 446,000 are refugees.

It was invaded by Israel 1956, reoccupied 1967, and retained 1973. Clashes between the Israeli authorities and the Palestinian people escalated to intifada (uprising) 1988.

Gdańsk (German ***Danzig***) Polish port; population (1985) 467,000. It was in almost continuous Prussian possession 1793–1919, when it again became a free city under the protection of the League of Nations. Annexed by Germany 1939, it reverted to Poland 1945, when the churches and old merchant houses were restored. In the 1980s there were repeated anti-government strikes at the Lenin shipyards.

General Agreement on Tariffs and Trade (GATT) an organization within the United Nations founded 1948 with the aim of encouraging ◊free trade between nations through low tariffs, abolitions of quotas, and curbs on subsidies.

general strike a refusal to work by employees in several key industries, with the intention of paralyzing the economic life of a country.

In British history, the General Strike refers to a nationwide strike called by the Trade Union Congress on 3 May 1926 in support of the miners' union. The immediate cause of the 1926 General Strike was the report of a royal commission on the coal mining industry (Samuel Report 1926) which, among other things, recommended a cut in wages. The mine-owners wanted longer hours as well as lower wages. The miners' union under the leadership of A J Cook resisted with the slogan 'not a penny off the pay, not a minute on the day'. A coal strike started in early May 1926 and the miners asked the TUC to bring all major industries out on strike in support of the action; eventually it included more than two million workers. The conservative government under Stanley Baldwin used troops, volunteers, and special constables to maintain food supplies and essential services, and had a monopoly on the information services including BBC radio. After nine days the TUC ended the general strike, leaving the miners – who felt betrayed by the TUC – to remain on strike, unsuccessfully, until Nov 1926. The Trades Disputes Act of 1927 made general strikes illegal.

Geneva Convention international agreement 1864 regulating the treatment of those wounded in war, and later extended to cover the types of weapons allowed, the treatment of prisoners and the sick, and the protection of civilians in wartime. The rules were revised at conventions held 1906, 1929, and 1949, and by the 1977 Additional Protocols.

Geneva Protocol international agreement 1925 designed to prohibit the use of poisonous gases, chemical weapons, and bacteriological methods of warfare. It came into force 1928 but was not ratified by the USA until 1974.

genocide the deliberate and systematic extermination of a national, racial, religious, or ethnic group defined by the exterminators as undesirable.

The term is commonly applied to the policies of the Nazis during World War II (what they called the 'final solution' – the extermination of all 'undesirables' in occupied Europe). At the end of World War II the United Nations' indictment of 24 Nazi leaders brought the word genocide into more common usage and coined a new term in international law. In 1948 the United Nations General Assembly adopted a convention on the prevention and punishment of genocide, as well as the Universal Declaration of ◊Human Rights.

George V 1865–1936. King of Great Britain from 1910, when he succeeded his father Edward VII. He was the second son, and became heir 1892 on the death of his elder brother Albert, Duke of Clarence. In 1893, he married Princess Victoria Mary of Teck (Queen Mary), formerly engaged to his brother. During World War I he made several visits to the front. In 1917, he abandoned all German titles for himself and his family. The name of the royal house was changed from Saxe-Coburg-Gotha (popularly known as Brunswick or Hanover) to Windsor.

George VI 1895–1952. King of Great Britain from 1936, when he succeeded after the abdication of his brother Edward VIII, who had succeeded their father George V. Created Duke of York 1920, he married in 1923 Lady Elizabeth Bowes-Lyon (1900–), and their children are Elizabeth II and Princess Margaret. During World War II, he visited the Normandy and Italian battlefields.

German Spring offensive Germany's final offensive on the Western Front during World War I. By early 1918, German forces outnumbered the Allies on the Western Front. Germany staged three separate offensives, which culminated in the Second Battle of the Marne fought between July 15 – Aug 6. It marked the turning point of World War I. After winning the battle the Allies advanced steadily, and, by September, Germany had lost all the territory it had gained during Spring.

Germany, East former country in E Europe, bounded to the N by the Baltic Sea, E by Poland, S by Czechoslovakia, and SW and W by West Germany.

history Formerly the Soviet zone of occupation in the partition of Germany, the German Democratic Republic was established 1949, becoming a sovereign state 1954. It was recognized at first only by the Communist powers. In 1973, however, following the adoption by the Federal Republic of the new policy of ◊Ostpolitik, a Basic Treaty governing relations between East and West Germany was ratified by both states. The treaty fell short of full recognition by the Federal Republic, permanent missions rather than ambassadors being stationed in the respective nations. It led, however, to East Germany's admission to the ◊United Nations and to its full recognition by other Western states.

sovietization The years immediately after 1949 saw the rapid establishment of a Communist regime on the Soviet model, involving the creation of a one-party political system, the nationalization of industry, and the formation of agricultural collectives. Opposition to such Sovietization led, during food shortages, to demonstrations and a general strike 1953, which was suppressed by Soviet troops. In 1961 the ◊Berlin Wall was erected to stem the growing movement of refugees to the Federal Republic. Economic reforms boosted the East German growth rate in the 1960s, significantly improving living conditions. During the following decade, with the replacement of the Stalinist Socialist Unity Party (SED) leader Walter ◊Ulbricht by the pragmatic Erich Honecker, a more moderate political approach was adopted at home, while economic and diplomatic relations with the West were extended. The German Democratic Republic was a loyal and vital member of ◊Comecon and the ◊Warsaw Pact (Soviet medium-range nuclear missiles being stationed on its soil) during the ◊Brezhnev era. From 1987 Honecker was urged by the USSR to accelerate the pace of domestic economical and political reform. However, he refused to do so, and grassroots pressure for liberalization mounted.

New Forum In Sept 1989, after the violent suppression of a church and civil rights activists' demonstration in Leipzig, an umbrella dissident organization, *Neue Forum* ('New Forum'), was illegally formed. The regime was further destabilized between Aug and Oct 1989 both by the exodus of more than 30,000 of its citizens to West Germany through Hungary, which had opened its borders with Austria in May, and by the illness of Honecker during the same period. On 6 and 7 Oct the Soviet leader Mikhail ◊Gorbachev visited East Berlin, and made plain his desire to see greater reform. This catalysed the growing reform movement and a wave of demonstrations, the first since 1953, swept East Berlin, Dresden, Leipzig, and smaller towns. Faced with the rising tide of protest and the increasing exodus to West Germany (between 5,000 and 10,000 people a day), which caused grave disruption to the economy, Honecker was replaced as party leader and head of state by Egon Krenz on 18–24 Oct.

reform movement Krenz sanctioned far-reaching reforms in Nov 1989 that effectively ended the SED monopoly of power and laid the foundations for a pluralist system. The Politburo was purged of conservative members; Modrow became prime minister and a new cabinet was formed; New Forum was legalized, and opposition parties allowed to form; borders with the West were opened and free travel allowed, with the Berlin Wall being effectively dismantled. Following revelations of high-level corruption during the Honecker regime, Krenz was forced to resign as SED leader and head of state, and was replaced by

Gregor Gysi and Manfred Gerlach respectively. Honecker was placed under house arrest awaiting trial on charges of treason, corruption, and abuse of power, and the Politburo was again purged.

political crisis An interim SED–opposition 'government of national responsibility' was formed Feb 1990. However, the political crisis continued to deepen, with the opposition divided over reunification with West Germany, while the popular reform movement showed signs of running out of control following the storming in Jan of the former security-police (*Stasi*) headquarters in East Berlin. The economy deteriorated further following the exodus of 344,000 people to West Germany in 1989, with a further 1,500 leaving each day, while country-wide work stoppages increased.

German reunification Elections in Mar 1990 were won by the centre-right Alliance for Germany, a three-party coalition led by the Christian Democrat Union (CDU). A treaty committing East and West Germany to economic, monetary and social union under the West German system from July 1990 was signed in May 1990, and they formally united 3 October 1990.

Germany, West former country in W Europe, bounded to the N by the North Sea and Denmark, E by East Germany and Czechoslovakia, S by Austria and Switzerland, and W by France, Belgium, Luxembourg, and the Netherlands.

history The Federal Republic was formed 1949 from the British, US, and French occupation zones in the west of the German Empire which were under Allied military control following Germany's surrender 1945. A policy of demilitarization, decentralization, and democratization was instituted by the Allied control powers and a new, intentionally provisional, constitution framed, which included eventual German reunification.

the Berlin blockade West ◊Berlin was blockaded by the Soviet Union 1948–49, but survived to form a constituent *Land* in the Federal Republic, after an airlift operation by the Allied powers. Politics during the Federal Republic's first decade were dominated by the CDU (the Christian Democratic Union), led by the popular Konrad ◊Adenauer.

growth and reconstruction Chancellor Adenauer and his economics minister, Ludwig Erhard, established a successful approach to economic management, termed the 'social market economy', which combined the encouragement of free market forces with strategic state intervention on the grounds of social justice. This new approach, combined with ◊Marshall Aid and the enterprise of the labour force (many of whom were refugees from the partitioned East), brought rapid growth and reconstruction during the 1950s and 1960s, an era termed the 'miracle years'. During this period, West Germany was also reintegrated into the international community. It gained full sovereignty 1954, entered ◊NATO 1955, emerging as a loyal supporter of the USA, and, under Adenauer's lead, joined the new ◊European Economic Community 1957. Close relations with France enabled the Saarland to be transferred to German sovereignty 1957.

In 1961, East Germany's construction of the ◊Berlin Wall to prevent refugees from leaving the East created a political crisis that vaulted West Berlin's mayor, Willy ◊Brandt, to international prominence. Domestically, Brandt played a major role in shifting the SPD (the Social Democratic Party) away from its traditional Marxist affiliation towards a more moderate position. Support for the SPD steadily increased after this policy switch and the party joined the CDU in a 'Grand Coalition' 1966–69, before gaining power itself, with the support of the FDP (the Free Democratic Party), under Brandt's leadership 1969.

eastern policy As chancellor, Brandt introduced the foreign policy of ◊Ostpolitik, which sought reconciliation with Eastern Europe as a means of improving contacts between East and West Germany. Treaties 1970 normalized relations with the Soviet Union and Poland, and recognized the Oder–Neisse border line, while in 1972 a basic treaty was effected with East Germany, acknowledging East Germany's borders and separate existence and enabling both countries to enter the UN 1973. Brandt resigned as chancellor 1974. His successor, former finance minister, Helmut ◊Schmidt, adhered to Ostpolitik and emerged as a leading advocate of European cooperation. Chancellor Schmidt fought to maintain a moderate, centrist course but the FDP eventually withdrew from the federal coalition 1982 and joined forces with the CDU, led by Dr Helmut ◊Kohl, to unseat the chancellor in a 'positive vote of no confidence'. Helmut Schmidt immediately retired from politics. The new Kohl administration adhered closely to the external policy of the previous chancellorship. At home a freer market approach was introduced. With unemployment rising to 2.5 million in 1984, problems of social unrest emerged, while violent demonstrations greeted the installation of US nuclear missiles on German soil 1983–84. Internally, the Kohl administration was rocked by scandals over illegal party funding. However, a strong recovery in the German economy from 1985 enabled the CDU–CSU–FDP coalition to gain re-election in the federal election 1987.

German reunification During 1988–89, following the death of the CSU's Franz-Josef Strauss, support for the far-right Republican party increased. In 1989–90 events in East Germany and elsewhere in Eastern Europe caused half a million economic and political refugees to enter the Federal Republic, as well as re-opening the debate on reunification (*Wiedervereinigung*). The CDU gave strong support to 'confederative' reunification, if desired, following free elections in East Germany, Chancellor Kohl unveiling a ten-point plan Dec 1989. The SPD were more cautious and divided over the issue. Official reunification came about on 3 Oct 1990, with Berlin as the capital (though the seat of government remained in Bonn). In mid-Oct new *Länder* elections were held in former East Germany, in which the conservative parties did well. The first all-German elections since 1932 took place 2 Dec 1990, resulting in victory for Chancellor Kohl and a coalition government comprising the CDU, CSU and FDP parties. In Berlin, which became a *Land*, the ruling SPD lost control of the city council to a new coalition government. Besides the addition of Berlin as a *Land*, the former states of East Germany resumed their status as *Länder* – Brandenburg, Saxony-Anhalt, Saxony, Mecklenburg-West Pomerania, and Thuringia.

Gestapo abbreviated form of ***Geheime Staatspolizei***, Nazi Germany's secret police, formed 1933, and under the direction of Heinrich Himmler from 1936.

The Gestapo used torture and terrorism to stamp out anti-Nazi resistance. It was declared a criminal organization at the Nuremberg Trials 1946.

Ghana country in W Africa, bounded to the N by Burkina Faso, E by Togo, S by the Gulf of Guinea, and W by the Ivory Coast.

history The area now known as Ghana was once made up of several separate kingdoms, including those of the Fanti on the coast and the Ashanti further inland.

the Gold Coast In 1874 the coastal region became the British colony of The Gold Coast, and after continued fighting, the inland region to the north of Ashanti 1898, and the Ashanti kingdom 1901, were made British protectorates. After 1917 the W part of Togoland, previously governed by Germany, was administered with The Gold Coast. Britain thus controlled both coastal and inland territories, and in 1957 they, together with British Togoland, became the independent Republic of Ghana.

'African socialism' Dr Kwame Nkrumah, a former prime minister of The Gold Coast, became president. He embarked on a policy of what he called 'African socialism' and established an authoritarian regime. In 1964 he declared Ghana a one-party state, with the Convention People's Party (CPP), which he led, as the only political organization. He then dropped his stance of nonalignment and forged links with the USSR and other Communist countries. In 1966, while visiting China, he was deposed in a coup led by General Joseph Ankrah, whose national liberation council released many political prisoners and purged CPP supporters. In 1969 Ankrah was replaced by General Akwasi Afrifa, who announced plans for a return to civilian government. A new constitution established an elected national assembly and a non-executive presidency. The Progress Party (PP) won a big majority in the assembly, and its leader, Kofi Busia, became prime minister. In 1970 Edward Akufo-Addo became the civilian president.

political coups Following economic problems, the army seized power again 1972. The constitution was suspended and all political institutions replaced by a National Redemption Council (NRC), under Col Ignatius Acheampong. In 1976 he too promised a return to civilian rule but critics doubted his sincerity and he was replaced by his deputy, Frederick Akuffo, in a bloodless coup 1978. Like his predecessors, he announced a speedy return to civilian government, but before elections could be held he, in turn, was deposed by junior officers led by Flight-Lt Jerry Rawlings, claiming that previous governments had been corrupt and had mismanaged the economy. Civilian rule was restored 1979, but two years later Rawlings led another coup, again complaining of the government's incompetence. He established a Provisional National Defence Council (PNDC), with himself as chair, again suspending the constitution, dissolving parliament, and banning political parties. Although Rawlings' policies were initially supported by workers and students, his failure to revive the economy caused discontent, and he has had to deal with a number of demonstrations and attempted coups, including one in Oct 1989.

Gibraltar British dependency, situated on a narrow rocky promontory in S Spain, area 6.5 sq km/2.5 sq mi; population (1988) 30,000. Captured from Spain 1704, it was ceded to Britain under the Treaty of Utrecht 1713. A referendum 1967 confirmed the wish of the people to remain in association with the UK, but Spain continues to claim sovereignty, and closed the border 1969–85. In 1989, the UK government announced it would reduce the military garrison by half.

Giscard d'Estaing Valéry 1926– . French conservative politician, president 1974–81. He was finance minister to Charles de Gaulle 1962–66 and Georges Pompidou 1969–74. As leader of the Union pour la Démocratie Française, which he formed in 1978, Giscard sought to project himself as leader of a 'new centre'.

Giscard was active in the wartime Resistance. After a distinguished academic career, he worked in the Ministry of Finance and entered the National Assembly for Puy de Dôme in 1956 as an Independent Republican. After Pompidou's death he was narrowly elected president in 1974, in difficult economic circumstances; he was defeated by the socialist François Mitterrand in 1981. He returned to the National Assembly in 1984. In 1989 he resigned from the National Assembly to play a leading role in the European Parliament.

glasnost (Russian 'openness') Soviet leader Mikhail ◊Gorbachev's policy of liberalizing various aspects of Soviet life, such as introducing greater freedom of expression and information, and opening up relations with Western countries.

Glasnost has involved the lifting of bans on books, plays, and films, the release of political ◊dissidents, the tolerance of religious worship, a reappraisal of Soviet history (destalinization), the encouragement of investigative journalism to uncover political corruption, and the sanctioning of greater candour in the reporting of social problems and disasters (such as ◊Chernobyl).

Under legislation introduced 1990, censorship of mass media was abolished; however, publication of state secrets, calls for the overthrow of the state by force, incitement of national or religious hatred, and interference in people's private lives are prohibited. Journalists' rights to access are enshrined, and there is a right of reply. Citizens have the right to receive information from abroad.

Goebbels Paul Josef 1897–1945. German Nazi leader. He was born in the Rhineland, became a journalist, joined the Nazi party in its early days, and was given control of its propaganda 1929. As minister of propaganda from 1933, he brought all cultural and educational activities under Nazi control and built up sympathetic movements abroad to carry on the 'war of nerves' against Hitler's intended victims. On the capture of Berlin by the Allies, he poisoned himself.

Goering (German ***Göring***) Hermann Wilhelm 1893–1946. Nazi leader, German field marshal from 1938. He was part of Hitler's inner circle, and with Hitler's rise to power in 1933, he established the Gestapo and concentration camps. Appointed successor to Hitler in 1939, he built a vast economic empire in occupied Europe, but later lost favour and was expelled from the party in 1945. Tried at Nuremberg for war crimes, he poisoned himself before he could be executed.

Goering was born in Bavaria. He was a renowned fighter pilot in World War I, and joined the Nazi party in 1922. He was elected to the Reichstag in 1928 and became its president in 1932. As commissioner for aviation from 1933 he built up the Luftwaffe (airforce). In 1936 he took charge of the four-year plan for war preparations.

gold standard system under which a country's currency is exchangeable for a fixed weight of gold on demand at the central bank. It was almost universally applied 1870–1914, but by 1937 no single country was on the full gold standard. Britain abandoned the gold standard 1931; the USA abandoned it 1971. Holdings of gold are still retained because it is an internationally recognized commodity, which cannot be legislated upon or manipulated by interested countries.

The gold standard broke down in World War I, and attempted revivals were undermined by the Great Depression. After World War II the par values of the currency units of the ◊International Monetary Fund (which includes nearly all members of the United Nations not in the Soviet bloc) were fixed in terms of gold and the US dollar, but by 1976 floating exchange rates (already unofficially operating from 1971) were legalized.

Gomułka Władysław 1905–1982. Polish Communist politician, party leader 1943–48 and 1956–70. He introduced moderate reforms, including private farming and tolerance for Roman Catholicism.

Gomułka, born in Krosno in SE Poland, was involved in underground resistance to the Germans during World War II, taking part in the defence of Warsaw. Leader of the Communist Party in Poland from 1943, he was ousted by the Moscow-backed Bolesław Bierut (1892–1956) in 1948, but was restored to the leadership in 1956, following riots in Poznań. Gomułka was forced to resign in Dec 1970 after sudden food-price rises induced a new wave of strikes and riots.

Gorbachev Mikhail Sergeyevich 1931– . Soviet president, in power from 1985. He was a member of the Politburo from 1980 and, during the Chernenko administration 1984–85, was chair of the Foreign Affairs Commission.

Gorbachev, born in the N Caucasus, studied

Gorbachev *President of the USSR and Communist Party leader Mikhail Gorbachev. He has introduced wide-ranging reform.*

law at Moscow University and joined the CPSU 1952. In 1955–62 he worked for the Komsomol (Communist Youth League) before being appointed regional agriculture secretary. As Stavropol party leader from 1970 he impressed Andropov, and was brought into the Communist Party (CPSU) secretariat 1978. Gorbachev was promoted into the Politburo in 1980 and in 1983, when Andropov was general secretary, took broader charge of the Soviet economy. On Chernenko's death 1985 he was appointed party leader and was president of the Supreme Soviet from 1988. He became head of state 1989 and in March 1990 he was formally elected to a five-year term as executive president with greater powers. He initiated wide-ranging liberal reforms and broad economic restructuring (◊perestroika and ◊glasnost) and introduced campaigns against alcoholism, corruption and inefficiency. He attempted to halt the arms race abroad. Gorbachev radically changed the style of Soviet leadership, despite opposition to the pace of change from both conservatives and radicals.

At home, his plans for economic reform failed to avert a food crisis in the winter of 1990–91 and his desire to preserve a single, centrally controlled USSR met with resistance from Soviet republics seeking more independent government systems. He was awarded the Nobel Peace Prize 1990, but his international reputation suffered in the light of the harsh repression of nationalist demonstrations in the Baltic states early in 1991.

government system whereby political authority is exercised. Modern systems of government distinguish between liberal democracies, totalitarian (one-party) states, and autocracies (authoritarian, relying on force rather than ideology). The Greek philosopher Aristotle was the first to attempt a systematic classification of governments. His main distinctions were between government by one person, by few, and by many (monarchy, oligarchy, and democracy), although the characteristics of each may vary between states and each may degenerate into tyranny (rule by an oppressive elite in the case of oligarchy or by the mob in the case of democracy).

Many of the words used (dictatorship, tyranny, totalitarian, democratic) have acquired negative or positive connotations that makes it difficult to use them objectively. The term ***liberal democracy*** was coined to distinguish Western types of democracy from the many other political systems that claimed to be democratic. Its principal characteristics are the existence of more than one political party, open processes of government and political debate, and a separation of powers. ***Totalitarian*** has been applied to both fascist and communist states and denotes a system where all power is centralized in the state, which in turn is controlled by a single party that derives its legitimacy from an exclusive ideology. ***Autocracy*** describes a form of government that has emerged in a number of Third World countries, where state power is in the hands either of an individual or of the army; normally ideology is not a central factor, individual freedoms tend to be suppressed where they may constitute a challenge to the authority of the ruling group, and there is a reliance upon force.

Great Leap Forward the change in the economic policy of the People's Republic of ◊China introduced by ◊Mao Zedong under the second five-year plan of 1958–62. The aim was to convert China into an industrially based economy by transferring resources away from agriculture. This coincided with the creation of people's communes. The inefficient and poorly planned allocation of state resources led to the collapse of the strategy by 1960 and a return to more adequate support for agricultural production.

Great Patriotic War (1941–45) during World War II, the war between the USSR and Germany. When Germany invaded the USSR in June 1941 the Russians retreated, carrying out a scorched-earth policy and relocating strategic industries beyond the Ural Mountains. Stalin remained in Moscow and the Russians, inspired to fight on by his patriotic speeches, launched a counter-offensive. The Allies tried to provide the USSR with vital supplies through Murmansk and Archangel despite German attempts to blockade the ports. In 1942 the Germans failed to take Leningrad and Moscow, and launched an attack towards the river Volga and to capture the oil wells at Baku. In August 1942 the Germans attacked Stalingrad but it was held by the Russians. The Germans were forced to surrender at Stalingrad in Jan 1943. The Red Army, under the command of Marshal Zhukov, gradually forced the Germans back and by February 1945 the Russians had reached the German border. In April 1945 the Russians, who had made tremendous sacrifices during the Great Patriotic War (20 million dead and millions more wounded) entered Berlin. In May 1945 the war ended.

Great War another name for ◊World War I.

Greece country in SE Europe, comprising the S Balkan peninsula, bounded N by Yugoslavia and Bulgaria, NE by Turkey, E by the Aegean Sea, S by the Mediterranean Sea, W by the Ionian Sea, NW by Albania, and numerous islands to the S and E.

government The 1975 constitution provides for a parliamentary system of government, with a president who is head of state, a prime minister who is head of government, and a single-chamber parliament elected by universal suffrage. The president, elected by parliament, appoints the prime minister and cabinet.

history Although independence from Turkey had been established in 1829, relations between the two states were embittered by the Greeks' desire to recover Macedonia, Crete, and other Turkish territories with Greek populations. A war 1897 ended in disaster, but the ◊Balkan Wars 1912–13 won most of the disputed areas for Greece. In a period of internal conflict from 1914, two monarchs were deposed, and there was a republic 1923–25, when a military coup restored George II, who in the following year established a dictatorship under Joannis Metaxas. An Italian invasion 1940 was successfully resisted, but an intensive attack by Germany 1941 overwhelmed the Greeks. During the German occupation of Greece 1941–44, a Communist-dominated resistance movement armed and trained a guerrilla army, and after World War II the National Liberation Front, as it was called, wanted to create a Socialist state. If the Greek royalist army had not had massive assistance from the USA, under the provisions of the ◊Truman doctrine, this undoubtedly would have happened. The monarchy was re-established under King Paul, who was succeeded by his son Constantine 1964. Dissatisfaction with the government and conflicts between the king and his ministers resulted in a coup 1967, replacing the monarchy with a new regime, which, despite its democratic pretensions, was little more than a military dictatorship, with Col George Papadopoulos as its head. All political activity was banned, and opponents of the government were forced out of public life. In 1973 Greece declared itself a republic, and Papadopoulos became president. A civilian cabinet was appointed, but before the year was out another coup brought Lt-Gen Phaidon Ghizikis to the presidency, with Adamantios Androutsopoulos as prime minister.

democratic republic The government's failure to prevent the Turkish invasion of Cyprus led to its downfall, and a former prime minister, Constantine Karamanlis, was recalled from exile to form a new Government of National Salvation. He immediately ended martial law, press censorship, and the ban on political parties, and in the 1974 general election his Party, ND, won a decisive majority in parliament. A referendum the same year rejected the return of the monarchy, and in 1975 a new constitution for a democratic 'Hellenic Republic' was adopted, with Constantine Tsatsos as president. ND won the 1977 general election with a reduced majority, and in 1980 Karamanlis resigned as prime minister and was elected president. The following year Greece became a full member of the EC. Meanwhile, the ND was faced with a growing challenge from PASOK, which won an absolute majority in parliament in the 1981 general election. Its leader, Andreas Papandreou, became Greece's first Socialist prime minister.

Greek socialism PASOK had been elected on a radical Socialist platform, which included withdrawal from the EC, the removal of US military bases, and a programme of domestic reform. However, Papandreou was content to obtain a modification of the terms of EC entry, and, rather than close US bases, he signed an agreement on military and economic cooperation. In 1983 he also signed a ten-year economic cooperation agreement with the USSR. Despite introducing austerity measures to deal with rising inflation, PASOK won a comfortable majority in the 1985 elections. In 1986 the constitution was amended, limiting the powers of the president in relation to those of the prime minister. The 1989 general election proved inconclusive and eventually

Tzannis Tzannatakis, an ND backbencher, formed Greece's first all-party government. However, this soon broke up and after months of negotiation Xenophon Zolotas (PASOK) put together a government of unity, comprising communists, socialists, conservatives, and non-political figures. In July 1990 an agreement on the siting of US bases in Greece was signed.

greenhouse effect a phenomenon of the Earth's atmosphere by which solar radiation, absorbed by the Earth and re-emitted from the surface, is prevented from escaping by carbon dioxide in the air. The result is a rise in the Earth's temperature; in a garden greenhouse, the glass walls have the same effect. The concentration of carbon dioxide in the atmosphere is estimated to have risen by 25% since the Industrial Revolution (which began in the 19th century), and 10% since 1950; the rate of increase is now 0.5% a year. The United Nations Environment Programme estimates an increase in average world temperatures of 1.5°C/2.7°F with a consequent rise of 20 cm/7.7 in in sea level by 2025.

The French mathematician, Joseph Fourier warned, in 1827, that the generation of carbon dioxide waste could warm the atmosphere and affect the climate; at the end of the 19th century, Swedish scientist Svante Arrhenius coined the phrase 'the greenhouse effect'.

Green Party political party aiming to 'preserve the planet and its people', based on the premise that incessant economic growth is unsustainable. The leaderless party structure reflects a general commitment to decentralization. Green parties sprang up in W Europe in the 1970s and spread in the 1980s. Parties in different countries are linked to one another but unaffiliated to any pressure group.

The British Green Party was founded 1973 as the Ecology Party (initially solely environmental). In the 1989 European elections, the British Greens polled over two million votes but received no seats in Parliament, because Britain was the only country in Europe not to have some form of proportional representation.

Group Areas Act in South Africa, an Act of 1950, under which the different races in South Africa were assigned to separate areas. Demonstrations and inter-ethnic riots resulted from such measures of segregation.

guerrilla irregular soldier fighting in a small unofficial unit, typically against an established or occupying power, and engaging in sabotage, ambush, and the like, rather than pitched battles against an opposing army. Guerrilla tactics have been used both by resistance armies in wartime (for example, the Vietnam War) and in peacetime by national liberation groups and militant political extremists (for example the ◊PLO; Tamil Tigers).

The term was first applied to the Spanish and Portuguese resistance to French occupation during the Peninsular War (1808–14). Guerrilla techniques were widely used in World War II – for example, in Greece and the Balkans. Political activists who resort to violence, particularly ***urban guerrillas***, tend to be called 'freedom fighters' by those who support their cause, 'terrorists' by those who oppose it.

Examples of guerrillas active in recent years include Amal Shi'ite muslim militia in Lebanon; the Contras of Nicaragua; ETA, the Basque separatist movement in northern Spain; and the IRA (Irish Republican Army) an organization advocating a unified Irish republic.

Guevara 'Che' Ernesto 1928–1967. Latin American revolutionary. He was born in Argentina and trained there as a doctor, but in 1953 left his homeland because of his opposition to the right-wing president Perón. In effecting the Cuban revolution of 1959, he was second only to Castro and Castro's brother Raúl. In 1965 he went to the Congo to fight against white mercenaries, and then to Bolivia, where he was killed in an unsuccessful attempt to lead a peasant rising. He was an orthodox Marxist, and renowned for his guerrilla techniques.

gulag a Russian term used to describe the forced labour camps, in particular during the Stalin era. In these remote camps thousands of prisoners, many of them dissidents and opponents of the regime, died from the harsh conditions.

Gulf War hostilities between the United Nations Security Forces and Iraq culminating in war 15 Jan–28 Feb 1991. In Aug 1990, Saddam Hussein's Iraqi troops invaded and annexed neighbouring Kuwait. Resolutions made by the UN Security Council for his immediate withdrawal went unheeded and, in response to requests for help from King Fahd of Saudi Arabia, a large multi-national force was assembled near the Saudi-Kuwait border. Efforts to avert war by the enforcement of sanctions were considered unsuccessful by the United Nations, and war began shortly after Iraq's failure to respond to the UN deadline for withdrawal by 15 Jan 1991. It ended six weeks later with the United Nations' forces successfully routing Iraqi occupying forces from Kuwait. Iraq faced serious political uprisings, from the Kurds and Shi'ites before restoring order to Iraq in the postwar aftermath.

It is also another name for the Iran–Iraq war 1980–88. See also under ◊Iraq.

Guomindang Chinese National People's Party, founded 1894 by Sun Yat-sen (Sun Zhong Shan), which overthrew the Manchu Empire 1912. By 1927 the right wing, led by ◊Chiang Kai-shek (Jiang Jie Shi), was in conflict with the left, led by Mao Zedong until the Communist victory 1949 (except for the period of the Japanese invasion 1937–45). It survives as the sole political party of Taiwan, where it is still spelled ***Kuomintang***.

H

Haig Douglas, 1st Earl Haig 1861–1928. British army officer, commander in chief in World War I. His Somme (France) offensive in the summer of 1916 made considerable advances only at enormous cost to human life, and his Passchendaele (Belgium) offensive (July–Nov 1917) achieved little at a similar huge loss. He was created field marshal 1917.

He was awarded the Order of Merit, an earldom, and £100,000 1919. Haig retired 1921 and devoted himself to ex-service interests as first president of the British Legion (an organization promoting the welfare of British war veterans). He was born in Edinburgh. He served in the Omdurman and South African campaigns, and in World War I commanded the 1st Army Corps 1914–15, and the 1st Army 1915 until he succeeded Sir John French as commander-in-chief the same year. He then loyally supported the French marshal Foch in his appointment as supreme commander of the Allied armies and in his victorious 1918 offensive, and it was Haig's foresight that persuaded Foch to extend his attack north, so breaking the Hindenburg Line (the German western line of fortifications). He has been stringently criticized by some modern historians for the appalling losses on the Somme and at Passchendaele.

Haile Selassie Ras (Prince) Tafari ('the Lion of Judah') 1892–1975. Emperor of Ethiopia 1930–74. He pleaded unsuccessfully to the League of Nations against Italian conquest of his country 1935–36, and lived in the UK until his restoration in 1941. He was deposed by a military coup in 1974 and died in captivity the following year. Followers of the Rastafarian religion believe that he was the Messiah, the incarnation of God (Jah).

Hammarskjöld Dag 1905–1961. Swedish secretary general of the United Nations 1953–61. Over the ◊Suez Crisis 1956 he opposed Britain. His attempts to solve the problem of the Congo (now Zaïre), where he was killed in a plane crash, were criticized by the USSR. Nobel Peace Prize 1961.

Havel Vaclav 1936– . Czech playwright and politician, president from Dec 1989.

The son of a Prague engineer, his critical works were banned throughout Eastern Europe from 1968. He became the leading spokesman for the Charter 77 human rights movement and founded the Committee for the Defence of the Unjustly Persecuted (VONS). For such 'subversive' and 'anti-state' activities he was imprisoned in 1977 and again in 1979–83 and placed under house arrest between 1977–79. In 1988 he founded the ◊samizdat monthly 'Lidove Noviny' (People's Newspaper) and in 1989 served a further four months in prison after laying flowers on the twentieth anniversary of the death of Jan Palach, the student who burnt himself to death in protest against the Soviet invasion of 1968.

In 1989, he became a presidential candidate after the resignation of the Communist Gustav Husák. Following the overthrow of the communist regime, he was elected state president by the federal assembly Dec 1989.

health service government provision of medical care on a national scale.

In the UK the National Health Service Act 1946 was largely the work of Aneurin ◊Bevan, Labour minister of Health. It instituted a health service from July 1948 that sought to provide free medicine, dental, and optical treatment as a right. Successive governments, both Labour and Conservative, introduced charges for some services. The ***National Health Service*** (NHS) now includes hospital care, but nominal fees are made for ordinary doctors' prescriptions, eye tests and spectacles, and dental treatment, except for children and people on very low incomes. A White Paper published Jan 1989 by the Conservative government proposed legislation for decentralizing the control of hospitals and changes in general practice giving doctors greater scope for management.

Heath Edward (Richard George) 1916– . British Conservative politician, party leader 1965–75. As prime minister 1970–74 he took the UK into the European Community but was brought down by economic and industrial relations crises at home. In 1990 he undertook a mission to Iraq and successfully secured the release of several British hostages prior to the Gulf War.

Heath entered Parliament 1950, was

minister of Labour 1959–60, and as Lord Privy Seal 1960–63 conducted abortive negotiations for Common Market (European Community) membership. He succeeded Alec Douglas-Home as Conservative leader 1965, the first elected leader of his party. Defeated in the general election 1966, he achieved a surprise victory 1970, but his confrontation with the striking miners as part of his campaign to control inflation led to his defeat Feb 1974 and again Oct 1974. He was replaced as party leader by Margaret Thatcher 1975, and has since become increasingly critical of her policies and her opposition to the UK's full participation in the EC.

Helsinki Conference international conference 1975 at which 35 countries, including the USSR and the USA, attempted to reach agreement on cooperation in security, economics, science, technology, and human rights.

Some regarded the conference as marking the end of the ◊Cold War. Others felt it legitimized the division of Europe that had been a fact since the end of World War II. Human-rights groups contend that there have been many violations of the provisions of the accords. Its full title is the Helsinki Conference on Security and Cooperation in Europe (CSCE).

The Soviet military intervention in Afghanistan 1979 which caused US president Carter to shelve SALT II (Strategic Arms Limitation Treaty), and President Reagan's announcement 1983 of the Strategic Defense Initiative (SDI), or 'Star Wars', which, according to the USSR, would violate the 1972 Anti-Ballistic Missile Treaty, further slowed progress towards closer relations between the superpowers. Alleged Soviet violations of human rights, especially of Soviet Jews seeking to emigrate, coupled with US anticommunist intervention in Central America, did likewise. However, reforms under the Soviet leader Gorbachev, especially the Soviet commitment to withdrawal from Afghanistan, have helped to improve relations between the USA and the USSR, which led to a treaty 1987 eliminating some nuclear weapons.

Himmler Heinrich 1900–1945. German Nazi leader, head of the ◊SS elite corps from 1929, the police and the ◊Gestapo secret police from 1936, and supervisor of the extermination of the Jews in E Europe. During World War II he replaced Hermann Goering as Hitler's second-in-command. He was captured May 1945 and committed suicide.

Born in Munich, he joined the Nazi Party in 1925 and became chief of the Bavarian police 1933. His accumulation of offices meant he had command of all German police forces by 1936, which made him one of the most powerful people in Germany. In Apr 1945 he made a proposal to the Allies that Germany should surrender to the USA and Britain but not to the USSR, which was rejected.

Hindenburg Paul Ludwig Hans von Beneckendorf und Hindenburg 1847–1934. German field marshal and right-wing politician. During World War I he was supreme commander and, with Erich von Ludendorff, practically directed Germany's policy until the end of the war. He was president of Germany 1925–33.

Born in Posen of a Prussian Junker (aristocratic landowner) family, he was commissioned 1866, served in the Austro-Prussian and Franco-German wars, and retired 1911. Given the command in East Prussia Aug 1914, he received the credit for the defeat of the Russians at Tannenberg and was promoted to supreme commander and field marshal. Re-elected president 1932, he was compelled to invite Hitler to assume the chancellorship Jan 1933.

Hiroshima industrial city and port on the S coast of Honshu, Japan, destroyed by the first wartime use of an atomic bomb 6 Aug 1945 by the US. The city has largely been rebuilt since the war; population (1987) 1,034,000.

More than 10 sq km/4 sq mi was obliterated, with very heavy damage outside that area. Casualties totalled at least 137,000 out of a population of 343,000: 78,150 were found dead, others died later.

Hirohito 1901–1989. Emperor of Japan from 1926. He succeeded his father Yoshihito. After the defeat of Japan in World War II 1945, he was stripped of his divine powers and made constitutional monarch by the US-backed 1946 constitution. He was believed to have played a reluctant role in politician Hideki ◊Tojo's pre-war expansion plans. Hirohito ruled post-war occupied Japan with dignity. He was a scholar of botany and zoology and the author of books on marine biology. He was succeeded by his son Akihito.

Hitler Adolf 1889–1945. German Nazi dictator, born in Austria. Führer (leader) of the Nazi party from 1921, he led Germany in World War II.

The son of a customs official, he spent his early years in poverty in Vienna and Munich. After serving as a volunteer in the German army during World War I, he was employed as a spy by the military authorities in Munich and in 1919 joined, in this capacity, the German Workers' Party. By 1921 he had assumed its leadership, renamed it the National Socialist German Workers' Party

Hitler *German Nazi leader Adolf Hitler at Berchtesgaden, Bavaria.*

(Nazi Party for short), and provided it with a programme that mixed nationalism with ◊anti-Semitism. Having led an unsuccessful uprising in Munich 1923, he was sentenced to nine months' imprisonment during which he wrote his political testament, *Mein Kampf/My Struggle* 1925–27. The party did not achieve national importance until the elections of 1930. By 1932, although Field Marshal Hindenburg defeated Hitler in the presidential elections, it formed the largest group in the Reichstag (parliament). As the result of an intrigue directed by Chancellor Franz von Papen, Hitler became chancellor in a Nazi–Nationalist coalition 30 Jan 1933. Hitler rapidly created a dictatorship by playing party and state institutions against each other and continually creating new offices and appointments. He succeeded in suppressing opposition and removing Nationalists from government. The Nazis were declared the only legal party and in 1934 Hitler succeeded Paul Hindenburg as head of state.

Meanwhile the drive to war began: Germany left the League of Nations, conscription was reintroduced, and in 1936 the Rhineland was reoccupied. Hitler and the Italian fascist leader Mussolini, who were already both involved in in the Spanish civil war, formed an alliance (the Axis) 1936, joined by Japan 1940. He annexed Austria 1938, and occupied the Sudentenland under the ◊Munich Agreement. The rest of Czechoslovakia was annexed Mar 1939, and in Aug 1939 Hitler signed a non-aggression pact with the USSR, which secretly allowed for the partition of Poland between the two countries and which formed a sufficient security in the east for Hitler's invasion of Poland in Sept 1939, following which Britain and France declared war.

Hitler conducted the war in a ruthless but idiosyncratic way, took and ruled most of the neighbouring countries with repressive occupation forces, and had millions of Slavs, Jews, Gypsies, homosexuals, and political enemies killed in concentration camps and massacres. He narrowly escaped death 1944 from a bomb explosion at a staff meeting, prepared by high-ranking officers. On 29 April 1945, when Berlin was largely in Soviet hands, he married his mistress Eva Braun in his bunker under the chancellory building and on the following day committed suicide with her.

Hoare–Laval Pact plan for a peaceful settlement to the Italian invasion of Ethiopia in Oct 1935. It was devised by Samuel Hoare (1880–1959), British foreign secretary, and Pierre Laval, French premier, at the request of the ◊League of Nations. Realizing no European country was willing to go to war over Ethiopia, Hoare and Laval proposed official recognition of Italian claims. Public outcry in Britain against the pact's seeming approval of Italian aggression was so great that the pact had to be disowned and Hoare was forced to resign.

Ho Chi Minh adopted name of Nguyen That Tan 1890–1969. North Vietnamese Communist politician, premier and president 1954–69. Having trained in Moscow shortly

Ho Chi Minh *President Ho Chi Minh of Vietnam visiting Prague, Czechoslovakia, July 1957.*

after the ◊Russian Revolution, he headed the communist ◊Vietminh from 1941 and fought against the French during the Indochina War 1946–54, becoming president and prime minister of the republic at the armistice. Aided by the Communist bloc, he did much to develop industrial potential. He relinquished the premiership 1955, but continued as president. In the years before his death, Ho successfully led his country's fight against US-aided South Vietnam in the Vietnam War 1954–75.

Hollywood district in the city of Los Angeles, California; the centre of the US film industry from 1911. Home of the legendary film studios such as 20th Century- Fox, MGM, Paramount, Columbia Pictures, United Artists, Disney, and Warner Brothers. From the 1920s Hollywood's name became synonymous with luxury and glamour, and was influential in promoting US values during the 1930s and 1940s.

Holocaust, the the annihilation of more than 16 million people by the Hitler regime 1933–45 in the numerous extermination and ◊concentration camps, most notably Auschwitz, Sobibor, Treblinka, and Maidanek in Poland, and Belsen, Buchenwald, and Dachau in Germany. Of the victims, more than six million were Jews (over 67% of European Jewry); 10 million Ukrainian, Polish, and Russian civilians and prisoners-of-war, Romanies, socialists, homosexuals, and others (labelled 'defectives') were also imprisoned and/or exterminated. Victims were variously starved, tortured, experimented on, and worked to death. Many thousands were executed in gas chambers, shot, or hanged. It was euphemistically termed the final solution.

home front a term describing the organized sectors of domestic activity in wartime, mainly associated with World Wars I and II. Features of the home front in World War II included the organization of the black-out, evacuation, air raid shelters, ARP posts, the 'home guard', rationing, and distribution of gas masks. With many men on active military service, women were called upon to carry out jobs previously only undertaken by men.

Home Guard unpaid force formed in Britain May 1940 to repel the expected German invasion, and known until July 1940 as the Local Defence Volunteers. It consisted of men aged 17–65 who had not been called up, who formed part of the armed forces of the crown, and were subject to military law. Over two million strong in 1944, it was disbanded 31 Dec 1945, but revived 1951, then placed on a reserve basis 1955, and ceased activities 1957.

Homelands Policy South Africa's apartheid policy which set aside ◊Black National States for black Africans.

Home Rule, Irish the movement to repeal the Act of Union 1801 that joined Ireland to Britain and established an Irish parliament responsible for internal affairs. In 1870 Isaac Butt (1813–1879) formed the Home Rule Association and the movement was led in Parliament from 1880 by Charles Parnell. After 1918 the demand for an independent Irish republic replaced that for home rule.

Gladstone's Home Rule bills 1886 and 1893 were both defeated. A third bill was introduced by the Liberals in 1912, which aroused opposition in Ireland where the Protestant minority in Ulster feared domination by the Catholic majority. Ireland appeared on the brink of civil war but the outbreak of World War I rendered further consideration of Home Rule inopportune. In 1920 the Government of Ireland Act introduced separate parliaments in the North and South.

Hong Kong British crown colony in SE Asia, comprising Hong Kong island, the Kowloon peninsula, and the mainland New Territories. It is due to revert to Chinese control 1997.

history formerly part of China, Hong Kong island was occupied by Britain 1841, and ceded by China under the 1842 Treaty of Nanking. The Kowloon Peninsula was acquired under the 1860 Peking (Beijing) Convention and the New Territories secured on a 99-year lease from 1898. The colony, which developed into a major market place for Sino-British trade during the late 19th and early 20th centuries, was occupied by Japan 1941–45. The restored British administration promised, after 1946, to increase self-government. These plans were shelved, however, after the 1949 Communist revolution in China. During the 1950s almost 1,000,000 Chinese (predominantly Cantonese) refugees fled to Hong Kong. Immigration continued during the 1960s and 1970s, raising the colony's population from 1,000,000 in 1946 to 5,000,000 in 1980, and forcing the imposition of strict border controls during the 1980s. Since 1975, 160,000 Vietnamese 'boat people' have fled to Hong Kong; in 1989 50,000 remained, and the UK government began forced repatriation (51 forced, 630 voluntary by Dec 1989). Hong Kong's economy expanded rapidly during the corresponding period, however, and the colony became one of Asia's major commercial, financial, and industrial centres. As the date (1997) for the termination of the New Territories' lease approached, negotiations on Hong Kong's future were opened between Britain and China 1982. These culminated in a unique agreement, signed in Beijing 1984, in which Britain agreed to transfer full sovereignty of the

Islands and New Territories to China 1997 in return for Chinese assurance that Hong Kong's social and economic freedom and capitalist lifestyle would be preserved for at least 50 years.

Hoover Herbert Clark 1874–1964. The 31st president of the USA 1929–33, a Republican. Secretary of commerce 1921–28. He lost public confidence after the stock-market crash of 1929, when he opposed direct government aid for the unemployed in the Depression that followed.

He defeated the Democratic candidate for the presidency, Al Smith, by a wide margin. The shantytowns or ***Hoovervilles*** of the homeless that sprang up around large cities were evidence of his failure to cope with the effects of the Depression. He was severely criticized for his adamant opposition to federal relief for the unemployed, even after the funds of states, cities, and charities were exhausted. In 1933, he was succeeded by F D ◊Roosevelt.

House of Commons the lower chamber of the UK Parliament. It consists of 650 elected members of Parliament, each of whom represents a constituency. Its functions are to debate, legislate, and to scrutinize the activities of government. Constituencies are kept under continuous review by the Parliamentary Boundary Commissions 1944. The House of Commons is presided over by the Speaker. Proceedings in the House of Commons were televised from Nov 1989.

House of Lords the upper chamber of the UK Parliament. Its members are unelected and comprise the ***temporal peers***: all hereditary peers of England created to 1707, all hereditary peers of Great Britain created 1707–1800, and all hereditary peers of the UK from 1801 onwards; all hereditary Scottish peers (under the Peerage Act 1963); all peeresses in their own right (under the same act); all life peers (both the law lords and those created under the Life Peerages Act 1958); and the ***spiritual peers***: the two archbishops and 24 of the bishops (London, Durham, and Winchester by right, and the rest by seniority). Since the Parliament Act 1911 the powers of the Lords have been restricted in that they may delay a bill passed by the Commons but not reject it. The Lords are presided over by the Lord Chancellor.

housing the provision of residential accommodation. All states have now found some degree of state housing provision or subsidy essential, even in free-enterprise economies such as the USA. In the UK flats and houses to rent (intended for people with low incomes) are built by local authorities under the direction of the secretary of state for environment.

Housing legislation in Britain began with the Artisan's Dwellings Act of 1875, which gave powers to local councils to condemn properties and clear slums within their boundaries. The Housing of the Working Classes Act 1890 strengthened earlier acts and encouraged local councils to undertake housing improvement schemes. Under an act of 1919, the government offered a subsidy for houses built by a local council for rent. The introduction of rent control in 1915 began a long-term decline in the amount of rented accommodation, and tax relief on mortgages encouraged private ownership; 14 million Britons were home-owners in 1986. In 1980 legislation was introduced to enable council tenants to buy their homes, and nearly one million council houses had been sold by 1986. In the USSR in 1990 President Gorbachev's first presidential decree allowed private ownership of property and the buying and selling of houses.

Hua Guofeng formerly ***Hua Kuofeng*** 1920– . Chinese politician, leader of the Chinese Communist Party (CCP) 1976–81, premier 1976–80. He dominated Chinese politics 1976–77, seeking economic modernization without major structural reform. From 1978 he was gradually eclipsed by Deng Xiaoping. Hua was ousted from the Politburo Sept 1982 but remained a member of the CCP Central Committee.

Hua, born in Shanxi into a peasant family, fought under Zhu De, the Red Army leader, during the liberation war 1937–49. He entered the CCP Central Committee 1969 and the Politburo 1973. An orthodox, loyal Maoist, Hua was selected to succeed Zhou Enlai as prime minister Jan 1976 and became party leader on Mao Zedong's death Sept 1976. He was replaced as prime minister by Zhao Ziyang Sept 1980 and as CCP chair by Hu Yaobang June 1981.

Human Rights, Universal Declaration of charter of civil and political rights drawn up by the ◊United Nations 1948. They include the right to life, liberty, education, and equality before the law; to freedom of movement, religion, association, and information; and to a nationality. Under the European Convention of Human Rights 1950, the Council of Europe established the ***European Commission of Human Rights*** (headquarters in Strasbourg, France), which investigates complaints by states or individuals, and its findings are examined by the ***European Court of Human Rights*** (established 1959), whose compulsory jurisdiction has been recognized by a number of states, including the UK.

The declaration is not legally binding, and the frequent contraventions are monitored by organizations such as ◊Amnesty International. Human rights were also an issue at the Helsinki Conference of 1975, an international gathering where countries attempted to reach agreement on cooperation on a series of issues.

In 1988 the European Court condemned as unlawful the UK procedure of holding those suspected of terrorism for up to seven days with no judicial control.

Hundred Days, the in European history, the period 20 March–28 June 1815, marking the French emperor Napoleon's escape from imprisonment on Elba to his departure from Paris after losing the battle of Waterloo 18 June.

The phrase also describes other periods of new administration. For example, in 1898 Emperor Te Tsung of China attempted 100 days of reform (11 June–16th Sept), under the guidance of K'ang Yu-wei. In 1931 Mussolini and G Forzano wrote *The 100 Days*. It is also applied to the reform period in the administration of US President F D Roosevelt from his inauguration on 4 March 1933 when much of the legislation for his New Deal programme was initiated.

Hungary country in central Europe, bordered to the N by Czechoslovakia, NE by the USSR, E by Romania, S by Yugoslavia, and W by Austria.

history The revolution of 1848–49 proclaimed a Hungarian republic and abolished serfdom, but Austria suppressed the revolt with Russian help.

Austro-Hungarian Empire In 1867 the Austro-Hungarian empire was established, giving Hungary self-government. During World War I, Hungary fought on the German side, and after the collapse of the Austro-Hungarian empire, became an independent state 1918.

For 133 days in 1919, Hungary was a Communist republic under Béla Kun but this was brought to an end by intervention from Romania and Czechoslovakia. From 1920–44, Hungary was ruled by Admiral Horthy, acting as regent for an unnamed king. After 1933, he fell more and more under German influence and joined Hitler in the invasion of the USSR 1941.

communism Hungary was overrun by Communist forces 1944–45. Horthy fled, and a provisional government, including the Communist agriculture minister, Imre Nagy, was formed, distributing land to the peasants. An elected assembly inaugurated a republic 1946, but it soon fell under Soviet domination. Under Communist Party leader Matyas Rakosi, a Stalinist regime was imposed 1946–53, a Soviet-style constitution being adopted 1949, industry nationalized, land collectivized, and a wave of secret police terror launched.

Hungarian national uprising Liberalization in the economic sphere was experienced 1953–55 when Imre Nagy, supported by Soviet premier Malenkov, replaced Rákosi as prime minister. Nagy was removed from office 1955, after the fall of Malenkov, but in 1956, in the wake of the general secetary of the Soviet communist party, Khrushchev's, denunciation of Stalin in his 'secret speech', pressure for democratization mounted. Rakosi stepped down as Communist Party leader and, following student and worker demonstrations in Budapest, Nagy was recalled as prime minister, and János Kádár appointed general secretary of the renamed Hungarian Socialist Workers' Party (HSWP). Nagy lifted restrictions on the formation of political parties, released the anti-Communist primate Cardinal Mindszenty, and announced plans for Hungary to withdraw from the ◊Warsaw Pact and become a neutral power. These changes were, however, opposed by Kádár, who set up a counter-government in E Hungary before returning to Budapest with Soviet tanks to overthrow the Nagy government 4 Nov. Some 200,000 fled to the West during the 1956 'Hungarian National Uprising'. After a period of strict repression, Kádár proceeded to introduce pragmatic liberalizing reforms after 1960. Hungary remained, however, a loyal member of the Warsaw Pact and ◊Comecon.

reform Its relations with Moscow significantly improved during the post-Brezhnev era, with Hungary's 'market socialism' experiment influencing Mikhail Gorbachev's ◊perestroika programme. Further reforms introduced 1987–88 included additional price deregulation, the establishment of 'enterprise councils', the introduction of value-added tax (VAT), and the creation of a stock market.

Kádár stepped down as HSWP general secretary May 1988, being replaced by the prime minister Karoly Grosz, while two radical reformers, Rezso Nyers and Imre Pozsgay, were brought into the Politburo. A period of far-reaching political reform began in which the right to demonstrate freely, and to form rival political parties and trade unions, was ceded; the official verdict on the 1956 events was revised radically; and a new 'socialist pluralist' constitution was outlined.

The Hungarian Democratic Forum was formed Sept 1988 as an umbrella movement for opposition groups, and several dozen other political parties were formed 1989–90. Two months later Grosz was forced to cede power to the more radical reformist troika of Nyers (party president), Pozsgay, and Miklos Nemeth (prime minister since Nov 1988), who joined Grosz in a new four-person ruling presidium. In Oct 1989 a series of constitutional changes were approved by the national assembly. These included the adoption of a new set of electoral rules, banning of workplace party cells, and the deletion of the word 'People's' from the country's name. Also in Oct the HSWP changed its name to the Hungarian Socialist Party (HSP), and adopted Poszgay as its presidential candidate. Conservatives, including Grosz, refused to play an active role in the new party, which had become essentially a social democratic party committed to multi-party democracy. Despite these changes, the HSP's standing was seriously damaged in the 'Danubegate' scandal of Jan 1990, when it was revealed that the secret police had bugged opposition parties and passed the information obtained to the HSP. In Feb 1990 talks were held with the USSR to discuss the withdrawal of Soviet troops stationed in Hungary. In June 1990 the Hungarian government announced the country's decision no longer to participate in Warsaw Pact military exercises and its intention to withdraw altogether from the Pact's structures by the end of 1991. As the first step in the privatization programme, a stock exchange was opened in Budapest.

Hussein Saddam 1937– . Iraqi politician, in power from 1968, president from 1979. Ruthless in the pursuit of his objectives, he fought a bitter war against Iran 1980–88 and dealt harshly with Kurdish rebels seeking a degree of independence. In 1990 he ordered the invasion and annexation of ◊Kuwait, provoking a United Nations embargo and an international ◊Gulf War Jan 15–Feb 28 1991.

Hussein joined the Arab Ba'ath Socialist Party as a young man and soon became involved in revolutionary activities. In 1959 he was sentenced to death and took refuge in Egypt, but a coup in 1963 made his return possible, although in the following year he was imprisoned for plotting to overthrow the regime he had helped to instal. After his release he took a leading part in the 1968 revolution, removing the civilian government and establishing a Revolutionary Command Council (RCC). In 1977 Saddam Hussein al-Tikriti abolished the use of surnames in Iraq to conceal the fact that a large number of people in the government and ruling party all came from the village of Tikrit and therefore bore the same surname. At first discreetly, and then more openly, Hussein strengthened his position and in 1979 became RCC chair and state president. The 1990–91 Kuwait annexation followed a long-running border dispute and was prompted by the need for more oil resources after the expensive war against Iran. Despite his efforts to rally Arab support for a holy war or 'jihad', the Allied forces of the United Nations successfully routed Iraqi troops from Kuwait. Saddam then faced political rebellion from the Kurds and the Shi'ites which was brutally supressed, provoking a Kurdish refugee crisis.

Hussein *The president of Iraq, Saddam Hussein. He has ruled the country with an iron fist since coming to power in 1979*

I

Ibn Saud 1880–1953. First king of Saudi Arabia from 1932. His father was the son of the sultan of Nejd, at whose capital, Riyadh, Ibn Saud was born. In 1891 a rival group seized Riyadh, and Ibn Saud went into exile with his father, who resigned his claim to the throne in his son's favour. In 1902 Ibn Saud recaptured Riyadh and recovered the kingdom, and by 1921 he had brought all central Arabia under his rule. In 1924 he invaded the Hejaz, of which he was proclaimed king in 1926.

Nejd and the Hejaz were united in 1932 in the kingdom of Saudi Arabia. Ibn Saud introduced programmes for modernization with revenue from oil, which was discovered in 1936.

IMF abbreviation for ◊***International Monetary Fund.***

immigration and emigration the movement of people from one country to another. Immigration is movement to a country; emigration is movement from a country. Immigration or emigration on a large scale is often for economic reasons or because of religious, political or social persecution (which may create refugees), and often prompts restrictive legislation by individual countries. The USA has received immigrants on a larger scale than any other country, more than 50 million during its history.

In the UK, Commonwealth Immigration Acts were passed in 1962 and 1968, and replaced by a single system of control under the Immigration Act of 1971. The British Nationality Act 1981 further restricted immigration by ruling that only a British citizen has the right to live in the United Kingdom.

imperialism the policy of extending the power and rule of a government beyond its own boundaries. A country may attempt to dominate others by direct rule or by less obvious means such as control of markets for goods or raw materials. The latter is often called neo-colonialism.

In the 19th century imperialism was synonymous with the establishment of colonies (see ◊British Empire). Many socialist thinkers believe that the role of Western (especially US) finance capital in the Third World constitutes a form of imperialism.

Independent Labour Party (ILP) British socialist party, founded in Bradford 1893 by the Scottish member of Parliament Keir Hardie. In 1900 it joined with trades unions and Fabians in founding the Labour Representation Committee, the nucleus of the ◊Labour Party. Many members left the ILP to join the Communist Party 1921, and in 1932 all connections with the Labour Party were severed. After World War II the ILP dwindled, eventually becoming extinct. James Maxton (1885–1946) was its chair 1926–46.

India country in S Asia, bounded N by Afghanistan, China, Nepál, and Bhutan; E by Myanmar; NW by Pakistan; surrounded to the SE, S, and SW by the Indian Ocean; situated in the NE corner of India, N of the Bay of Bengal, is Bangladesh.

government India was established as a federal republic in 1949. it comprises 25 self-governing states. In times of crisis, central rule ('president's rule') can be imposed. There are also seven union territories, administered by a lieutenant-governor appointed by the federal president. The central (federal) government has sole responsibility in military and foreign affairs and plays a key role in economic affairs.

The titular, executive head of the federal government is the president. However, real executive power is held by a prime minister and cabinet drawn from the majority party or coalition within the federal parliament. The dominant national-level party in India, which until 1989 had held power for all but three years (1977–79) since independence, is the Congress Party, today termed Indian National Congress (I or Indira).

history The earliest Indian civilization evolved in the Indus Valley. Many other sites developed along the rivers from the Himalayas to the Arabian sea, forming the largest unitary civilization in the ancient world. The India National Congress was founded (see ◊Congress Party) in 1885 as a focus for nationalism, and resistance to UK rule was organized under the leadership of Mohandas ◊Gandhi from 1915. In 1947 British India was divided into the independent dominions of

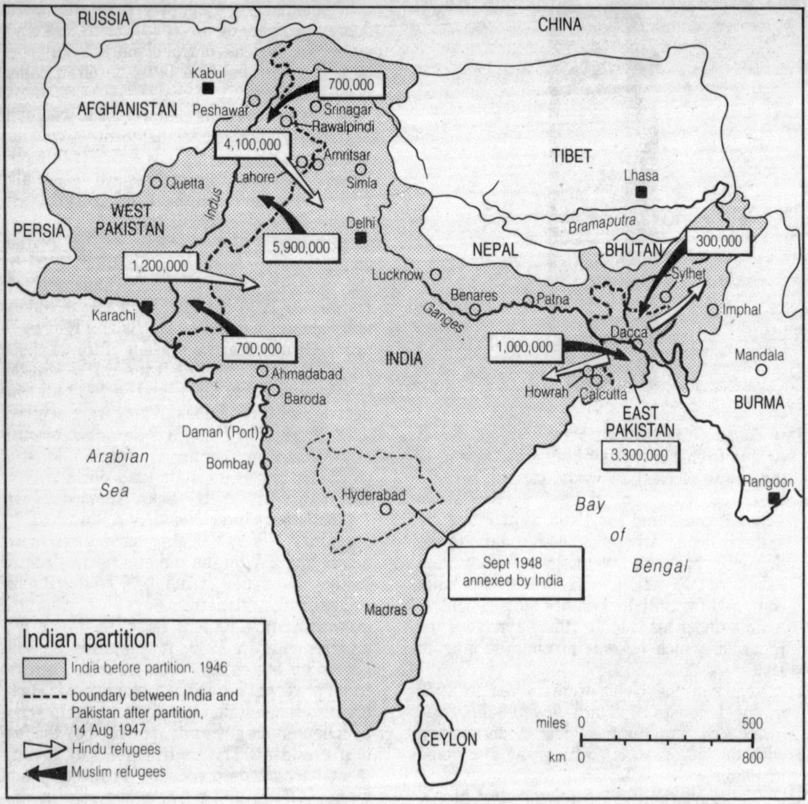

India (predominantly Hindu) and ◊Pakistan (predominantly Muslim). Between 1947 and 1949 India temporarily remained under the supervision of a governor general appointed by the British monarch while a new constitution was framed and approved. Former princely states were integrated, and the old British provinces restructured into new states; in 1950 India was proclaimed a fully independent federal republic.

independent republic During its early years the republic faced the problem of resettling refugees from Pakistan and was involved in border skirmishes over Kashmir. Under the leadership of Prime Minister Nehru, land reforms and a new socialist economic programme (involving protectionism), and an emphasis on heavy industries and government planning, were introduced, while sovereignty of parts of India held by France and Portugal was recovered 1950–61.

foreign affairs In foreign affairs, India remained within the ◊Commonwealth, was involved in border clashes with China 1962, and played a leading role in the formation of the ◊nonaligned movement 1961. In 1964, Nehru died and was succeeded as prime minister by Lal Bahadur Shastri. There was a second war with Pakistan over Kashmir 1964. The new prime minister, Indira ◊Gandhi (Nehru's daughter), came to power on Shastri's death 1966 and kept broadly to her father's policy programme, but drew closer to the Soviet Union with the signing of a 15-year economic and military assistance agreement 1973. In 1971 Indian troops invaded East Pakistan in support of separatist groups. They defeated Pakistan's troops and oversaw the creation of independent ◊Bangladesh.

regional unrest In 1975, having been found guilty of electoral malpractice, Indira Gandhi imposed a 'state of emergency' and imprisoned almost 1,000 political opponents. She was cleared of malpractice by the Supreme Court Nov 1975, but the 'emergency' continued for two years, during which period a harsh compulsory birth control programme was introduced under the supervision of Sanjay Gandhi (Indira's youngest son). The 'state of emergency' was lifted March 1977 for elections in which the Janata opposition party was swept to power, its leader Morarji Desai defeating Indira Gandhi in her home constituency. The new government was undermined by economic difficulties and internal factional strife, which led to the defection of many members to a new party, the *Lok Dal*, led by Raj Narain and Charan Singh. Desai was toppled as prime minister 1979, and a coalition, under Charan Singh, assumed power. After only 24 days in Aug 1979 Singh's government was overthrown, and in Jan 1980 the Congress (I) Party, led by Indira Gandhi and promising firmer government, was returned to power with a landslide victory. The new Gandhi administration was economically successful, but the problems of intercaste violence and regional unrest, were such that the Congress (I) Party lost control of a number of states.

Amritsar massacre The greatest unrest was in Punjab, where Sikh demands for greater religious recognition escalated into calls for the creation of a separate state of 'Khalistan'. In 1984, troops were sent into the Sikh's most holy shrine, the Golden Temple at Amritsar, to dislodge the armed Sikh extremist leader Sant Jarnail Singh Bhindranwale, resulting in the deaths of Bhindranwale and hundreds of his supporters. The ensuing Sikh backlash brought troop mutinies, culminating in the assassination of Indira Gandhi by her Sikh bodyguards Oct 1984. In Delhi, retaliating Hindus massacred 3,000 Sikhs before the new prime minister, Rajiv Gandhi (Indira's eldest son), restored order.

reform In the elections of Dec 1984, Congress (I) gained a record victory. As prime minister, Rajiv Gandhi pledged to modernize the Indian economy and to resolve the Punjab, Assam, and Kashmir disputes. Some progress was made; however, Gandhi was unable to resolve the Punjab problem, with Sikh-Hindu ethnic conflict continuing, while in N India Hindi-Muslim relations deteriorated. Gandhi's enthusiasm for economic reform also waned from 1986 and his personal reputation was sullied by the uncovering of a financial scandal (the 'Bofors scandal'), by finance minister V P Singh.

coalition government Despite bumper harvests 1988–89, Gandhi's popularity continued to fall. V P Singh, who was dismissed from Congress (I) in 1987, attacked his increasingly dictatorial style and became the recognized leader of the opposition forces, which united under the Janata Dal umbrella Oct 1988. In the general election of Nov 1989 a broad anti-Congress electoral pact was forged, embracing the Janata Dal, BJP, Communist Party, and Teluga Desam. Gandhi resigned from office and V P Singh, widely respected for his incorruptibility, took over at the head of a minority 'National Front' coalition.

separatist violence Singh's major objective was the lowering of racial tensions. However, in Jan 1990 Muslim separatist violence erupted in Kashmir, forcing the imposition of direct rule and leading to a deterioration of relations with Pakistan. President's rule was imposed over Jammu and Kashmir in July 1990 and over Assam in Nov 1990, as a result of the rising tide of separatist violence. Punjab, where inter-ethnic murders climbed to record heights from Nov, was already under president's rule. On 7 Nov, after troops had fired on Hindu fanatics who were attempting to storm the Ajodhya mosque, the Singh government was voted out of office. A new minority government was formed by Chandra Shekar, who led a tiny Janata Dal socialist faction comprising 56 deputies, and who was assured of outside support by the Congress Party of Rajiv Gandhi (Gandhi having declined the president's invitation to head a government of his own). With the economy badly hit by the Gulf Crisis' impact upon oil prices, and caste communalist and separatist violence continuing, the minority government appeared insecure.

India of the Princes the 562 Indian states ruled by princes during the period of British control. They occupied an area of 715,964 sq mi (45% of the total area of pre-partition India) and had a population of over 93 million. At the partition of British India in 1947 the princes were given independence by the British government but were advised to adhere to either India or Pakistan. Between 1947 and 1950 all except Kashmir were incorporated in either country. Most of the states were Hindu.

Indochina French former collective name for ◊Cambodia, Laos, and ◊Vietnam, which became independent after World War II.

Indochina War successful war of independence 1946–1954 between the Nationalist forces of what was to become Vietnam and France, the occupying colonial power.

In 1945 Vietnamese Nationalist communist leader Ho Chi Minh proclaimed an independent Vietnamese republic, which soon began an armed struggle against French forces.

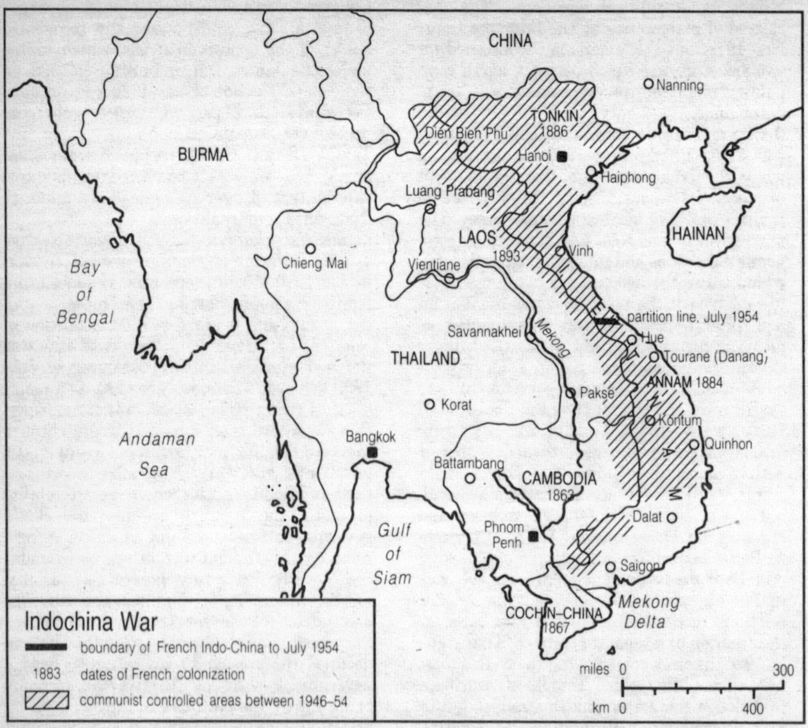

France in turn set up a Noncommunist state four years later. In 1954, after the siege of Dien Bien Phu, a ceasefire was agreed between France and China that resulted in the establishment of two separate Vietnamese states, North and South Vietnam, divided by the 17th parallel. Attempts at reunification of the country led subsequently to the ◊Vietnam War.

Indonesia country in SE Asia, made up of over 13,000 islands situated on the equator, between the Indian and Pacific oceans.

history In the 17th century the Dutch managed to establish trading centres, while Indonesian kingdoms dominated the region, but by the 18th–19th centuries their control was complete, and the islands were proclaimed a Dutch colony 1816. A nationalist movement developed during the 1920s under the pro-communist Indonesian Nationalist Party (PNI), headed by Achmed Sukarno. This was suppressed by the Dutch, but in 1942, after Japan's occupation of the islands, the PNI was installed in power as an anti-Western puppet government. When Japan surrendered to the Allies 1945, President Sukarno proclaimed Indonesia's independence. The Dutch challenged this by launching military expeditions before agreeing to transfer sovereignty 1949. A 'special union' was established between the two countries but was annulled by Indonesia 1956.

the republic The new republic was planned as a federation of 16 constituent regions but was made unitary 1950. This led to dominance by Java (which has two-thirds of Indonesia's population), provoking revolts in Sumatra and the predominantly Christian South Moluccas. The paramount political figure in the new republic was President Sukarno, who ruled in an authoritarian manner and pursued an ambitious and expansionist foreign policy. He effected the transfer of Netherlands New Guinea (Irian Jaya) to Indonesia 1963 but failed in a confrontation with Malaysia over claims to Sabah and Sarawak. With the economy deteriorating, in 1965 an attempted coup against Sukarno by groups connected with the Indonesian Communist Party was firmly put down by army Chief of Staff General

◊Suharto, who then assumed power as emergency ruler 1966. Suharto coordinated the massacre by the army of between 200,000 and 700,000 people in 1965; it was later revealed that US intelligence was directly linked to this massacre as it had provided the Indonesian military with lists of around 5,000 members of the Indonesian Communist Party.

the 'New Order' Suharto ended hostility over Sabah and Sarawak and formally replaced Sukarno as president 1967. He proceeded to institute what was termed a 'New Order'. This involved the concentration of political power in the hands of a coterie of army and security-force officers, the propagation of *Pancasila*, which stressed unity and social justice, the pursuit of a liberal economic programme, and the fierce suppression of communist activity.

Rising oil exports brought significant industrial and agricultural growth to Indonesia during the 1970s, and self-sufficiency in rice production was attained by the 1980s. In addition, its borders were extended by the forcible annexation of the former Portuguese colony of East Timor 1976. Suharto's authoritarian approach met with opposition from left-wing groups, from radical Muslims, from separatist groups in outlying islands (most especially in Irian Jaya), and S Moluccas. In Irian Jaya, following the supression of a rebellion organized by the Free Papua Movement (OPM), a 'transmigration' programme was instituted by the Suharto government, with the aim of resettling 65 million Javanese. This encountered strong opposition from native Melanesians, prompting the emigration of more than 10,000 refugees to neighbouring Papua New Guinea. In East Timor, tens of thousands died from famine and continuing warfare; although travel restrictions were partly eased 1988, the UN refused to recognize Indonesia's sovereignty over the area. In recent years, economic problems have mounted as a result of the fall in world prices of oil, which provides 70% of Indonesia's foreign exchange earnings. Indonesia has long pursued a ◊nonaligned foreign policy, hosting the Bandung Conference of Third World nations 1955, and is a member of ◊ASEAN. Under General Suharto, its relations with the West have become closer.

industrialization a policy usually associated with modernization of developing countries where the process normally starts with the manufacture of simple goods that can replace imports. It is essential for economic development and largely responsible for the growth of cities.

industry the extraction and conversion of raw materials, the manufacture of goods, and the provision of services. Industry can be either low technology, unspecialized and labour-intensive as in the less developed countries, or highly automated, mechanized, and specialized, using advanced technology, as in the 'industrialized' countries. Major trends in industrial activity 1960–90 were the growth of electronic, robotic, and microelectronic technologies, the expansion of the offshore oil industry, and the prominence of Japan and the Pacific region countries in manufacturing and distributing electronics, computers, and motor vehicles.

world industry On the global scale, the period after World War II has been marked by the development of traditional industry such as shipbuilding and motor manufacture in the low-cost countries, particularly Japan, Korea, and the Pacific region generally. This has been followed by moves into new industrial products, such as electronics and computers, in which these countries have dominated the world. In the West, the USA has been most successful partly because of the great size of its home market, while the USSR, and to a lesser extent Europe, have resorted to protectionist tariff and quota barriers, and attempts to implement economic planning as a tool for economic growth.

British industry The prominent trends in industrial activity in Britain from the 1970s onwards have been the growth of the offshore oil and gas industries, the rapid growth of electronic and microelectronic technologies, and a continuous rise in the share of total employment of service industries. Recessions in 1974–75 and 1980–81, due in part to fluctuating energy costs, have been offset by increased productivity, but these gains mean that the increased output was achieved with fewer workers, and unemployment has been a persistent feature of the period. The government-owned public sector includes coal, steel, British Rail, and the Post Office. Conservative government policy is to encourage economic recovery by improving performance in the face of the open market, through the ◊privatization (selling shares to the public) of public sector industry. British Telecom was sold in 1985, British Gas in 1986, British Airways in early 1987, and the water boards in 1989. As a member of the European Community (EC), Britain has received grants from the European Regional Development Fund, which was established in 1975 to assist in the development of new or declining industrial regions.

inflation in economics, a rise in the general level of prices. The many causes include ***cost-push inflation*** that occurred in 1974 as a

Inflation *Laundry baskets were needed to collect wages during a period of hyperinflation in Germany 1923.*

result of the world price increase in oil, thus increasing production costs. ***Demand-pull inflation*** results when overall demand exceeds supply. Suppressed inflation occurs in controlled economies and is reflected in rationing, shortages, and black market prices.

In the 20th century inflation has been marked in many countries, and at times price increases have occurred so rapidly that a state of 'hyperinflation' has resulted. Such were the conditions in Germany 1923, and in Hungary 1946 when prices doubled each day.

For almost 50 years inflation has been continuous in the UK and in the USA. The acceleration in inflation at the end of the 1960s was common to most major indutrialized countries. In 1973–74 a sharp increase in world inflation was experienced by all the major economies reflecting the rising prices of raw materials in world markets, especially of oil.

From the 1960s to the 1980s inflation was generally more rapid in the UK than in other major economies. Between 1980–85, the UK remained at or near the top of the international inflation league, despite some successes in the government's anti-inflation strategy.

Deflation, a fall in the general level of prices, is the reverse of inflation. Deflation prevailed in most countries from the early 1920s to the mid-1930s.

Inkatha South African political organization formed 1975 by Chief Gatsha Buthelezi, leader of six million Zulus, the country's biggest ethnic group. Inkatha aims to create a nonracial democratic political situation. Because Inkatha has tried to work with the white regime, Buthelezi has been regarded as a collaborator by blacks and the United Democratic Front. Fighting between Inkatha and African National Congress members cost more than 1,000 lives in the first five months of 1990. The term Inkatha is from the grass coil worn by Zulu women for carrying head loads; its many strands give it strength.

INLA abbreviation for ◊Irish National Liberation Army.

integrated circuit (IC), popularly called ***silicon chip*** a miniaturized electronic circuit produced on a single crystal, or chip, of a semiconducting material such as silicon. It may contain many thousands of components and yet measure only 5 mm square and 1 mm thick. The discovery in the early 1970s of the means to produce such circuits, superseding the printed circuit, began the so-called computer revolution.

intelligence in military and political affairs, information, often secretly or illegally obtained, about other countries. ***Counter-intelligence*** is information on the activities of hostile agents. Much intelligence is gained by technical means, such as satellites and the electronic interception of data.

The British secret intelligence service is M(ilitary) I(ntelligence) 6 and its agents operate abroad; the US equivalent is the ◊Central Intelligence Agency. In the UK the counter-intelligence service MI5 has as its executive arm Scotland Yard's Special Branch. In the USA, the ◊Federal Bureau of Investigation is responsible for counter-intelligence; in the USSR, the ◊KGB.

International Court of Justice the main judicial organ of the ◊United Nations, at The Hague, the Netherlands.

International Labour Organization (ILO) an agency of the United Nations, established in 1919, which formulates standards for labour and social conditions. Its headquarters are in Geneva. It was awarded the Nobel Peace Prize 1969.

International Monetary Fund (IMF) specialized agency of the United Nations, headquarters Washington DC, established under the 1944 Bretton Woods agreement and operational since 1947. It seeks to promote international monetary cooperation and the growth of world trade, and to smooth multilateral payment arrangements among member states. IMF stand-by loans are available to members in balance of payments difficulties (the amount being governed by the member's quota), usually on the basis of acceptance of instruction on stipulated corrective measures.

The Fund also operates other drawing facilities, including several designed to provide preferential credit to developing countries with liquidity problems. Having previously operated in US dollars linked to gold, since 1972, the IMF has used the special drawing right (SDR) as its standard unit of account, valued in terms of a weighted 'basket' of major currencies. Since the 1971 Smithsonian agreement permitting wider fluctuations from specified currency parities, IMF rules have been progressively adapted to the increasing prevalence of fully floating exchange rates.

In 1986, in conjunction with the World Bank, the IMF set up a huge fund to assist the world's poorest countries.

IRA abbreviation for ◊Irish Republican Army.

Iran country in SW Asia, bounded N by the USSR and the Caspian Sea, E by Afghanistan and Pakistan, S and SW by the Gulf of Oman, W by Iraq, and NW by Turkey.

history Revolutions in 1905 and 1909 resulted in the establishment of a parliamentary regime. During World War I the country was occupied by British and Russian forces. An officer, Col Reza Khan, seized power 1921, and a coup 1925 made him the shah, allowing him to carry out a massive programme of modernization to bring Persia, as it was then called, into the 20th century. During World War II, Iran, as it had become known, was occupied by British, US, and Soviet troops until 1946. Anti-British and anti- American feeling grew, and in 1951 the newly elected prime minister, Dr Muhammad Mossadeq, obtained legislative approval for the nationalization of Iran's largely foreign-owned petroleum industry. With US connivance, he was deposed in a 1953 coup, and the dispute over nationalization was settled the following year when oil-drilling concessions were granted to a consortium of eight companies. The shah took complete control of the government, and during 1965–1977 Iran enjoyed a period of political stability and economic growth, based on oil revenue.

Iranian revolution By 1975 the shah had introduced a one-party system, based on the Iran National Resurgence Party *Rastakhis*, but opposition to his regime was growing. The most effective opposition came from the religious leader, Ayatollah Khomeini, who campaigned from exile in France. He demanded a return to the principles of Islam, and pressure on the shah became so great that in 1979 he left the country, leaving the way open for Khomeini's return. He appointed a provisional government, but power was placed essentially in the hands of the 15-member Islamic Revolutionary Council, controlled by Khomeini.

Islamic republic Iran was declared an Islamic republic, and a new constitution, based on Islamic principles, was adopted. Relations with the USA were badly affected when a group of Iranian students took 63 Americans hostage at the US embassy in Tehran, demanding that the shah return to face trial. Even the death of the shah, in Egypt 1980, did little to resolve the crisis, which ended when all the hostages were released Jan 1981.

the Iran–Iraq War Externally, the war with Iraq, that broke out 1980 after a border dispute, continued with considerable loss of life on both sides. By 1985 the failure to end the Gulf War and the harshness of the Islamic codes were increasing opposition to Khomeini's regime but his position remained secure. In Aug 1988, under heavy domestic and international pressure, Iran accepted the provisions for a UN-sponsored ceasefire. Full diplomatic relations with the UK were restored Dec 1988, but the issuing of a death threat to the author Salman Rushdie caused a severance March 1989.

Khomeini's death in June 1989 provoked a power struggle between hardline revolutionaries and so-called pragmatists who recognized a need for trade and cooperation with the West. Revelations in 1989 that Iran had negotiated secret oil sales to Israel reflected Iran's need for hard currency to rebuild its economy as well as a desire to counter Iraq. Struggle for succession began, ending with the confirmation of the former Speaker of the *Majlis*, Hoshemi Rafsanjani, as president with increased powers. Despite his reputation for moderation and pragmatism, Iran's relations with the West, and particularly the UK, were slow to improve. In Aug 1990 Iran accepted Iraq's peace terms, which virtually gave back everything Iraq had claimed at the start of the Iran-Iraq war.

Irangate US political scandal involving senior members of the Reagan administration (called this to echo the Nixon administation's ◊Watergate).

Arms, including Hawk missiles, were sold to Iran via Israel (at a time when the USA was publicly calling for a worldwide ban on sending arms to Iran), violating the law prohibiting the sale of US weapons for resale to a third country listed as a 'terrorist nation', as well as the law requiring sales above $14 million to be reported to Congress. The negotiator in the field was Lt Col Oliver North, a military aide to the National Security Council, reporting in the White House to the national-security adviser (first Robert McFarlane, then John Poindexter). North and his associates were also channelling donations to the Contras from individuals and from other countries, including $2 million from Taiwan, $10 million from the sultan of Brunei, and $32 million from Saudi Arabia.

The Congressional Joint Investigative Committee reported, in Nov 1987, that the president bore 'ultimate responsibility' for allowing a 'cabal of zealots' to seize control of the administration's policy, but found no firm evidence that President Reagan had actually been aware of the Contra diversion. Reagan persistently claimed to have no recall of events, and some evidence was withheld on grounds of 'national security'. North was tried and convicted in May 1989 on charges of obstructing Congress and unlawfully destroying government documents. Poindexter was found guilty on all counts in 1990.

Iraq country in SW Asia, bounded N by Turkey, E by Iran; S by the Persian Gulf, Kuwait, and Saudi Arabia; SW by Jordan; and W by Syria.

history Occupied by Britain in World War I, Iraq was placed under British administration by the League of Nations 1920. In 1932 Iraq became a fully independent kingdom, and in 1933 the reigning king, Faisal I, died and was succeeded by his son, Ghazi. The leading figure behind the throne was the strongly pro-Western General Nuri-el-Said, who was prime minister 1930–58. In 1939 King Ghazi died in an accident, and Faisal II became king at the age of three, his uncle Prince Abdul Ilah acting as regent until 1953 when the king assumed full powers. In 1955 Iraq signed the Baghdad Pact, a regional collective security agreement, with the USSR seen as the main potential threat, and in 1958 joined Jordan in an Arab Federation, with King Faisal as head of state. In July of that year, a revolution overthrew the monarchy, and King Faisal, Prince Abdul Ilah, and General Nuri were all killed.

the republic The constitution was suspended, and Iraq was declared a republic, with Brig Abdul Karim Kassem as head of a left-wing military regime. He withdrew from the Baghdad Pact 1959 and, after tenuously holding power for five years, was killed 1963 in a coup led by Col Salem Aref, who established a new government, ended martial law, and within two years had introduced a civilian administration. He died in an air crash 1966, and his brother, who succeeded him, was ousted 1968 and replaced by Maj-Gen al-Bakr. He concentrated power in the hands of a Revolutionary Command Council (RCC) and made himself head of state, head of government, and chair of the RCC. In 1979 Saddam ◊Hussein who for several years had been the real power in Iraq, replaced al-Bakr as RCC chair and state president. In 1980 he introduced a National Charter, reaffirming a policy of nonalignment and a constitution that provided for an elected national assembly. The first elections took place that year. Iraq had, since 1970, enjoyed a fluctuating relationship with Syria, sometimes distant and sometimes close enough to contemplate a complete political and economic union. By 1980, however, the atmosphere was cool.

the Iran–Iraq War Relations between Iraq and Iran had been tense for some years, with disagreement over their shared border, which runs down the Shatt-al-Arab waterway. The 1979 Iranian revolution made Iraq more suspicious of Iran's intentions, and in 1980 a full-scale war broke out. Hundreds of thousands of lives were lost on both sides and incalculable damage to industry and property sustained. Following Iranian acceptance of UN ceasefire provisions, the war came to an end 1988. Hussein took advantage of the end of hostilities to turn his combat-hardened army against Kurdish separatists, many of whom had sided with Iran.

Gulf War In 1990 Hussein re-opened a long-standing territorial dispute with neighbouring Kuwait while seeking to assume leadership of the Arab world. Following increasing diplomatic pressure, on 2 Aug Iraqi troops invaded and annexed Kuwait, installing a puppet government and declaring it part of Iraq. As Iraqi troops massed on his borders, King Fahd of Saudi Arabia requested help from the USA and the UK and a rapid build-up of US ground and air power and British aircraft began. Meanwhile the UN Security Council condemned the invasion, demanded Iraq's withdrawal, and imposed comprehensive sanctions. To ensure the safety of his border, President Hussein hastily concluded a permanent peace treaty with Iran, under which he conceded virtually everything for which he had fought the Iran–Iraq war and both countries agreed to release all detained prisoners.

In Dec 1990 the UN Security Council set a Jan 15 1991 deadline for Iraq's withdrawal from Kuwait, after which force could be used. On Jan 16 the US-led Allied forces began the aerial bombardment of Baghdad as the first phase of operation 'Desert Storm', the military campaign to liberate Kuwait; the Iraqi military response during the air campaign was largely limited to the firing of 'Scud' missiles into Israel and Saudi Arabia. A last-minute peace initiative by the Soviet Union to avoid a land battle failed, and on Feb 23 the Allied land offensive began, with thousands of Iraqi troops immediately surrendering without a fight to the advancing Allied armies. By Feb 28 Allied troops had successfully liberated Kuwait from the occupying Iraqi forces and the war was officially declared over. Iraq dealt harshly with Kurdish and Shi'ite rebels in the period of political turmoil and near civil war that followed. Despite world condemnation, many thousands of civilian men, women, and children were killed in Saddam's attempt to restore his authority. This led to a mass exodus of Kurdish refugees from the North, into neighbouring Iran, and Turkey. A 'safe haven' in northern Iraq was established for Kurdish protection under United Nations' auspices.

Ireland: history The Tudor monarchs adopted a policy of conquest, confiscation of Irish land, and plantation by English settlers, and further imposed the Reformation and English law on Ireland. The most important of the plantations was that of Ulster, carried out under James I 1610. In 1800 William Pitt induced the Irish parliament to vote itself out of existence by the Act of Union, effective 1 Jan 1801, which gave Ireland parliamentary representation at Westminster. During the famine 1845–46, 1.5 million people emigrated, mostly to the USA. By the 1880s there was a strong movement for home rule for Ireland; Gladstone supported it but was defeated by the British parliament. By 1914, home rule was conceded but World War I delayed implementation. The ***Easter Rising*** took place in Apr 1916, when nationalists seized the Dublin general post office and proclaimed a republic. After a week of fighting, the revolt was suppressed by the British army and most of the leaders executed. From 1918–21 there was guerrilla warfare against the British army, especially by the ◊Irish Republican Army (IRA), formed by Michael Collins 1919. This led to a split in the rebel forces, but in 1921 the Anglo-Irish Treaty resulted in partition and the creation of the Irish Free State in S Ireland. For history since that date, see ◊Ireland, Republic of; ◊Ireland, Northern.

Ireland, Northern constituent part of the UK ***government*** because of the outbreak of violence, there has been direct rule from the UK since 1972. Northern Ireland is entitled to send 12 members to the Westminster Parliament. Under the Anglo-Irish Agreement 1985,

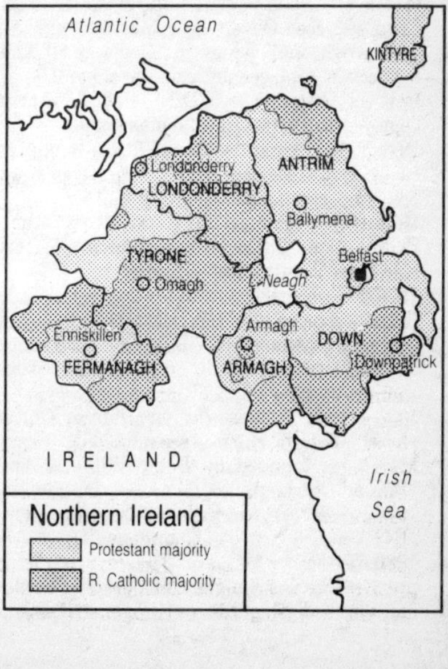

the Republic of Ireland was given a consultative role (via an Anglo-Irish conference) in the government of Northern Ireland, but agreed that there should be no change in its status except by majority consent, and that there should be greater cooperation against terrorism. The agreement was approved by Parliament, but all 12 Ulster members gave up their seats, so that by-elections could be fought as a form of 'referendum' on the views of the province itself. A similar boycotting of the Northern Ireland Assembly since the Anglo-Irish agreement led to its dissolution 1986 by the UK government.

history For history pre-1921, see ◊Ireland, history. The creation of Northern Ireland dates from 1921 when the mainly Protestant counties of Ulster withdrew from the newly established Irish Free State. Spasmodic outbreaks of violence by the ◊IRA continued, but only in 1968–69 were there serious disturbances arising from Protestant political dominance and discrimination against the Roman Catholic minority in employment and housing.

1967 Northern Ireland Civil Rights Association set up to press for equal treatment for Catholics in the provinces.

1968 Series of civil rights marches sparked off rioting and violence, especially in Londonderry.

1969 Election results weakened Terence O'Neil's Unionist government. Further rioting led to call-up of (protestant based) B-Specials to Royal Ulster Constabulary. Chichester-Clark replaced O'Neil. IRA split into 'official' and 'provisional' wings. RUC disarmed and B-Specials replaced by non-sectarian Ulster Defence Regiment (UDR). British Army deployed in Belfast and Londonderry.

1971 First British soldier killed. Faulkner replaced Chichester-Clark. IRA stepped up bombing campaign.

1972 'Bloody Sunday' in Londonderry when British Army killed 13 demonstrators. Direct rule from Westminster introduced.

1974 'Power sharing' between Protestant and Catholic groups tried but failed. IRA extended bombing campaign to UK mainland. Bombs in Guildford and Birmingham caused a substantial number of fatalities.

1976 British Ambassador in Dublin, Christopher Ewart Biggs, assassinated. Peace Movement founded by Betty Williams and Mairead Corrigan.

1978 British MP Airey Neave assassinated by ◊INLA at the House of Commons.

1980 Meeting of Margaret Thatcher and Irish premier Charles Haughey on a peaceful settlement to the Irish question. Hunger strikes and 'dirty protests' started by Republican prisoners in pursuit of political status.

1981 Hunger strikes led to deaths of Bobby Sands and Francis Hughes; Anglo-Irish Intergovernmental Council formed.

1982 Northern Ireland Assembly created to devolve legislative and executive powers back to the province. Social Democratic and Labour Party (SDLP) (19%) and Sinn Féin (10%) boycotted the asssembly.

1984 Series of reports from various groups on the future of the province. IRA bomb at Conservative Party conference in Brighton killed five people. Second Anglo-Irish Intergovernmental Council summit meeting agreed to oppose violence and cooperate on security; Britain rejected ideas of confederation or joint sovereignty.

1985 Meeting of Margaret Thatcher and Irish premier Garrett Fitzgerald at Hillsborough produced Anglo-Irish agreement on the future of Ulster; regarded as a sell-out by Unionists.

1986 Unionist opposition to Anglo-Irish agreement included protests and strikes. Loyalist violence against police and Unionist MPs boycotted Westminster.

1987 IRA bombed British Army base in West Germany. Unionist boycott of Westminster ended. Extradition clauses of Anglo-Irish Agreement approved in Eire. IRA bombed Remembrance Day service at Enniskillen – later admitted it to be a 'mistake'.

1988 Three IRA bombers killed by security forces on Gibraltar.

1989 After serving fourteen years in prison, the 'Guildford Four' were released when their convictions were ruled unsound by the Court of Appeal.

1990 Anglo-Irish Agreement threatened when Eire refused extraditions.

1991 IRA renewed bombing campaign on British mainland, targetting cabinet meeting in Downing Street and mainline railway stations. Release of 'Birmingham Six' after going to the Court of Appeal.

Ireland, Republic of country occupying the main part of the island of Ireland, off the NW coast of Europe. It is bounded E by the Irish Sea, S and W by the Atlantic, and NE by Northern Ireland.

government The 1937 constitution provides for a president, elected by universal suffrage, and a two-chamber national parliament, consisting of a senate, *Seanad Eireann*, and a house of representatives, *Dail Eireann*. The *Dail* is elected by universal suffrage through a system of proportional representation. The president appoints a prime minister who is nominated by the *Dail*, which is subject to dissolution by the president if the cabinet loses its confidence within the five-year term. Proportional representation encourages the existence of several parties, the most significant being ◊Fianna Fáil, Fine Gael (United Ireland Party), the Labour Party, and the Progressive Democrats.

history For history pre-1921, see ◊Ireland, history. In 1921 a treaty gave Southern Ireland dominion status within the ◊Commonwealth, while six out of the nine counties of Ulster remained part of the UK, with limited self-government. The Irish Free State, as Southern Ireland was formally called 1922, was accepted by IRA leader Michael Collins but not by many of his colleagues, who shifted their allegiance to Fianna Fáil leader, Eamonn de Valera; the latter eventually acknowledged the partition as well in 1937 when a new constitution established the country as a sovereign state under the name of Eire. The IRA continued its fight for an independent, unified Ireland through a campaign of violence, mainly in Northern Ireland but also on the British mainland and, to a lesser extent, in the Irish republic. Eire remained part of the Commonwealth until 1949, when it left, declaring itself the Republic of Ireland, while Northern Ireland remained a constituent part of the UK. In 1973 Fianna Fáil, having held office for over 40 years, was defeated, and Liam Cosgrave formed a coalition of the Fine Gael and Labour parties. In 1977 Fianna Fáil returned to power, with Jack Lynch as prime minister. In 1979 IRA violence intensified with the killing of Earl Mountbatten in Ireland and 18 British soldiers in Northern Ireland. Lynch resigned later the same year, and was succeeded by Charles Haughey. His aim was a united Ireland, with considerable independence for the six northern counties. After the 1981 election Garrett FitzGerald, leader of Fine Gael, formed another coalition with Labour but was defeated the following year on budget proposals and resigned. Haughey returned to office with a minority government, but he, too, had to resign later that year, resulting in the return of FitzGerald.

Anglo-Irish Agreement In 1983 all the main Irish and Northern Irish political parties initiated the New Ireland Forum as a vehicle for discussion. Its report was rejected by Margaret Thatcher's Conservative government in the UK, but discussions between London and Dublin resulted in the signing of the Anglo-Irish Agreement 1985, providing for regular consultation and exchange of information on political, legal, security, and cross-border matters. The agreement also said that the status of Northern Ireland would not be changed without the consent of a majority of the people. The agreement was criticized by the Unionist parties of Northern Ireland, who asked that it be repealed. FitzGerald's coalition ended 1986, and the Feb 1987 election again returned Fianna Fáil and Charles Haughey. In 1988 relations between the Republic of Ireland and the UK were at a low ebb because of disagreements over extradition decisions. In 1989, Haughey failed to win a majority at the election and entered into a coalition with the Progressive Democrats (a breakaway party from Fianna Fáil), putting two of their members into the cabinet. In Nov 1990, after being sacked as deputy prime minister, Brian Lenihan was defeated in the presidential election by the left-wing backed Mary Robinson. In the same month Alan Dukes resigned the leadership of the Fine Gael, to be replaced by the right-winger John Bruton.

Irish nationalism political movement objecting to British rule of Ireland (which had no elected government of its own but sent members to the British Parliament in Westminster) and campaigning for ◊Home Rule.

In the ◊Easter Rising 1916 an armed rebellion that aimed to secure Irish independence from British rule was crushed by the British army. In 1919 fighting broke out in Ireland between the British army and the ◊Irish Republican Army (IRA), a guerrilla unit formed by the political group Sinn Fein. In the 1921 treaty partitioning Ireland, southern Ireland became independent (Irish Free State 1922) with the province of Northern Ireland voting to remain part of Britain.

Irish National Liberation Army (INLA) guerrilla organization committed to the end of British rule in Northern Ireland and the incorporation of Ulster into the Irish Republic. The INLA was a 1974 offshoot of the Irish Republican Army. Among the INLA's activities was the killing of British politician Airey Neave in 1979.

Irish Republican Army (IRA) militant Irish nationalist organization whose aim is to create a united Irish socialist republic including Ulster. The paramilitary wing of ◊Sinn Féin, it was founded 1919 by Michael Collins and fought a successful war against Britain 1919–21. It came to the fore again 1939 with a bombing campaign in Britain, and was declared illegal in Eire. Its activities intensified from 1968 onwards, as the civil-rights disorders ('the Troubles') in Northern Ireland developed. In 1970 a group in the north broke away to become the ***Provisional IRA***; their commitment is to the expulsion of the British from Northern Ireland.

In 1974 a further breakaway occurred, of

the left-wing Irish Republican Socialist Party with its paramilitary wing, the Irish National Liberation Army.

The IRA is committed to the use of force in trying to achieve its objectives, and it regularly carries out bombings and shootings. In 1979 it murdered Louis Mountbatten, and its bomb attacks in Britain have included: Birmingham, Guildford, and Woolwich pub bombs 1974; Chelsea Barracks, London, 1981; Harrods department store, London, 1983; and Brighton 1984 (an attempt to kill members of the UK cabinet during the Conservative Party conference). The IRA admitted responsibility for a Remembrance Day bomb explosion in Enniskillen, Northern Ireland, 1987. The movement gained some sympathy, though shortlived, after the shooting of three IRA activists by the SAS in Gibraltar, 1988. Another attempt to kill members of the cabinet in Downing Street, was followed by a renewed bombing campaign on London's mainline railway stations 1991.

Iron Curtain in Europe after World War II, the symbolic boundary of the ◊Cold War between capitalist West and communist East. The term was popularized by the UK prime minister Winston Churchill from 1945.

Islam (Arabic 'submission', that is, to the will of Allah) religion founded in the Arabian peninsula in the early 7th century AD. It emphasizes the oneness of God, his omnipotence, beneficence, and inscrutability. The sacred book is the ***Koran*** of the prophet Muhammad, the Prophet or Messenger of Allah. There are two main Muslim sects: ***Sunni*** and ***Shi'ite***. Other schools include ***Sufism***, a mystical movement originating in the 8th century. Islam embodies a secular law (the ***Shar'ia***).

history Islam began as a militant and missionary religion, and between 711 and 1492 spread east into India, west over N Africa, then north across Gibraltar into the Iberian peninsula. Islam was seen as an enemy of Christianity by European countries during the Crusades of the Middle Ages. Driven from Europe, Islam remained established in N Africa and the Middle East. Islam is a major force in the Arab world and is a focus for nationalism among the peoples of Soviet Central Asia. It is also a significant factor in Pakistan, Indonesia, Malaysia, and parts of Africa. It is the second largest religion in the UK. Since World War II there has been a resurgence of fundamentalist Islam (often passionately opposed to the ideas of the West) in Iran, Libya, Afghanistan, and elsewhere. In the UK 1987 the manifesto *The Muslim Voice* demanded rights for Muslim views on education (such as single-sex teaching) and on the avoidance of dancing, mixed bathing, and sex education.

isolationism in politics, concentration on internal rather than foreign affairs; a foreign policy having no interest in international affairs that do not affect the country's own interests. In the USA, isolationism is usually associated with the Republican Party, especially politicians of the Midwest (for example, the Neutrality Acts 1935–39). Intervention by the USA in both World Wars was initially resisted. In the 1960s some Republicans demanded the removal of the ◊United Nations from American soil.

Israel country in SW Asia, bounded N by Lebanon, E by Syria and Jordan, S by the Gulf of Aqaba, and W by Egypt and the Mediterranean.

history The Zionist movement, calling for an independent community for Jews in their historic homeland of Palestine, began in the 19th century, and in 1917 Britain declared its support for the idea. In 1920 the ◊League of Nations placed Palestine under British administration, and the British government was immediately faced with the rival claims of Jews who wished to settle there and the indigenous Arabs who opposed them. In 1937 Britain proposed separate Arab and Jewish communities; this was accepted by the Jews but not by the Arabs, and fighting broke out between them. In Europe, the Nazi Holocaust killed about 6 million Jews, and hundreds of thousands tried to get to Palestine before, during, and after World War II 1939–45. Many survivors could no longer live in Europe.

creation of Israel In 1947 the British plan for partition was supported by the UN, and when Britain ended its Palestinian mandate 1948, an independent State of Israel was proclaimed, with David ◊Ben-Gurion as prime minister. Neighbouring Arab states sent forces to crush Israel but failed, and when a cease-fire agreement was reached in 1949, Israel controlled more land than had been originally allocated to it. The non-Jewish-occupied remainder of Palestine, known as the West Bank, was occupied by Jordan. The creation of Israel encouraged Jewish immigration on a large scale, about 2 million having arrived from all over the world by 1962. Hundreds of thousands of Arab residents fled from Israel to neigbouring countries, such as Jordan and Lebanon. In 1964 a number of Palestinian Arabs in exile founded the ◊Palestine Liberation Organization (PLO), aiming to overthrow Israel.

Arab-Israeli Wars During the 1960s there was considerable tension between Israel and

***Israel** Towards the end of the British mandate over the lands that are now Israel, Jewish immigration was restricted. In 1947, the year before the Jewish state of Israel was proclaimed, the* Theodore Herzl *carrying immigrants to their promised land was shot at by the British Navy.*

Egypt, which, under President ◊Nasser, had become a leader in the Arab world. His nationalization of the ◊Suez Canal in 1956 provided an opportunity for Israel, with Britain and France, to attack Egypt and occupy a part of Palestine that Egypt had controlled since 1949, the Gaza Strip, from which Israel was forced by UN and US pressure to withdraw in 1957. Ten years later, in the Six Day War, Israel gained the whole of Jerusalem, the West Bank area of Jordan, the Sinai Peninsula in Egypt, and the Golan Heights in Syria. All were placed under Israeli law, although the Sinai was returned to Egypt under the terms of the ◊Camp David agreements. Ben-Gurion resigned in 1963 and was succeeded by Levi Eshkol, leading a coalition government; in 1968 three of the coalition parties combined to form the Israel Labour Party. In 1969 Golda Meir became Labour Party prime minister. Towards the end of her administration another Arab-Israeli war broke out, on Yom Kippur, the holiest day of the Jewish year. Israel was attacked by Egypt and Syria, and after nearly three weeks of fighting, with heavy losses, a ceasefire was agreed. Golda Meir resigned in 1974 and was succeeded by General Itzhak Rabin, heading a Labour-led coalition. In the 1977 elections the Consolidation (Likud) bloc, led by Menachem Begin, won an unexpected victory, and Begin became prime minister.

Camp David Agreements Within five months relations between Egypt and Israel changed dramatically, mainly owing to initiatives by President ◊Sadat of Egypt, encouraged by US president Jimmy Carter. Setting a historical precedent for an Arab leader, Sadat visited Israel to address the *Knesset* 1977, and the following year the Egyptian and Israeli leaders met at Camp David, in the USA, to sign agreements for peace in the Middle East. A treaty was signed in 1979, and in 1980 Egypt and Israel exchanged ambassadors, to the dismay of most of the Arab world. Israel withdrew from Sinai by 1982 but continued to occupy the Golan Heights. In the same year Israel, without consulting Egypt, entered Lebanon and surrounded W Beirut, in pursuit of 6,000 PLO fighters who were trapped there. A split between Egypt and Israel was avoided by the efforts of the US special negotiator, Philip Habib, who secured the evacuation from Beirut to other Arab countries of about 15,000 PLO and Syrian fighters in Aug 1982. Israel's alleged complicity in massacres in two Palestinian refugee camps increased Arab hostility. Talks between Israel and Lebanon, between Dec 1982 and May 1983, resulted in an agreement, drawn up by US secretary of state George Shultz, calling for the withdrawal of all foreign forces from Lebanon within three months. Syria refused to acknowledge the agreement, and left some 30,000 troops, with about 7,000 PLO members, in the northeast; Israel retaliated by refusing to withdraw its forces from the south. Meanwhile, the problems in Lebanon continued. In 1984, under pressure from Syria, President Gemayel of Lebanon revoked the 1983 treaty with Israel. Israel retaliated by attacking Shi'ite villages. Most of the withdrawal was complete by June 1985. Several peace initiatives by King Hussein of Jordan failed. Prime Minister Peres met King Hussein secretly, and, in a speech to the UN, Peres said he would not rule out the possibility of an international conference on the Middle East. PLO leader Yasser ◊Arafat also had talks with Hussein and later, in Cairo, renounced PLO guerrilla activity outside Israeli-occupied territory. Domestically, the government of national unity was having some success with its economic policies, inflation falling in 1986 to manageable levels. The Nov 1988 general election resulted in a hung parliament; after lengthy negotiations, Shamir formed a coalition with Peres and the Labour Party. Shamir's harsh handling of Palestinian protests, and differences over dealings with the PLO, broke the partnership in Mar 1990 when the coalition fell after a vote of no confidence. Egyptian president Hosini Mubarak proposed a 10-point programme for elections in the occupied territories leading towards an unspecified form of autonomous self-rule. Labour quickly agreed to the provisions, and the US approved the plan. In 1989 Likud accepted some of the provisions but remained opposed to any PLO role in the negotiations. In Oct 1990 the killing of at least 19 Palestinians by Israeli troops on Jerusalem's Temple Mount drew widespread international condemnation.

Italy country in S Europe, bounded N by Switzerland and Austria, E by Yugoslavia and the Adriatic Sea, S by the Ionian and Mediterranean seas, and W by the Tyrrhenian Sea and France. It includes the Mediterranean islands of Sardinia and Sicily.

government The 1948 constitution provides for a two-chamber parliament consisting of a senate and a chamber of deputies. Both are elected by universal suffrage, through a

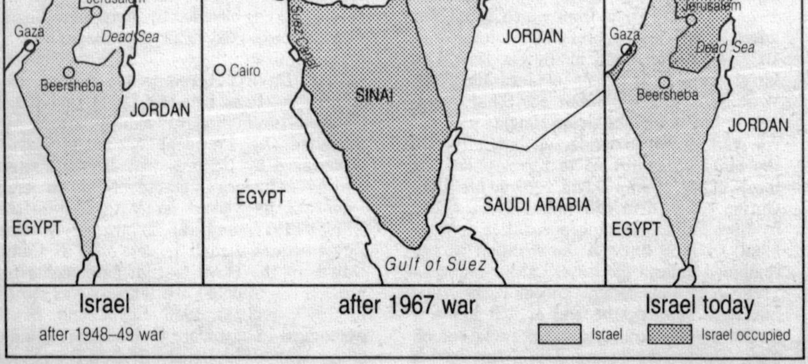

system of proportional representation, and have equal powers. The president is constitutional head of state and is elected by an electoral college consisting of both houses of parliament and 58 regional representatives. The president appoints the prime minister and cabinet (council of ministers), and they are collectively responsible to parliament.

Although Italy is not a federal state, each of its 20 regions enjoys a high degree of autonomy, with a regional council elected for a five-year term by universal suffrage. The voting system encourages a multiplicity of political parties.

history In 1870 the unification of Italy was completed and the Pope ceased to be a temporal ruler until 1929 when the Vatican City State was established. The formation of a colonial empire began in 1869 with the purchase of land on the Bay of Assab, on the Red Sea, from the local sultan. In the next 20 years the Italians occupied all Eritrea, which was made a colony in 1889. An attempt to seize Ethiopia was decisively defeated at Adowa in 1896. War with Turkey 1911–12 gave Italy Tripoli and Cyrenaica. Italy's intervention on the Allied side in World War I secured it Trieste, the Trentino, and S Tirol.

The postwar period was marked by intense political and industrial unrest, culminating in 1922 in the establishment of ◊Mussolini's Fascist dictatorship. The regime embraced a policy of aggression with the conquest of Ethiopia 1935–36 and Albania 1939.

World War II Italy entered World War II in 1940 as an ally of Germany. Defeat in Africa 1941–43 and the Allied conquest of Sicily 1943 resulted in Mussolini's downfall; the new government declared war on Germany, and until 1945 Italy was a battlefield of German occupying forces and the advancing Allies.

the republic In 1946 Victor Emmanuel III, who had been king since 1900, abdicated in favour of his son Humbert (Umberto) II. The monarchy was abolished after a referendum in 1946, and the country became a republic, adopting a new constitution in 1948. Between 1946 and 1986 there were nine parliaments and 45 administrations. The Christian Democrats were dominant until 1963 and after this participated in most coalition governments.

coalition government In 1983, the leader of the Socialist Party, Bettino Craxi, became the republic's first Socialist prime minister, leading a coalition of Christian Democrats, Socialists, Republicans, Social Democrats, and Liberals. Despite criticism of Craxi's strong-willed style of leadership, the coalition parties could find no acceptable alternative and so continued to support him. Under Craxi's government the state of the economy improved, although the north–south divide in productivity and prosperity persists, despite attempts to increase investment in the south. In foreign affairs Italy has demonstrated its commitment to the EC, NATO, and the UN, and in 1983 played an important part in the multinational peace-keeping force in Beirut. In 1987 the Christian Democrat Giovanni Goria formed a coalition government, that fell when the Liberal Party withdrew some three months later. He was succeeded by Ciriaco De Mita, who formed a new Christian Democrat–Socialist–Liberal coalition, but resigned a few months later after disagreements within the government. After lengthy negotiations the veteran Giulio Andreotti put together a new coalition of Christian Democrats, Socialists, and minor parties.

Iwo Jima, Battle of scene of intense fighting between Japanese and US forces 19 Feb–17 Mar 1945 during World War II. In Feb 1945, US marines landed on the island of Iwo Jima, a Japanese air base, intending to use it to prepare for a planned final assault on mainland Japan. The Japanese defences were so strong that 5,000 marines were killed and 15,000 wounded.

J

Japan country in E Asia, occupying a group of islands of which the four main ones are Hokkaido, Honshu, Kyushu, and Shikoku. Japan is situated in the N Pacific, E of North and South Korea.

history From 1867, the privileges of the feudal nobility were gradually abolished, a uniform code of law was introduced and a constitution was established 1889. The army was modernized and a powerful navy founded. Industry developed steadily, and a considerable export trade was built up.

Japanese expansion In 1894 a war with China secured Japanese control of Formosa and S Manchuria, as well as Korea, which was formally annexed 1910. A victory over Russia 1904–05 gave Japan the southern half of Sakhalin and compelled the Russians to evacuate Manchuria. Japan formed an alliance with Britain 1902 and joined the Allies in World War I. At the peace settlement it received the German islands in the N Pacific as mandates. The 1920s saw an advance towards democracy and party government, but after 1932 the government assumed a semi-Fascist form. As a result of successful aggression against China 1931–32, a Japanese puppet monarchy under P'u-i, the last emperor of China, was established in Manchuria; war with China was renewed 1937.

World War II Japan entered World War II with the attack on Pearl Harbor 7 Dec 1941 and at first won a succession of victories in the Philippines, the Malay Peninsula, Burma, (now Myanmar) and the Netherlands Indies. Japan was finally compelled to surrender 15 Aug 1945, following the detonation of atomic bombs at ◊Hiroshima and ◊Nagasaki. An allied control commission took charge, and Japan was placed under military occupation by Allied (chiefly US) troops under General Douglas ◊MacArthur until 1952, when the Japanese Peace Treaty came into force and full sovereignty was regained.

After Japan's defeat, Korea was made independent; Manchuria and Formosa (Taiwan) were returned to China; and the islands mandated to Japan after World War I were placed by the United Nations under US trusteeship. Japan regained the Ryukyu Islands 1972 and the Boninj and Volcano Islands 1968 from the USA, and continues to agitate for the return of the Northern Territories (the islands of the Shikotan and Habomai Group) and the southernmost Kurils (Kunashiri and Etorofu).

democratization and reconstruction During Allied rule, Aug 1945–April 1952, a major 'democratization campaign' was launched, involving radical land, social, and educational reform and the framing of a new 'Peace Constitution' 1946 in which Emperor Hirohito renounced his claims to divinity and became a powerless figurehead ruler, and the nation committed itself to a pacific foreign policy. Japan concentrated during the early postwar years on economic reconstruction, tending towards neutralism in foreign affairs under the protection provided by the 1951 Security Pact. Through a paternalist, guided approach to economic development, epitomized by the operations of the Ministry for International Trade and Industry (MITI), the Japanese economy expanded dramatically during the 1950s and 1960s, with gross national product (GNP) increasing by 10% per year. During this period, Japan was rehabilitated within the international community, entering the UN 1958 and establishing diplomatic relations with Western nations and with Communist China 1972. Japan's internal politics were rocked 1960 and 1968–69 by violent attacks by the anarchic Red Army guerrilla organization protesting against US domination and in 1974 by the resignation of Prime Minister Kakuei Tanaka after a bribery scandal involving the US Lockheed Corporation. The LDP remained in power, however, as the largest single party in parliament. Japanese economic growth was maintained during the 1970s, and made a major impact in the markets of North America and Europe as an exporter of electronics, machinery, and motor vehicles. This created resentment overseas as economic recession began to grip Europe and the USA during the later 1970s, and led to calls for Japan to open up its internal market to foreign exporters and to assume a greater share of the defence burden for the Asia-Pacific region.

liberalization A review of policy was

instituted by Prime Minister Yasuhiro Nakasone, who assumed power 1982. He favoured a strengthening of Japan's military capability, a re-evaluation of attitudes towards the country's past, and the introduction of a more liberal, open-market economic strategy at home. His policy departures were controversial and only partly implemented. During 1987 his plans for tax reform, including the introduction of a 5% value-added tax (VAT), were overturned by the Diet (parliament). Despite this defeat Nakasone remained popular and was able to select Noboru Takeshita as his successor.

Heisei era Takeshita continued Nakasone's domestic and foreign policies, introducing a 3% sales tax 1988 and lowering income-tax levels to boost domestic consumption. The new sales tax was electorally unpopular, and the government's standing during 1988–89 was further undermined by the Recruit-Cosmos insider share-dealing scandal, in which more than 40 senior LDP and opposition figures, including Takeshita, Nakasone, the deputy prime minister, and the finance and justice ministers, were implicated. The last three were forced to resign, as, eventually, was Takeshita in June 1989. This marked an inauspicious start to the new *Heisei* ('achievement of universal peace') era proclaimed on the death Jan 1989 of Hirohito (Showa) and the accession of his son Akihito as emperor. The new prime minister, Sosuke Uno, dogged by scandal and the LDP's unprecedented loss of its majority in the house of councillors, resigned Aug 1989. He was replaced by Toshiki Kaifu. Kaifu formed a new cabinet whose members were comparatively young and included two women. Kaifu having partly repaired the damage done to the LDP by the Recruit scandal, parliament was dissolved Jan 1990 and elections called for Feb. They were won by the LDP, but with large gains for the JSP. Kaifu's government was weakened when, in Nov 1990, it failed to secure parliamentary approval for the despatch of (unarmed) Japanese Self Defence Forces to the Gulf. On 12 Nov Akihito was enthroned as Japan's 125th emperor.

Jarrow Crusade a march in 1936, from Jarrow to London, protesting at the high level of unemployment following the closure of Palmer's shipyard in the town.

The march was led by Labour MP Ellen Wilkinson, and it proved a landmark event of the 1930s ◊Depression. In 1986, on the 50th anniversary of the event, a similar march was held to protest at the high levels of unemployment in the 1980s.

Jaruzelski Wojciech 1923– . Polish general, communist leader from 1981, president from 1985. He imposed martial law for the first year of his rule, suppressed the opposition, and banned trade-union activity, but later released many political prisoners. In 1989, elections in favour of the free trade union Solidarity forced Jaruzelski to speed up democratic reforms, overseeing a transition to a new form of 'socialist pluralist' democracy, stepping down as president 1990.

Jaruzelski, who served with the Soviet army 1939–43, was defence minister 1968–83 and entered the Politburo 1971. At the height of the crisis of 1980–81 he assumed power as prime minister and the Polish United Workers' Party (PUWP) first secretary; in 1985 he resigned as prime minister to become president, but remained the dominant political figure in Poland. His attempts to solve Poland's economic problems were unsuccessful.

Jellicoe John Rushworth, 1st Earl 1859–1935. British admiral who commanded the Grand Fleet 1914–16 during World War I; the only action he fought was the inconclusive battle of ◊Jutland. He was First Sea Lord 1916–17, when he failed to push the introduction of the convoy system to combat U-boat attack. Created 1st Earl 1925.

Jewish Autonomous Region part of the Khabarovsk Territory, USSR, capital Birobidzhan; area 36,000 sq km/13,900 sq mi; population (1986) 211,000. Industries include textiles, leather, metallurgy, light engineering, agriculture, and timber. It was established as a Jewish National District 1928 and became an Autonomous Region 1934 but became only nominally Jewish after the Stalinist purges 1936–47 and 1948–49.

Jiang Qing formerly ***Chiang Ching*** 1913– . Chinese communist politician, wife of the party leader Mao Zedong. In 1960 she became minister for culture, and played a key role in the 1966–69 Cultural Revolution as the leading member of the Shanghai-based ◊Gang of Four, who attempted to seize power 1976. Jiang was imprisoned.

Jiang was a Shanghai actress when in 1937 she met Mao Zedong at the communist headquarters in Yan'an; she became his third wife 1939. She emerged as a radical, egalitarian Maoist. Her influence waned during the early 1970s and her relationship with Mao became embittered. On Mao's death Sept 1976, the ◊Gang of Four with Jiang as a leading figure, sought to seize power by organizing military coups in Shanghai and Beijing. They were arrested for treason by Mao's successor Hua Guofeng and tried 1980–81. The Gang were blamed for the excesses of the Cultural

Jinnah *Muslim leader Muhammad Ali Jinnah, first governor general of the state of Pakistan.*

Revolution, but Jiang asserted during her trial that she had only followed Mao's orders as an obedient wife. This was rejected, and Jiang received a death sentence Jan 1981, which was subsequently commuted to life imprisonment.

Jinnah Muhammad Ali 1876–1948. Indian politician, Pakistan's first governor general from 1947. He was president of the ◊Muslim League from 1934, and by 1940 was advocating the need for a separate state of Pakistan; at the 1946 conferences in London he insisted on the partition of British India into Hindu and Muslim states.

John XXIII Angelo Giuseppe Roncalli 1881–1963. Pope from 1958. He improved relations with the USSR in line with his encyclical *Pacem in Terris/Peace on Earth* 1963, established Roman Catholic hierarchies in newly emergent states, and summoned the Second Vatican Council, which reformed church liturgy and backed the ecumenical movement.

John Paul II Karol Wojtyla 1920– . Pope 1978– , the first non-Italian to be elected pope since 1522. He was born near Kraków, Poland. He has upheld the tradition of papal infallibility, condemned artificial contraception, women priests, married priests, and modern dress for monks and nuns, measures which have aroused criticism from liberalizing elements in the Church. He has warned against involvement of priests in political activity.

Johnson Amy 1904–1941. British aviator. She made a solo flight from England to Australia 1930, in 19½ days, and in 1932 made the fastest ever solo flight from England to Cape Town, South Africa. Her plane disappeared over the English Channel in World War II while she was serving with the Air Transport Auxiliary.

Johnson Lyndon Baines 1908–1973. The 36th president of the USA 1963–69, a Democrat. He was born in Stonewall, Texas, elected to Congress 1937–49 and the Senate 1949–60. His persuasive powers and hard work on domestic issues led J F Kennedy to ask him to be his vice presidential running mate 1960. Johnson brought critical Southern support which won a narrow victory.

After the Tonkin Gulf Incident (in which two US destroyers were fired upon), the escalation of US involvement in the ◊Vietnam War eventually dissipated the support won by his Great Society legislation (civil rights, education, alleviation of poverty), and he declined to run for re-election 1968.

Jordan country in SW Asia, bordered N by Syria, NE by Iraq, E and SE by Saudi Arabia, S by the Gulf of Aqaba, and W by Israel.

history Palestine (the West Bank of present-day Jordan) and Transjordan (the present-day East Bank) were part of the Turkish Ottoman Empire until its dissolution after World War I. Both were then placed under British administration by the League of Nations. Transjordan acquired greater control of its own affairs than Palestine and separated from it in 1923,

Johnson *Lyndon B Johnson became president of the USA after J F Kennedy's assassination in 1963.*

achieving full independence when the British mandate expired in 1946. The mandate for Palestine ran out in 1948, whereupon Jewish leaders claimed it for a new state of Israel. The Arabs attacked Israel and fighting continued until a cease-fire was agreed in 1949. By then Transjordan forces had occupied part of Palestine to add to what they called the new state of Jordan. The following year they annexed the West Bank. In 1953 Hussein ibn Talai came to the Jordanian throne at the age of 17. In 1958 Jordan and Iraq formed an Arab Federation, that ended five months later when the Iraqi monarchy was overthrown.

the search for peace After Israel's invasion of Lebanon in 1982, Hussein played a key role in attempts to bring peace to the area, establishing a relationship with ◊Palestine Liberation Organization (PLO) leader, Yasser ◊Arafat. By 1984 the Arab world was split into two camps, with the moderates represented by Jordan, Egypt, and Arafat's PLO, and the militant radicals by Syria, Libya, and the rebel wing of the PLO. In 1985 Hussein and Arafat put together a framework for a Middle East peace settlement. It would involve bringing together all interested parties, including the PLO, but Israel objected to the PLO representation. Further progress was hampered by the PLO's alleged complicity in a number of guerrilla operations in that year. Hussein tried to revive the search for peace by secretly meeting the Israeli prime minister in France and persuading Yasser Arafat to renounce publicly, PLO violence in territories not occupied by Israel. The role of Jordan, through King Hussein, could be vital in any future peacemaking moves. In response to mounting unrest within Jordan in 1989, Hussein promised greater democratization and in Nov elections to an 80-member parliament were held. Soon afterwards the veteran politician Mudar Badran was made prime minister; he announced the lifting of martial law Dec 1989. Following the Iraqi invasion and annexation of Kuwait in Aug 1990, under popular pressure from his own country, Hussein unsuccessfully attempted to act as a mediator. Meanwhile the UN trade embargo on Iraq and the exodus of thousands of refugees into Jordan strained Jordan's resources.

July Plot or ***July Conspiracy*** an unsuccessful attempt to assassinate the German dictator Adolf Hitler and to overthrow the Nazi regime 20 July 1944. Col von Stauffenberg planted a bomb under the conference table at Hitler's headquarters at Rastenburg, East Prussia. Believing that Hitler had been killed, Stauffenberg flew to Berlin to join Field Marshall von Witzleben and General von Beck to proclaim a government headed by resistance leader and former lord mayor of Leipzig Carl Goerdeler. Hitler was only injured, telephone communications remained intact, and counter measures were taken in Berlin by Major Ernst Remer. Reprisals were savage: 150 alleged conspirators were executed, while fifteen prominent personalities, including Field Marshall Rommel, committed suicide.

Jutland, Battle of major naval battle of World War I, fought between England and Germany on 31 May 1916, off the W coast of Jutland. Despite the British having 50% more ships than the Germans, accurate German gunnery inflicted heavier casualties on the British side and the German fleet were able to return to port. The outcome of the battle was indecisive, but the German fleet remained in port for the rest of the war.

K

Kaifu Japanese conservative politician, prime minister from 1989, Toshiki Kaifu.

Kádár János 1912–1989. Hungarian Communist leader, in power 1956–88, after suppressing the national uprising. As Hungarian Socialist Workers' Party (HSWP) leader and prime minister 1956–58 and 1961–65, Kádár introduced a series of market-socialist economic reforms, while retaining cordial political relations with the USSR.

Kádár was a mechanic before joining the outlawed Communist Party and working as an underground resistance organizer in World War II. After the war he was elected to the National Assembly, served as minister for internal affairs 1948–50, and became a prominent member of the Hungarian Workers' Party (HSP). Imprisoned 1951–53 for deviation from Stalinism, Kádár was rehabilitated 1955, becoming party leader in Budapest, and in Nov 1956, at the height of the Hungarian national rising, he was appointed head of the new HSWP. With the help of Soviet troops, he suppressed the revolt. He was ousted as party general secretary May 1988, and forced into retirement May 1989.

Kaifu Toshiki 1932– . Japanese conservative politician, prime minister from 1989. A protégé of former premier Takeo Miki, he was selected as a compromise choice as Liberal Democratic Party president and prime minister in Aug 1989, following the resignation of Sosuke Uno.

Kaifu entered politics 1961, was deputy chief secretary 1974–76 in the Miki cabinet, and was education minister under Yasuhiro Nakasone. He is a member of the minor Komoto faction. In 1987 he received what he claimed were legitimate political donations amounting to £40,000 from a company later accused of bribing a number of Liberal Democratic Party (LDP) politicians. His popularity was dented by the unconstitutional proposal, defeated in the Diet, to contribute Japanese forces to the Western army in the Persian Gulf area after Iraq's annexation of Kuwait 1990.

kamikaze (Japanese 'wind of the gods') the pilots of the Japanese air force in World War II who deliberately crash-dived their planes, loaded with bombs, usually onto ships of the US Navy.

Kampuchea former name (1975-89) of Cambodia.

Katyn Massacre execution of 4,500 Polish prisoners of war in Katyn Forest near Smolensk, USSR, during World War II. In 1943, the Nazis claimed that German troops had found the mass graves of Polish officers, and accused the USSR of the massacre: the prisoners of war were captured in the German-Soviet partition of Poland 1940. 10,000 others were killed elsewhere. In 1989 the USSR accepted responsibility for the massacre.

Kaunda Kenneth (David) 1924– . Zambian politician. Imprisoned in 1958–60 as founder of the Zambia African National Congress, he became in 1964 first prime minister of Northern Rhodesia, then first president of Zambia. In 1973 he introduced one-party rule. He supported the nationalist movement in Southern Rhodesia, now ◊Zimbabwe, and survived a coup attempt 1980 thought to have been promoted by South Africa. He was elected chair of the Organization of African Unity 1987. In 1990 his popularity fell and he was faced with wide anti-government demonstrations.

Kellogg–Briand pact agreement 1927 (signed 1928) between the USA and France to renounce war and seek settlement of disputes by peaceful means. It took its name from the US secretary of state Frank B Kellogg (1856–1937) and the French foreign minister Aristide Briand. Other powers signed in Aug 1928, making a total of 67 signatories. Some successes were achieved in settling South American disputes, but the pact made no provision for measures against aggressors and became ineffective in the 1930s, with Japan in Manchuria, Italy in Ethiopia, and Hitler in central Europe.

Kennedy John F(itzgerald) 1917–1963. The 35th president of the USA 1961–63, a Democrat. Kennedy was the first Roman Catholic and the youngest person to be elected president. In foreign policy he carried through the unsuccessful ◊Bay of Pigs invasion of Cuba, and in 1963 secured the withdrawal of Soviet missiles from the island. His programme for reforms at home, called the ***New Frontier***, was posthumously executed by Lyndon Johnson. Kennedy was assassinated while on a state visit to Dallas, Texas, on 22 Nov 1963 by Lee Harvey Oswald (1939–1963), who was in turn shot dead by Jack Ruby.

Son of Joseph Kennedy, he was born in Brookline, Massachusetts, and served in the navy in the Pacific during World War II. He was elected to Congress 1946 and to the Senate 1952. In 1960 he defeated Richard Nixon for the presidency, partly as a result of televised debates, and brought academics and intellectuals to Washington as advisers.

Kennedy *The 35th president of the USA, John F Kennedy, the youngest person to hold the office. He was assassinated after less than three years in power.*

Kenya country in E Africa, bordered N by Sudan and Ethiopia, E by Somalia, SE by the Indian Ocean, SW by Tanzania, and W by Uganda.

history Kenya was a British colony 1895–1964, when it achieved full independence within the ◊Commonwealth. There was near civil war during the 20 years before independence, as nationalist groups carried out a campaign of violence. The Kenya African Union (KAU) was founded in 1944, and in 1947 Jomo ◊Kenyatta, a member of Kenya's largest ethnic group, the Kikuyu, became its president. Three years later a secret society of young Kikuyu militants was formed, called Mau Mau, that had the same aims as KAU but sought to achieve them by violent means. Although Kenyatta dissociated himself from Mau Mau, the British authorities distrusted him and imprisoned him in 1953. By 1956 the guerrilla campaign had largely ended, the state of emergency was lifted and Kenyatta was released.

independence Kenya was granted internal self-government in 1963, and Kenyatta, who had become leader of the Kenya African National Union (KANU), became prime minister and then president after full independence in 1964. Kenyatta continued as president until his death in 1978, during which time the country achieved considerable stability. He was succeeded by Vice-President Daniel arap Moi, who built on Kenyatta's achievements, launching an impressive four-year development plan.

one-party state An attempted coup by junior air force officers in 1982 was foiled and resulted in political detentions and press censorship. The air force and Nairobi University were temporarily dissolved. In the same year the national assembly declared Kenya a one-party state. President Moi was re-elected in 1983, and for a third successive term 1988; successfully tackling corruption and inefficiency in the public services and, externally, re-establishing good relations with most of his E African neighbours. In June 1989 Moi unexpectedly announced the release of all known political detainees. Kenya led the effort 1989 to ban trading in ivory after poaching became uncontrollable. The deaths of several US tourists on safari provoked President Moi to declare a war against poachers. In July 1990 there were widespread anti-government riots while more moderate elements called for a

Kenyatta *The first president of independent Kenya, Jomo Kenyatta.*

multi-party system; this has been resisted by President Moi.

Kenyatta Jomo. Assumed name of Kamau Ngengi c. 1894–1978. Kenyan nationalist politician, prime minister from 1963, as well as first president of Kenya from 1964 until his death. He led the Kenya African Union from 1947 and was active in liberating Kenya from British rule.

A member of the Kikuyu ethnic group, Kenyatta joined the Kikuyu Central Association (KCA), devoted to recovery of Kikuyu lands from white settlers, and became its president. He spent some years in Britain, returning to Kenya in 1946. He became president of the Kenya African Union (successor to the banned KCA 1947). In 1953 he was sentenced to seven years' imprisonment for his management of the guerrilla organization ◊Mau Mau, though some doubt has been cast on his complicity. Released to exile in N Kenya in 1958, he was allowed to return to Kikuyuland 1961 and in 1963 became prime minister (also president from 1964) of independent Kenya. His slogans were *'Uhuru na moja'* (Freedom and unity) and *'Harambee'* (Let's get going).

Kerensky Alexandr Feodorovich 1881–1970. Russian revolutionary politician, prime minister of the second provisional government before its collapse Nov 1917, during the ◊Russian Revolution. He was overthrown by the Bolshevik revolution, since he insisted on staying in World War I and mismanaged internal economic affairs. He fled to France 1918 and to the USA 1940.

Keynes John Maynard, 1st Baron Keynes 1883–1946. English economist, whose *The General Theory of Employment, Interest, and Money* 1936 proposed the prevention of financial crises and unemployment by adjusting demand through government control of credit and currency. He is responsible for that part of economics now known as macroeconomics.

Keynes led the British delegation at the Bretton Woods Conference 1944, which set up the International Monetary Fund. His theories were widely accepted in the aftermath of World War II, and he was one of the most influential economists of the 20th century. His ideas are today often contrasted with those of ◊monetarism.

Keynes was Fellow of King's College, Cambridge. He worked at the Treasury during World War I, and took part in the peace conference as chief Treasury representative, but resigned in protest against the financial terms of the treaty. He justified his action in *The Economic Consequences of the Peace* 1919. His later economic works aroused much controversy. Created 1st Baron 1942.

KGB the Soviet secret police, the ***Komitet Gosudarstvennoye Bezhopaznosti***/'Committee of State Security', in control of frontier and general security and the forced-labour system. KGB officers hold key appointments in all fields of daily life, reporting to administration offices in every major town. Many KGB officers are also said to hold diplomatic posts in embassies abroad. The headquarters is in Dzerzhinsky Square, Moscow.

Khaddhafi or ***Gaddafi*** or ***Qaddafi***, Moamer al 1942– . Libyan revolutionary leader. Overthrowing King Idris 1969, he became virtual president of a republic, although he nominally gave up all except an ideological role 1974. He favours territorial expansion in N Africa reaching as far as Zaïre, has supported rebels in Chad, and proposed mergers with a number of countries. His theories, based on those of the Chinese communist leader Mao Zedong, are contained in a *Green Book*.

Khmer Rouge Communist movement in Cambodia (Kampuchea) that formed the largest opposition group to the US-backed regime led by Lon Nol 1970–75. By 1974 the Khmer Rouge controlled the countryside, and in 1975 the capital, Phnom Penh, was captured and Sihanouk installed as head of state. Internal disagreements led to the creation of the Pol Pot government 1976 and mass deportations and executions. From 1978, when Vietnam invaded the country, the Khmer Rouge conducted a guerrilla campaign against the Vietnamese forces. Pol Pot retired as military leader 1985 and was succeeded by the more moderate Khieu Samphan. Following the withdrawal of Vietnamese forces in 1989, the Khmer Rouge continued its warfare against the Vietnamese-backed government making substantial advances during 1990. Its future, however, seemed imperilled by the possibility of the withdrawal of Chinese support.

Khomeini Ayatollah Ruhollah 1900–1989. Iranian Shi'ite Muslim leader, born in Khomein, central Iran. Exiled for opposition to the shah from 1964, he returned when the shah left the country 1979, and established a fundamentalist Islamic republic. His rule was marked by a protracted war with Iraq, and suppression of opposition within Iran, executing thousands of opponents.

Khrushchev Nikita Sergeyevich 1894–1971. Soviet politician, secretary general of the Communist Party 1953–64, premier 1958–64. He emerged as leader from the power struggle following ◊Stalin's death and was the first official to denounce Stalin, in 1956. His destalinization programme gave rise to revolts in Poland and Hungary 1956. Because of problems with the economy and foreign affairs (a breach with China 1960; conflict with the USA in the ◊Cuban missile crisis 1962), he was ousted by Leonid Brezhnev and Alexei Kosygin.

Born near Kursk, the son of a miner, Khrushchev fought in the post-Revolutionary civil war 1917–20, and in World War II organized the guerrilla defence of his native Ukraine. He denounced Stalinism in a secret session of the party Feb 1956. Many victims of the purges of the 1930s were either released or posthumously rehabilitated, but when Hungary revolted in Oct against Soviet domination, there was immediate Soviet intervention. In 1958 Khrushchev succeeded Bulganin as chair of the council of ministers (prime minister). His policy of competition with capitalism was successful in the space programme, which launched the world's first satellite (*Sputnik*). Because of the Cuban crisis and the personal feud with Mao Zedong that led to the Sino-Soviet split, he was compelled to resign 1964, although by 1965 his reputation was to some extent officially restored. In Apr 1989 his Feb 1956 'secret speech' against Stalin was officially published for the first time.

Kim Il Sung 1912–. North Korean Communist politician and marshal. He became prime minister 1948 and president 1972, retaining the presidency of the Communist Workers' Party. He likes to be known as the 'Great Leader' and has campaigned constantly for the reunification of Korea. His son ***Kim Jong Il*** (1942–), known as the 'Dear Leader', has been named as his successor.

King Martin Luther Jr 1929–1968. US ◊civil-rights campaigner, black leader, and Baptist minister. He first came to national attention as leader of the Montgomery, Alabama, bus boycott 1955, and was one of the organizers of the massive (200,000 people) march on Washington DC 1963 to demand racial equality. An advocate of ◊nonviolence, he was awarded the Nobel Peace Prize 1964. He was assassinated in Memphis, Tennessee by James Earl Ray. King's birthday (15 Jan) is observed on the third Monday in Jan as a public holiday in the USA.

Born in Atlanta, Georgia, son of a Baptist minister, King founded the Southern Christian Leadership Conference 1957. A brilliant and moving speaker, he was the symbol of, and leading figure in, the campaign for integration and equal rights in the late 1950s and early 1960s. In the mid-1960s his moderate approach was criticized by black militants. He was the target of intensive investigation by the federal authorities, especially the FBI under J Edgar Hoover. His personal life was scrutinized and criticized by those opposed to his policies.

Kinnock Neil 1942– . British Labour politician, party leader from 1983. Born and educated in Wales, he was elected to represent a Welsh constituency in Parliament 1970 (Islwyn from 1983). He was further left than prime ministers Harold Wilson and James Callaghan, but as party leader (in succession to Michael Foot) adopted a moderate position, he initiated the expulsion of the left-wing Militant Tendency members from the Labour Party 1986, and introduced a major policy review 1988–89.

Kissinger Henry 1923– . German-born US diplomat. He was appointed assistant for National Security Affairs in 1969 by President Nixon, and was secretary of state 1973–77. His missions to the USSR and China improved US relations with both countries, and he took part in negotiating US withdrawal from Vietnam 1973 and in Arab-Israeli peace negotiations 1973–75. Nobel Peace Prize 1973.

Born in Bavaria, Kissinger emigrated to the USA in 1938. After working in Germany for army counterintelligence, he won a scholarship to Harvard, and subsequently became a government consultant. His secret trips to Beijing and Moscow led to Nixon's visits to both countries and a general détente. In 1973 he shared a Nobel Peace Prize with Le Duc Tho, the North Vietnamese Politburo member, for his part in the Vietnamese peace negotiations, and in 1976 he was involved in the negotiations in Africa arising from the Angola and Rhodesia crises. In 1983, President Reagan appointed him to head a joint commission on Central America. He was widely regarded as the most powerful member of Nixon's administration.

Khrushchev *The Soviet politician Nikita Khrushchev at the Quai d'Orsay, Paris.*

Kohl Helmut 1930– . German conservative politician, leader of the Christian Democratic Union (CDU) from 1976, West German chancellor 1982–90 and chancellor of the newly united Germany from 1990.

Elected to the Rhineland-Palatinate *Land* (state) parliament 1959, he became state premier 1969. After the 1976 Bundestag (federal parliament) elections Kohl led the CDU in opposition. He became federal chancellor (prime minister) 1982, when the Free Democratic Party (FDP) withdrew support from the socialist Schmidt government, and was elected as the head of a new coalition that included the FDP. From 1984 Kohl was implicated in the Flick bribes scandal over the illegal business funding of political parties, but he was cleared of all charges in 1986, and was reelected chancellor Jan 1987. During 1989–90 he oversaw the reunification of Germany. In 1990 he won a resounding victory and became the first chancellor of a reunited Germany.

Komsomol Russian name for the USSR's All-Union Leninist Communist Youth League. Founded in 1918, it acts as the youth section of the Communist Party. Its activities include all forms of national service, for example, the rebuilding of Stalingrad in 1942. Membership is open to all between the ages of 14 and 26 and numbers several millions.

Korean War war 1950–53 between North Korea (supported by China) and South Korea, aided by the United Nations (the troops were mainly US). North Korean forces invaded the South 25 June 1950, and the Security Council of the United Nations, owing to a walk-out by the USSR, voted to oppose them.

By Sept 1950 the North Koreans had overrun most of the south, with the UN forces holding a small area, the Pusan perimeter, in the south east. The course of the war changed after the surprise landing of US troops later the same month at Inchon on South Korea's NW coast. The troops, led by General Douglas MacArthur, fought their way through North Korea to the Chinese border in little over a month. On 25 Oct 1950 Chinese troops attacked across the Yalu River, driving the UN forces below the 38th parallel. Truce talks began in July 1951, and the war ended two years later, with the restoration of the original boundary on the 38th parallel.

Kosygin Alexei Nikolaievich 1904–1980. Soviet politician, prime minister 1964–80. He was elected to the Supreme Soviet 1938, became a member of the Politburo 1946, deputy prime minister 1960, and succeeded Khrushchev as premier (while Brezhnev succeeded him as party secretary). In the late 1960s Kosygin's influence declined.

Kronstadt uprising revolt in Mar 1921 by sailors of the Russian Baltic Fleet at their headquarters in Kronstadt, outside Petrograd (now Leningrad). On the orders of the leading Bolshevik Leon Trotsky, Red Army troops, dressed in white camouflage, crossed the ice to the naval base and captured it on 18 Mar. The leaders were subsequently shot.

Following a strike by Petrograd workers in Feb 1921, the Kronstadt sailors reaffirmed their demands for the rights obtained in theory by the Revolution of 1917. The sailors were thus labelled the 'conscience of the Revolution' for demanding what had been promised, but not delivered, by the Bolsheviks. The sailors were also perceived as a threat by the Bolsheviks, because of their detection and resentment of the growing Bolshevik monopoly of power.

Ku Klux Klan US secret society dedicated to white supremacy, founded 1866 in the southern states of the USA to oppose Reconstruction after the Civil War and to deny political rights to the black population. Members wore hooded white robes to hide their identity, and burned crosses as a rite of intimidation. It was active in the 1960s in terrorizing civil-rights activists and organizing racist demonstrations.

kulak Russian term for a peasant who could afford to hire labour and often acted as village usurer. The kulaks resisted the Soviet government's policy of collectivization, and in 1930 they were 'liquidated as a class', with up to 5 million being either killed or deported to Siberia.

Kuomintang original name of Chinese nationalist party, now known (outside Taiwan) as ◊Guomindang.

Kursk capital city of Kursk region of the USSR; site of a railway junction occupied by the German army 1941. In World War II it was close to the site of a major tank battle 5–15 July 1943 between the Red Army and Hitler's German forces. The Germans, under General Model, launched their last Russian offensive ('Operation Citadel') against the railway junction at Kursk. The Russians had, under Marshal Zhukov, anticipated the German plan, and completely overwhelmed their forces. The German losses of 70,000 men, 1,000 tanks, and 1,000 aircraft made it impossible for them to renew an offensive on the Eastern Front.

Kuwait country in SW Asia, bordered N and NW by Iraq, E by the Persian Gulf, and S and SW by Saudi Arabia.

history The region was part of the Turkish ◊Ottoman Empire from the 16th century; the ruling family founded the sheikdom of Kuwait 1756. The ruler made a treaty with Britain 1899 enabling it to become a self-governing protectorate until it achieved full independence 1961. Oil was first discovered 1938, and its large-scale exploitation began after 1945, transforming Kuwait City from a small fishing port into a thriving commercial centre. The oil revenues have enabled ambitious public works and education programmes to be undertaken. Sheik Abdullah al-Salem al-Sabah took the title of emir 1961 when he assumed full executive powers. He died 1965 and was succeeded by his brother, Sheik Sabah al-Salem al-Sabah. He, in turn, died 1977 and was succeeded by Crown Prince Jabir, who appointed Sheik Saad al-Abdullah al-Salem al-Sabah as his heir apparent. In Jan 1990 pro-democracy demonstrations were dispersed by the police. Kuwait has used its considerable wealth not only to improve its infrastructure and social services but also to secure its borders, making, for example, substantial donations to Iraq, which in the past had made territorial claims on it. It has also been a strong supporter of the Arab cause generally.

the Iran–Iraq War During the 1980–88 Iran–Iraq war, Kuwait was the target of destabilization efforts by the revolutionary Iranian government. Shi'ite terrorists conducted a bombing campaign as part of an effort to incite the Shi'ite minority in Kuwait. Seventeen were arrested 1983 and their freedom was the demand in several hijacking incidents that followed. In 1987 Kuwait sought US protection for its tankers in the wake of attacks on Gulf shipping. Several Kuwaiti tankers were 'reflagged', and the US Navy conducted convoys through the Gulf. Iranian missiles also struck Kuwaiti installations, provoking fears of an expansion of the conflict. Kuwait released two of the convicted bombers Feb 1989.

the Gulf War On 2 Aug 1990 President Hussein of Iraq reactivated a long-standing territorial dispute and invaded and occupied the country. The emir and most of his family escaped to Saudi Arabia. The occupation 2 Aug 1990–27 Feb 1991 was characterized by brutal repression and terrorizing of the inhabitants. Before its expulsion Feb 1991 by coalition forces acting under UN authority, Iraqi forces had caused huge structural and ecological damage. The resumption of normal life will be a severe test of Kuwait's absolutist form of government.

L

Labor Party in Australia, political party based on socialist principles. It was founded 1891 and first held office 1904. It formed governments 1929–31 and 1939–49, but in the intervening periods internal discord provoked splits, and reduced its effectiveness. It returned to power under Gough Whitlam 1972–75, and again under Bob Hawke from 1983.

Labour Party UK political party based on socialist principles, originally formed to represent workers. It was founded 1900 and first held office 1924. The first majority Labour government 1945–51 introduced ◊nationalization and the National ◊Health Service, and expanded ◊social security. Labour was again in power 1964–70 and 1974–79. The party leader is elected by Labour members of Parliament. Neil Kinnock became leader 1983.

The Labour Party, the Trades Union Congress, and the cooperative movement together form the National Council of Labour, whose aims are to coordinate political activities and take joint action on specific issues.

Although the Scottish socialist Keir Hardie and John Burns, a workers' leader, entered Parliament independently as Labour members 1892, it was not until 1900 that a conference representing the trade unions, the Independent Labour Party (ILP), and the Fabian Society founded the Labour Party, known until 1906, when 29 seats were gained, as the Labour Representation Committee. All but a pacifist minority of the Labour Party supported World War I, and in 1918 a socialist programme was first adopted, with local branches of the party set up to which individual members were admitted.

By 1922 the Labour Party was recognized as the official opposition, and in 1924 formed a minority government (with Liberal support) for a few months under the party's first secretary Ramsay MacDonald. A second minority government 1929 followed a conservative policy, and in 1931 MacDonald and other leaders, faced with a financial crisis, left the party to support the national government. The ILP withdrew 1932. In 1936–39 there was internal dissension on foreign policy; the leadership's support of nonintervention in Spain was strongly criticized and Stafford Cripps, Aneurin Bevan, and others were expelled for advocating an alliance of all left-wing parties against Neville Chamberlain's government.

The Labour Party supported Churchill's wartime coalition, but then withdrew and took office for the first time as a majority government under Clement Attlee, party leader from 1935, after the 1945 elections. The welfare state was developed by nationalization of essential services and industries, a system of national insurance 1946, and the National Health Service 1948. Defeated 1951, Labour was split by disagreements on further nationalization, and unilateral or multilateral disarmament, but achieved unity under Hugh Gaitskell's leadership 1955–63.

Under Harold Wilson the party returned to power 1964–70 and, with a very slender majority, 1974–79. James Callaghan, who had succeeded Wilson 1976, was forced to a general election 1979 and lost. Michael Foot was elected to the leadership 1980; Neil Kinnock succeeded him 1983 after Labour had lost another general election. The party adopted a policy of unilateral nuclear disarmament 1986 and expelled the left-wing faction Militant Tendency, but rifts remained. Labour lost the 1987 general election, a major reason being their non-nuclear policy.

Lahore Resolution a meeting in Lahore March 1940 at which the Indian politician Muhammad Ali Jinnah led the ◊Muslim League in demanding the eventual partition of India and the creation of a muslim state of 'Pakistan'.

Laos landlocked country in SE Asia, bordered N by China, E by Vietnam, S by Cambodia, and W by Thailand.

history Laos became an independent kingdom in the 14th century and was first visited by Europeans in the 17th century, becoming a French protectorate 1893–1945. After a brief period of Japanese occupation, France re-established control 1946 despite opposition from the Chinese-backed Lao Issara (Free Laos) nationalist movement. The country became semi-autonomous 1950, when, under the constitutional monarchy of the king of

Luang Prabang, it became an associated state of the French Union.

civil war In 1954, after the Geneva Agreements, Laos gained full independence. Civil war broke out between two factions of former Lao Issara supporters: a moderate, royalist-neutralist group led by Prince Souvanna Phouma, which had supported the 1950 French compromise and was the recognized government for most of the country; and a more extreme Communist resistance group, the Pathet Lao (Land of the Lao), led by ex-Prince Souphanouvong (the half-brother of Prince Souvanna) and supported by China and the ◊Vietminh, which controlled much of N Laos. A coalition government was established after the 1957 Vientiane Agreement. This soon collapsed, and in 1960 a third, right-wing force emerged when General Phoumi Nosavan, backed by the royal army, overthrew Souvanna Phouma and set up a pro-Western government headed by Prince Boun Gum. A new Geneva Agreement 1962 established a tripartite (right-left-neutral) government under the leadership of Prince Souvanna Phouma. Fighting continued, however, between the North Vietnamese–backed Pathet Lao and the US-backed neutralists and right wing, until the 1973 Vientiane Agreement established a ceasefire line dividing the country NW to SE, giving the Communists two-thirds of the country, including the Plain of Jars and the Bolovens Plateau in the south, but giving the Souvanna Phouma government two-thirds of the population. All foreign forces (North Vietnamese, Thai, and US) were to be withdrawn, and both sides received equal representation in Souvanna Phouma's provisional government 1974.

the republic In 1975 the Communist Pathet Lao (renamed the Lao People's Front) seized power. King Savang Vatthana (1908–80), who had succeeded 1959, abdicated, and Laos became a People's Democratic Republic under the presidency of Prince Souphanouvong. Prince Souvanna Phouma remained as an 'adviser' to the government, but the real controlling force was now the prime minister and communist party leader, Kaysone Phomvihane.

reform The new administration, which inherited a poor, war-ravaged economy, attempted to reorganize the country along Socialist lines, nationalizing businesses and industries and collectivizing agriculture. Further 'liberalization' followed from 1985 under the prompting of the Soviet leader Mikhail Gorbachev, with a new profit-related 'socialist business accounting system' being adopted. In March 1989, multi-party elections were held for the first time since the Communists came to power 1975, with the Communists retaining political control. In Aug 1989 party-to-party relations were established with China after a ten-year break. A draft constitution was published June 1990.

Lateran Treaties series of agreements that marked the reconciliation of the Italian state with the papacy 1929. They were hailed as a propaganda victory for the Fascist regime. The treaties involved recognition of the sovereignty of the ◊Vatican City State, the payment of an indemnity for papal possessions lost during unification in 1870, and agreement on the role of the Catholic church within the Italian state in the form of a concordat between Pope Pius XI and the dictator Mussolini.

Lausanne, Treaty of peace settlement 1923 between Greece and Turkey after Turkey refused to accept the terms of the Treaty of Sèvres 1920, which would have made peace with the western Allies. It involved the surrender by Greece of Smyrna (now Izmir) to Turkey and the enforced exchange of the Greek population of Smyrna for the Turkish population of Greece.

Laval Pierre 1883–1945. French right-wing politician. He was prime minister and foreign secretary 1931–32, and again 1935–36. In World War II he joined Henri Pétain's ◊Vichy government as vice-premier June 1940; dismissed Dec 1940, he was reinstated by Hitler's orders as head of the government and foreign minister 1942.

Laval, born near Vichy, entered the chamber of deputies 1914 as a socialist, but after World War I moved towards the right. His second period as prime minister was marked by the ◊Hoare–Laval Pact for concessions to Italy in Abyssinia (Ethiopia). His part in the deportation of French labour to Germany during World War II made him universally hated. When the Allies invaded, he fled the country but was arrested in Austria, tried for treason, and shot after trying to poison himself.

Lawrence T(homas) E(dward), known as ***Lawrence of Arabia*** 1888–1935. British soldier and writer. Appointed to the military intelligence department in Cairo, Egypt, during World War I, he took part in negotiations for an Arab revolt against the Ottoman Turks, and in 1916 attached himself to the emir Faisal. He became a guerrilla leader of genius, combining raids on Turkish communications with the organization of a joint Arab revolt, described in *The Seven Pillars of Wisdom* 1935.

League of Nations international organization formed after World War I to solve international disputes by arbitration. The league included representatives from states throughout the world, but was severely weakened by the US decision not to become a member, and had no power to enforce its decisions. It was dissolved 1946.

The League of Nations was suggested in US president Woodrow Wilson's 'Fourteen Points' 1917 as part of the peace settlement for World War I. The league covenant was drawn up by the Paris peace conference 1919 and incorporated into the Versailles and other peace treaties. The member states undertook to preserve the territorial integrity of all, and to submit international disputes to the league. There were a number of important subsidiary organizations:

International Labour Organization (ILO) formed 1920, based in Geneva and concerned primarily with working conditions and social welfare.

High Commission for Refugees (Nansen Office) created to assist refugees, primarily from the USSR and Eastern Europe. Built on the work of the Norwegian explorer Fridtjof Nansen as first high commissioner, the High Commission declined in importance after his death and the entry of the USSR to the league. It formed the basis for post-1945 refugee work by the United Nations.

Permanent Court of Justice created in The Hague 1921 and based on ideas for some form of international court put forward at the Hague congress 1907; now known as the International Court of Justice (see ◊United Nations).

The league enjoyed some success in the humanitarian field (international action against epidemics, drug traffic, and the slave trade), in organizing population exchanges after the Paris peace conferences had established new national boundaries, and in deferring arguments over disputed territories and former German colonies by mandating a league member to act as a caretaker of administration for a specified period of time, or until a permanent solution could be found. Mandates were created for Palestine (Britain), SW Africa (South Africa), and the free city of Danzig (Gdańsk).

In the political and diplomatic field, the league was permanently hampered by internal rivalries and the necessity for unanimity in the decision-making process. No action was taken against Japan's aggression in Manchuria 1931; attempts to impose sanctions against Italy for the invasion of Ethiopia 1935–36 collapsed; no actions were taken when Germany annexed Austria and Czechoslovakia, nor when Poland was invaded. Japan 1932 and Germany 1933 simply withdrew from the league, and the expulsion of the USSR 1939 had no effect on the Russo-Finnish war. Long before the outbreak of World War II, diplomacy had abandoned international security and reverted to a system of direct negotiation and individual alliances.

Lebanon country in W Asia, bordered N and E by Syria, S by Israel, and W by the Mediterranean.

history Lebanon was part of the Ottoman Empire from the 16th century, until administered by France under a League of Nations mandate 1920–41. It was declared independent 1941 and achieved full autonomy 1944. Lebanon has a great variety of religions, including Christianity and many Islamic sects. For many years these coexisted peacefully, giving Lebanon a stability that enabled it, until the mid-1970s, to be a commercial and financial centre.

period of turmoil After the establishment of Israel 1948, thousands of Palestinian refugees fled to Lebanon. The presence of the Palestinian Liberation Organization in Lebanon has been the main reason for Israeli invasions and much of the subsequent civil strife. Fighting has been largely between left-wing Muslims of the Progressive Socialist Party, and conservative Christian groups, mainly members of the Phalangist Party. There have also been differences between pro-Iranian traditional Muslims, such as the Shi'ites and Syrian-backed Muslims, such as the Druse. The turmoil and armed conflict between the various factions has contributed to, and been exacerbated by, foreign intervention at various times by the USA, Syria, and Israel, and also by the United Nations. Lebanon, and particularly Beirut, has seen its infrastructure and earlier prosperity virtually destroyed as it continues to be a battlefield for rival factions.

Lebensraum (German 'living space') theory developed by Hitler for the expansion of Germany into E Europe, and in the 1930s used by the Nazis to justify their annexation of neighbouring states on the grounds that Germany was overpopulated.

left wing in politics, the socialist parties. The term originated in the French National Assembly 1789, where the nobles sat in the place of honour to the right of the president, and the commons sat to the left. It is also usual to speak of the right, left, and centre, when referring to the different elements composing a single party.

lend-lease an Act of the US congress Mar 1941 that gave the president power to order 'any defense article for the government of any country whose defense the president deemed vital to the defense of the USA'. During World War II, the USA negotiated many Lend-Lease agreements, most notably with Britain and the Soviet Union.

The aim of such agreements was to ignore trade balances among the participating countries during the war effort and to aid the Allied war effort without fanning isolationist sentiments. Lend-lease was officially stopped Aug 1945, by which time goods and services to the value of $42 billion had been supplied in this way, of which the British Empire had received 65% and the Soviet Union 23%.

Lenin Vladimir Ilyich. Adopted name of Vladimir Ilyich Ulyanov 1870–1924. Russian revolutionary, first leader of the USSR, and communist theoretician. Active in the 1905 Revolution, Lenin had to leave Russia when it failed, settling in Switzerland 1914. He returned to Russia after the February revolution of 1917 (see ◊Russian Revolution). He led the Bolshevik revolution in Nov 1917 and became leader of a Soviet government, concluded peace with Germany, and organized a successful resistance to White Russian (protsarist) uprisings and foreign intervention 1918–20. His modification of traditional Marxist doctrine to fit conditions prevailing in Russia became known as ***Marxism-Leninism***, the basis of communist ideology.

Lenin was born in Simbirsk (now renamed Ulyanovsk), and became a lawyer in St Petersburg (now Leningrad). His brother was executed in 1887 for attempting to assassinate Tsar Alexander III. A Marxist from 1889, Lenin was sent to Siberia for spreading revolutionary propaganda 1895–1900. He then edited the political paper *Iskra* ('The Spark') from abroad, and visited London several times. In *What Is to be Done?* 1902 he advocated a professional core of Social Democratic Party activists to spearhead the revolution in Russia, a suggestion accepted by the majority (*bolsheviki*) at the London party congress 1903. From Switzerland he attacked socialist support for World War I as aiding an 'imperialist' struggle, and wrote *Imperialism* 1917. After the renewed outbreak of revolution in Feb/Mar 1917, he returned to Russia in Apr and called for the transfer of power to the soviets (workers' councils). From the overthrow of the provisional government Nov 1917 until his death, Lenin effectively controlled the Soviet Union, although an assassination attempt 1918 injured his health. He founded the Third (Communist) International in 1919. Communism proving inadequate to put the country on its feet, in 1921 he introduced the private-enterprise ◊New Economic Policy. His embalmed body is in a mausoleum in Red Square, Moscow.

Leningrad capital of the Leningrad region, at the head of the Gulf of Finland. Originally called ***St Petersburg***, it was renamed ***Petrograd*** 1914 and ***Leningrad*** 1924.

history During the German invasion in World War II the city withstood siege and bombardment Sept 1941–Jan 1944. Over 100,000 bombs were dropped by the Luftwaffe, and 150,000–200,000 shells were fired, but most deaths (estimate 1 million) resulted from famine and cold. In 1943 Soviet counter attacks began but the siege was not completely lifted until Jan 1944.

less developed country any country late in developing an industrial base, and dependent on cash crops and unprocessed minerals. The Group of 77 was established 1964 to pressure industrialized countries into giving greater aid to less developed countries.

liberalism political and social theory that favours representative government, freedom of the press, speech, and worship, the abolition of class privileges, the use of state resources to protect the welfare of the individual, and international ◊free trade. It is historically associated with the Liberal Party in the UK and the Democratic Party in the USA.

Liberalism developed during the 17th–19th centuries as the distinctive theory of the industrial and commercial classes in their struggle against the power of the monarchy, the church, and the feudal landowners. Economically it was associated with *laissez-faire*, or nonintervention. In the late 19th and early 20th centuries its ideas were modified by the acceptance of universal suffrage and a certain amount of state intervention in economic affairs, in order to ensure a minimum standard of living and to remove extremes of poverty and wealth. The classic statement of liberal principles is found in *On Liberty* and other works of the British philosopher J S Mill.

Liberal Party in the UK, a political party, the successor to the Whig Party, with an ideology of liberalism. In the 19th century it was the party of the left, representing the interests of commerce and industry. From 1914 it declined, and the rise of the Labour Party pushed the Liberals into the middle ground. The Liberals joined forces with the Social Democratic Party (SDP) as the Alliance for the 1983 and 1987 elections. In 1988, a majority of the SDP voted to merge with the Liberals to form the Social and Liberal Democrats.

In 1906, after 11 years in opposition, the Liberals came to power with a huge majority, reinforced by Labour and Irish support. Old-age pensions, National Insurance, limitation of the powers of the Lords, and the Irish Home Rule Bill followed. David Lloyd George's alliance with the Conservatives 1916–22 divided them between him and his predecessor Henry Asquith, and although reunited by 1923 the Liberals continued to lose votes. They briefly joined the National Government 1931–32. After World War II they were reduced to a handful of members of Parliament. A revival began under the leadership 1956–67 of Jo Grimond and continued under Jeremy Thorpe, who resigned after a period of controversy within the party 1976. After a caretaker return by Grimond, David Steel became the first party leader in British politics to be elected by party members who were not MPs. In 1977–78 Steel entered into an agreement to support Labour in any vote of confidence in return for consultation on measures undertaken. He resigned 1988 and was replaced by Paddy Ashdown.

Libya country in N Africa, bordered N by the Mediterranean, E by Egypt, SE by Sudan, S by Chad and Niger, and W by Algeria and Tunisia.

history From the 16th century Libya was part of the Turkish Ottoman Empire. In 1911 it was conquered by Italy, becoming known as Libya from 1934. After being the scene of much fighting during World War II, in 1942 it was divided into three provinces: Fezzan, which was placed under French control; Cyrenaica; and Tripolitania, which was placed under British control. In 1951 it achieved independence as the United Kingdom of Libya, Muhammad Idris-as-Sanusi becoming King Idris. The country enjoyed internal and external stability until a bloodless revolution 1969, led by young nationalist officers, deposed the king and proclaimed a Libyan Arab Republic. Power was vested in a Revolution Command Council (RCC), chaired by Col Moamer al-Khaddhafi, with the Arab Socialist Union (ASU) as the only political party. Khaddhafi soon began proposing schemes for Arab unity, none of which was permanently adopted. In 1972 he planned a federation of Libya, Syria, and Egypt and later that year a merger between Libya and Egypt. In 1980 he proposed a union with Syria and in 1981 with Chad.

Islamic socialism Khaddhafi tried to run the country on Socialist Islamic lines, with people's committees pledged to socialism and the teachings of the Koran. The 1977 constitution made him secretary-general of the general secretariat of the GPC, but in 1979 he resigned the post in order to devote more time to 'preserving the revolution'. His attempts to establish himself as a leader of the Arab world have brought him into conflict with Western powers, particularly the USA. The Reagan administration objected to Libya's presence in Chad and its attempts to unseat the French-US-sponsored government of President Habré.

In Jan 1989 Khaddaffi resisted the urge to respond to the shooting-down of two of his fighters off the Libyan coast by the US navy and has worked steadily at improving external relations, particularly in the Arab world, effecting a reconciliation with Egypt in Oct 1989. For the USA and other western nations, Khaddhafi remains suspect, and US intelligence official released evidence that Libya intended to produce chemical weapons.

Lidice Czechoslovak mining village, destroyed by the Nazis 10 June 1942 as a reprisal for the assassination of Reinhard Heydrich. The men were shot, the women sent to concentration camps, and the children taken to Germany. The officer responsible was hanged 1946. The village of Lezaky was also destroyed.

Li Xiannian 1905–. Chinese politician, member of the Chinese Communist Party (CCP) Politburo from 1956. He fell from favour during the 1966–69 Cultural Revolution, but was rehabilitated as finance minister 1973, supporting cautious economic reform. He was state president 1983–88.

Li, born into a poor peasant family in Hubei province, joined the CCP 1927 and served as a political commissar during the ◊Long March of 1934–36. During the 1950s and early 1960s Li was vice premier to the State Council and minister for finance and was inducted into the CCP Politburo and secretariat in 1956 and 1958 respectively. He retains a seat on the Politburo's standing committee and chairs the Chinese People's Political Consultative Conference.

Lloyd George David 1863–1945. Welsh Liberal politician, prime minister 1916–22. A pioneer of social reform, as chancellor of the Exchequer 1908–15 he introduced old-age pensions 1908 and health and unemployment insurance 1911. High unemployment, intervention in the Russian Civil War, and use of the military police force (the Black and Tans) in Ireland eroded his support as prime minister, and creation of the Irish Free State 1921 and his pro-Greek policy against the Turks caused the collapse of his coalition government.

Lloyd George was born in Manchester, became a solicitor, and was member of Parliament for Caernarvon Boroughs from 1890. During the Boer War, he was prominent as a pro-Boer. His 1909 Peoples' Budget (with graduated direct taxes and taxing land values) provoked the Lords to reject it, and resulted in the Act of 1911 limiting their powers. He held ministerial posts during World War I until 1916 when there was an open breach between him and prime minister Henry ◊Asquith, and he became prime minister of a coalition government. Securing a unified Allied command, he enabled the Allies to withstand the last German offensive and achieve victory. After World War I he had a major role in the ◊Versailles peace treaty.

Locarno, Pact of series of diplomatic documents initialled in Locarno 16 Oct 1925 and formally signed in London 1 Dec 1925. The pact settled the question of French security, and the signatories – Britain, France, Belgium, Italy, and Germany – guaranteed Germany's existing frontiers with France and Belgium. Following the signing of the pact, Germany was admitted to the ◊League of Nations. Hitler disregarded the 'spirit of Locarno' when he sent his troops in to the demobilized Rhinelands in 1936.

London, Treaty of secret treaty signed 26 Apr 1915 between Britain, France, Russia, and Italy. It promised Italy territorial gains (at the expense of Austria-Hungary) on condition that it entered World War I on the side of the Triple Entente (Britain, France, and Russia). Italy's intervention did not achieve the rapid victories expected, and the terms of the treaty (revealed by Russia 1918), angered the USA. Britain and France refused to honour the treaty and, in the post-war peace treaties, Italy received far less territory than promised.

Long Huey 1893–1935. US Democratic politician, nicknamed 'the Kingfish', governor of Louisiana 1928–31, US senator for Louisiana 1930–35. A legendary public speaker, he was popular with poor white voters for his programme of social and economic reform, which he called the 'Share Our Wealth' programme, and which represented a significant challenge to Roosevelt's ◊New Deal economic programme, but his own extravagance, including the state capitol building at Baton Rouge built of bronze and marble, was widely criticized, and he was also accused of corruption. He was assassinated.

Long March in Chinese history, the 10,000 km/6,000 mi trek undertaken 1934–35 by ◊Mao Zedong and his Communist forces from SE to NW China, under harassment from the Nationalist army.

Some 100,000 Communists left Jiangxi, Mao's first headquarters, in Oct 1934 and only 8,000 lasted the journey to arrive about a year later in Shanxi, which became their new base. The march cemented Mao Zedong's control of the movement. See also ◊Chinese Revolution.

The ***New Long March*** is China's plan to achieve world leadership in science and technology by the year 2000.

Ludendorff Erich von 1865–1937. German general, chief of staff to ◊Hindenburg in World War I, and responsible for the eastern-front victory at the Battle of ◊Tannenberg 1914. After Hindenburg's appointment as chief of general staff and Ludendorff's as quartermaster-general 1916, he was also politically influential. He took part in the Nazi rising in Munich 1923 and sat in the Reichstag (parliament) as a right-wing Nationalist.

Lusitania ocean liner sunk by a German submarine 7 May 1915 with the loss of 1,200 lives, including some Americans; its destruction helped bring the USA into World War I.

Luxemburg Rosa 1870–1919. Polish-born German communist, a leader of the left wing of the German Social Democratic Party from 1898 and collaborator with Karl Liebknecht in founding the communist Spartacus League in 1918 (see ◊Spartacist). She was murdered with him by army officers during the Jan 1919 Berlin workers' revolt.

M

MacArthur Douglas 1880–1964. US general in World War II, commander of US forces in the Far East and, from Mar 1942, of the Allied forces in the SW Pacific. After the surrender of Japan he commanded the Allied occupation forces there.

The son of an army officer, born in Arkansas, MacArthur became chief of staff 1930–35. He defended the Philippines against the Japanese 1941–42 and escaped to Australia. He was responsible for the reconquest of New Guinea 1942–45 and of the Philippines 1944–45, being appointed general of the army 1944. As commander of the UN forces in the Korean War, he invaded the North 1950 until beaten back by Chinese troops; his threats to bomb China were seen as liable to start another world war and he was removed from command by President Truman in Apr 1951, but received a hero's welcome on his return to the USA.

MacArthur US general Douglas MacArthur in 1945. He had been Allied commander in the SW Pacific area since 1942 and helped mastermind the defeat of Japan in World War II.

McCarthy Eugene Joseph 1916– . US politician. Born in Watkins, Minnesota, McCarthy received a master's degree in economics from the University of Minnesota. Active in the Democratic-Farmer-Labor party, he was elected to the US House of Representatives 1948 and to the US Senate 1958. An early opponent of the Vietnam War, he consolidated widespread opposition to the war when he ran for president 1968. Although his victory in the New Hampshire primary forced incumbent Lyndon Johnson out of the race, McCarthy lost the presidential nomination to Hubert Humphrey.

McCarthy Joe (Joseph Raymond) 1908–1957. US right-wing Republican politician, whose unsubstantiated claim 1950 that the State Department and US army had been infiltrated by Communists started a wave of anticommunist hysteria, wild accusations, and blacklists, which continued until he was discredited 1954. He was censured by the US senate for misconduct.

A lawyer, McCarthy became senator for his native Wisconsin in 1946, and in Feb 1950 caused a sensation by claiming to hold a list of about 200 Communist party members working in the State Department. McCarthy continued a witch-hunting campaign against, amongst others, members of President ◊Truman's administration. When he turned his attention to the army, and it was shown that he and his aides had been falsifying evidence, then President Eisenhower renounced him and his tactics. By this time, however, many people in public life and the arts had been unofficially blacklisted as suspected Communists or fellow travellers (Communist sympathizers). ***McCarthyism*** came to represent the practice of using innuendo and unsubstantiated accusations against political adversaries.

MacDonald (James) Ramsay 1866–1937. British politician, first Labour prime minister Jan–Oct 1924 and 1929–31. He joined the ◊Independent Labour Party 1894, and became first secretary of the new Labour Party 1900. In Parliament he led the party 1906–14 and 1922–31 and was prime minister of the first two Labour governments. Failing to deal with worsening economic conditions, he left the party to form a coalition government 1931, which was increasingly dominated by Conservatives, until he was replaced by Stanley Baldwin 1935.

MacDonald was born in Scotland, the son of a labourer. He was elected to Parliament 1906, and led the party until 1914, when his opposition to World War I lost him the leadership. This he recovered 1922, and in Jan 1924 he formed a government dependent on the support of the Liberal Party. When this was withdrawn in Oct the same year, he was forced to resign. He returned to office 1929, again as leader of a minority government, which collapsed 1931 as a result of the economic crisis. MacDonald left the Labour Party to form a national government with backing from both Liberal and Conservative parties. He resigned the premiership 1935.

Macmillan (Maurice) Harold, 1st Earl of Stockton 1894–1986. British prime minister 1957–63. Conservative MP for Stockton 1924–29 and 1931–45; and for Bromley 1945–64. As minister of housing 1951–54 he achieved the construction of 300,000 new houses a year. He became foreign secretary 1955 and was chancellor of the Exchequer 1955–57. He became prime minister on the resignation of Anthony Eden after the Suez crisis. Macmillan led the Conservative Party to victory in the 1959 elections on the slogan 'You've never had it so good' (the phrase was borrowed from a US election campaign). Internationally, his realization of the 'wind of change' in Africa advanced the independence of former colonies. In 1963 he attempted to negotiate British entry to the European Economic Community, but was blocked by the French president de Gaulle. Much of his career as prime minister was spent trying to maintain a UK nuclear weapon, and he was responsible for the purchase of US Polaris missiles 1962. Macmillan's nickname Supermac was coined by the cartoonist Vicky. Created 1st Earl of Stockton 1984.

Mafia (Italian 'swank') secret society reputed to control organized crime such as gambling, loansharking, drug traffic, prostitution, and protection. It originated in 15th-century Sicily and now operates chiefly there and in US cities; connected with the Camorra (a secret society) of Naples.

It began as a secret society that avenged wrongs against Sicilian peasants by means of terror and vendetta. In 19th-century Sicily the Mafia was employed by absentee landlords to manage their *latifundia* (landed estates), and through intimidation it soon became the unofficial ruling group. The *latifundia* were dispossessed and divided up after World War II; however, the Mafia remains powerful in Sicily. The Italian government has waged periodic campaigns of suppression, notably 1927, when the Fascist leader Mussolini appointed Cesare Mori (1872–?) as prefect of Palermo. Mori's methods were, however, as suspect as those of the people he was arresting, and he was fired 1929. A further campaign was waged 1963–64.

The Mafia spread through immigration, mainly to the USA, where it grew during ◊Prohibition. Main centres are New York, Las Vegas, Miami, Atlantic City, and Chicago. A code of loyalty and secrecy, combined with the intimidation of witnesses, makes it difficult to bring criminal charges against its members.

Maginot Line French fortification system along the German frontier from Switzerland to Luxembourg built 1929–36 under the direction of the war minister, André Maginot. It consisted of semi-underground forts joined by underground passages, and protected by anti-tank defences; lighter fortifications continued the line to the sea. In 1940 German forces pierced the Belgian frontier line and outflanked the Maginot Line.

Major John 1943– . British Conservative politician, foreign secretary 1989, chancellor of the Exchequer 1989–90, and elected prime minister in the Conservative party leadership election in November 1990.

Formerly a banker, he became member of Parliament for Huntingdonshire in 1979 and

Major *British Conservative prime minister, John Major, elected in the Conservative party leadership election of November 1990.*

joined the government in 1981, becoming deputy to Chancellor Nigel Lawson 1987. In 1989 Major was promoted to foreign secretary and, after Lawson's resignation, to chancellor, within the space of six months. As chancellor he led Britain into the European Exchange Rate Mechanism (ERM) in Oct 1990. He was elected prime minister in a leadership contest with Michael Heseltine and Douglas Hurd following the resignation of Margaret Thatcher the previous month. His stated policies aim for an open, compassionate society and a reduction in inflation, and he brings a positive yet compromising approach to economic and monetary union with Europe.

Makarios III 1913–1977. Cypriot politician, Greek Orthodox archbishop 1950–77. A leader of the Resistance organization ◊EOKA, he was exiled by the British to the Seychelles 1956–57 for supporting armed action to achieve union with Greece (*enosis*). He was president of the republic of Cyprus 1960–77 (briefly deposed by a Greek military coup July–Dec 1974).

Malawi country in SE Africa, bordered N and NE by Tanzania; E, S and W by Mozambique; and W by Zambia.

history The Portuguese, in the 17th century, were the first Europeans to visit the area, but Britain intervened and, in 1891 annexed the country, making it the British protectorate of Nyasaland from 1907. Between 1953 and 1964 it was part of the Federation of Rhodesia and Nyasaland, which comprised the territory that is now Zimbabwe, Zambia, and Malawi.

independence Dr Hastings Banda, through the Malawi Congress Party, led a campaign for independence, and in 1963 the federation was dissolved. Nyasaland became independent as Malawi in 1964 and two years later became a republic and a one-party state, with Banda as its first president. He has governed his country in a very individual way, tolerating no opposition, and his foreign policies have at times been rather idiosyncratic. He astonished his black African colleagues in 1967 by officially recognizing the Republic of South Africa, and in 1971 became the first African head of state to visit that country. In 1976, however, he also recognized the Communist government in Angola. Banda keeps a tight control over his government colleagues, and, as yet, no successor has emerged. In 1977 he embarked upon a policy of cautious liberalism, releasing some political detainees and allowing greater press freedom. His external policies are based on a mixture of national self-interest and practical reality and have enabled Malawi to live in reasonable harmony with its neighbours. Malawi adopted an 'open-door' policy towards refugees fleeing the civil war in neighbouring Mozambique; about 70,000 refugees crossed the border Sept 1986. By 1988 one in ten of the population of eight million was a Mozambican.

Malaysia country in SE Asia, comprising the Malay Peninsula, bordered N by Thailand, and surrounded E, S, and W by the South China Sea; and the states of Sabah and Sarawak in the northern part of the island of Borneo (S Borneo is part of Indonesia).

history The areas that comprise present-day Malaysia were part of a powerful Muslim empire. Malacca later came under Portuguese, Dutch and finally British control. Britain succeeded in unifying its protectorates in Borneo and the Malay Peninsula after World War II, making them a crown colony under the name of the Federation of Malaya in 1948.

The Federation of Malaysia was formed 1963 by the union of the 11 states of the Federation of Malaya with the British crown colonies of N Borneo (then renamed Sabah) and Sarawak, and Singapore, which seceded from the federation in 1965. Since 1966 the 11 states on the Malay Peninsula have been known as West Malaysia, and Sabah and Sarawak, as East Malaysia. The two regions are separated by 400 miles of the South China Sea. The establishment of the federation was opposed by guerrillas backed by Sukarno of Indonesia 1963–66, while the Philippines disputed the sovereignty of East Malaysia in 1968 through their claim on Sabah. Tunku Abdul Rahman was Malaysia's first prime minister 1963–69, and his multiracial style of government was successful until anti-Chinese riots in Kuala Lumpur in 1969 prompted the formation of an emergency administration. They provoked the resignation of Tunku Abdul Rahman in 1970 and the creation by his successor, Tun Abdul Razak, of a broader National Front governing coalition, including previous opposition parties in its ranks.

new economic policy A 'new economic policy' was launched in 1971, with the aim of raising the percentage of Malay-owned businesses from 4% to 30% by 1990 and to extend the use of pro-Malay 'affirmative action' quota systems for university entrance and company employment. During the 1970s Malaysia enjoyed economic growth, but relations with the Chinese community became uneasy later in the decade as a result of the federal government's refusal to welcome Vietnamese refugees. Even more serious has been a revival in fundamentalist Islam in the west and north. Dr Mahathir bin Mohamad became the new leader of the UMNO and prime minister in 1981 and pursued a more narrowly Islamic and Malay strategy than his predecessors. He also launched an ambitious industrialization programme, seeking to emulate Japan. He was re-elected in 1982 and 1986 but has encountered opposition from his Malaysian Chinese Association coalition partners, Christian-Muslim conflict in Sabah, and slower economic growth as a result of the fall in world tin, rubber, and palm-oil prices. In 1987, in the wake of worsening Malay-Chinese relations, Mahathir ordered the arrest of opposition activists, and tightened press censorship. These moves precipitated a rift in the UMNO, with the former premier Tunku Abdul Rahman and former trade and industry minister Razaleigh Hamzah leaving to form a new multiracial party grouping, Semangat '46, in 1989. In 1988 a reconstituted New UMNO had been set up by Mahathir following a high-court ruling that, as a result of irregularities in its 1987 leadership election, the existing UMNO was an 'unlawful body'. The prime minister also announced some relaxation of the 1971 'new economic policy' as part of the 'Malay unity' programme. Malaysia joined ◊ASEAN in 1967 and originally adopted a pro-Western, anti-Communist position. During recent years, while close economic links have been developed with Japan and joint ventures encouraged, relations with the communist powers and with Islamic nations have also become closer. In Oct 1990 federal and state elections were held. Prime Minister Mahathir bin Mohamad's ruling National Front coalition captured 70% of the National Assembly seats.

Malenkov Georgi Maximilianovich 1902–1988. Soviet prime minister 1953–55, Stalin's designated successor but abruptly ousted as Communist Party secretary within two weeks of Stalin's death by ◊Khrushchev, and forced out as prime minister in 1955 by Nikolai Bulganin. Malenkov subsequently occupied minor party posts. He was expelled from the Central Committee 1957 and from the Communist Party 1961.

Malta island in the Mediterranean, S of Sicily, E of Tunisia, and N of Libya.

history After requesting British protection, Malta was annexed by Britain 1814 and became a leading naval base. A vital link in World War II, Malta came under heavy attack and was awarded the George Cross decoration. The island was made self-governing 1947, and in 1955 Dom Mintoff, leader of the Malta Labour Party (MLP), became prime minister. In 1956 the MLP's proposal for integration with the UK was approved by a referendum but opposed by the conservative Nationalist Party, led by Dr Giorgio Borg Olivier. In 1958 Mintoff rejected the British proposals and resigned, causing a constitutional crisis. By 1961 both parties favoured independence, and talks began 1962, with Borg Olivier as prime minister.

independence Malta became a fully independent state within the ◊Commonwealth and under the British crown in 1964, having signed a ten-year military and economic aid treaty with the UK. In 1971 Mintoff and the MLP returned to power with a policy of international nonalignment. He declared the 1964 treaty invalid and began to negotiate a new arrangement for leasing the Maltese NATO base and obtaining the maximum economic benefit from it for his country.

the republic A seven-year agreement was signed 1972. Malta became a republic 1974, and in the 1976 general election the MLP was returned with a reduced majority. It again won a narrow majority in the House of Representatives 1981. At the end of 1984 Mintoff announced his retirement, and Dr Mifsud Bonnici succeeded him as MLP leader and prime minister. The Nationalist Party was elected in 1987 and its leader, Edward Fenech Adami, became prime minister. Malta was the site of the Dec 1989 summit meeting between US President Bush and Soviet President Gorbachev. In Oct 1990 Malta formally applied for EC membership.

Manchuria European name for the NE region of China, comprising the provinces of Heilongjiang, Jilin, and Liaoning. It was united with China by the Manchu dynasty 1644, but as the Chinese Empire declined, Japan and Russia were rivals for its control. Chinese colonization of Manchuria began in the 18th century (80% of the population by 1900). The Russians were expelled after the ◊Russo-Japanese War 1904-05, and in 1932 Japan consolidated its position by creating a puppet state, ***Manchukuo***, which disintegrated on the defeat of Japan in World War II. Manchukuo was then ruled by the former Chinese emperor Henry P'u-i; its capital was Hsinking (modern Chinese Changchun). After World War II Japanese settlers were expelled.

mandate a territory whose administration was entrusted to Allied states by the League of Nations under the Treaty of Versailles after World War I. Mandated territories were former German and Turkish possessions (including Iraq, Syria, Lebanon, and Palestine). When the ◊United Nations replaced the League of Nations in 1945, mandates that had not achieved independence became known as trust territories.

Mandela Nelson (Rolihlahla) 1918– . South African politician and lawyer. As organizer of the banned ◊African National Congress (ANC), he was acquitted of treason 1961, but was given a life sentence 1964 on charges of sabotage and plotting to overthrow the government. In prison he became a symbol of unity for the worldwide anti-apartheid movement. In Feb 1990 he was released, after the ban on the ANC was lifted.

Mandela Winnie (Nomzamo) 1934– . Civil-rights activist in South Africa and wife of Nelson Mandela. A leading spokesperson for the African National Congress during her husband's imprisonment 1964–90, she has been jailed for a year and put under house arrest several times. In 1989 she was involved in the abduction of four youths, one of whom, Stompie Seipei, was later murdered. Winnie Mandela was convicted of kidnapping and assault, and given a six year jail sentence May 1991.

Manhattan Project code name for the development of the ◊atom bomb in the USA in World War II, to which the physicists Enrico Fermi and J Robert Oppenheimer contributed.

Maoism form of communism based on the ideas and teachings of the Chinese communist leader ◊Mao Zedong. It involves an adaptation of ◊Marxism to suit conditions in China and apportions a much greater role to agriculture and the peasantry in the building of socialism, thus effectively bypassing the capitalist (industrial) stage envisaged by Marx.

***Mandela** Vice president of the African National Congress, Nelson Mandela.*

Mao Zedong or ***Mao Tse-tung*** 1893–1976. Chinese political leader and Marxist theoretician. A founder of the Chinese Communist Party (CCP) 1921, Mao soon emerged as its leader. He organized the ◊Long March 1934–36 and the war of liberation 1937–49, following which he established a People's Republic and Communist rule in China; he headed the CCP and government until his death. His influence diminished with the failure of his 1958–60 ◊Great Leap Forward, but he became dominant again during the 1966–69 ◊Cultural Revolution. Mao adapted communism to Chinese conditions, as set out in the *Little Red Book*.

Mao, son of a peasant farmer in Hunan province, was once library assistant at Beijing University and a headmaster at Changsha. He became chief of CCP propaganda under the Guomindang (Nationalist) leader Sun Yat-sen (Sun Zhong Shan) until dismissed by Sun's successor Chiang Kai-shek (Jiang Jie Shi). In 1931–34 Mao set up a Communist republic at Jiangxi and, together with Zhu De, marshalled the Red Army and organised the Long March to Shaanxi to evade Nationalist suppressive tactics. CCP head from 1935, Mao secured an alliance with the Nationalist forces 1936–45 aimed at repelling the Japanese invaders. At Yen'an, he built up a people's republic 1936–47 and married his third wife ◊Jiang Qing 1939. Civil war with the Nationalists was renewed from 1946 until 1949 when Mao defeated them at Nanking and established the People's Republic and Communist party rule under his leadership. During the civil war, he successfully employed mobile, rural-based guerrilla tactics.

Mao served as party head until his death Sept 1976 and as state president until 1959. After the damages of the Cultural Revolution, the Great Helmsman, as he was called, working with his prime minister Zhou Enlai, oversaw a period of reconstruction from 1970 until deteriorating health weakened his political grip in the final years.

Mao's writings and thoughts dominated the functioning of the People's Republic 1949–76. He wrote some 2,300 publications, comprising 3 million words; 740 million copies of his *Quotations* have been printed. He stressed the need for rural rather than urban-based revolutions in Asia, for reducing rural-urban differences, and for perpetual revolution to prevent the emergence of new elites. Mao helped precipitate the Sino-Soviet split 1960 and was a firm advocate of a ◊nonaligned Third World strategy. Since 1978, the leadership of Deng

Xiaoping has reinterpreted Maoism, and criticized its policy excesses, and commercialized the nation, but many of Mao's ideas remain valued.

March on Rome the means by which Fascist leader, Benito Mussolini came to power in Italy 1922. A protracted crisis in government and the threat of civil war enabled Mussolini to demand the formation of a fascist government to restore order. On 29 Oct 1922, King Victor Emmanuel III invited Mussolini to come to Rome to take power. The 'march' was a fascist propaganda myth: Mussolini travelled overnight by train from Milan to Rome where he formed a government the following day, 30 Oct. 25,000 fascist Blackshirts were also transported to the city where they marched in a ceremonial parade on 31 Oct.

Marne, Battles of the in World War I, two unsuccessful German offensives: ***First Battle*** 5–12 Sept 1914, marked the failure of the German Schlieffen Plan. The German armies under General Alexander von Kluck had advanced with little opposition until they reached the river Marne. The French General Joffre rapidly moved his troops out of Paris to the river Marne where they attacked the advancing Germans. The battle itself was indecisive but the Germans ultimately withdrew. It marked a turning point from a war of rapidly moving armies into a long period of trench warfare on the ◊Western Front.

The ***Second Battle*** 15 July–7 Aug 1918, marked an Allied victory. Although the German forces under General Ludendorff had launched the attack on 15 July and crossed the Marne river, the French General Foch quickly counter-attacked and forced the Germans to retreat. The Allied counter-offensive frustrated Ludendorff's plan for a great attack in Flanders.

Marshall Plan a programme of US financial aid to Europe, set up at the end of World War II, totalling $13,000 billion 1948–52. Officially known as the European Recovery Programme, it was announced by secretary of state George Marshall in a speech at Harvard in June 1947, but it was in fact the work of a State Department group led by Dean Acheson. The danger of communist takeover in postwar Europe was the major motivation for the aid effort.

Marxism philosophical system, developed by the 19th-century German social theorists Karl Marx and Friedrich Engels, also known as ***dialectical materialism***, under which matter gives rise to mind (materialism) and all is subject to change. As applied to history, it supposes that the succession of feudalism, capitalism, socialism, and finally the classless society is inevitable. The stubborn resistance of any existing system to change necessitates its complete overthrow in the ***class struggle*** – in the case of capitalism, by the proletariat – rather than gradual modification.

Social and political institutions progressively change their nature as economic developments transform material conditions. The orthodox belief is that each successive form is 'higher' than the last; perfect socialism is seen as the ultimate rational system, and it is alleged that the state would then wither away. Marxism has proved one of the most powerful and debated theories in modern history, inspiring both dedicated exponents (Lenin, Trotsky, Stalin, Mao) and bitter opponents. It is the basis of ◊communism.

Masurian Lakes, battle of lakes in Poland (former East Prussia) which in 1914–15 were the scene of battles in which the Germans defeated the Russians.

Mau Mau a Kenyan secret guerrilla movement 1952–60, an offshoot of the Kikuyu Central Association banned in World War II. Its aim was to end British colonial rule. This was achieved in 1964 with the granting of Kenyan independence and the election of Jomo ◊Kenyatta as Kenya's first president.

A state of emergency was declared in 1952, and by 1956 colonial government forces had killed more than 11,000 Kikuyu. More than 100 Europeans and Asians and 2,000 pro-government Kikuyu were killed by the Mau Mau. The state of emergency was ended in 1960, and in 1963 Kenya was granted internal self-government, with full independence following a year later. Jomo Kenyatta, who was convicted of being the leader of the Mau Mau, became the country's first prime minister in 1963 and president after independence.

means test a method of assessing the amount to be paid in social security benefits, which takes into account all sources of personal or family income.

In 1931 an Act was passed in the UK Parliament that restricted the use of the employment insurance fund to the payment of limited, short-term benefits. The longer-term unemployed and those not covered by the scheme were to receive assistance only after a 'means test' had been applied and the amount of unemployment benefit assessed. The Unemployment Act 1934 retained the means test as a method of administering unemployment benefit.

medicine the science of preventing, diagnosing, alleviating, or curing disease, both physical and mental; also any substance used in the treatment of disease. The basis of medicine is anatomy (the structure and form of the body) and physiology (the study of the body's functions).

In the West, medicine increasingly relies on new drugs and sophisticated surgical techniques, while diagnosis of disease is more and more by noninvasive procedures. The time and cost of Western-type medical training makes it inaccessible to many parts of the ◊Third World; where health care of this kind is provided it is often by auxiliary medical helpers trained in hygiene and the administration of a limited number of standard drugs for the prevalent diseases of a particular region.

1798 Edward Jenner published his work on vaccination.
1877 Patrick Manson, Scottish parasitologist, worked on animal carriers of infectious diseases.
1882 Robert Koch isolated the tuberculosis bacillus.
1884 Edwin Klebs, German pathologist, isolated the diphtheria bacillus.
1885 Louis Pasteur produced the rabies vaccine.
1890 Joseph Lister demonstrated antiseptic surgery.
1897 Martinus Beijerinck, Dutch botanist, discovered viruses.
1899 German doctor Felix Hoffman developed aspirin; Sigmund Freud founded psychiatry.
1910 Paul Ehrlich synthesized the first specific bacterial agent, salvarsan (cure for syphilis).
1922 Insulin was first used to treat diabetes.
1928 Alexander Fleming discovered the antibiotic penicillin.
1930s Electro-convulsive therapy (ECT) was developed.
1932 Gerhard Domagk, German bacteriologist and pathologist, began work on the sulphonamide drugs, a kind of antibiotic.
1940s Lithium treatment for depression was developed.
1950 Proof of a link between cigarette smoking and lung cancer was established.
1950s Major development of antidepressant drugs and beta-blockers for heart disease; Medawar's work on the immune system.
1950–75 Manipulation of the molecules of synthetic chemicals, the main source of new drugs.
1953 Vaccine for polio developed by Jonas Salk.
1960s Heart-transplant surgery began with the work of Christiaan Barnard; new generation of minor tranquillizers called benzodiazepenes developed.
1971 Viroids, disease-causing organisms even smaller than viruses, were isolated outside the living body.
1975 Nuclear medicine, for example positron-emission tomography (Hounsfield), came into practical use.
1978 Birth of the first 'test-tube baby', Louise Brown, in England.
1980s AIDS (acquired immune-deficiency syndrome) first recognized in the USA; recognition of the discovery of the transposable gene by Barbara McClintock, US geneticist.
1980 Smallpox eradicated by the World Health Organization.
1984 Vaccine for leprosy developed; discovery of the human immuno-deficiency virus (HIV), responsible for AIDS, at the Institut Pasteur in Paris and in the USA.
1987 World's longest-surviving heart-transplant patient died in France, 18 years after his operation.
1989 Patient with Parkinson's disease first treated by graft of fetal brain tissue.

medicine, alternative forms of medical treatment that do not use synthetic drugs or surgery in response to the symptoms of a disease, but aim to treat the patient as a whole (holism). The emphasis is on maintaining health (with diet and exercise) and on dealing with the underlying causes rather than just the symptoms of illness. It may involve the use of herbal remedies and techniques like acupuncture, homeopathy, and chiropractic.

Meiji Mutsuhito 1852–1912. Emperor of Japan from 1867, when he took the title *meiji tennō* ('enlightened sovereign'). During his reign Japan became a world industrial and naval power. He abolished the feudal system and discrimination against the lowest caste, established state schools, and introduced conscription, the Western calendar, and other measures in an attempt to modernize Japan, including a constitution 1889.

Mein Kampf (German 'my struggle') book written by Adolf ◊Hitler 1924 during his jail sentence for his part in the abortive 1923 Munich beer-hall putsch. Part autobiography, part political philosophy, the book presents Hitler's ideas of German expansion, anticommunism, and anti-Semitism.

Meir Golda 1898–1978. Israeli Labour (*Mapai*) politician. Born in Russia, she emigrated to the USA 1906, and in 1921 went to Palestine. She was foreign minister 1956–66 and prime minister 1969–74. Criticism of the Israelis' lack of preparation for the 1973 Arab-Israeli War led to election losses for Labour and, unable to form a government, she resigned.

Menshevik member of the minority (Russian *menshinstvo* 'minority') of the Russian Social Democratic Party, who split from the ◊Bolsheviks 1903. The Mensheviks believed in a large, loosely organized party and that, before socialist revolution could occur in Russia, capitalist society had to develop further. During the Russian Revolution they had limited power and set up a government in Georgia, but were suppressed 1922.

microchip popular name for the silicon chip or ◊integrated circuit.

microcomputer or ***micro*** a small desktop or portable computer, typically designed to be used by one person at a time. Microcomputers are the smallest of the four classes of computer (the others are supercomputer, mainframe, and minicomputer). Since the appearance in 1975 of the first commercially available microcomputer, the Altair 8800, micros have become widely accepted in commerce and industry.

Midway Islands two islands in the Pacific, 1,800 km/1,120 mi NW of Honolulu. They were annexed by the USA 1867, and are now administered by the US Navy. The naval ***Battle of Midway*** 3–6 June 1942, between the USA and Japan, was a turning point in World War II: the US victory marked the end of Japanese expansion in the Pacific.

militarism the prevalence of military sentiment or ideals among a people, state, or nation. It is sometimes marked by the predominance of the military class in government or administration; examples include 19th century Prussia and interwar Japan. With industrialization, the characteristics of militarism have become associated with a growing number of states.

Mitterrand François 1916– . French socialist politician, president from 1981. He held ministerial posts in 11 governments 1947–1958. He founded the French Socialist Party (PS) 1971. In 1985 he introduced proportional representation, allegedly to weaken the growing opposition from left and right.

Mitterrand studied law and politics in Paris. During World War II he was prominent in the Resistance. He entered the National Assembly as a centre-left deputy for Nièvre. Opposed to General de Gaulle's creation of the Fifth Republic 1958, he formed the centre-left anti-Gaullist Federation of the Left in the 1960s. In 1971 he became leader of the new PS. An electoral union with the Communist Party 1972–77 established the PS as the most popular party in France.

Mitterrand was elected president 1981. His programme of reform was hampered by deteriorating economic conditions after 1983. When the socialists lost their majority Mar 1986, he was compelled to work with a right-wing prime minister, Jacques Chirac, and grew in popularity. He defeated Chirac to secure a second term in the presidential election May 1988.

Mitterrand *French socialist president François Mitterrand, May 1989.*

mixed economy combines the private enterprise of capitalism with a degree of state monopoly. In mixed economies, governments seek to control the public services, the basic industries, and those industries that cannot raise sufficient capital investment from private sources. Thus a measure of economic planning can be combined with a measure of free enterprise. A notable example was US President F D Roosevelt's ◊New Deal in the 1930s.

mobilization the preparation of armed forces (land, sea, air) for active service.

Mobutu Sese-Seko-Kuku-Ngbeandu-Wa-Za-Banga 1930– . Zaïrean president from 1965. He assumed the presidency by coup, and created a unitary state under his centralized government. He abolished secret voting in elections 1976 in favour of a system of acclamation at mass rallies. His personal wealth is estimated at $3–4 billion, and more money is spent on the presidency than on the entire social-services budget. The harshness of some of his policies and charges of corruption have attracted widespread international criticism.

Modernism in the arts, a general term used to describe the 20th century's conscious attempt to break with the artistic traditions of the 19th century; it is based on a concern with form and the exploration of technique as opposed to content and narrative.

In the visual arts, direct representationalism gave way to abstraction: for example, Russian artist Wassily Kandinsky's work. In literature, writers such as James Joyce and Virginia Woolf experimented with alternatives to orthodox sequential storytelling, as in the 'stream of consciousness' technique. In music, the traditional concept of key was challenged by atonality: Austrian composer Arnold Schoenberg is an example. In architecture, Functionalism (the conscious exclusion of all that serves no practical purpose) ousted decorativeness as a central objective: French architect, Charles Le Corbusier was Functionalism's prime exponent. Critics of Modernism have found in it an austerity that is seen as dehumanizing.

monetarism an economic policy, advocated by the economist Milton Friedman and the Chicago school of economists, that proposes control of a country's money supply to keep it in step with the country's ability to produce goods, with the aim of curbing inflation. Cutting government spending is advocated, and the long-term aim is to return as much of the economy as possible to the private sector, allegedly in the interests of efficiency.

Central banks – in the USA, the Federal Reserve Bank – use the discount rate and other tools to restrict or expand the supply of money to the economy. Unemployment may result from some efforts to withdraw government 'safety nets,' but monetarists claim it is less than eventually occurs if the methods of ◊Keynesian economics are adopted. Monetarist policies were widely adopted in the 1980s in response to the inflation problems caused by spiralling oil prices in 1979.

Mongolia country in E Central Asia, bounded N by the USSR and S by China.

history Formerly inhabited by nomads from N Asia, the area was part of China from 1689.

revolution After the revolution of 1911–12 Mongolia became autonomous under the Lamaist religious ruler Jebsten Damba Khutukhtu (the Living Buddha). From 1915 it increasingly fell under Chinese influence and not until 1921, with the support of the USSR, were Mongolian nationalists able to cast off the Chinese yoke.

'Sovietization' In 1924 it adopted the Soviet system of government and, after proclaiming itself a people's republic, launched a programme of 'defeudalization'. In 1931, when two provinces revolted against the Communist Party, religious buildings were destroyed and mass executions carried out on the Soviet dictator Stalin's orders. An armed uprising by anti-government forces in 1932 was suppressed with Soviet assistance. China recognized its independence in 1946, but relations deteriorated as Mongolia took the Soviet side in the Sino-Soviet dispute. In 1966 Mongolia signed a 20-year friendship, cooperation and mutual-assistance pact with the USSR, and some 60,000 Soviet troops based in the country caused China to see it as a Russian colony.

economic change Isolated from the outside world during the 1970s, under the leadership of Yumjaagiyn Tsedenbal – the nation's dominant figure since 1958 – Mongolia underwent great economic change as urban industries developed and settled agriculture on the collective system spread. Tsedenbal was deposed 1984.

nationalist revival After the accession to power in the USSR of Mikhail Gorbachev, Mongolia was encouraged to broaden its outside contacts. Cultural exchanges with China increased, diplomatic relations were established with the USA, and between 1987 and 1990 the number of Soviet troops stationed in the country was reduced from 80,000 to 15,000. A Mongolian nationalist revival developed, with increasing study and use of the Mongolian script, which was nationally readopted to replace the Cyrillic in 1990. Influenced by events in Eastern Europe, an opposition grouping, the Mongolian Democratic Union, was illegally formed Dec 1989 by the Moscow University–educated Sanjasuren Zorig (1962–). During 1990 it spearheaded a campaign demanding greater democratization and the return of Tsedenbal (from exile in Moscow) to face trial.

free elections Free multiparty national elections and local municipal and people's hurals were held on 29 July 1990. The MPRP secured 83% of the seats of the central parliament and 62% of the seats in the Little Hural. The principal opposition body, the Democratic Party (MDP), led by Erdenijn Bat-Uul, captured only 5% of the seats. In Sept 1990 the new assembly elected the MPRP's Punsalmaagiyn Ochirbat as president and Dashiyn Byambasuren as prime minister.

Montgomery Bernard Law, 1st Viscount Montgomery of Alamein 1887–1976. British field marshal. In World War II he commanded the 8th Army in N Africa in the Second Battle of El ◊Alamein 1942. As commander of British troops in N Europe from 1944, he received the German surrender on 3 May 1945.

At the start of World War II he commanded part of the British Expeditionary Force in France 1939–40 and took part in the evacuation from Dunkirk. In Aug 1942 he took command of the 8th Army in N Africa, then barring the German advance on Cairo; the victory of El ◊Alamein in Oct turned the tide in N Africa and was followed by the expulsion of Field Marshal Rommel from Egypt and rapid Allied advance into Tunisia. In Feb 1943

Montgomery's forces came under US general Eisenhower's command, and they took part in the conquest of Tunisia and Sicily and the invasion of Italy. Montgomery was promoted to field marshal in 1944. In 1948 he became permanent military chair of the Commanders-in-Chief Committee for W European defence, and 1951–58 was deputy Supreme Commander Europe.

Montgomery commanded the Allied armies during the opening phase of the invasion of France in Jun 1944, and from Aug the British and imperial troops that liberated the Netherlands, overran N Germany, and entered Denmark. At his 21st Army Group headquarters on Lüneberg Heath, he received the German surrender on 3 May 1945. He was in command of the British occupation force in Germany until Feb 1946, when he was appointed chief of the Imperial General Staff. Created 1st Viscount Montgomery of Alamein 1946.

Moroccan Crises two periods of international tension 1905 and 1911 following German objections to French expansion in Morocco. Their wider purpose was to break up the Anglo-French entente 1904, but both crises served to reinforce the entente and isolate Germany.

Morocco country in N Africa, bordered N and NW by the Mediterranean, E and SE by Algeria, and S by Western Sahara.

history European influence began in the 19th century, with Morocco being divided in 1912 into French and Spanish protectorates. It became fully independent as the Sultanate of Morocco in 1956 under Mohammed V (sultan since 1927). The former Spanish protectorate joined the new state, with Tangier, which had previously been an international zone. The sultan was restyled king of Morocco in 1957. After his death in 1961 he was succeeded by King Hassan II, who has survived several attempted coups and assassinations. Between 1960 and 1972 several constitutions were formulated in an attempt to balance personal royal rule with demands for greater democracy.

Western Sahara dispute Hassan's reign has been dominated by the dispute over Western Sahara, a former Spanish colony seen as historically Moroccan. In 1975 Spain ceded it to Morocco and Mauritania, leaving them to divide it. The inhabitants, who had not been consulted, reacted violently through an independence movement, the Polisario Front. Less than a year later, Morocco and Mauritania were involved in a guerrilla war.

the 'Sahrahwi Arab Democratic Republic' With Algerian support, Polisario set up a government in exile in Algiers, the Sahrahwi Arab Democratic Republic (SADR). This prompted Hassan to sever diplomatic relations with Algeria in 1976. In 1979 Mauritania agreed a peace treaty with Polisario, and Morocco annexed the part of Western Sahara that Mauritania had vacated. Polisario reacted by intensifying its operations. In 1983 the Organization of African Unity (OAU) proposed a cease-fire, direct negotiations between Morocco and Polisario, and a referendum in Western Sahara. Morocco agreed but refused to deal directly with Polisario. Although the war was costly, it allowed Hassan to capitalize on the patriotism it generated in his country. In 1984 he unexpectedly signed an agreement with Col Khaddhafi of Libya, who had been helping Polisario, for economic and political cooperation and mutual defence. Meanwhile, Morocco was becoming more isolated as SADR gained wider recognition. Towards the end of 1987 the Polisario guerrillas agreed a cease-fire and in Aug 1988 a United Nations peace plan was accepted by both sides, calling for a referendum to permit the area's inhabitants to choose independence or incorporation into Morocco. Full diplomatic relations with Algeria were restored in May 1988, and with Syria in Jan 1989.

motorcar another term for ◊car.

motorway main road for fast traffic, with separate carriageways for traffic moving in opposite directions, and limited access points. The first motorway (85 km/53 mi) ran from Milan to Varese, Italy, and was completed 1924, and by 1939 there was some 500 km/300 mi of motorway (*autostrada*). In Germany some 2,100 km/1,310 mi of *Autobahnen* had been completed by 1942. The first motorway in the UK, the Preston by-pass (now part of the M6) was opened 1958, and the first section of the M1 was opened in 1959.

Mountbatten Louis, 1st Earl Mountbatten of Burma 1900–1979. British admiral and administrator. In World War II he became chief of combined operations 1942 and commander in chief in SE Asia 1943. As last viceroy of India 1947 and first governor general of India until 1948, he oversaw that country's transition to independence.

He entered the navy in 1913 and was present at the Battle of ◊Jutland. In World War II at the battle of Crete the ship he commanded, HMS *Kelly*, was sunk, and he was picked up from the sea. He was criticized for the heavy loss of Allied lives at Dieppe. He was chief of UK Defence Staff 1959–65. He was killed by an Irish Republican Army bomb aboard his yacht in the Republic of Ireland.

Mubarak Hosni 1928– . Egyptian politician,

president from 1981. He commanded the air force 1972–75 (and was responsible for the initial victories in the Egyptian campaign of 1973 against Israel), when he became an active vice president to Anwar Sadat, and succeeded him on his assassination. He has continued to pursue Sadat's moderate policies, and has significantly increased the freedom of the press and of political association, while trying to repress the growing Islamic fundamentalist movement.

Mugabe Robert (Gabriel) 1925– . Zimbabwean politician, prime minister from 1980 and president from 1987. He was in detention in Rhodesia for nationalist activities 1964–74, then carried on guerrilla warfare from Mozambique. As leader of ZANU (Zimbabwe African National Union) he was in an uneasy alliance with Joshua ◊Nkomo of ZAPU (Zimbabwe African People's Union) from 1976. The two parties merged 1987.

He is a member of the Shona people, and was educated at Fort Hare University, South Africa. In 1985 he postponed the introduction of a multiparty state for five years.

Mukden, Battle of the taking of Mukden (now Shenyang), NE China, from Russian occupation by the Japanese 1905, during the ◊Russo-Japanese War. Mukden was later the scene of a surprise attack (the ***Mukden Incident***) 18 Sept 1931 by the Japanese on the Chinese garrison, which marked the beginning of their invasion of China.

Munich Agreement pact signed on 29 Sept 1938 by the leaders of the UK (Neville Chamberlain), France (Edouard Daladier), Germany (Adolf Hitler), and Italy (Benito Mussolini), under which Czechoslovakia was compelled to surrender its Sudeten-German districts (the ***Sudetenland***) to Germany. Chamberlain claimed it would guarantee 'peace in our time', but it did not prevent Hitler from seizing the rest of Czechoslovakia in Mar 1939.

Most districts were not given the option of a plebiscite under the agreement. After World War II the Sudetenland was returned to Czechoslovakia, and over 2 million German-speaking people were expelled from the country.

Munich Putsch an unsuccessful uprising led by Adolf Hitler, attempting to overthrow the government of Bavaria in Nov 1923. More than 2,000 Nazi demonstrators were met by armed police, who opened fire killing 16 of Hitler's supporters. At the subsequent trial for treason, General Ludendorff, who had supported Hitler, was acquitted. Hitler was sentenced to prison, during which time he wrote ◊*Mein Kampf*.

Muslim Brotherhood movement founded by members of the Sunni branch of Islam in Egypt in 1928. It aims at the establishment of an Islamic state ruled according to religious principle (theocracy) and is headed by a 'supreme guide'. It is also active in Jordan, Sudan, and Syria.

Muslim League Indian political organization. The All India Muslim League was founded 1906 under the leadership of the Aga Khan. In 1940 the League demanded an independent Muslim state. The Congress Party and the Muslim League won most seats in the 1945 elections for an Indian Central Legislative Assembly. In 1946 the Indian Constituent Assembly League was boycotted by the Muslim League. It was partly the activities of the League that led to the establishment of ◊Pakistan.

Mussolini Benito 1883–1945. Italian dictator 1925–43. As founder of the Fascist Movement (see ◊fascism) 1919 and prime minister from 1922, he became known as *Il Duce* ('the leader'). He invaded Ethiopia 1935–36, intervened in the Spanish Civil War 1936–39 in support of Franco, and conquered Albania 1939. In June 1940 Italy entered World War II supporting Hitler. Forced by military and domestic setbacks to resign 1943, Mussolini established a breakaway government in N Italy 1944–45, but was killed trying to flee the country.

Mussolini was born in the Romagna, the

Mussolini *Italian Fascist dictator 1925–43, Benito Mussolini.*

son of a blacksmith, and worked in early life as a teacher and journalist. He became active in the socialist movement, from which he was expelled 1914 for advocating Italian intervention in World War I. In 1919 he founded the Fascist Movement, whose programme combined violent nationalism with demagogic republican and anticapitalist slogans, and launched a campaign of terrorism against the socialists. This movement was backed by many landowners and industrialists and by the heads of the army and police, and in Oct 1922 Mussolini was in power as prime minister at the head of a coalition government. In 1925 he assumed dictatorial powers, and in 1926 all opposition parties were banned. During the years that followed, the political, legal, and education systems were remodelled on Fascist lines.

Mussolini's Blackshirt followers were the forerunners of Hitler's Brownshirts, and his career of conquest drew him into close cooperation with Nazi Germany. Italy and Germany formed the ◊Axis alliance 1936. During World War II, Italian defeats in N Africa and Greece, the Allied invasion of Sicily, and discontent at home destroyed Mussolini's prestige, and in July 1943 he was compelled to resign by his own Fascist Grand Council. He was released from prison by German parachutists in Sept 1943 and set up a 'Republican Fascist' government in N Italy. In Apr 1945 he and his mistress, Clara Petacci, were captured by partisans at Lake Como while heading for the Swiss border, and shot. Their bodies were taken to Milan and hung upside down in a public square.

Myanmar formerly (until 1989) ***Burma***) country in SE Asia, bordered NW by India, NE by China, SE by Laos and Thailand, and SW by the Bay of Bengal.

history The Burmese date their era from AD 638, when they had arrived from the region where China meets Tibet. By 850 they had organized a state in the centre of the plain at Pagan. In a series of wars in the nineteenth century, Britain gained control, and the country was united as a province of India until 1937, when it was made a crown colony with a degree of self-government.

World War II Burma was occupied 1942–45 by Japan, under a government of anti-British nationalists. The nationalists, led by Aung San and U Nu, later founded the Anti-Fascist People's Freedom League (AFPFL). Burma was liberated 1945 and achieved full independence outside the Commonwealth 1948.

the republic A parliamentary democracy was established under the Socialist AFPFL led by Prime Minister U Nu. The republic was weakened by civil war between Karens, Communist guerrillas, and ethnic group separatists. Splits within the AFPFL forced the formation of an emergency caretaker government by General Ne Win (1911–) 1958–60, leading to a military coup 1962 and abolition of the parliamentary system. Ne Win became head of a revolutionary council and established a strong one-party state. In 1974 a new presidential constitution was adopted, and the revolutionary council was dissolved. The military leaders became civilian rulers. Ne Win became president and was re-elected 1978, before stepping down to be replaced by U San Yu (1918–) 1981.

'Burmese Socialism' The post-1962 government adopted a foreign policy of neutralist isolationism while at home it pursued its unique, self-reliant, Buddhist-influenced 'Burmese Way towards Socialism', founded upon state ownership in the commercial-industrial sector and strict agricultural price control. Internal opposition by armed separatist groups continued after 1962, causing the economy to deteriorate. The Burmese Communist Party, which received Chinese funding during the 1960s, established control over parts of the N; the Karen National Liberation Army in the SE; and the Kachin Independence Army in the NE. In 1975 the non-Communist ethnic separatist groups joined together to form the broad National Democratic Front with the aim of creating a federal union. In 1974 and 1976 worsening economic conditions prompted a wave of food riots and in Sept 1987, with rice prices spiralling, student demonstrations broke out in Yangon. Worker's riots followed in the spring of 1988. Initially they were violently supressed, at the cost of several hundred lives. In the summer of 1988 San Yu and Ne Win, the leader of the ruling party, were forced to resign, as was the newly appointed president, Brig-Gen Sein Lwin, following the murder of 3,000 unarmed demonstrators.

military coup With the government control crumbling, as a widely supported pro-democracy movement swept the nation, the more reformist Maung Maung took over as president and free multi-party elections were promised 'within three months'. However, in Sept 1988 a military coup was staged by General Saw Maung, with the constitution being suspended, martial law imposed, and authority transferred to a 19-member State Law and Order Restoration Council. The new regime proceeded to pursue a more liberal economic course and to legalize the formation of political parties. Popular opposition leaders, including Suu Kyi (1945– , the daughter of the late Aung San) and U Nu, were harassed and debarred from standing in the elections that were promised in May 1990. Behind the scenes, Ne Win remained in control. In June 1989 the government announced the change in the country's name; it was recognized by the UN in the same month. Elections in May 1990 resulted in an overwhelming victory by opposition parties. Foreign observers remained cautious about whether the military would surrender power as promised.

My Lai massacre the killing of 109 civilians in My Lai, a village in South Vietnam, by US troops in Mar 1968. An investigation in 1969 was followed by the conviction of Lieutenant William Calley, commander of the platoon.

Sentenced to life imprisonment 1971, Calley was later released on parole. His superior officer was acquitted but the trial revealed a US Army policy of punitive tactics against civilians. News of the massacre contributed to domestic pressure for the USA to end its involvement in Vietnam.

N

Nagasaki industrial port on Kyushu island, Japan. An atom bomb was dropped on it 9 Aug 1945, three days after one was dropped on ◊Hiroshima. Of Nagasaki's population of 212,000, 73,884 were killed and 76,796 injured, not counting the long-term victims of radiation.

Nagy Imre 1896–1958. Hungarian politician, prime minister 1953–55 and 1956. He led the Hungarian revolt against Soviet domination in 1956, for which he was executed.

Nagy, an Austro-Hungarian prisoner of war in Siberia during World War I, became a Soviet citizen after the Russian Revolution, and lived in the USSR 1930–44. In 1953, after Stalin's death, he became prime minister in Hungary introducing liberal measures such as encouraging the production of consumer goods, but was dismissed 1955 by hardline Stalinist premier Rákosi. Reappointed Oct 1956 during the Hungarian uprising, he began taking liberalization further than the Soviets wanted; for example, announcing Hungarian withdrawal from the Warsaw Pact. Soviet troops entered Budapest, and Nagy was dismissed Nov 1956. He was captured by the KGB and executed. In 1989 the Hungarian Supreme Court recognized his leadership of a legitimate government and quashed his conviction for treachery.

Namibia formerly (to 1968) ***South West Africa*** country in SW Africa, bounded N by Angola and Zambia, E by Botswana and South Africa, and W by the Atlantic Ocean. Much of the land is desert.

history Annexed, with the exception of the British Cape Colony enclave of Walvis Bay, by Germany 1884, it was occupied in World War I by South African forces under L Botha, and was mandated to South Africa 1920. South Africa did not accept the termination of the mandate by the United Nations 1966, although briefly accepting the principle of ultimate independence 1978 (UN Security Council Resolution 435); in 1968 the UN renamed the territory Namibia. South Africa's apartheid laws were extended to the colony in 1966 and in opposition to such racial discrimination Sam Nujoma, an Ovambu, led a political (from 1958) and then (from mid-1960s) an armed resistance campaign for independence, forming the South-West Africa People's Organization (SWAPO) and the People's Liberation Army of Namibia (PLAN). Following harassment, he was forced into exile in 1960, establishing guerrilla bases in Angola and Zambia. Military conflict in Namibia escalated from the mid-1970s as the Pretoria regime attempted to topple the Marxist government in neighbouring Angola. In 1985 South Africa installed a puppet regime in Namibia, the Transitional Government of National Unity (TGNU), a multi-racial body, but including only one Ovambo minister. It attempted to reform the apartheid system but was internally divided between moderate reformist and conservative wings, and failed to secure UN recognition.

peace settlement In 1988 progress was finally made towards a peace settlement in Namibia as a result of both South Africa and the USSR's (via Cuba) tiring of the cost of their proxy military involvement in the civil wars of both the colony and neighbouring Angola. In Aug 1988 the South African and Angolan governments signed an agreement that provided for an immediate ceasefire, followed by the rapid withdrawal of South African forces from Angola and, during 1989, the phased withdrawal of Cuba's troops from Angola and South Africa's from Namibia. From April 1989, a UN peacekeeping force was stationed in Namibia to oversee the holding of multi-party elections in Nov. These were won by SWAPO, but its 57% share of the seats in the constituent assembly, which had the task of framing a new 'independence constitution', fell short of the two-thirds majority required for it to dominate the proceedings. As a consequence, a moderate multiparty constitution was adopted in Feb 1990. Sam Nujoma was unanimously elected Namibia's first president by the assembly on 16 Feb 1990, and was formally sworn in by the UN secretary general on independence day, 21 March 1990.

Nasser Gamal Abdel 1918–1970. Egyptian politician, prime minister 1954–56 and from 1956 president of Egypt (the United Arab Republic 1958–71). In 1952 he was the driving

Nasser *Egyptian politician and prime minister Gamal Abdel Nasser, Oct 1964.*

power behind the Neguib coup, which ended the monarchy. His nationalization of the Suez Canal 1956 led to an Anglo-French invasion and the ◊Suez Crisis), and his ambitions for an Egyptian-led union of Arab states led to disquiet in the Middle East (and in the West). Nasser was also an early and influential leader of the ◊nonaligned movement.

National Government in British politics, a government of Labour, Liberal and Conservative MPs formed in 1931, and consequent upon a rapidly declining financial situation which had led to a split in the Labour government. The Labour leader, Ramsay Macdonald, was prime minister of the National Government but the majority of his own party refused to support him. Thus the National Government was mainly Conservative, and Macdonald (who resigned in 1935) was succeeded as prime minister by the Conservative leader Stanley Baldwin.

National Health Service (NHS) UK government medical scheme; see ◊health service.

national insurance in the UK, state social security scheme which provides child allowances, maternity benefits, and payments to the unemployed, sick, and retired, and also covers medical treatment. It is paid for by weekly contributions from employees and employers.

National Insurance Act UK act of Parliament 1911, introduced by Lloyd George, Liberal chancellor, which first provided insurance for workers against ill health and unemployment.

Part I of the act introduced compulsory health insurance for all manual workers aged between 16 and 70 and nonmanual workers with incomes below £250 a year who did not claim exemption. Part II of the act provided insurance against unemployment for 2 million workers but excluded domestic servants, agricultural workers, and nonmanual workers exempt from Part I. The schemes were contributory, with employer, employee, and the state making regular contributions. The act provided for medical assistance and maternity benefits and supplemented recently introduced welfare provisions for disabilities and pensions.

nationalism in politics, a movement that consciously aims to unify a nation, create a state, or liberate it from foreign rule. Nationalist movements became a potent factor in European politics during the 19th century; since 1900 nationalism has become a strong force in Asia and Africa and in the late 1980s revived strongly in E Europe. In the second half of the 20th century a strongly national literary and political movement has developed in Scotland and Wales.

nationalization policy of bringing a country's essential services and industries under public ownership. It was pursued, for example, by the UK Labour government 1945–51. In recent years the trend towards nationalization has slowed and in many countries such as the UK, France, and Japan reversed (◊privatization). Assets in the hands of foreign governments or companies may also be nationalized; for example, Iran's oil industry, the Suez Canal, and US-owned fruit plantations in Guatemala, all in the 1950s.

In the UK, acts were passed nationalizing the Bank of England, coal, and most hospitals in 1946; transport and electricity in 1947; gas in 1948; and iron and steel in 1949. In 1953 the succeeding Conservative government provided for the return of road haulage to private enterprise and for decentralization of the railways. It also denationalized iron and steel in 1953, but these were renationalized by the next Labour government in 1967. In 1977 Callaghan's Labour government nationalized the aircraft and shipbuilding industries.

National Socialism official name for the

Nazi movement in Germany; see also ◊fascism.

NATO abbreviation for ◊***North Atlantic Treaty Organization***.

Nazism ideology based on racism, nationalism, and the supremacy of the state over the individual. The German Nazi party, the ***Nationalsozialistiche Deutsche Arbeiterpartei*** (National Socialist German Workers' Party), was formed from the German Workers' Party (founded 1919) and led by Adolf ◊Hitler 1921–45.

During the 1930s, many similar parties were created throughout Europe and the USA, although only those of Austria, Hungary, and Sudetenland were of major importance. These parties collaborated with the German occupation of Europe 1939–45. After the Nazi atrocities of World War II (see ◊concentration camp), the party was banned in Germany, but today parties with Nazi or neo-Nazi ideologies exist in many countries.

Nazi-related movements were founded in the UK 1932 by Oswald Mosley and 1962 by Colin Jordan (National Socialist Movement), and in 1967 the National Front was formed. In the USA the American Nazi Party was founded 1958 by George Lincoln Rockwell.

A neo-fascist group in Italy claimed responsibility for a bomb that killed 76 people in Bologna 1980.

Nazi-Soviet pact a non-aggression treaty signed by Germany and the USSR on 23 August 1939. Under the terms of the treaty both countries agreed to remain neutral and to refrain from acts of aggression against each other if either went to war. Secret clauses allowed for the partition of Poland – Hitler was to acquire western Poland, Stalin the eastern part. On 1 Sept 1939 Hitler invaded Poland. The Pact ended when Hitler invaded Russia on 22 June 1941. See also ◊World War II.

Nehru Jawaharlal 1889–1964. Indian nationalist politician, prime minister from 1947. Before the partition (the division of British India into India and Pakistan) he led the socialist wing of the Nationalist ◊Congress Party, and was second in influence only to Mohandas ◊Gandhi. He was imprisoned nine times by the British 1921–45 for political activities. As prime minister from the creation of the dominion (later republic) of India Aug 1947, he originated the idea of ◊nonalignment (neutrality towards major powers). His daughter was Prime Minister Indira ◊Gandhi.

neocolonialism disguised form of ◊imperialism, by which a country may grant independence to another country but continue to dominate it by control of markets for goods or raw materials.

This system was analysed in the Ghanaian leader Kwame Nkrumah's book *Neo-Colonialism, the Last Stage of Imperialism* 1965.

NEP abbreviation for the Soviet leader Lenin's ◊New Economic Policy.

Netherlands, the country in W Europe on the North Sea, bounded E by Germany and S by Belgium.

government The Netherlands is an hereditary monarchy. Its constitution 1983, based on that of 1814, provides for a two-chamber legislature called the States-General, consisting of a First Chamber and a Second Chamber. Members of the First Chamber are indirectly elected by representatives of 11 provincial councils, and Second Chamber members are elected by universal adult suffrage, through a system of proportional representation. Legislation is introduced and bills amended in the Second Chamber, while the First has the right to approve or reject.

The monarch appoints a prime minister as head of government, and the prime minister chooses the cabinet, all appointed for life. The sovereign is its formal president but appoints a vice president to chair it. Although not a federal state, the Netherlands gives considerable autonomy to its 11 provinces, each of which has an appointed governor and an elected council.

history During the 19th century the Netherlands followed a path of strict neutrality, but its brutal occupation by Germany 1940–45 persuaded it to adopt a policy of cooperation with its neighbours. It became a member of the Western European Union, the North Atlantic Treaty Organization (NATO), the Benelux customs union, the European Coal and Steel Community, the European Atomic Energy Community (Euratom), and the European Community. In 1980 Queen Juliana, who had reigned since 1948, abdicated in favour of her eldest daughter, Beatrix. The granting of independence to former colonies (Indonesia 1949, with the addition of W New Guinea 1963; Suriname 1975) increased immigration and unemployment. All governments since 1945 have been coalitions, with the parties differing mainly over economic policies. The three significant parties are the Christian Democratic Appeal (CDA) the Labour Party (PvdA), and the Liberal Party. In Sept 1989 elections were fought largely on environmental issues, Ruud Lubbers' Christian Democrats won the most parliamentary seats. Lubbers formed a coalition government with the leftist Labour Party.

New Deal in the USA, programme introduced

by President F D Roosevelt 1933 to counter the ◊depression of 1929, including employment on public works, farm loans at low rates, and social reforms such as old-age and unemployment insurance, prevention of child labour, protection of employees against unfair practices by employers, and loans to local authorities for slum clearance. In the first 100 days of Roosevelt's administration, he introduced and pushed through Congress hundreds of programmes and economic initiatives. Critics from the right called his approach too socialistic.. Many of its provisions were declared unconstitutional by the Supreme Court 1935–36, and full employment was not established until the military-industrial needs of World War II.

The ***Public Works Administration*** was given $3.3 billion to spend on roads, public buildings, and similar developments (the ◊Tennessee Valley Authority was a separate project). The ***Agricultural Adjustment Administration*** raised agricultural prices by restriction of output. In 1935 Harry L Hopkins was put in charge of a new agency, the ***Works Progress Administration*** (WPA), which in addition to taking over the public works created something of a cultural revolution with its federal theatre, writers', and arts projects. When the WPA was disbanded 1943 it had found employment for 8.5 million people.

The New Deal encouraged the growth of trade-union membership, brought previously unregulated areas of the US economy under federal control, and revitalized cultural life and community spirit. Although it did not succeed in restoring full prosperity, it did bring political stability to the industrial-capitalist system.

New Economic Policy (NEP) economic policy of the USSR 1921–29 devised by the Soviet leader ◊Lenin. Rather than requisitioning all agricultural produce above a stated subsistence allowance, the state requisitioned only a fixed proportion of the surplus; the rest could be traded freely by the peasant. The NEP thus reinstated a limited form of free-market trading, although the state retained complete control of major industries.

The NEP was introduced in Mar 1921 after a series of peasant revolts and the Kronstadt uprising, a revolt by sailors who demanded the rights obtained in theory by the 1917 revolution. Aimed at re-establishing an alliance with the peasantry, it began as an agricultural measure to act as an incentive for peasants to produce more food. The policy was ended in 1928 by Stalin's first Five-Year Plan, which began the collectivization of agriculture.

newspaper a daily or weekly publication in the form of folded sheets containing news and comment. In recent years, production costs have fallen with the introduction of new technology.

The invention of the Linotype machine that cast whole lines of type, introduced in Britain 1896, together with better train services, first made national breakfast-time circulation possible. There were nine evening papers in the London area at the end of the 19th century, and by 1920, 50% of British adults read a daily paper. The first generation of press barons, William Beaverbrook, Alfred Northcliffe, and Harold Rothermere in the UK, and William Hearst in the USA, used their power to propagate their own political opinions.

Newspapers in the first half of the 20th century reinforced the traditional class model of British society, being aimed at upper, middle, or working-class readers. During World War II and until 1958, newsprint rationing prevented market forces from killing off the weaker papers. Polarization into 'quality' and 'tabloid' newspapers followed. The sales of the mass-circulation papers are boosted by lotteries and photographs of women in states of undress; their news content is small. British newspapers cover a political spectrum from the moderate left to the far right. Investigative reporting is restricted by stringent laws of libel and contempt of court and by the Official Secrets Act. The Press Council was established 1953 to foster 'integrity and a sense of responsibility to the public', but has no power to enforce its recommendations. In Dec 1989 all major national newspapers agreed on a new code of conduct to prevent possible new legislation by instituting a right of reply, a readers representative and prompt correction of mistakes.

new town a planned urban area. In the UK, new towns were partly designed to accomodate the overspill from large cities and towns with provision for housing, employment and other amenities after World War II, when the population was rapidly expanding and city centres had either decayed or been destroyed. In 1976 the policy, which had been criticized for disrupting family groupings and local communities, destroying small shops and specialist industries, and leading to the decay of city centres, was abandoned.

In order to stimulate employment in depressed areas, 14 new towns were planned 1946–50, with populations of 25–60,000, among them Cwmbran and Peterlee, and eight near London to relieve congestion there. Another 15, with populations up to 250,000, were established 1951–75, but by then a static population and cuts in government spending halted their creation.

Nicholas II 1868–1918. Tsar of Russia 1894–1917. He was dominated by his wife, Princess Alix of Hessen (Tsarina Alexandra), who was under the influence of 'holy man' Gregory ◊Rasputin. His mismanagement of the ◊Russo-Japanese War and of internal affairs led to the revolution of 1905, which he suppressed, although he was forced to grant limited constitutional reforms. He took Russia into World War I in 1914, was forced to abdicate in 1917 (see ◊Russian Revolution) and was executed with his family.

Nigeria country in W Africa on the Gulf of Guinea, bounded N by Niger, E by Chad and Cameroon, and W by Benin.

history Nigeria has been inhabited since about 700 BC. In the Muslim north, Portuguese and British slave traders raided from the 15th century. In 1900 two protectorates were set up by the British: N Nigeria and S Nigeria, with Lagos joined to S Nigeria 1906. Britain's largest African colony, Nigeria, was united 1914.

republic Nigeria became a federation 1954 and achieved full independence, as a constitutional monarchy within the ◊Commonwealth, in 1960. In 1963 it became a republic, based on a federal structure so as to accommodate the many different ethnic groups. Nigeria's first president was Dr Nnamdi Azikiwe, a banker and proprietor of a newspaper group, who had played a leading part in the movement for independence. He came from the Ibo tribe. His chief rival was Abubakar Tafawa Balewa, who was prime minister from 1957 until he was assassinated in a military coup in 1966. The coup had been led mainly by Ibo junior officers from the eastern region, which had become richer after the discovery of oil there in 1958. The offices of president and prime minister were suspended, and it was announced that the state's federal structure would be abandoned. Before this could be done, the new military government was overturned in a counter-coup by a mostly Christian group from the north, led by Col Yakubu Gowon. He re-established the federal system and appointed a military governor for each region. Soon afterwards tens of thousands of Ibos in the north were killed.

civil war In 1967 a conflict developed between Gowon and the military governor of the eastern region, Col Chukwuemeka Odumegwu-Ojukwu, about the distribution of oil revenues, which resulted in Ojukwu's declaration of an independent Ibo state of Biafra. Gowon, after failing to pacify the Ibos, ordered federal troops into the eastern region, and a civil war began, lasting until Jan 1970, when Biafra surrendered to the federal forces. It was the first war among black Africans, and it left the economy gravely weakened. Warfare and famine together took an estimated one million lives.

bloodless coups In 1975, while he was out of the country, Gowon was replaced in a bloodless coup led by Brigadier Murtala Mohammad, but he was killed within a month and replaced by General Olusegun Obasanjo. He announced a gradual return to civilian rule, and in 1979 the leader of the National Party of Nigeria, Shehu Shagari, became president. In Dec 1983, with the economy suffering from falling oil prices, Shagari's civilian government was deposed in another bloodless coup, led by Maj-Gen Muhammadu Buhari. In 1985 another peaceful coup replaced Buhari with a new military government, led by Major-General Ibrahim Babangida, the army Chief of Staff. At the end of the year an attempted coup by rival officers was thwarted. President Babangida promised a return to a democratic civilian government in 1992, although in an effort to end corruption, he banned all persons who ever held elective office from being candidates for the new civilian government. The ban on political activity was also lifted May 1989, but the government has rejected the applications of former political associations for recognition as political parties, instead creating two official parties, one to the left and one to the right of the political spectrum. In 1990 inflation was running at 51%. Austerity measures, prescribed by the IMF in response to economic assistance, created widespread dissatisfaction with the government.

Night of the Long Knives a purge of the German Nazi party to root out possible opposition to Adolf Hitler. On the night of 29–30 June 1934 (and the following two days) the SS units under Heinrich Himmler were used by Hitler to exterminate the Nazi private army Sturm-Abteilung (SA or the Brownshirts) under Captain Ernst Roehm. Others were also executed for alleged conspiracy against Hitler (including Kurt von Schleicher). The Nazi purge enabled Hitler to gain the acceptance of the German Officer Corps and, when President Hindenburg died five weeks later, to become head of state.

The phrase 'Night of the Long Knives' was first used by Hitler on 13 July 1934 in a speech delivered at the Kroll Opera House, in Berlin. It was also used to describe the British prime minister Harold Macmillan's dismissal of seven members of his cabinet on 13 July 1962 in an attempt to retrieve Conservative fortunes.

Nixon *US President Richard Milhous Nixon. He resigned in mid-term while under threat of impeachment as his involvement in the Watergate Scandal was revealed.*

Nixon Richard (Milhous) 1913– . The 37th president of the USA 1969–74, a Republican. He attracted attention as a member of the Un-American Activities Committee 1948, and was vice president to Eisenhower 1953–61. As president he was résponsible for US withdrawal from Vietnam, and forged new links with China, but at home his culpability in the cover-up of the ◊Watergate scandal and the existence of a 'slush fund' for political machinations during his re-election campaign 1972 led to his resignation 1974 after being threatened with impeachment.

Of Quaker family, Nixon grew up in Whittier, California; he became a lawyer, entered Congress in 1947, and in 1948, as a member of the Un-American Activities Committee, pressed for the investigation of Alger Hiss, accused of being a spy. Nixon was senator for California from 1951 until elected vice president. He lost the presidential election 1960 to J F Kennedy, partly because televised electoral debates put him at a disadvantage. He did not seek presidential nomination in 1964, but in a 'law and order' campaign defeated Vice-President Humphrey 1968 in one of the most closely contested elections in US history.

In 1969 he formulated the Nixon Doctrine abandoning close involvement with Asian countries, but escalated the war in Cambodia by massive bombing. Re-elected 1972 in a landslide victory over George McGovern, he resigned 1974, the first US president to do so, under threat of impeachment on three counts: obstruction of the administration of justice in the investigation of Watergate; violation of constitutional rights of citizens, for example attempting to use the Internal Revenue Service, ◊Federal Bureau of Investigation, and Central Intelligence Agency as weapons against political opponents; and failure to produce 'papers and things' as ordered by the Judiciary Committee. He was granted a pardon 1974 by President Ford.

Nkomo Joshua 1917– . Zimbabwean politician, president of ZAPU (Zimbabwe African People's Union) from 1961 and a leader of the black nationalist movement against the white Rhodesian regime. He was a member of Robert ◊Mugabe's cabinet in 1980–82 and from 1987.

After completing his education in South Africa, Joshua Nkomo became a welfare officer on Rhodesian Railways and later organizing secretary of the Rhodesian African Railway Workers' Union. He entered politics 1950 and rose to become president of ZAPU. He was soon arrested, with other black African politicians, and was in detention during 1963–74. After his release he joined forces with Robert Mugabe as a joint leader of the Patriotic Front 1976, opposing the white-dominated regime of Ian Smith. Nkomo took part in the Lancaster House Conference, which led to Rhodesia's independence as the new state of Zimbabwe, and became a cabinet minister and vice president.

Nkrumah Kwame 1909–1972. Ghanaian nationalist politician, prime minister of the

Nkomo *Zimbabwean politician and cabinet member Joshua Nkomo.*

Nkrumah *The first president of Ghana, Kwame Nkrumah.*

Gold Coast (Ghana's former name) 1952–57 and of newly independent Ghana 1957–60. He became Ghana's first president 1960 but was overthrown in a coup 1966. His policy of 'African socialism' led to links with the Communist bloc.

Originally a teacher, he studied later in both Britain and the USA, and on returning to Africa formed the Convention People's Party (CPP) 1949 with the aim of immediate self-government. He was imprisoned in 1950 for incitement of illegal strikes, but was released the same year. As president he established an authoritarian regime and made Ghana a one-party (CPP) state 1964. He then dropped his stance of nonalignment and drew closer to the USSR and other communist countries. Deposed from the presidency while on a visit to Beijing (Peking) 1966, he remained in exile in Guinea, where he was made a co-head of state until his death, but was posthumously 'rehabilitated' 1973.

nonaligned movement strategic and political position of neutrality ('nonalignment') towards major powers, specifically the USA and USSR. Although originally used by poorer states, the nonaligned position was later adopted by oil-producing nations. The 1989 summit in Belgrade was attended by 102 member states.

The term was originally used by the Indian prime minister Nehru, and was adopted 1961 at an international conference in Belgrade, Yugoslavia, by the country's president Tito, in general opposition to colonialism, neocolonialism, and imperialism, and to the dominance of dangerously conflicting East and West alliances. However, many members were in receipt of aid from either East or West or both, and some went to war with one another (Vietnam–Cambodia, Ethiopia–Somalia).

nonviolence the principle or practice of abstaining from the use of violence. The Indian nationalist leader Mahatma Gandhi adopted a campaign of passive resistance 1907–14 in response to the attempts by the Transvaal Government to discriminate against Indians in South Africa. Later, in India, Gandhi employed nonviolent methods, including the boycotting of British goods and hunger strikes. Martin Luther ◊King led a nonviolent ◊civil-rights movement in the USA. He organized a boycott against segregated seating on the buses in Montgomery, Alabama. In June 1963 he led a peaceful demonstration in Washington and in March 1965 led a civil-rights march from Selina to Montgomery.

Normandy landings in World War II the Normandy beaches, NW France, were the site of the Allied invasion on ◊D-day, 6 June 1944.

North Africa Campaign Allied military campaign 1940–42 during World War II. Shortly after Italy declared war on France and Britain June 1940, an Italian offensive was launched from Libya towards Egypt and the Suez Canal. In Dec 1940 Britian launched a successful counter-offensive and captured Cyrenaica. Following agreement between Mussolini and Hitler the German Afrikakorps was established under General Rommel. During 1941 and early 1942 the ◊Axis powers advanced, recaptured Tobruk, and crossed the Egyptian border before halting at El Alamein. The British 8th Army under General Montgomery won a decisive Allied victory against Rommel's forces at El Alamein on 4 Nov 1942, followed by advances across Libya from Tunisia. British and US troops advanced from French North West Africa and the Allied armies in N Africa converged on Tunis. After a last ditch defence the Axis forces surrendered in May 1943.

North Atlantic Treaty Organization (NATO) association set up 1949 to provide for the collective defence of the major W European and North American states against the perceived threat from the USSR. Its chief body is the Council of Foreign Ministers (who have representatives in permanent session), and there is an international secretariat in Brussels, Belgium, and also the Military Committee consisting of the Chiefs of Staff. The military headquarters SHAPE (Supreme Headquarters Allied Powers, Europe) is in Chièvres, near Mons, Belgium.

Both the Supreme Allied Commanders (Europe and Atlantic) are from the USA, but there is also an Allied Commander, Channel (a British admiral). In 1960 a permanent multinational ***Allied Mobile Force*** (AMF) was established to move immediately to any NATO country under threat of attack; headquarters in Heidelberg, Germany.

France withdrew from the military integration (not the alliance) 1966; Greece withdrew politically but not militarily 1974. In 1980 Turkey was opposed to Greek re-entry because of differences over rights in the Aegean Sea. NATO has encountered numerous problems since its inception over such issues as the dominant position of the USA, the presence in Europe of US nuclear weapons, burden sharing, and standardization of weapons. In 1990, after a meeting in London, NATO declared that nuclear weapons were 'weapons of last resort' rather than 'flexible response', and offered to withdraw all nuclear artillery shells from Europe if the USSR did the same. NATO's counterpart is the ◊Warsaw Pact.

Original signatories of the North Atlantic Treaty 1949 were Belgium, Canada, Denmark, France, Iceland, Italy, Luxembourg, Netherlands, Norway, Portugal, the UK, and the USA. Greece and Turkey were admitted as parties to the treaty 1952, West Germany 1955, and Spain 1982.

North–South divide the North–South geographical division of the world which theoretically demarcates the rich from the poor. The South includes all of Asia (except Japan, Australia, and New Zealand), all of Africa, the Middle East, Central and South America. The North includes Europe, the USA, Canada, and the USSR.

Many of the countrics in the South, particularly the relatively newly industrialized ones such as South Korea and Taiwan could be said to have more in common with the developed than developing ◊Third World counties.

Norway country in NW Europe, on the Scandinavian peninsula, bounded E by Sweden and NE by Finland and the USSR.

history The experience of German occupation 1940–45 persuaded the Norwegians to abandon their traditional neutral stance and join NATO 1949, the Nordic Council 1952, and the European Free Trade Area (EFTA) 1960. Norway was accepted into membership of the European Community 1972, but a referendum held that year rejected the proposal and the application was withdrawn. Its exploitation of North Sea oil and gas resources have given it a higher income per head of population than most of its European neighbours, and during the Cold War it succeeded in maintaining good relations with the USSR without damaging its commitments in the West. Norway has enjoyed stability under a series of coalition governments. In Nov 1988 Prime Minister Gro Harlem Brundtland was awarded the annual Third World Prize for her work on environmental issues but in the Sept 1989 election her party lost seats to the far-right and the far-left. Following a vote of no confidence, she resigned in Oct 1989 and was succeeded by the conservative Jan P Syse. In Oct 1990 the Syse coalition collapsed and Mrs Brundtland returned to power, leading a minority Labour government.

nuclear energy energy from the inner core or nucleus of the atom, as opposed to energy released in chemical processes, which is derived from the electrons surrounding the nucleus.

Nuclear fission, as in an atom bomb, is achieved by allowing a neutron to strike the nucleus of an atom of uranium-235, which then splits apart to release two or three other neutrons. If the uranium-235 is pure, a chain reaction is set up when these neutrons in turn strike other nuclei. This happens very quickly, resulting in the burst of energy seen in the atomic bomb.

Nuclear fusion is the process that occurs in the hydrogen bomb, and in the sun and other stars, whereby hydrogen nuclei fuse to form helium nuclei with an accompanying release of energy. Attempts to harness fusion for commercial power production have so far been unsuccessful. In the UK atomic energy and its uses are controlled by the United Kingdom Atomic Energy Authority. The first large-scale nuclear power station was at Calder Hall, Cumbria 1956. By the 1980s, the UK was generating 15% of its electricity in 18 nuclear power stations.

nuclear safety the use of nuclear energy has given rise to concern over safety. Anxiety has been heightened by accidents such as Windscale, UK; Five Mile Island, USA; and Chernobyl, USSR. There has also been mounting concern about the production and disposal of ◊nuclear waste, the toxic by-products of the nuclear energy industry. Nuclear waste may have an active life of several thousand years and there are no guarantees of the safety of the various methods of disposal. In 1990 a scientific study revealed an increased risk of leukemia in children whose fathers had worked at Sellafield between 1950 and 1985. Sellafield (UK) is the world's greatest discharger of radioactive waste.

nuclear warfare war involving the use of nuclear weapons. Nuclear-weapons research began in Britain 1940, but was transferred to the USA after it entered World War II. The research programme, known as the Manhattan Project, was directed by J Robert

Oppenheimer. The worldwide total of nuclear weapons in 1989 was about 50,000, and the number of countries possessing nuclear weapons stood officially at five – USA, USSR, UK, France, and China – although many other nations were thought either to have a usable stockpile of these weapons (Israel, South Africa) or the ability to produce them quickly (India, Pakistan, and others).

atom bomb The original weapon relied on the use of a chemical explosion to trigger a chain reaction. The first test explosion was at Alamogordo, New Mexico, 16 Jul 1945; the first use in war was by the USA against Japan 6 Aug 1945 over Hiroshima and three days later at Nagasaki.

hydrogen bomb A much more powerful weapon than the atom bomb, it relies on the release of thermonuclear energy by the condensation of hydrogen nuclei to helium nuclei (as happens in the Sun). The first detonation was at Eniwetok Atoll, Pacific Ocean, 1952 by the USA.

neutron bomb or ***enhanced radiation weapon*** (ERW). It is a very small hydrogen bomb that has relatively high radiation but relatively low blast, designed to kill (in up to six days) by a brief neutron radiation that leaves buildings and weaponry intact.

Nuclear methods of attack now include aircraft bombs, rocket-propelled missiles with nuclear warheads (long- or short-range, surface-to-surface, and surface-to-air), depth charges, and high-powered landmines ('atomic demolition munitions' to blast craters in the path of an advancing enemy army). The major subjects of Soviet-US negotiation are: ***intercontinental ballistic missiles*** (ICBMs), which since 1968, have been equipped with clusters of warheads.

Nuclear methods of defence include: ***antiballistic missile*** (ABM) Earth-based systems with two types of missile, one short-range with high acceleration, and one comparatively long-range for interception above the atmosphere; ***Strategic Defense Initiative*** (announced by the USA 1983 to be operative from 2000; popularly known as the 'Star Wars' programme) 'directed energy weapons' firing laser beams would be mounted on space stations, and by burning holes in incoming missiles would either collapse them or detonate their fuel tanks.

nuclear waste the radioactive and toxic by-products of the nuclear-energy and nuclear-weapons industries. Reactor waste is of three types: high-level spent fuel, or the residue when nuclear fuel has been removed from a reactor and reprocessed; intermediate, which may be long- or short-lived; and low-level, but bulky, waste from reactors, which has only short-lived radioactivity. Disposal, by burial on land or at sea, has raised problems of safety, environmental pollution, and security. In absolute terms, nuclear waste cannot be safely relocated or disposed of.

reprocessing About one-third of the fuel from nuclear reactors becomes spent each year. It is removed to a reprocessing plant where radioactive waste products are chemically separated from remaining uranium and plutonium, in an expensive and dangerous process. This practice increases the volume of radioactive waste more than a hundred times.

nuclear winter an expected long-term effect of a widespread nuclear war. In the wake of the destruction caused by nuclear blasts and the subsequent radiation, it has been suggested that atmospheric pollution by dust, smoke, soot, and ash could prevent the Sun's rays from penetrating for a period of time sufficient to eradicate most plant life on which other life depends, and create a new Ice Age.

Even after it had settled, ash would still reflect the Sun's rays and delay the planet's return to normal warmth. Insects, grasses, and sea life would have the best prospects of survival, as well as microorganisms.

Nuremberg trials after World War II, the trials of the 24 chief ◊Nazi war criminals Nov 1945–Oct 1946 by an international military tribunal consisting of four judges and four prosecutors: one of each from the USA, UK, USSR, and France. An appendix accused the German cabinet, general staff, high command, Nazi leadership corps, ◊SS, Sturmabteilung, and ◊Gestapo of criminal behaviour.

The main charges in the indictment were: (1) conspiracy to wage wars of aggression; (2) crimes against peace; (3) war crimes, for example, murder and ill-treatment of civilians and prisoners of war, deportation of civilians for slave labour, and killing of hostages; (4) crimes against humanity, for example, mass murder of the Jews and other peoples, and murder and ill-treatment of political opponents.

Of the accused, Alfred Krupp was too ill to be tried; Ley committed suicide during the trial; and Martin Bormann, who had fled, was sentenced to death in his absence. Fritsche, Hjalmar Schacht and Franz von Papen were acquitted. The other 18 were found guilty on one or more counts. Rudolf Hess, Walther Funk, and Erich Raeder were sentenced to life imprisonment; Shirach and Albert Speer to 20 years; Konstantin von Neurath to 15 years;

and Doenitz to 10 years. The remaining 11 men, sentenced to death by hanging, were Hans Frank, Wilhelm Frick, Hermann Goering (who committed suicide before he could be executed), Alfred Jodl, Ernst Kaltenbrunner, Wilhelm Keitel, Joachim Ribbentrop, Alfred Rosenberg, Fritz Sauckel, Arthur Seyss-Inquart, and Julius Streicher. The SS and Gestapo were declared criminal organizations.

Nyerere Julius (Kambarage) 1922– . Tanzanian socialist politician, president 1964–85. Originally a teacher, he devoted himself from 1954 to the formation of the Tanganyika African National Union and subsequent campaigning for independence. He became chief minister 1960, was prime minister of Tanganyika 1961–62, president of the newly formed Tanganyika Republic 1962–64, and first president of Tanzania 1964–85. Nyerere is a prominent advocate of African unity; he became head of the Organization of African Unity 1984. Under his leadership Tanzania sent troops to support the overthrow of President Idi Amin of Uganda 1979.

Nyerere *Tanzanian politician and premier Dr Julius Nyerere, in London, 1960.*

O

OAU abbreviation for ◊***Organization of African Unity***.

Obote (Apollo) Milton 1924– . Ugandan politician who led the independence movement from 1961. He became prime minister 1962 and was president 1966–71 and 1980–85, being overthrown by first Idi Amin and then Lt-Gen Tito Okello.

October Revolution the second stage of the ◊Russian Revolution 1917, when, on 24 Oct (6 Nov Western calendar), the Red Guards under Trotsky, and on orders from Lenin, seized the Winter Palace and arrested members of the Provisional Government. The following day the Second All-Russian Congress of Soviets handed over power to the ◊Bolsheviks.

Oder-Neisse Line border between Poland and East Germany provisionally agreed at the Yalta Conference, and confirmed at the Potsdam Conference in 1945 at the end of World War II. It was named after the two rivers that form the frontier.

Approximately 6 million Germans were expelled from the territory handed over to Poland, which was subsequently resettled by the Poles.

oil natural mineral oil, a thick greenish-brown flammable liquid found underground. From crude oil or ◊petroleum, various products are made by distillation and other processes; for example, fuel oil, gasoline (petrol), kerosene, diesel, lubricating oil, paraffin wax, and petroleum jelly.

The burning of fuels derived from petroleum is a major cause of air pollution. Its transport can lead to major catastrophes – for example, the *Torrey Canyon* tanker lost off SW England, 1967, which led to an agreement by the international oil companies 1968 to pay compensation for massive shore pollution. The 1989 oil spill in Alaska from the *Exxon Valdez* damaged the area's fragile environment, despite clean-up efforts. The 1991 oil spill released into the Persian Gulf during the Gulf War likewise threatened the delicately balanced ecosystem in the locality. The problems associated with petroleum have led to various alternative energy technologies. See ◊Organization of the Petroleum Exporting Countries.

Okinawa largest of the Japanese Ryukyu Islands in the W Pacific. It was captured by the USA in the ***Battle of Okinawa*** 1 Apr–21 June 1945, with 47,000 US casualties (12,000 dead) and 60,000 Japanese (only a few hundred survived as prisoners); the island was returned to Japan 1972.

old-age pension a regular payment made by the state or by a private institution, to those who have reached a specified age and are eligible for such assistance. In Germany, the Old Age and Invalidity Insurance Law 1889 provided pensions as part of chancellor Otto von Bismarck's 'state socialism'. The costs were divided between employers, employees, and the state. In Britain, the Old Age Pensions Act 1908 provided a weekly pension of five shillings to people over 70 years of age (7s 6d for a married couple) with an income of less than ten shillings a week.

one-party state a state in which there is a ban, constitutional or unofficial, on the number of political parties permitted to stand for election. In some cases there may be no legal alternative parties. For example: in the USSR members of only one political party stand for election; in others there may be limited tolerance of a few token members of an opposition party, as in Mexico; or one party may be permanently in power with no elections.

Organization for Economic Cooperation and Development (OECD) Paris-based international organization of 24 industrialized countries, which coordinates member states' economic policy strategies. The OECD's subsidiary bodies include the International Energy Agency 1974, set up in the face of a world oil crisis.

It superseded the Organization for European Economic Cooperation (established 1948 to promote European recovery under the ◊Marshall Plan) 1961, when the USA and Canada became members and its scope was extended to include development aid. The OECD members are: Australia, Austria, Belgium, Canada, Denmark, Finland, France, Germany, Greece, Iceland, Ireland, Italy, Japan, Luxembourg, Netherlands, New Zealand, Norway, Portugal, Spain, Sweden, Switzerland, Turkey, UK, and USA.

Organization of African Unity (OAU) association of African States established at the Pan-African Conference in Addis Ababa 1963 to eradicate colonialism and improve economic, cultural, and political cooperation in Africa; headquarters Addis Ababa, Ethiopia. The secretary-general is Salim Ahmed Salim (deputy prime minister of Tanzania). The French-speaking ***Joint African and Mauritian Organization/Organisation Commune Africaine et Mauritienne: OCAM*** (1962) works within the framework of the OAU for African solidarity; headquarters Yaoundé, Cameroon.

Organization of the Petroleum Exporting Countries (OPEC) body established 1960 to coordinate price and supply policies of oil-producing states, and also to improve the position of ◊Third World states by forcing Western states to open their markets to the resultant products. Its concerted action in raising prices in the 1970s triggered worldwide recession but also lessened demand so that its influence was reduced by the mid-1980s. OPEC members include: Algeria, Ecuador, Gabon, Indonesia, Iran, Iraq, Kuwait, Libya, Nigeria, Qatar, Saudi Arabia, United Arab Emirates, and Venezuela.

OPEC's importance in the world market was reflected in its ability to implement oil price increases from $3 a barrel in 1973 to $30 a barrel in 1980. In the 1980s, OPEC's dominant position was undermined by reduced demand for oil in industrialized countries, increased non-OPEC oil supplies, and production of alternative energy. These factors contributed to the dramatic fall in world oil prices to $10 a barrel in July 1986 from $28 at the beginning of the year. OPEC's efforts to stabilize oil prices through mandatory reduced production have been resisted by various members.

Orwell George. Pen name of Eric Arthur Blair 1903–1950, English author. His books include the satire *Animal Farm* 1945, which included such sayings as 'All animals are equal, but some are more equal than others', and the prophetic *Nineteen Eighty-Four* 1949, portraying the dangers of excessive state control over the individual. Life as a dishwasher and tramp were related in *Down and Out in Paris and London*, and service for the Republican cause in the Spanish Civil War in *Homage to Catalonia*.

Osborne Judgement UK legal ruling of 1909 that prevented ◊trade unions from using membership subscriptions to finance the ◊Labour Party. In 1913 the judgement was negated by the Trade Union Act, which permitted them to raise political levies and provide financial support to the Labour Party. Individual trade unionists could 'contract out' of the political levy by signing a form saying they did not wish to pay.

W V Osborne, the secretary of the Walthamstow branch of the Amalgamated Society of Railway Servants and a member of the Liberal Party, took legal action to restrain the union and prohibit financial support for political parties. He won on an appeal that was upheld in the House of Lords.

Ostpolitik (German 'eastern policy') West German chancellor Willy ◊Brandt's policy of reconciliation with the communist bloc from 1971, pursued to a modified extent by his successors Schmidt and Kohl. The policy attained its goal with the reunification of Germany in 1990.

Ottawa agreements the trade agreements concluded at the Imperial Economic Conference, held in Ottawa 1932, between Britain and its dependent territories. The Dominions agreed to lower their preferential tariffs on British manufactures, while Britain admitted almost all Dominion produce free of duty, granted preferences to the rest, and increased duties on foreign imports competing with Dominion produce.

Ottoman Empire Muslim empire of the Turks 1300–1920. Its capital was Istanbul (formerly Constantinople). At its greatest extent its boundaries were Europe as far as Hungary, part of S Russia, Iran, the Palestinian coastline, Egypt, and N Africa. From the 17th century it was in decline. There was an attempted revival and reform under the Young Turk party 1908, but the regime crumbled when Turkey sided with Germany in World War I. The sultanate was abolished by Kemal Atatürk 1922; the last sultan was Muhammad VI.

P

Pakistan country in S Asia, stretching from the Himalayas to the Arabian Sea, bounded W by Iran, NW by Afghanistan, NE by China, and E by India.

history For history before 1947, see ◊India. Fear of domination by the Hindu majority in India led in 1940 to a serious demand for a separate Muslim state, which delayed for some years India's independence. In 1947 British India was divided into two dominions, India and Pakistan. Ater the death of its leader Muhammad ◊Jinnah 1948, Pakistan remained a dominion with the British monarch as head of state until being declared a republic March 1956. Its new constitution was repealed Oct 1958, and military rule was imposed through a coup by General Muhammad Ayub Khan. The country experienced rapid economic growth during the 1960s, but regional tension mounted between demographically dominant East Pakistan and West Pakistan, where political and military power was concentrated.

civil war After serious strikes and riots March 1969, General Ayub Khan stepped down and was replaced by the commander-in-chief, General Agha Muhammad Yahya Khan. Pakistan's first elections with universal suffrage were held Dec 1970 to elect an assembly to frame a new constitution. Sheikh Mujib ur-Rahman's Awami League, which proposed autonomy, gained a majority of seats in East Pakistan, and the Pakistan People's Party (or PPP) in West Pakistan. East Pakistan declared its independence from the West, March 1971, precipitating a civil war. India intervened on East Pakistan's side Dec 1971, and the independent republic of ◊Bangladesh emerged.

General Yahya Khan resigned, passing power in (W) Pakistan to the People's Party leader Zulfiqar Ali ◊Bhutto, who introduced a new federal parliamentary constitution April 1973 and a Socialist economic programme of land reform and nationalization. From the mid-1970s Bhutto faced deteriorating economic conditions and growing regional opposition. Bhutto won a majority in the March 1977 Assembly elections but was accused of ballot-rigging by the Pakistan National Alliance opposition. Riots ensued, and the Punjabi Muslim army Chief of Staff, General Zia ul-Haq, seized power in a bloodless coup July 1977. Martial law was imposed; Bhutto was imprisoned for alleged murder and hanged April 1979.

Islamization programme Between 1979 and 1981 General Zia imposed severe restrictions on political activity. He introduced a broad Islamization programme, which was opposed by middle-class professionals and by the Shi'ite minority. In March 1981, nine banned opposition parties, including the People's Party of Pakistan, formed the Movement for the Restoration of Democracy. The campaign resulted in considerable anti-government violence in Sind province 1983. In Dec 1985, martial law and the ban on political parties were lifted. A government was formed by the Pagaro faction of the Pakistan Muslim League led by Mohammad Khan Junejo, which supported, and was subservient to General Zia. Benazir ◊Bhutto, the daughter of Zulfiqar Ali Bhutto and leader of the Pakistan People's Party (PPP), returned from self-exile in London April 1986 to launch a popular campaign for immediate open elections. Riots erupted in Lahore, Karachi, and rural Sind, where troops were sent in, and PPP leaders were arrested. In May 1988, concerned with the deteriorating state of the economy and anxious to accelerate the Islamization process, President Zia dismissed the Junejo government and dissolved the National Assembly. Ruling by ordinance, Zia decreed, in July 1988, that the Sharia, the Islamic legal code, would immediately become the country's supreme law. A month later, the president was killed in a military air crash. Sabotage was suspected. Benazir Bhutto (PPP) became prime minister in Dec 1988, and Ghulam Ishaq Khan was elected as president. In March 1989 Nusrat Bhutto, the mother of Benazir Bhutto and widow of Zulfikar Ali Bhutto, was brought into the cabinet as deputy prime minister. The new Bhutto administration pledged itself to a free market economic programme. In Oct 1989 the MQM withdrew from the ruling coalition and allied itself with the opposition Islamic Democratic Alliance.

foreign affairs In foreign affairs, Pakistan's relations with India have been strained since independence, with border wars over Kashmir 1965 and East Pakistan 1971. It left the Commonwealth 1972, when the new state of Bangladesh was accepted, but rejoined in 1989. As a result of shared hostility to India, Pakistan has been allied with China since the 1950s; during the 1970s it developed close relations with the USA, providing support for the US-backed Afghan rebels, while at the same time joining the ◊nonaligned movement (1979) and drawing closer to the Islamic states of the Middle East and Africa.

Benazir Bhutto's government was dismissed from office by president Ghulam Ishaq Khan in Aug 1990 accused of incompetence, corruption, and abuse of power. The National Assemblies were also dissolved. On 24 Oct 1990 the opposition was swept to victory and Nawaz Sharif, Bhutto's former chief minister of Punjab province, was sworn in as prime minister. Sharif promised to pursue a free market economic programme and was supported by the military, state bureaucracy, and mullahs.

Palestine (Arabic *Falastin* 'Philistines') (also called the ***Holy Land*** because of its links with Judaism, Christianity, and Islam) the area between the Mediterranean and the river Jordan, with Lebanon to the north and Sinai to the south. Today it forms part of Israel. The Palestinian people (about 500,000 in the West Bank, E Jerusalem, and the Gaza Strip; 1.2 million in Jordan; 1.2 million in Israel; 300,000 in Lebanon; and 100,000 in the USA) are descendants of the people of Canaan.

1880–1914 Jewish immigration increased sharply as a result of pogroms in Russia and Poland

1897 At the first Zionist Congress, Jews called for a permanent homeland in Palestine

1909 Tel Aviv, the first all-Jewish town in Palestine was built

1917–18 Turks driven out by British Field Marshal Henry Allenby in World War I

1922 Britain received Palestine as a League of Nations mandate to administer both historic Palestine and lands across the river Jordan that were recognized 1923 as the Hashimite Kingdom of Jordan

1929 and ***1936–38*** Arab revolts fuelled by Jewish immigration (300,000 during 1920–39)

1937 Peel Commission report; Pan-Arab Congress

1938 Woodhead Commission

1939 British plan for Palestine

1939–45 Both Arab and Jewish Palestinians served in the Allied forces in World War II

1947 Following Jewish guerrilla activities, prompted by restriction of Jewish immigration, Britain put the question before the United Nations, which voted for partition

1948 15 May (eight hours before Britain's renunciation of the mandate was due) a Jewish state of ◊Israel was proclaimed. A series of ◊Arab-Israeli Wars resulted in the total loss of the Palestinian state, and the displacement of large numbers of Palestinian Arabs

1964 The Palestine Liberation Organization (PLO) was formed and a guerilla war was waged against the Jewish state

1974 The Palestine Liberation Organization became the first nongovernmental delegation to be admitted to a plenary session of the United Nations General Assembly

1987 The ***intifada***, a popular uprising against Israeli occupation began

1988 PLO leader Yasser Arafat renounces terrorism; USA agrees to meetings

1989 Israeli prime minister Yitzhak Shamir proposed Palestinian elections in the West Bank/Gaza Strip.

Palestine Liberation Organization (PLO) Arab organization founded 1964 to bring about an independent state of Palestine. It consists of several distinct groupings, the chief of which is al-Fatah, led by Yasser ◊Arafat, the president of the PLO since 1969. To achieve its ends it has pursued diplomatic initiatives, but also operates as a guerrilla army. In 1988, the Palestine National Council voted to create a state of Palestine, but at the same time endorsed United Nations resolution 242, recognizing Israel's right to exist.

Beirut, Lebanon became PLO headquarters 1970–71 after its defeat in the Jordanian civil war. In 1974 the PLO became the first nongovernmental delegation to be admitted to a session of the United Nations General Assembly. When Israel invaded Lebanon 1982 the PLO had to abandon its headquarters there; it moved on to Tunis, Tunisia and in 1986 to Baghdad, Iraq. PLO members who remained in Lebanon after the expulsion were later drawn into the internal conflict (see ◊Arab-Israeli Wars). In 1986 Jordan suspended 'political coordination' with the PLO and expelled Arafat's deputy, dealing instead directly with Palestinians in Israeli-occupied territories.

Palestine wars another name for the ◊Arab-Israeli wars.

Panama country in Central America, on a narrow isthmus between the Caribbean and the Pacific Ocean, bounded W by Costa Rica and E by Colombia.

history Panama achieved full independence 1903 with US support. At the same time the USA bought the rights to build the Panama Canal and was given control of a ten-mile-wide strip of territory, known as the Canal Zone, in perpetuity. Panama was guaranteed US protection and an annuity. In 1939 Panama's protectorate status was ended by mutual agreement, and in 1977 two treaties were signed by Panama's president (1968–78), General Omar Torrijos Herara, and US President Carter. One transferred ownership of the canal to Panama effective 1999 and the other guaranteed its subsequent neutrality, with the conditions that only Panamanian forces would be stationed in the zone, and that the USA would have the right to use force to keep the canal open if it became obstructed.

economy deterioration The 1980s saw a deterioration in the state of Panama's economy, with opposition to the government's austerity measures. Unade won 40 seats in the 1984 general election ADO won 27 seats. Dr Nicolas Ardito Barletta, the Democratic Revolutionary Party (PRD) candidate, was declared president, but in 1985 he resigned. Relations between Panama and the USA deteriorated with his departure: the Reagan administration cut and later suspended its financial aid.

Barletta was succeeded by Eric Arturo del Valle, but the country was, from 1983, effectively ruled by the army Commander in Chief, General Manuel Noriega. Although the 1977 Torrijos-Carter Canal Treaties specified that US forces in Panama were present purely to defend the canal, Noriega cooperated in allowing the US to use Panama as an intelligence, training, resupply, and weapons base for the Reagan administration's campaigns in Nicaragua and El Salvador.

US intervention In 1987 Noriega was accused of corruption. Noriega's forces were allegedly responsible for up to a dozen political killings between 1983 and 1989. Political parties, labour and student unions, and business groups united as the National Civic Crusade to campaign for his removal; demonstrations were suppressed by riot police. In July 1987 Noriega successfully resisted calls for his removal, despite the suspension of US military and economic aid. He declared the May 1989 assembly elections invalid and in Sept Francisco Rodriguez, with army backing, was made president. In the following month an attempted coup against Noriega was put down. In Dec 1989, after mounting harassment of Americans in the Canal Zone, US president Bush ordered troops to invade the country with the declared object of arresting Noriega and bringing him to trial. An estimated 7,000 people were killed and more than 15,000 made homeless in the US invasion. The US and Panamanian forces raided newspaper offices and rounded up hundreds of dissidents, many of whom were imprisoned without charge. Noriega took refuge in the Vatican embassy but eventually surrendered and was taken to the USA to answer charges relating to drug trafficking. The US authorities installed Guillermo Endara as president.

Panama Canal canal across the Panama isthmus in Central America, connecting the Pacific and Atlantic oceans; length 80 km/50 mi, with 12 locks. Built by the USA 1904–14, it was formally opened 1920. The ***Panama Canal Zone*** was acquired 'in perpetuity' by the USA 1903, comprising land extending about 5 km/3 mi on either side of the canal. The zone passed to Panama 1979, and control of the canal itself was ceded to Panama by the USA in Jan 1990 under the terms of the Panama Canal Treaty 1977.

It runs SE from Cristóbal on the Atlantic to Balboa on the Pacific. The original construction company, headed by the French engineer Ferdinand de Lesseps, began construction 1879, but collapsed 1889 because of financial scandals. It was designed to ensure free passage to international shipping in a turbulent area, but in the 1960s was the focus of US strategy in South America as a training for special forces devised by President Kennedy to fight irregular wars. Nationalist feeling in Panama led to anti-US riots 1964, and under the treaty of 1978 negotiated by President Carter, the zone passed to Panama 1979.

Pankhurst Emmeline (born Goulden) 1858–1928. English suffragette. Founder of the Women's Social and Political Union 1903, she launched the militant suffragette campaign 1905. In 1926 she joined the Conservative Party and was a prospective Parliamentary candidate.

She started as a Liberal, became a Fabian, then joined the Independent Labour Party, founded the WSPU, then became a Conservative. She became the prospective parliamentary candidate for the Whitechapel district of London. Her daughter Sylvia Pankhurst (1882–1960) was imprisoned nine times under the 'Cat and Mouse Act', was a pacifist in World War I, and a staunch supporter of the Ethiopian cause against Italy.

Papen Franz von 1879–1969. German right-wing politician. As chancellor 1932, he negotiated the Nazi-Conservative alliance that made Hitler chancellor 1933. He was envoy to

Austria 1934–38 and ambassador to Turkey 1939–44. Although acquitted at the ◊Nuremberg trials, he was imprisoned by a German denazification court for three years.

Paris, Treaty of any of various peace treaties signed in Paris; they include:

1919–20 The conference preparing the Treaty of ◊Versailles at the end of World War I was held in Paris.

1946 After World War II the peace treaties between the ◊Allies and Italy, Romania, Hungary, Bulgaria, and Finland.

1951 Treaty signed by France, West Germany, Italy, Belgium, Netherlands and Luxembourg, embodying the Schuman Plan to set up a single coal and steel authority.

1973 Ending US participation in the ◊Vietnam War.

parliament the legislative body of a country. The Supreme Soviet of the USSR, with 1,500 members, may be the world's largest legislature.

In the UK, Parliament is the supreme legislature, comprising the ◊House of Commons and the ◊House of Lords. The origins of Parliament are in the 13th century, but its powers were not established until the late 17th century. The English parliament was united with the Irish 1801–1922. The powers of the Lords were curtailed 1911, and the duration of parliaments was fixed at five years maximum, but any parliament may extend its own life, as happened during both world wars. It meets in the Palace of Westminster, London.

1832 Reform Act involves redistribution of parliamentary seats from 'rotten boroughs' to urban constituencies. Franchise extended to householders paying £10 per year rent in towns and 40-shilling freeholders in counties. (Electorate 813,000 = 7% of pop.)

1867 Reform Act involves further redistribution of seats and extension of franchise to all ratepayers in boroughs. (Electorate 2,500,000 = 16% of pop.)

1872 Ballot Act introduces secret ballots for elections.

1883 Corrupt and Illegal Practices Act sets limits to election expenses.

1884 Reform Act again involves redistribution of seats and equalisation of franchise for boroughs and counties, to include all householders and ratepayers. (Electorate 5,600,000 = 28.5% of pop.)

1885 Further redistribution of parliamentary seats.

1918 Representation of the People Act gives vote to all men over 21 and all women ratepayers (or wives of ratepayers) over 30. (Electorate 74% of pop.)

1928 Representation of the People (Equal Franchise) Act gives vote to all women over 21. (Electorate 97% of pop.)

1948 Plural voting abolished. Permanent Boundary Commission established.

1969 Voting age reduced to 18.

1979 Constituencies established for direct election to European Parliament in Strasbourg.

partition the division of a country into two or more nations. Ireland was divided into Northern Ireland and the Irish Republic under the Government of Ireland Act 1920. The division of the Indian subcontinent into India and Pakistan took place in 1947. Other examples of partition include Korea 1953 and Vietnam 1954.

Passchendaele village in W Flanders, Belgium, near Ypres. The Passchendaele ridge before ◊Ypres was the object of a costly and unsuccessful British offensive in World War I, between July and Nov 1917; British casualties numbered over 300,000.

Pasternak Boris Leonidovich 1890–1960. Russian poet and novelist. His volumes of lyric poems include *A Twin Cloud* 1914 and *On Early Trains* 1943, and he translated Shakespeare's tragedies. His novel *Dr Zhivago* 1957 was banned in the USSR as a 'hostile act', and followed by a Nobel prize (which he declined). *Dr Zhivago* has since been unbanned and Pasternak posthumously rehabilitated.

Patton George (Smith) 1885–1945. US general in World War II, known as 'Blood and Guts'. He commanded the 2nd Armoured Division 1940, and in 1942 led the Western Task Force that landed at Casablanca, Morocco. After commanding the 7th Army, he led the 3rd Army across France and into Germany, and in 1945 took over the 15th Army.

Pearl Harbor US Pacific naval base in Oahu, Hawaii, USA, the scene of a Japanese attack 7 Dec 1941, which brought the USA into World War II. It took place while Japanese envoys were holding so-called peace talks in Washington. More than 2,000 US servicemen were killed, and a large part of the US Pacific fleet was destroyed or damaged during the attack.

The Japanese, angered by US embargoes of oil and other military supplies and convinced that US entry into the war was inevitable, opted to strike a major blow in hopes of forcing US concessions. The attack galvanized public opinion and raised anti-Japanese sentiment to a fever pitch, with war declared thereafter. The local commanders Admiral Kummel and Lt-Gen Short were relieved of their posts and held responsible for the fact that the base was totally unprepared at the time of the attack, but recent information indicates that warnings of the attack given to the USA (by British intelligence and others) were withheld from Kummel and Short by President F D Roosevelt. US public opinion was very much against entering the war, and Roosevelt wanted an excuse to change popular sentiments and take the USA into the war.

peasant a country-dweller engaged in small-scale farming. A peasant normally owns or rents a small amount of land, aiming to be self-sufficient and to sell surplus supplies locally.

In the UK, the move towards larger farms in the 18th century resulted in the disappearance of the independent peasantry, although the custom survives in smallholdings and Scottish crofts. Landowners in countries such as France, Spain, and Italy showed less direct interest in agriculture, so the tradition of small independent landholding remains a distinctive way of life today. See also ◊commune and ◊kulak.

People's Budget the UK Liberal government's budget of 1909 to finance social reforms and naval rearmament. The chancellor of the Exchequer David Lloyd George proposed graded and increased income tax and a 'supertax' on high incomes. The budget aroused great debate and precipitated a constitutional crisis.

The People's Budget was passed in the House of Commons but rejected by the House of Lords. The prime minister Herbert Asquith denounced the House of Lords for a breach of the constitution over the finance bill and obtained the dissolution of Parliament. The Liberals were returned to power in the general election 1910. In 1911 the Parliament Act greatly reduced the power of the House of Lords.

perestroika (Russian 'restructuring') in Soviet politics, the wide-ranging economic and political reforms initiated during Mikhail Gorbachev's leadership of the Soviet state. It is also the title of a book by Gorbachev 1987.

The term was first proposed at the 26th Party Congress in 1979 and actively promoted by Gorbachev from 1985. Originally, in the economic sphere, perestroika was conceived as involving the 'switching onto a track of intensive development' by automation and improved labour efficiency. It has evolved to attend increasingly to market indicators and incentives ('market socialism') and a gradual dismantlement of the Stalinist central-planning system, with decision-taking authority being devolved to self-financing enterprises.

Pérez de Cuéllar Javier 1920– . Peruvian diplomat, secretary-general of the ◊United Nations from 1982. A delegate to the first UN General Assembly 1946–47, he subsequently held several ambassadorial posts. He raised the standing of the UN by his successful diplomacy in ending the Iran–Iraq war in 1988 and securing the independence of Namibia 1989. He was, however, unable to resolve the Gulf conflict resulting from Iraq's invasion of Kuwait 1990, leading to the ◊Gulf War 15 Jan–28 Feb 1991.

Pérez de Cuéllar *Peruvian diplomat and secretary-general of the United Nations since 1982, General Javier Pérez de Cuéllar, Mexico City, 1984.*

permissive society a society in which the prevailing ethic is one of tolerance, liberalism, and sexual freedom. The term often describes the years in the West from the 1950s to the 1970s.

Perón Juan (Domingo) 1895–1974. Argentine politician, dictator 1946–55 and from 1973 until his death. He took part in the military coup 1943, and his popularity with the *descamisados* ('shirtless ones') led to his election as president 1946. He instituted social reforms, but encountered economic difficulties. After the death of his second wife Eva Perón he lost popularity, and was deposed in a military coup 1955. He returned from exile to the presidency 1973, but died in office 1974, and was succeeded by his third wife Isabel Perón.

persecution the unjust harassment, often with cruelty, of a person or people. Examples in the 20th century include the persecution of the Jews in central and eastern Europe (particularly in Nazi Germany 1933–45) and the persecution of the Kenyan Asians in the 1960s.

Peru country in South America, on the Pacific, bounded N by Ecuador and Colombia, E by Brazil and Bolivia, and S by Chile.

history In the Pacific War against Chile

1879–83, Peru was defeated and lost three provinces (one, Tacna, was returned 1929). Other boundary disputes were settled by arbitration 1902 with Bolivia, 1927 with Colombia, and 1942 with Ecuador. Peru declared war on Germany and Japan Feb 1945.

military rule In 1948 a group of army officers led by General Manuel Odría ousted the elected government, temporarily banned APRA, and installed a military junta. Odría became president 1950 and remained in power until 1956. In 1963 military rule ended, and Fernando Belaúnde Terry, the joint candidate of the Popular Action (AP) and Christian Democrats (PDC) parties, won the presidency, while APRA took the largest share of the Chamber of Deputies seats. After economic problems and industrial unrest, Belaúnde was deposed in a bloodless coup 1968, and the army returned to government led by General Velasco Alvarado. Velasco introduced land reform, with private estates being turned into cooperative farms, but he failed to return any land to Indian peasant communities, and the Maoist guerrillas of *Sendero Luminoso* ('Shining Path') became increasingly active in the Indian region of S Peru.

economic and social crisis Another bloodless coup, 1975, brought in General Morales Bermúdez. He called elections for the presidency and both chambers of Congress May 1980, and Belaúnde was re-elected. Belaúnde introduced agrarian and industrial reform, but by 1985, the country was again in a state of economic and social crisis. His successor, Social Democrat, Alan García Pérez, tried to expand the economy with price and exchange controls. In July 1987 he announced his intention to nationalize the banks and insurance companies but delayed the move in Aug, after a vigorous campaign against the proposal. In 1989 the International Development Bank suspended credit to Peru because it was six months behind in debt payments. The annual inflation rate to April was 4,329%. With the president fast losing popularity, Alberto Fujimoro, the son of Japanese immigrants and leader of a new party, Change 90, won a substantial victory in the June 1990 elections. In Aug 1990 an attempt to assassinate the president failed.

Pétain Henri Philippe 1856–1951. French general and right-wing politician. His defence of Verdun 1916 during World War I made him a national hero. In World War II he became prime minister June 1940 and signed an armistice with Germany which disarmed French forces and placed much of France under German occupation. Removing the seat of government to ◊Vichy, he established an authoritarian regime. On the Allied invasion he was taken to Germany, but returned 1945 and was sentenced to death for treason, the sentence being commuted to life imprisonment.

petroleum natural mineral ◊oil, a thick greenish-brown flammable liquid found underground. The exploitation of oilfields began with the first commercial well in Pennsylvania 1859. The USA led in production until the 1960s, when the Middle East outproduced other areas, their immense reserves leading to a worldwide dependence on cheap oil for transport and industry. In 1961 the Organization of the Petroleum Exporting Countries (OPEC) was established to avoid exploitation of member countries; after OPEC's price rises in 1973, the International Energy Agency (IEA) was established 1974 to protect the interests of oil-consuming countries. New technologies were introduced to pump oil from offshore and from the Arctic (the Alaska pipeline) in an effort to avoid a monopoly by OPEC.

Philippines country on an archipelago E of the Pacific Ocean and W of the South China Sea.

history During the 19th century there were a series of armed nationalist revolts. These continued after the islands were ceded by Spain to the USA in 1898, and increasing self-government was granted in 1916 and 1935. The Philippines were occupied by Japan 1942–45, before becoming a fully independent republic in 1946. A succession of presidents drawn from the islands' wealthy estate-owning elite followed, doing little to improve the lot of the peasant.

In 1965 President Diosdado Macapagal was defeated by Ferdinand Marcos, the leader of the Nationalist Party. Marcos initiated rapid economic development and some land reform. He was re-elected in 1969, but encountered growing opposition. Marcos's authoritarian leadership was criticized for corruption, and in 1977 the opposition leader, Benigno Aquino, was jailed under sentence of death for alleged subversion. In 1978 martial law was relaxed, the 1972 ban on political parties was lifted, and elections for an interim National Assembly were held, resulting in an overwhelming victory for Marcos.

In Jan 1981 martial law was lifted completely, and hundreds of political prisoners released. Marcos then won approval, by referendum, for a partial return to democratic government with himself as president, working with a prime minister and executive council. Political and economic conditions deteriorated, Communist guerrilla insurgency escalated, unemployment climbed to over 30%. In 1983 Benigno Aquino, returning from self-imposed exile in the USA, was shot dead on his arrival at Manila airport. In 1986 the main anti-Marcos movement, United Nationalist Democratic Organization (UNIDO), chose Corazón Aquino, Benigno's widow, to contest new elections for the presidency that Marcos had been persuaded to hold as a means of maintaining vital US economic and diplomatic support.

'people's power' On 16 Feb 1986 the National Assembly declared Marcos the winner, a result disputed by an independent electoral watchdog, the National Citizens' Movement for Free Elections (Namfrel). Corazón Aquino began a non-violent protest, termed 'people's power', which gathered massive popular support, backed by the Roman Catholic church; President Marcos came under strong international pressure, particularly from the USA, to step down. On 22 Feb 1986 the army, led by Chief of Staff Lt-Gen Fidel Ramos and defence minister Juan Enrile, declared its support for Aquino, and on 25 Feb Marcos left for exile in Hawaii.

On assuming the presidency, Corazón Aquino dissolved the pro-Marcos National Assembly. She proceeded to govern in a conciliatory fashion, working with a coalition cabinet team comprising opposition politicians and senior military figures. She freed 500 political prisoners and granted an amnesty to the New People's Army (NPA) Communist guerrillas in an effort to end the 17-year-old insurgency and introduced a major rural-employment economic programme, with land reforms opposed by property owners.

freedom constitution The new administration endured a series of attempted coups by pro-Marcos supporters and faced serious opposition from Juan Enrile, dismissed in Nov 1986. In Feb 1987 a new 'freedom constitution' was overwhelmingly approved in a national plebiscite. This gave Aquino a mandate to rule as president until 30 June 1992. In the subsequent congressional elections, held in May 1987, Aquino's People's Power coalition won over 90% of the elected seats. However, in Aug 1987 the government was rocked by a coup attempt led by Col Gregorio 'Gringo' Honasan. In response, Aquino effected a major cabinet reshuffle in Sept 1987 that signalled a shift to the right in the government's policy, with tougher measures being instituted towards the NPA. Vice President Salvador Laurel, the former leader of UNIDO, was replaced as foreign minister. In Aug 1988 Laurel formed a new right-of-centre opposition force, the Union for National Action (UNA) and became president of the revived Nationalist Party in May 1989. Aquino endured a further reverse in Nov 1989 when a regional referendum proposing the merging of the 13 southern provinces, into an 'autonomous region' was rejected. This initiative had been made in an attempt to end the two decades long Muslim separatist struggle led by Moro National Liberation Front (MNLF).

Since becoming president, Corazón Aquino has enjoyed firm backing from the USA. US economic and military aid to the Philippines between 1985 and 1989 was approximately $1.5 billion. In Dec 1989 US air support was provided to help foil a further Honasan-planned coup attempt. Aquino declared a state of emergency, giving her broad powers to impose order. President Aquino survived another coup attempt in Oct 1990.

phoney war the period in World War II between Sept 1939, when the Germans had occupied Poland, and Apr 1940, when the invasions of Denmark and Norway took place. During this time there were few signs of hostilities in Western Europe; indeed, Hitler made some attempts to arrange a peace settlement with Britain and France.

Piłsudski Józef (Klemens) 1867–1935. Polish nationalist politician, dictator from 1926. Born in Russian Poland, he founded the Polish Socialist Party 1892 and was twice imprisoned for anti-Russian activities. During World War I he commanded a Polish force to fight for Germany but fell under suspicion of intriguing with the Allies and in 1917–18 was imprisoned by the Germans. When Poland became independent 1919, he was elected chief of state, and led an unsuccessful Polish attack on the USSR 1920. He retired 1923, but in 1926 led a military coup that established his dictatorship until his death.

PLO abbreviation for ◊***Palestine Liberation Organization***.

pogrom (Russian 'destruction') unprovoked violent attack on an ethnic group, particularly Jews, carried out with official sanction. The Russian pogroms against Jews began 1881, after the assassination of Tsar Alexander II, and again in 1903–06; persecution of the Jews remained constant until the Russian Revolution. Later there were pogroms in E Europe, especially in Poland after 1918, and in Germany under Hitler (see ◊Holocaust).

Poland country in E Europe, bounded E by the USSR, S by Czechoslovakia, and W by the Federal Republic of Germany.

history After years of occupation and partition by Prussia and Russia, Poland was revived as an independent republic 1918 under the leadership of Józef Piłsudski, the founder of the PPS, (Polish Socialist Party). Poland and the USSR then agreed on a frontier E of the Curzon Line.

the post-independence years Politically, the initial post-independence years were characterized by instability, 14 multi-party coalition governments holding power 1918–26. Piłsudski seized complete power in a coup and proceeded to govern in an increasingly authoritarian manner until his death in 1935. He was succeeded by a military regime headed by Smigly-Rydz.

World War II In April 1939 the UK and France concluded a pact with Poland to render military aid if it was attacked, and at the beginning of Sept Germany invaded (see ◊World War II). During the war, Western Poland was incorporated into the Nazi Reich, while the remainder, after a brief Soviet occupation of the east (1940–41), was treated as a colony. The country endured the full brunt of Nazi barbarism: a third of the educated elite were 'liquidated' and, in all, six million Poles lost their lives, half of them Jews slaughtered in concentration camps. A treaty between Poland and the USSR Aug 1945 (ratified 1946) established Poland's eastern frontier at the Curzon Line. Poland lost 181,350 sq km/70,000 sq mi in the east to the USSR but gained 101,000 sq km/39,000 sq mi in the west from Germany.

people's republic After elections, a 'people's republic' was established Feb 1947, and Poland joined ◊Comecon 1949 and the ◊Warsaw Pact 1955, remaining under close Soviet supervision, with the Soviet marshal Rokossovsky serving as minister for war 1949–56. A harsh Stalinist form of rule was instituted under the leadership of Boleslaw Bierut (1892–1956), involving rural collectivization, and the persecution of Catholic church opposition.

civil unrest In June 1956, serious strikes and riots, leading to 53 deaths, broke out in Poznan in opposition to Soviet 'exploitation' and food shortages. The more pragmatic Wladyslaw Gomulka took over as PUWP leader, reintroduced private farming, and released Cardinal Wyszynski. A further outbreak of strikes and rioting in Gdańsk, Gdynia, and Szczecin Dec 1970 followed sudden food-price rises. This led to Gomulka's replacement as PUWP leader by the Silesia party boss Edward Gierek, whose programme aimed at raising living standards and consumer-goods production. The country's foreign debt grew, and food prices again triggered strikes and demonstrations June 1976. Opposition to the Gierek regime, which was accused of corruption, mounted 1979 after a visit to his homeland by the recently elected Pope John Paul II. Strikes in Warsaw 1980, following a poor harvest and meat price increases, rapidly spread across the country.

the rise of Solidarity The government attempted to appease workers by entering into pay negotiations with unofficial strike committees, but at the Gdańsk shipyards demands emerged for permission to form free, independent trade unions. The government conceded the right to strike, and in Gdańsk 1980 the ◊Solidarity (Solidarność) union was formed under the leadership of Lech ◊Wałesa. In Sept 1980, Gierek was replaced as PUWP leader by Stanislaw Kania, but unrest continued as the 10-million member Solidarity campaigned for a five-day working week and established a rural section. With food shortages mounting and PUWP control slipping, Kania was replaced as PUWP leader Oct 1981 by the prime minister, General Wojciech ◊Jaruzelski; the Soviet army was active on Poland's borders; and martial law was imposed 13 Dec 1981. Trade-union activity was banned, the leaders of Solidarity arrested, a night curfew imposed, and the Military Council of National Salvation established, headed by Jaruzelski. Five months of severe repression ensued, resulting in 15 deaths and 10,000 arrests. The USA imposed economic sanctions. In June 1982, curfew restrictions were eased, prompting further serious rioting in Aug. In Nov Wałesa was released, and in Dec 1982 martial law was suspended (lifted 1983). The pope visited Poland 1983 and called for conciliation. The authorities responded by dissolving the Military Council and granting an amnesty to political prisoners and activists. In 1984, 35,000 prisoners and detainees were released on the 40th anniversary of the People's Republic, and the USA relaxed its economic sanctions. The Jaruzelski administration pursued pragmatic reform, including liberalization of the electoral system. Economic conditions and farm output slowly improved, but Poland's foreign debt remained huge. In Sept 1986, with the release of further prominent dissidents and the establishment of the broad new Consultative Council, the Jaruzelski administration sought to regain the public's trust. However, in Nov 1987 the regime failed to gain the necessary level (50% of the electorate) of support for a referendum on further liberalization reforms. During the following year the nation's shipyards, coalmines, ports, and steelworks were paralysed by a wave of Solidarity-led strikes for higher wages to offset the effect of recent price rises. With its economic strategy in tatters, the government of prime minister Zbigniew Messner resigned, being replaced, in Dec 1988, by a new administration headed by the reformist communist Mieczyslaw Rakowski.

socialist pluralism An historic accord was reached in April 1989 under whose terms Solidarity was re-legalized, the formation of opposition political associations tolerated, legal rights conferred upon the Catholic Church, the state's media monopoly lifted, and a new 'socialist pluralist' constitution adopted. In the subsequent national assembly elections, held in June 1989, Solidarity captured all but one of *Sejm* and Senate seats for which they were entitled to contest. In Sept 1989 a grand 'coalition' was formed with Tadeusz Mazowiecki, editor of Solidarity's newspaper, who became prime minister. Jaruzelski continued as president, and was re-elected in July. The new government, which attracted generous financial aid from Western powers, largely the USA and West Germany, proceeded to dismantle the command economy and encourage the private sector: a stock exchange was opened in Oct 1989, and a privatization programme launched. A tough ◊IMF-approved austerity programme was also instituted to solve the problem of hyperinflation running up to 550% in 1989. Censorship was abolished in April. In 1990 living standards in Poland fell by 40%. Unemployment rose to over one million. In July 1990, the Citizens' Movement of Democratic Action Party (ROAD) was established under Zbigniew Bujak and Wladyslaw Frasyniuk to provide a credible alternative to the Wałesa-orientated Solidarity Centre Alliance (SCA) established in May. Wałesa accused the government of delaying political and economic reform and forcing workers to bear the brunt of the austerity programme. In July 100 SCA deputies and senators petitioned Jaruzelski to stand down to make way for Wałesa. In the first round of presidential elections, held on 25 Nov 1990, the rupture within Solidarity was exposed by both Prime Minister Mazowiecki and Lech Wałesa contesting for the position. Having run a populist campaign, Wałesa topped the poll with a 40% vote share, and Mazowiecki, defending an unpopular government, finished in third position, with 18% of the vote, behind Stanislav Tyminski, a previously obscure right-wing, returned-emigrant Canadian businessman, who captured 23% of the vote. (In Dec Mazowiecki resigned as prime minister). In the second round, held on 9 Dec, Wałesa defeated Tyminski. Under a new constitution to be ratified May 1991, Walesa wishes to enhance the authority of the president, according him the power to issue decrees and make laws.

Politburo contraction of 'political bureau', a subcommittee (known as the Praesidium 1952–66) of the Central Committee of the Communist Party in the USSR and some other communist states, which lays down party policy. It consists of about 12 voting and six candidate (nonvoting) members.

pollution the harmful effect on the environment of by-products of human activity, principally industrial and agricultural processes—for example noise, smoke, car emissions, chemical effluents in seas and rivers, pesticides, sewage, and household waste. Pollution contributes to the ◊greenhouse effect.

Pollution control involves higher production costs for the industries concerned, but failure to implement adequate controls may result in irreversible environmental damage and an increase in the incidence of diseases such as cancer.

In the UK 1987 air pollution caused by carbon monoxide emission from road transport was measured at 5.26 million tonnes. In Feb 1990 the UK had failed to apply 21 European Community Laws on air and water pollution and faced prosecution before the European Court of Justice on 31 of the 160 EC directives in force.

Pol Pot (also known as ***Saloth Sar, Tol Saut,*** and ***Pol Porth***) 1925– . Cambodian politician and Communist party leader; a member of the anti-French resistance under Ho Chi Minh in the 1940s. As leader of the Khmer Rouge, he overthrew the government 1975 and proclaimed Democratic Kampuchea with himself as premier. His policies were to evacuate cities and put people to work in the countryside. The Khmer Rouge also carried out a systematic large-scale extermination of the Western-influenced educated and middle classes (3–4 million) before the regime was overthrown by a Vietnamese invasion 1979. Pol Pot continued to help lead the Khmer Rouge until their withdrawal in 1989; in that year too he resigned from his last position within the Khmer Rouge.

Pop art movement of young artists in the mid-1950s and 1960s, reacting against the elitism of abstract art. Pop art used popular imagery drawn from advertising, comic strips, film, and television. It originated in Britain 1956 with Richard Hamilton, Peter Blake, and others, and broke through in the USA with the paintings of flags and numbers by Jasper Johns 1958 and Andy Warhol's first series of soup cans 1962.

Portugal country in SW Europe, on the Atlantic Ocean, bounded N and E by Spain.

government The 1976 constitution, revised 1982, provides for a president and a single-chamber assembly elected by universal suffrage. The president, an active politician rather than a figurehead, appoints a prime minister who chooses the council of ministers, responsible to the assembly. A council of state, chaired by the president, acts as a supreme national advisory body.

history After a civil war 1828–34, constitutional government was established. Carlos I was assassinated 1908; his son Manuel II was driven from the country by a revolution 1910, and a republic was proclaimed. Portugal remained economically weak and corrupt until the start of the dictatorship of Dr Antonio de Oliveira Salazar, prime minister from 1928. Social conditions were improved at the cost of personal liberties. Salazar was succeeded as prime minister 1968 by Dr Marcello Caetano, who proved unable to liberalize the political system or deal with the costly wars in Portugal's colonies of Angola and Mozambique. Criticisms of his administration led to a military coup April 1974 to 'save the nation from government'. The Junta of National Salvation was set up, headed by General Antonio Ribeiro de Spinola. He became president a month later, with a military colleague replacing the civilian prime minister. The new president promised liberal reforms, but after disagreements within the Junta, Spinola resigned Sept 1974 and was replaced by General Francisco da Costa Gomes. In 1975 there was a swing to the left among the military and President Gomes narrowly avoided a Communist coup by collaborating with the leader of the moderate Socialist Party (PS), Mario Soares. In 1976 Portugal's first free assembly elections in 50 years were held. The PS won 36% of the vote, and Soares formed a minority government. The army chief, General Antonio Ramalho Eanes, won the presidency, with the support of centre and left-of-centre parties.

After a period of political instability in Dec 1980, President Eanes invited Dr Francisco Balsemão, to form a centre-party coalition. Dr Balsemão survived many challenges to his leadership, and in Aug 1982 the assembly approved his draft of a new constitution, which would reduce the powers of the president and move the country to a fully civilian government. In 1983 Soares entered a coalition with the PSD, whose leader was now the former finance minister, Professor Aníbal Cavaco Silva. In June 1985 the PS-PSD coalition broke up, and a premature general election was called. Cavaco Silva formed a minority government and was able to form a majority government after a landslide victory for the PSD July 1987. He has increased economic growth and raised living standards, and favours a free market and privatization.

In the 1986 presidential election Soares became Portugal's first civilian president for 60 years. He promised an open and cooperative presidency. Portugal entered the European Community 1986 and is a member of NATO. In July 1987 the Social Democrats won an absolute majority in parliament, with the PRD and Communists both losing seats. In June 1989 the parliament approved a series of measures that denationalized major industries and renounced the 'Socialist economy'.

Potsdam Conference conference held at Potsdam (in former East Germany) 17 July–2 Aug 1945 between representatives of the USA, the UK, and the USSR. They established the political and economic principles governing the treatment of Germany in the initial period of Allied control at the end of World War II, and sent an ultimatum to Japan demanding unconditional surrender on pain of utter destruction.

poverty the condition that exists when the basic needs of human beings (shelter, food and clothing) are not being met.

In many countries, poverty is common and persistent, being reflected in poor nutrition, low life expectancy, and high levels of infant mortality. It may result from a country's complete lack of resources, and an inability to achieve economic development.

Many different definitions of poverty exist, since there is little agreement on the standard of living (known as the ***poverty level***) considered to be the minimum adequate level by the majority of people. In a survey of York *Poverty: A Study of Town Life 1900* Seebohm Rowntree explained that of the 20,000 people living 'in poverty' 13,000 were living in what he called 'secondary poverty', defined as meaning that the income of families was sufficient for the maintenance of physical need.

Prague Spring the programme of liberalization initiated by prime minister Alexander Dubček in ◊Czechoslovakia 1968. In Aug 1968 Soviet tanks invaded Czechoslovakia and entered the capital Prague to put down the liberalization movement. Dubček had earlier assured the USSR that his planned reforms would not threaten socialism. He was arrested but released soon afterwards. Most of the Prague Spring reforms were reversed.

privatization the policy or process of selling or transferring state-owned or public assets and services (nationalized industries) to private investors. The proponents of privatization argue for the public benefit from its theoretically greater efficiency in a competitive market, and the release of resources for more appropriate use by government. Those against privatization believe that it removes a country's assets from all the people to a minority, whereas public utilities such as gas and water become private monopolies, and that a profit-making state-owned company raises revenue for the government.

The policy has been pursued by the post-1979 Conservative administration in Britain, and by recent governments in France, Japan (Nippon Telegraph and Telephone Corporation 1985, Japan Railways 1987, Japan Air Lines 1987), Italy, and elsewhere. By 1988 the practice had spread worldwide with communist countries such as China and Cuba selling off housing to private tenants.

Industries in Britain privatized since 1979:
British Telecom
British Gas Corporation
British National Oil Corporation
British Airways
British Airports Authority
British Aerospace
British Shipbuilders
British Steel
British Transport Docks Board
British Water Board
National Freight Company
Enterprise Oil

Prohibition in US history, the period 1920–33 when alcohol was illegal, and which represented the culmination of a long campaign by church and women's organizations, temperance societies, and the Anti-Saloon League. This led to bootlegging (the illegal distribution of liquor, often illicitly distilled), to the financial advantage of organized crime. Public opinion insisted on repeal 1933. The prohibition amendment to the US constitution is known as the Volstead Act, after the congressman who introduced it.

propaganda the systematic spreading (propagation) of information or disinformation, usually to promote a religious or pol-

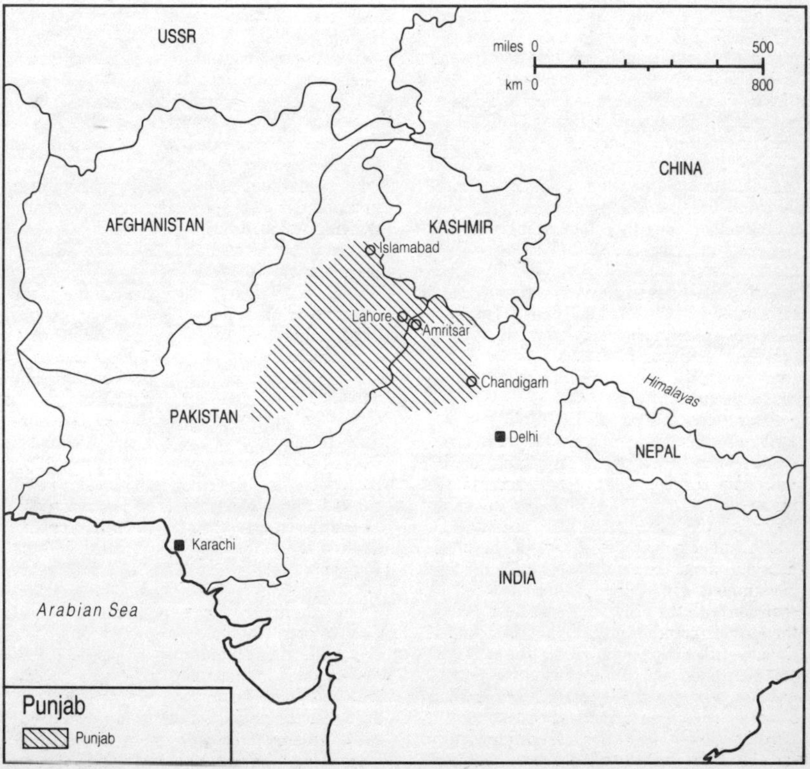

itical doctrine with the intention of instilling particular attitudes or responses.

Examples of the use of propaganda are the racial doctrines put forth by Nazism in World War II, and some of the ideas and strategies propagated by the USA and the Soviet Union during the ◊Cold War 1945–90. There are various forms of propaganda: black propaganda (a pack of lies), grey propaganda (half-truths and distortions), and white propaganda (the truth).

Punjab massacres the violence occurring after the partition of India 1947, in which more than a million people died whilst relocating in the Punjab. The eastern section became an Indian state, while the western area, dominated by the Muslims, went to Pakistan. Violence occurred as Muslims fled from eastern Punjab, and Hindus and Sikhs moved from Pakistan to ◊India.

purge the removal (for example from a political party) of suspected opponents or of persons regarded as undesirable. In 1934 the Nazis carried out a purge of their party and a number of party leaders were executed for an alleged plot against Hitler. During the 1930s purges were conducted in the USSR under Joseph Stalin, carried out by the secret police against political opponents, Communist Party members, minorities, civil servants, and large sections of the armed forces' officer corps. Some 10 million people were executed or deported to labour camps from 1934 to 1938. Later purges include Communist purges in Hungary (1949), Czechoslovakia (1951), and China (1955).

Q

Qaddafi alternative form of ◊Khaddhafi, Libyan leader.

Québec Conference two conferences of Allied leaders in the city of Québec during World War II. The ***first conference*** 1943 approved the British admiral Mountbatten as supreme Allied commander in SE Asia and made plans for the invasion of France, for which the US general Eisenhower was to be supreme commander. The allied leaders F D Roosevelt, Winston Churchill, William Mackenzie King and Tse-ven Soong were also present. The ***second conference*** Sept 1944 adopted plans for intensified air attacks on Germany, created a unified strategy against Japan, and established a postwar policy for a defeated Germany.

Quisling Vidkun 1887–1945. Norwegian politician. Leader from 1933 of the Norwegian Fascist Party, he aided the Nazi invasion of Norway 1940 by delaying mobilization and urging non-resistance. He was made premier by Hitler 1942, and was arrested and shot as a traitor by the Norwegians 1945. His name became a generic term for a traitor who aids an occupying force.

R

racism belief in, or set of implicit assumptions about, the superiority of one's own race or ethnic group, often accompanied by prejudice against members of an ethnic group different from one's own. Racism may be used to justify ◊discrimination, verbal or physical abuse, or even genocide, as in Nazi Germany, or as practised by European settlers against American Indians in both North and South America.

radio transmission and reception of radio waves. In radio transmission a microphone converts sound waves (pressure variations in the air) into electromagnetic waves that are then picked up by a receiving aerial and fed to a loudspeaker, which converts them back into sound waves.

The theory of electromagnetic waves was first developed by James Clerk Maxwell 1864, given practical confirmation in the laboratory 1888 by Heinrich Hertz, and put to practical use by Guglielmo Marconi, who in 1901 achieved reception of a signal in Newfoundland transmitted from Cornwall, England.

railway method of transport in which trains convey passengers and goods along a twin rail track (at first made of wood but later of iron or steel). Such railways were first used in NE Britain on the coalfields from the 17th century onwards. Following the work of English steam pioneers such as James Watt, George Stephenson built the first public steam railway, from Stockton to Darlington, 1825. This heralded extensive railway building in Britain, continental Europe, and North America, providing a fast and economical means of transport and communication. After World War II, steam was replaced by electric and diesel engines. At the same time, the growth of road building, air services, and car ownership destroyed the supremacy of the railways.

Four years after building the first steam railway, Stephenson opened the first steam passenger line, inaugurating it with his locomotive *Rocket*, which achieved speeds of 50 kph/30 mph. The railway construction that followed resulted in 250 separate companies in Britain, which resolved into four systems 1921 and became the nationalized British Railways 1948, known as British Rail from 1965. With the increasing use of private cars and government-encouraged road haulage after World War II, and the demise of steam, rising costs on the railways meant higher fares, fewer passengers, and declining freight traffic. During the 1960s and 1970s many rural rail services closed down, particularly after the Beeching Report 1963. From the 1970s national railway companies began investing in faster intercity services: in the UK, the diesel high-speed train (HST) was introduced; elsewhere such trains run on specially built tracks such as the Shinkansen (Japan) and TGV (France) networks.

1825 George Stephenson in England built the first public railway to carry steam trains – the Stockton and Darlington line – using his engine *Locomotion*.

1829 Stephenson designed his locomotive *Rocket*.

1830 Stephenson completed the Liverpool and Manchester Railway, the first steam passenger line. The first US-built locomotive, *Best Friend of Charleston*, went into service on the South Carolina Railroad.

1835 Germany pioneered steam railways in Europe, using *Der Adler*, a locomotive built by Stephenson.

1863 Robert Fairlie, a Scot, patented a locomotive with pivoting driving bogies, allowing tight curves in the track (this was later applied in the Garratt locomotives). London opened the world's first underground railway, powered by steam.

1869 The first US transcontinental railway was completed at Promontory, Utah, when the Union Pacific and the Central Pacific railroads met. George Westinghouse of the USA invented the compressed-air brake.

1879 Werner von Siemens demonstrated an electric train in Germany. Volk's Electric Railway along the Brighton seafront in England was the world's first public electric railway.

1883 Charles Lartique built the first monorail, in Ireland.

1885 The trans-Canada continental railway was completed, from Montreal in the east to Port Moody, British Columbia, in the west.

1890 The first electric underground railway opened in London.
1901 The world's most successful monorail, the Wuppertal Schwebebahn, went into service in Germany.
1912 The first diesel locomotive took to the rails in Germany.
1938 The British steam locomotive *Mallard* set a steam-rail speed record of 201 kph/125 mph.
1941 Swiss Federal Railways introduced a gas-turbine locomotive.
1964 Japan National Railways inaugurated the 515 km/320 mi New Tokaido line between Osaka and Tokyo, on which run the 210 kph/130 mph 'bullet' trains.
1973 British Rail's High Speed Train (HST) set a diesel rail speed record of 229 kph/142 mph.
1979 Japan National Railways' maglev test vehicle ML-500 attained a speed of 517 kph/321 mph.
1981 France's TGV superfast trains began operation between Paris and Lyons, regularly attaining a peak speed of 270 kph/168 mph.
1987 France and the UK began work on the Channel Tunnel, a railway link connecting the two countries, running beneath the English Channel.
1989 A new world rail-speed record of 482.4 kph/298 mph was established by a French TGV train in Dec 1989.

Raj, the British the period of British rule in ◊India before Independence in 1947.

Rapallo, Treaties of treaties were signed here 1920 (settling the common frontiers of Italy and Yugoslavia) and 1922 (cancelling German and Russian counter-claims for indemnities for World War I). German soldiers were also permitted to train in the USSR, in defiance of the Treaty of ◊Versailles.

Rasputin (Russian 'dissolute') Grigory Efimovich 1871–1916. Siberian Eastern Orthodox mystic and wandering 'holy man', the illiterate son of a peasant. He acquired influence over the tsarina Alexandra, wife of ◊Nicholas II, because of her faith in his power to ease her son's suffering from haemophilia, and he was able to make political and ecclesiastical appointments. His abuse of power and his notorious debauchery (reputedly including the tsarina) led to his being murdered by a group of nobles, who, when poison had no effect, dumped him in the river Neva after shooting him.

rationing a restricted allowance of provisions or other supplies in time of war or shortage. For example, food rationing was introduced in Germany and in Britain during World War I. During World War II food rationing, organized by the government, began in Britain in 1940. Each person was issued with a ration book of coupons. Bacon, butter, and sugar were restricted, followed by other goods including sweets, petrol, clothing, soap, and furniture. Some people tried to supplement their rations by buying goods on the black market. In 1946 the world wheat shortage led to bread rationing. Clothes rationing ended in Britain in 1949. During the Suez crisis of 1956 petrol rationing was introduced in Britain.

Reagan Ronald (Wilson) 1911– . 40th president of the USA 1981–89, a Republican. He was governor of California 1966–74, and a former Hollywood actor. Reagan was a hawkish and popular president. He adopted an aggressive policy in Central America, attempting to overthrow the government of Nicaragua, and invading Grenada 1983. In 1987, ◊Irangate was investigated by the Tower Commission; Reagan admitted that USA– Iran negotiations had become an 'arms for hostages deal', but denied knowledge of resultant funds being illegally sent to the Contras in Nicaragua. He increased military spending (sending the national budget deficit to record levels), cut social programmes, introduced deregulation of domestic markets, and cut taxes. His ◊Strategic Defense Initiative, announced 1983, proved controversial owing to the cost and unfeasibility. He was succeeded by George ◊Bush.

Reagan was born in Tampico, Illinois, the son of a shoe salesman who was bankrupted during the Depression. He became a Hollywood actor 1937 and appeared in 50 films,

Reagan *The Hollywood actor who became president of the USA, Ronald Reagan.*

including *Bedtime for Bonzo* 1951 and *The Killers* 1964. As president of the Screen Actors' Guild 1947–52, he became a conservative, critical of the bureaucratic stifling of free enterprise, and named names before the House Un-American Activities Committee. He joined the Republican Party 1962, and his term as governor of California was marked by battles against students. Having lost the Republican presidential nomination 1968 and 1976 to Nixon and Ford respectively, Reagan won it 1980 and defeated President Carter. He was wounded in an assassination attempt 1981. The invasion of Grenada, following a coup there, generated a revival of national patriotism, and Reagan was re-elected by a landslide 1984. His insistence on militarizing space through the Strategic Defense Initiative, popularly called Star Wars, prevented a disarmament agreement when he met the Soviet leader ◊Gorbachev 1985 and 1986, but a 4% reduction in nuclear weapons was agreed 1987. In 1986, he ordered the bombing of Tripoli, Libya, in retaliation for the killing of a US soldier in Berlin by a guerrilla group.

rearmament re-equipping a country with new armaments. The German dictator Adolf Hitler concentrated on rearmament in Germany after he achieved power in 1934. During the 1930s Britain followed a policy of rearmament.

Red Army former name of the army of the USSR. It developed from the ◊Red Guards, volunteers who carried out the Bolshevik revolution, and received its name because it fought under the red flag. It was officially renamed the ***Soviet Army*** 1946. The Chinese revolutionary army was also called the Red Army.

Red Cross, the international relief agency founded by the Geneva Convention 1864 at the instigation of the Swiss doctor Henri Dunant to assist the wounded and prisoners in war. Its symbol is a symmetrical red cross on a white ground. The Muslim equivalent is the ***Red Crescent***. In addition to dealing with associated problems of war, such as refugees and the care of the disabled, the Red Cross is increasingly concerned with victims of natural disasters – floods, earthquakes, epidemics, and accidents.

The British Red Cross Society was founded 1870, and incorporated 1908. It works in close association with the St John Ambulance Association.

Red Guards armed workers who took part in the ◊Russian Revolution of 1917. The name was also given to the school and college students, wearing red armbands, active in the Cultural Revolution in China 1966–68.

refugee a person fleeing from oppressive or dangerous conditions (such as political, religious, or military persecution) and seeking refuge in a foreign country. In 1990 there were an estimated 15 million refugees worldwide, whose resettlement and welfare were the responsibility of the United Nations High Commission for Refugees (UNCHR).

The term was originally applied to the French Huguenots who came to England after the revocation of the Edict of Nantes in 1685. Major refugee movements in 20th-century Europe include: Jews from the ◊pogroms of Russia 1881–1914 and again after the Revolution; White Russians from the USSR after 1917; Jews from Germany and other Nazi-dominated countries 1933–45; and the displaced people of World War II.

Elsewhere, the Palestinians represent the longest-running refugee problem. Many Chinese fled the mainland after the communist revolution of 1949, especially to Taiwan and Hong Kong; many Latin Americans fled from Cuba, Colombia, Brazil, Chile, Argentina, and Central America when new governments took power; and many people left Vietnam (the ***boat people***) after the victory of the North over the South. Refugee movements created by natural disasters and famine have been widespread, most notably in Ethiopia and Sudan. In 1990 the largest single refugee groupings were: Afghans (about 6 million, temporarily settled in Iran and Pakistan); Palestinians (2.3 million); Ethiopians (1.3 million, mostly Eritreans who have moved to Sudan); Mozambicans (1.2 million, displaced mostly to Malawi); Iraqis (600,000, predominantly Kurds who have settled in Iran); Somalis (400,000); Sudanese (400,000); Sri Lankan Tamils (300,000, who have fled to India); and Cambodians (300,000, who live in refugee camps in Thailand). A distinction is usually made by Western nations between 'political' and so-called 'economic' refugees, particularly when the refugees come from low-income countries such as the Vietnamese boat people.

Reichstag German parliament building and lower legislative house during the German Empire 1871–1918 and Weimar Republic 1919–33.

Reichstag Fire burning of the German parliament building in Berlin 27 Feb 1933, less than a month after the Nazi leader Adolf Hitler became chancellor. The fire was used as a justification for the suspension of many constitutional guarantees and also as an excuse to attack the communists. There is still debate over Nazi involvement in the crime, not least because they were the main beneficiaries.

The Nazi government maintained that the fire was the result of a communist conspiracy. Although three Bulgarians–Dimitrov, Popov, and Tanev–and a German, Torgler, were all indicted and tried in Leipzig, only a Dutch communist, Marinus van der Lubbe, was convicted, after being found at the scene of the crime and confessing.

reparation compensation for war damage paid by countries that start or are alleged to start wars in which they are defeated, as, for example, by Germany in both world wars.

At the end of World War I, Germany had to pay massive reparations. Under the terms of the 1919 Peace Treaty the Reparations Commission met. The question of reparations proved highly contentious leading to the occupation of the Ruhr valley 1923, the Dawes Plan 1924, and the Young Plan 1929, in which the payments were much reduced. After World War II, the Allies also imposed reparations on Italy, 1947.

Representation of the People Acts series of UK Acts of Parliament from 1867 that extended voting rights, creating universal suffrage in 1928.

The 1867 and 1884 Acts are known as the Second and Third Reform Acts. The 1918 Act gave the vote to men over the age of 21 and women over the age of 30, and the 1928 Act extended the vote to women over the age of 21. Certain people had the right to more than one vote; this was abolished by the 1948 Act. The 1969 Act reduced the minimum age of voting to 18.

Republican Party one of the USA's two main political parties (the other being the ◊Democrats), formed 1854 by a coalition of slavery opponents, who elected their first president, Abraham Lincoln, in 1860. The early Republican Party supported protective tariffs and favoured genuine settlers (homesteaders) over land speculators. Towards the end of the century the Republican Party was identified with US imperialism and industrial expansion. With few intermissions, the Republican Party controlled Congress from the 1860s until defeated by the New Deal Democrats 1932. After an isolationist period before World War II, the Republican Party adopted an active foreign policy under Richard ◊Nixon and Gerald Ford, but the latter was defeated by Jimmy Carter in the presidential election 1976. However, the party enjoyed landslide presidential victories for Ronald ◊Reagan and also carried the Senate 1980–86. George ◊Bush won the 1988 presidential election but faced a Democratic Senate and House of Representatives.

resistance movement opposition movement in a country occupied by an enemy or colonial power, especially in the 20th century. During World War II, resistance in E Europe took the form of ◊guerrilla warfare, for example in Yugoslavia, Greece, Poland, and by ***partisan*** bands behind the German lines in the USSR. In more industrialized countries, such as France (where the underground movement was called the ***maquis***), Belgium, and Czechoslovakia, sabotage in factories and on the railways, propaganda, and the assassination of Germans and collaborators were a priority.

Most resistance movements in World War II were based on an alliance of all anti-fascist parties, but there was internal conflict between those elements more intent on defeat of the enemy, and those who aimed at establishing communist regimes, as in Yugoslavia and Greece.

revolution any rapid, far-reaching, or violent change in the political, social, or economic structure of society. It is usually applied to political change: examples include the American Revolution 1775–83, where colonists broke free from their colonial ties and established a sovereign, independent nation; the French Revolution 1789–95, where an absolute monarchy was overthrown by opposition from inside the country and a popular uprising; and the ◊Russian Revolution 1917, where a repressive monarchy was overthrown by those seeking to institute widespread social and economic changes based on a socialist model.

While political revolutions are often associated with violence, other types of change can have just as much impact on society. Most notable is the Industrial Revolution of the mid-18th century, which caused massive economic and social changes. In the 1970s and 1980s a high-tech revolution based on the silicon chip took place, facilitating the widespread use of computers. In 1989–90 the Eastern Bloc nations demonstrated against and voted out the Communist party (see ◊Communism), and in many cases, creating a pro-democracy revolution.

Rhee Syngman 1875–1965. Korean right-wing politician. A rebel under Chinese and Japanese rule, he became president of South Korea from 1948 until riots forced him to resign and leave the country 1960. He established a repressive dictatorship and was an embarrassing ally for the USA.

Rhineland a former province of Prussia, ceded in 1815. Under the terms of the Treaty of Versailles 1919, following World War I, the Rhineland was to be occupied by Allied forces for 15 years, with a permanent demilitarized zone. Demilitarization was reaffirmed by the Treaties of Locarno, but German foreign minister Gustav Stresemann achieved the removal of the British forces 1926, and French troops 1930. Both treaties were violated when Adolf Hitler marched into the demilitarized zone of the Rhineland in 1936. Britain and France merely protested, and it remained under German occupation. It was the scene of heavy fighting 1944, and was recaptured by US troops in 1945, becoming one of the largest states of West Germany after the end of World War II.

Rhodesia former name of Zambia (North Rhodesia) and ◊Zimbabwe (South Rhodesia).

right wing the more conservative or reactionary section of a political party or spectrum. It originated in the French national assembly 1789, where the nobles sat in the place of honour on the president's right, whereas the commons were on his left (hence left wing).

Romania country in SE Europe, on the Black Sea, bounded N and E by the USSR, S by Bulgaria, SW by Yugoslavia, and NW by Hungary.

history After the Russo-Turkish war 1877–78, in which Romania sided with Russia, the great powers recognized Romania's independence, and in 1881 Prince Charles became King Carol I. Romania fought against Bulgaria in the Second ◊Balkan War 1913 and annexed S Dobruja. It entered World War I on the Allied side 1916, was occupied by the Germans 1917–18, but received Bessarabia from Russia and Bukovina and Transylvania from the dismembered Habsburg empire under the 1918 peace settlement, thus emerging as the largest state in the Balkans. During the late 1930s, to counter the growing popularity of the fascist Iron Guard movement, Carol II abolished the democratic constitution of 1923 and established his own dictatorship. In 1940 he was forced to surrender Bessarabia, N Transylvania, and S Dobruja to the USSR, Hungary, and Bulgaria respectively, and abdicated when Romania was occupied by Germany in Aug. Power was assumed by Ion Antonescu (1882–1946, ruling in the name of Carol's son King Michael), who signed the ◊Axis Pact Nov 1940 and declared war on the USSR June 1941. In Aug 1944, with the Red Army on Romania's borders, King Michael supported the ousting of the Antonescu government by a coalition of left and centre parties, including the communists. Romania subsequently joined the war against Germany and in the Paris peace treaties 1947 recovered Transylvania but lost Bessarabia and N Bukovina to the USSR and S Dobruja to Bulgaria.

the republic In the elections 1946 a Communist-led coalition achieved a majority and proceeded to force King Michael to abdicate. The new Romanian People's Republic was proclaimed Dec 1947 and dominated by the Romanian Communist Party, then termed the Romanian Workers' Party (RWP). Soviet-style constitutions were adopted in 1948 and 1952; Romania joined ◊Comecon 1949 and co-signed the ◊Warsaw Pact 1955; and a programme of nationalization and agricultural collectivization was launched. After a rapid purge of opposition leaders, the RWP became firmly established in power, enabling Soviet occupation forces to leave the country 1958. The dominant political personality 1945–65 was RWP leader and state president Gheorghe Gheorghiu-Dej. He was succeeded by Nicolae ◊Ceauşescu, who placed greater emphasis on national autonomy and proclaimed Romania a Socialist republic. Under Ceauşescu, Romania adopted a foreign-policy line independent of the USSR, condemned the 1968 invasion of Czechoslovakia and refused to participate directly in Warsaw Pact manoeuvres or allow Russian troops to enter the country. Ceauşescu called for multilateral nuclear disarmament and the creation of a Balkan nuclear-weapons-free zone and maintained warm relations with China.

austerity programme At home, the secret police (Securitate) maintained a tight Stalinist rein on dissident activities, while a Ceauşescu personality cult was propagated. Economic difficulties mounted as Ceauşescu, pledging himself to repay the country's accumulated foreign debt (achieved 1989), embarked on an austerity programme. This led to food shortages and widespread power cuts in the winters from 1985 onwards; the army occupied power plants and brutally crushed workers' demonstrations in Brasov in Nov 1987.

'systematization plan' After a referendum in 1986, military spending was cut by 5%. Ceauşescu was re-elected general secretary of the RCP and state president in 1984–85 and again in 1989. From 1985 he refused to follow the ◊Gorbachev path of political and economic reform, even calling in the spring of 1989 for Warsaw Pact nations to intervene to prevent the opposition Solidarity movement from assuming power in Poland. The country's relations with neighbouring Hungary also reached crisis point 1988–89 as a result of a Ceauşescu 'systematization plan' to demolish 7,000 villages and replace them with 500 agro-industrial complexes, in the process forcibly resettling and 'Romanizing' Transylvania-based ethnic Hungarians.

overthrow of Ceauşescu The unexpected overthrow of the Ceauşescu regime occurred in Dec 1989 when, in the city of Timisoara, sparked off by the government's plans to exile Laszlo Tokes (1952–), a dissident Protestant pastor, to a remote village, ethnic Hungarians and Romanians joined forces to form an anti-Ceauşescu protest movement. Hundreds of demonstrators were killed in the state's subsequent crackdown on 17 Dec. Four days later, an officially sponsored rally in Bucharest backfired when the crowd chanted anti-Ceauşescu slogans. Divisions between the military and Securitate rapidly emerged and on 22 Dec the army Chief of Staff, General Stefan Gusa, turned against the president and called on his soldiers to 'defend the uprising'. Ceauşescu attempted to flee, but was caught and summarily tried and executed on Christmas Day. Battles between Ceauşescu-loyal Securitate members and the army ensued in Bucharest, with several thousand being killed, but the army seizing the upper hand.

the National Salvation Front A National Salvation Front was established, embracing former dissident intellectuals, reform communists, and military leaders. At its head was Ion Iliescu (1930–), a Moscow-trained communist, while Petre Roman (1947–), an engineer without political experience, was appointed prime minister. The Front's council proceeded to re-legalize the formation of alternative political parties and draft a new constitution. Faced with grave economic problems, it initiated a ban on the export of foodstuffs, the abandonment of Ceauşescu's 'systematization programme', the dissolution of the Securitate, the abolition of the RCP's leading role, and the re-legalization of abortion and small-plot farming.

reform In April 1990 a new Romanian Intelligence Service (RIS), accountable to parliament, was set up to replace the disbanded Securitate. The government legalized the Eastern Rite Catholic Church and the Vatican re-established diplomatic relations. In July bills to create a legal market economy were presented to parliament by Petre Roman. In Nov the leu was devalued, subsidies cut, and prices allowed to float. Industrial exports slumped and strikes increased. In Sept 1990 Nicu Ceauşescu, the younger son of Nicolae, was sentenced by a miltary tribunal to 20 years in prison for ordering security forces to fire on demonstrators in Sibu the previous year. Refugees continued to leave the country.

Romanov dynasty rulers of Russia from 1613 to the ◊Russian Revolution 1917. Under the Romanovs, Russia developed into an absolutist empire. The last tsar, Nicholas II, abdicated Mar 1917 and was murdered in July 1918, together with his family.

Rome-Berlin Axis another name for the ◊Axis.

Rome, Treaties of two international agreements signed 25 March 1957 by Belgium, France, West Germany, Italy, Luxembourg, and the Netherlands, which established the European Economic Community (EEC) and the European Atomic Energy Commission (EURATOM). The terms of the treaty, which came into effect 1 Jan 1958, provided for economic cooperation, reduction (and eventual removal) of customs barriers, and the free movement of capital, goods, and labour between the member countries, together with common agricultural and trading policies. Subsequent new members of the European Community have been obliged to accept these terms.

Rommel Erwin 1891–1944. German field marshal. He served in World War I, and in World War II he played an important part in the invasions of central Europe and France. He was commander of the N African offensive from 1941 (when he was nicknamed 'Desert Fox') until defeated in the Battles of El ◊Alamein. He was commander in chief for a short time against the Allies in Europe 1944 but (as a sympathizer with the ◊Stauffenberg plot against Hitler) was forced to commit suicide.

Roosevelt Franklin Delano 1882–1945. The 32nd president of the USA 1933–45, a Democrat. He served as governor of New York 1929–33. Becoming president amid the ◊Depression, he launched the ◊***New Deal*** economic and social reform programme, which made him popular with the people. After the outbreak of World War II he introduced ◊Lend-Lease for the supply of war materials and services to the Allies and drew up the ◊Atlantic Charter of solidarity. Once the USA had entered the war 1941 he spent much time in meetings with Allied leaders planning the conduct of the war.

During the first hundred days of his administration, major legislation to facilitate industrial and agricultural recovery was enacted. In 1935 he introduced the Utilities Act, directed against abuses in the large holding companies, and the Social Security Act, providing for disability and retirement insurance. The presidential election 1936 was won entirely on the record of the New Deal. During 1935–36 Roosevelt was involved in a long conflict over the composition of the Supreme Court, following its nullification of major New Deal measures as unconstitutional. In 1938 he introduced measures for farm relief and the improvement of working conditions.

He participated in the Washington 1942 and Casablanca 1943 conferences to plan the

Roosevelt *US president Franklin Delano Roosevelt led his country through the Depression of the 1930s and World War II, and was elected for an unprecedented fourth term of office in 1944.*

Roosevelt *Teddy bears derive their name from Theodore Roosevelt, the 26th US president, who, despite being a big-game hunter, refused to shoot a bear cub.*

Mediterranean assault, and the conferences in Québec, Cairo, and Tehran 1943, and Yalta 1945, at which the final preparations were made for the Allied victory. He was re-elected for a fourth term 1944, but died 1945.

Roosevelt Theodore 1858–1919. 26th president of the USA 1901–09, a Republican. After serving as governor of New York 1898–1900 he became vice president to William McKinley, whom he succeeded as president on McKinley's assassination 1901. He campaigned against the great trusts (combines that reduce competition), while carrying on a jingoist foreign policy designed to enforce US supremacy over Latin America.

Roosevelt, born in New York, was elected to the state legislature 1881. He was assistant secretary of the Navy 1897–98, and during the Spanish-American War 1898 commanded a volunteer force of 'rough riders'. At age 42, Roosevelt was the youngest man to become president of the US. In office he became more liberal. He tackled business monopolies, initiated measures for the conservation of national resources, and introduced the Pure Food and Drug Act. He won the Nobel Peace Prize 1906 for his part in ending the Russo-Japanese war. Alienated after his retirement by the conservatism of his successor William Taft, Roosevelt formed the Progressive or 'Bull Moose' Party. As their candidate he unsuccessfully ran for the presidency 1912, polling more votes than Taft, but enabling the democrat, Woodrow Wilson to win, by his intervention. During World War I he strongly advocated US intervention.

Rowntree Benjamin Seebohm 1871–1954. British entrepreneur and philanthropist. Much of the money he acquired as chair (1925–41) of the family firm of confectioners, H I Rowntree, he used to fund investigations into social conditions. The three ***Rowntree Trusts***, which were founded by his father ***Joseph Rowntree*** (1836–1925) in 1904, fund research into housing, social care, and social policy, support projects relating to social justice, and give grants to pressure groups working in these areas.

Rowntree joined the York-based family business in 1889 after studying at Owens College (later the University of Manchester). The introduction of company pensions (1906), a five-day working week (1919), and an employee profit-sharing scheme (1923) gave him a reputation as an enlightened and paternalistic employer. An associate of David Lloyd George, he was director of the welfare department of the Ministry of Munitions during World War I.

His pioneering study of working-class households in York 1897–98, published as

Poverty, A Study of Town Life, 1900 was a landmark in empirical sociology; it showed that 28% of the population fell below an arbitrary level of minimum income, and 16% experienced 'primary poverty'. Rowntree also wrote on gambling, unemployment, and business organization.

Royal Air Force (RAF) the ◊air force of Britain. The RAF was formed 1918 by the merger of the Royal Naval Air Service and the Royal Flying Corps.

Rusk Dean 1909– . US Democrat politician. He was secretary of state to presidents Kennedy and L B Johnson 1961–69. During World War II he fought in Burma (now Myanmar) and China and became deputy chief of staff of US forces. After the war he served in the Department of State, and as assistant secretary of state for Far Eastern affairs was prominent in ◊Korean War negotiations. His involvement with the ◊Vietnam War made him unpopular.

Russia originally the name of the pre-revolutionary Russian Empire (until 1917), and now accurately restricted to the Russian Soviet Federal Socialist Republic only. It is incorrectly used to refer to the whole of the present ◊Union of Soviet Socialist Republics.

Russian Revolution, 1905 political upheaval centred in and around St Petersburg, Russia 1905–06, leading up to the February and October revolutions of 1917. On Jan 22 1905 thousands of striking unarmed workers marched to Tsar Nicholas II's Winter Palace in St Petersburg to ask for reforms. Government troops fired on the crowd killing many people. After this 'Bloody Sunday' slaughter the revolution gained strength, culminating in a general strike which paralyzed the whole country in Oct 1905. Revolutionaries in St Petersburg formed a 'soviet' (council) called the Soviet of Workers' Deputies. Nicholas II then granted the Duma (parliament) the power to pass or reject proposed laws. Although these measures satisfied the liberal element, the revolution continued to gain ground and came to a head when the army crushed a serious uprising in Dec 1905.

Russian Revolution two revolutions of Feb and Oct 1917 (Julian calendar) that began with the overthrow of the Romanov dynasty and ended with the establishment of a communist soviet (council) state, the Union of Socialist Soviet Republics (USSR). The ***February Revolution*** (Mar Western calendar) arose because of food and fuel shortages, the ongoing repressiveness of the tsarist government, and military incompetence in World War I. Riots in Petrograd led to the abdication of Tsar Nicholas II and the formation of a provisional government under Prince Lvov. They had little support as troops, communications, and transport were controlled by the Petrograd workers' and soldiers' council. ◊Lenin returned to Russia in Apr as head of the ◊Bolsheviks. Kerensky replaced Lvov as head of government in July. During this period, the Bolsheviks gained control of the soviets and advocated land reform (under the slogan 'All power to the Soviets') and an end to their involvement in World War I.

The ***October Revolution*** was a coup on the night of 25–26 Oct (6–7 Nov Western calendar). Bolshevik workers and sailors seized the government buildings and the Winter Palace, Petrograd. The second All-Russian Congress of Soviets, which met the following day, proclaimed itself the new government of Russia, and Lenin became leader. Bolsheviks soon took control of the cities, established worker control in factories, and nationalized the banks. The Cheka (secret police) was set up to silence the opposition. The government concluded peace with Germany early in 1918 through the Treaty of ◊Brest-Litovsk, but civil war broke out in that year when anti-Bolshevik elements within the army attempted to seize power. The war lasted until 1922, when the Red Army, organized by ◊Trotsky, finally overcame 'White' (Tsarist) opposition, but with huge losses, after which communist control was complete.

1894 Reign of Tsar Nicholas II begins.

1898 Formation of the Social Democratic Party among industrial workers under the influence of Plekhanov and Lenin.

1901 Formation of the Socialist Revolutionary Party.

1903 Split in Social Democratic Party at party's second congress (London Conference) into Bolsheviks and Mensheviks.

1905 Jan: 'Bloody Sunday', where repression of workers in St Petersburg leads to widespread strikes and '1905 Revolution'. Oct: strikes and the first 'soviet' (local revolutionary council) in St Petersburg. October constitution provides for new parliament (Duma). Dec: insurrection of workers in Moscow. Punitive repression by the 'Black Hundreds'.

1914 July: outbreak of war between Russia and the Central Powers.

1917 March: outbreak of riots in St Petersburg. Tsar Nicholas abdicates. Provisional government established under Prince Lvov. Power struggles between government and Petrograd (St Petersburg) soviet. April: Lenin arrives in Petrograd. Demands transfer of power to soviets; an end to the war; the seizure of land by the peasants; control of industry by the workers. July: Bolsheviks attempt to seize

Russian Revolution *Bolshevik workers and the Red Guard seizing the Winter Palace in Petrograd Nov 1917.*

power in Petrograd. Trotsky arrested and Lenin in hiding. Kerensky becomes head of provisional government. Sept: Kornilov coup, fails due to strike by workers. Kerensky's government weakened. Nov: Bolshevik Revolution. Military revolutionary committee and Red Guards seize government offices and the Winter Palace, arresting all the members of the provisional government. Second All-Russian Congress of Soviets creates the Council of Peoples Commissars as new governmental authority, led by Lenin, with Trotsky as Commissar for War and Stalin as Commissar for National Minorities. Land Decree orders immediate distribution of land to the peasants. Banks are nationalized and national debt repudiated. Elections to the Constituent Assembly give large majority to the Socialist Revolutionary Party. Bolsheviks a minority.
1918 Jan: Constituent Assembly meets in Petrograd but almost immediately broken up by Red Guards. March: Treaty of Brest-Litovsk marks end of war with Central Powers but with massive losses of territory. July: murder of tsar and his family.
1918–22 Civil War in Russia between Red Army led by Trotsky and White Russian forces. Red Army ultimately victorious.
1923 6 July: constitution of USSR adopted.

Russo-Japanese War war between Russia and Japan 1904–05, which arose from conflicting ambitions in Korea and Manchuria, specifically, the Russian occupation of Port Arthur (modern Lüda) 1896 and of the Amur province 1900. Japan successfully besieged Port Arthur May 1904–Jan 1905, took Mukden 29 Feb–10 Mar, and on 27 May defeated the Russian Baltic fleet, which had sailed halfway around the world to Tsushima Strait. A peace was signed in Portsmouth, New Hampshire, USA, 23 Aug 1905. Russia surrendered its lease on Port Arthur, ceded S Sakhalin to Japan, evacuated Manchuria, and recognized Japan's interests in Korea.

S

Saarland (French *Sarre*) *Land* (state) of Germany, crossed NW–S by the river Saar; area 2,570 sq km/992 sq mi. In 1919, the Saar district was administered by France under the auspices of the League of Nations; a plebiscite returned it to Germany 1935; Hitler gave it the name Saarbrücken. Part of the French zone of occupation 1945, it was part of the economic union with France 1947. It was returned to Germany 1957; it is the smallest and poorest of the West German *Länder*.

Sadat Anwar 1918–1981. Egyptian politician. Succeeding Gamal ◊Nasser as president 1970, he restored morale by his handling of the Egyptian campaign in the 1973 war against Israel. In 1974 his plan for economic, social, and political reform to transform Egypt was unanimously adopted in a referendum. In 1977 he visited Israel to reconcile the two countries, and shared the Nobel Peace Prize with Israeli prime minister Menachem Begin 1978. He was assassinated by Islamic fundamentalists.

Saigon former name (until 1976) of Ho Chi Minh City, Vietnam.

St Germain-en-Laye, Treaty of 1919 treaty condemning the war between Austria and the Allies, signed at St Germain-en-Laye, a town 21 km/13 mi W of Paris. Representatives of the USA signed it, but because the US Senate failed to ratify the Treaty of ◊Versailles, the Treaty of St Germain was not submitted to it. The USA made a separate peace with Austria in 1921.

Sakharov Andrei Dmitrievich 1921–1989. Soviet physicist, known both as the 'father of the Soviet H-bomb' and as an outspoken human-rights campaigner. Awarded the Nobel Peace Prize 1975. He was elected to the Congress of the USSR People's Deputies (CUPD) 1989, where he emerged as leader of its radical reform grouping.

Sakharov was exempted from military service because of his skill at physics. In 1948 he joined Igor Tamm in developing the hydrogen bomb; he later protested against Soviet nuclear tests and was a founder member of the Soviet Human Rights Committee. In 1980 he was arrested and sent to internal exile in Gorky, following his criticism of Soviet action in Afghanistan. At the end of 1986 he was freed from exile and allowed to return to Moscow and resume his place in the Soviet Academy of Sciences.

Salazar Antonio de Oliveira 1889–1970. Portuguese prime minister 1932–68 who exercised a virtual dictatorship. A corporative constitution on the Italian model was introduced 1933, and until 1945 Salazar's National Union, founded 1930, remained the only legal party. Salazar was also foreign minister 1936–47 and during World War II he maintained Portuguese neutrality. He fought long colonial wars in Africa (Angola and Mozambique) that impeded Portugal's economic development.

SALT abbreviation for ◊***Strategic Arms Limitation Talks***, a series of US-Soviet negotiations 1969–79.

Salt March an episode during the period of Indian nationalist agitation against British rule, forming part of Mahatma Gandhi's campaign of ◊civil disobedience.

On 11 Mar 1930 Gandhi and his followers set out to walk 387 km/241 mi to Dandi, to campaign against the Salt Tax imposed by the British government, which maintained its monopoly by making it illegal for Indians to make their own salt. After arriving at Dandi on 6 Apr, Gandhi and his followers defied the British government by making their own salt. On 4 May Gandhi announced that the government-owned Dharasana saltworks were to be taken over on behalf of the Indian people. Gandhi was arrested but his followers advanced on the saltworks as planned. As the marchers moved forward in columns they were beaten to the ground, offering no resistance.

samizdat (Russian 'self-published') in the USSR, and eastern Europe before the 1989 uprisings, written material circulated underground to evade state censorship, for example reviews of Solzhenitsyn's banned novel *August 1914* 1972.

sanction economic or military measure taken by a state or number of states to enforce international law. Examples of the use of sanctions are the attempted economic boycott of Italy (1935–6) during the Abyssinian War by the

League of Nations; of Rhodesia, after its unilateral declaration of independence 1965, by the United Nations; the call for measures against South Africa on human-rights grounds by the United Nations and other organizations from 1985; the economic boycott of Iraq 1990 in protest over its invasion of Kuwait, following resolutions passed by the United Nations.

San Francisco Conference 1945 conference attended by representatives from 50 nations who had declared war on Germany prior to 1 March 1945; held in San Francisco, California, USA. The conference drew up the United Nations Charter which was signed 26 June 1945. A treaty between the Western Allies and Japan was signed here in 1951.

Sarajevo capital of Bosnia and Herzegovinia Yugoslavia.

A Bosnian, Gavrilo Princip, assassinated Archduke Francis Ferdinand here 1914, thereby precipitating World War I.

satellite any small body that orbits a larger one, either natural or artificial. Natural satellites that orbit planets are called moons. The first ***artificial satellite***, *Sputnik 1*, was launched into orbit around the Earth by the USSR 1957. Artificial satellites are used for scientific purposes, communications, weather forecasting, and military purposes. The largest artificial satellites can be seen by the naked eye.

The USA launched 23 nuclear-powered satellites 1961–77, of which four malfunctioned. The ◊Strategic Defense Initiative (Star Wars) programme proposes sending as many as 100 nuclear reactors into space. The USSR has launched 39 nuclear reactors on orbiting satellites since 1965, of which six have malfunctioned.

satellite, applications the uses to which artificial satellites are put. These include:

scientific experiments and observation Many astronomical observations are best taken above the disturbing effect of the atmosphere. Satellite observations have been carried out by *IRAS* (*Infrared Astronomical Satellite*, 1983) which made a complete infrared survey of the skies, and *Solar Max* 1980, which observed solar flares. The *Hipparchos* satellite, launched 1989, is expected to measure the positions of the stars with unprecedented accuracy. Medical experiments are carried out aboard crewed satellites, such as the Soviet *Mir* and the US *Skylab*.

reconnaisance and mapping applications Apart from military use and routine mapmaking, the US *Landsat*, the French *SPOT*, and the equivalent USSR satellites have provided much useful information about water sources and drainage, vegetation, land use, geological structures, oil and mineral locations, and snow and ice.

weather monitoring The US NOAA series

Sarajevo *Archduke Franz Ferdinand and his wife, minutes before their assassination at Sarajevo, June 1914.*

of satellites, and others launched by the European space agency, Japan, and India, provide continuous worldwide observation of the atmosphere.

navigation The US Global Positioning System, when complete in 1993, will feature 18 Navstar satellites that will enable users (including walkers and motorists) to find their position to within 1.5 m/4.5 ft. The Transit system, launched in the 1960s, with 12 satellites in orbit, locates users to within 100 m/328 ft.

communications A complete worldwide communications network is now provided by satellites such as the US-run Intelsat system.

satellite television transmission of broadcast signals through artificial communications satellites. Satellites have been used since the 1960s to relay television pictures around the world. Higher-power satellites have more recently been developed to broadcast signals to cable systems or directly to people's homes.

Direct broadcasting began in the UK Feb 1989 with the introduction of Rupert Murdoch's Sky Television service; its rival British Satellite Broadcasting (BSB) went on the air early in 1990, and they merged in Nov the same year, creating a monopoly subject to challenge by the regulating authority.

satyagraha (Sanskrit 'insistence on truth') nonviolent resistance to British rule in India, as employed by Mahatma ◊Gandhi from 1918 to press for political reform; the idea owes much to the Russian writer Leo Tolstoy.

Saudi Arabia country on the Arabian peninsula, stretching from the Red Sea to the Arabian Gulf, bounded N by Jordan, Iraq, and Kuwait; E by Qatar and United Arab Emirates; SE by Oman; and S by Yemen.

history Present-day Saudi Arabia is almost entirely the creation of King Ibn Saud who, after the dissolution of the ◊Ottoman Empire in 1918, fought rival Arab rulers until, in 1926, he had established himself as the undisputed king of the Hejaz and sultan of Nejd. In 1932 Nejd and Hejaz became the United Kingdom of Saudi Arabia.

economic prosperity Oil was discovered in the 1930s, commercially exploited from the 1940s, and became the basis of the country's prosperity. Ibn Saud died 1953 and was succeeded by his eldest son, Saud. During King Saud's reign relations between Saudi Arabia and Egypt became strained, and criticisms of the king within the royal family grew, until in 1964 he abdicated in favour of his brother Faisal. Under King Faisal, Saudi Arabia became a leader among Arab oil producers. In 1975 Faisal was assassinated by one of his nephews, and his half-brother Khalid succeeded him. King Khalid died of a heart attack in 1982 and was succeeded by Fahd.

Middle-East affairs Saudi Arabia has drawn up proposals for a permanent settlement of the Arab-Israeli dispute. It gave financial support to Iraq in its war with Iran. The Iran-Iraq War (see under ◊Iran) also prompted Saudi Arabia to buy advanced missiles from the USA. Islamic fundamentalists staged demonstrations in Mecca in 1979 and 1987, leading to violence and worsening relations with Iran. In 1989 Saudi Arabia assumed a leading role in the search for a settlement of the Lebanese civil war, hosting a constitutional convention of Lebanese legislators in Taif. On 2 Aug 1990 Iraq invaded and occupied neighbouring Kuwait, threatening the security of Saudi Arabia. King Fahd turned to the USA and UK for protection and a massive build-up of ground and air strength began, alongside Saudi Arabia's own forces. In return, King Fahd agreed to increase his oil output to offset the loss of Kuwaiti and Iraqi production, and to pay a substantial part of the cost of maintaining US and British forces.

Schlieffen Plan military plan produced by German chief of general staff, General Count Alfred von Schlieffen (1833–1913) Dec 1905, that formed the basis of German military planning before World War I, and which inspired Hitler's plans for the conquest of Europe in World War II. It involved a simultaneous attack on Russia and France, the object being to defeat France quickly and then deploy all available resources against the Russians. A modified version of the plan was implemented 1914.

Schmidt Helmut 1918– . German socialist politician, member of the Social Democratic Party (SPD), chancellor of West Germany 1974–83. As chancellor, Schmidt introduced social reforms and continued Brandt's policy of ◊Ostpolitik. With the French president Giscard d'Estaing, he instigated annual world and European economic summits. He was a firm supporter of ◊NATO and of the deployment of US nuclear missiles in West Germany during the early 1980s.

Schmidt was elected to the Bundestag (federal parliament) in 1953. He was interior minister 1961–65, defence minister 1969–72, and finance minister 1972–74. He became federal chancellor (prime minister) on Willy Brandt's resignation in 1974. Re-elected 1980, he was defeated in the *Bundestag* in 1982 following the switch of allegiance by the SPD's coalition allies, the Free Democratic Party. Schmidt retired from federal politics at the general election of 1983, having encountered growing opposition from the SPD's left wing, who opposed his stance on military and economic issues.

science park site on which high-technology industrial businesses are housed near a university, so that they can benefit from the research expertise of the university's scientists. Science parks originated in the USA in the 1950s.

By 1985 the UK had 13, the first being Heriot Watt in Edinburgh and the most successful in Cambridge.

SDI abbreviation for ◊***Strategic Defense Initiative***.

Second Front the battleline opened against Germany on 6 June 1944 by the Allies (Britain and the USA). Following Germany's invasion of Russia in June 1941 (the 'first front'), Russian leader Joseph Stalin asked Britain to invade the European mainland, to relieve pressure on the ◊Red Army. An Anglo-American invasion fleet landed on the Normandy beaches and, after overcoming fierce German resistance, Paris was liberated by the Allied forces 25 Aug 1944.

Second World War alternative name for ◊World War II, 1939–45.

secret police government run intelligence organizations such as the UK's Secret Service, the Soviet ◊KGB, or the US ◊Central Intelligence Agency.

Serbia Serbo-Croat ***Srbija*** constituent republic of Yugoslavia, which includes Kosovo and Vojvodina.

history After a war with Turkey 1876–78, Serbia became an independent kingdom. The two ◊Balkan Wars 1912–13 greatly enlarged Serbia's territory at the expense of Turkey and Bulgaria. Serbia's designs on Bosnia and Herzegovina, backed by Russia, led to friction with Austria, culminating in the outbreak of war 1914. Serbia was completely overrun 1915–16 and was occupied until 1918, when it became the nucleus of the new kingdom of the Serbs, Croats, and Slovenes, later Yugoslavia. There is still rivalry between Croats and Serbs. Slobodan Milosevic was elected president May 1989.

Sèvres, Treaty of, 1920 the last of the treaties that ended World War I. Negotiated between the Allied powers and the Ottoman Empire, the treaty reduced the size of Turkey by making concessions to the Greeks, Kurds, and Armenians, as well as ending Turkish control of Arab lands. It was finalised in Aug 1920 but never ratified by the Turkish government. It was superseded by the Treaty of ◊Lausanne in 1923.

Sharpeville black township in South Africa, 65 km/40 mi S of Johannesburg and N of Vereeniging; 69 people were killed here when police fired on a crowd of anti-apartheid demonstrators on 21 Mar 1960.

The massacre took place during a campaign launched by the Pan- Africanist Congress against the pass laws (laws requiring non-white South Africans to carry identity papers). On the anniversary of the massacre in 1985, during funerals of people who had been killed protesting against unemployment, 19 people were shot by the police at Langa near Port Elizabeth.

Shi'ite or ***Shiah*** member of a sect of ◊Islam who believe that Ali was Muhammad's first true successor. They are doctrinally opposed to the ◊Sunni Muslims. Holy men have greater authority in the Shi'ite sect than in the Sunni sect. They are prominent in Iran and Lebanon and are also found in Iraq and Bahrain. Breakaway sub-sects include the ***Alawite*** sect, to which the ruling party in Syria belongs; and the ***Ismaili*** sect, with the Aga Khan IV (1936–) as its spiritual head.

Shinto the indigenous religion of Japan. It combines an empathetic oneness with natural forces and loyalty to the reigning dynasty as descendants of the Sun goddess, Amaterasu-Omikami. Traditional Shinto followers stressed obedience and devotion to the emperor, and an aggressive nationalistic aspect was developed. Today Shinto has discarded these aspects.

Sectarian Shinto consists of 130 sects; the sects are officially recognized but not state-supported (as was state Shinto until its disestablishment after World War II and Emperor Hirohito's disavowal of his divinity 1946).

This was symbolized by the ***Yasukuni*** shrine, near Tokyo, since 1945 a purely religious memorial to 2.5 million war dead. Nevertheless, a public visit by Premier Nakasone in 1985 aroused controversy.

Siegfried Line in ***World War I*** the defensive line from Lens to Rheims established 1918 by the Germans in France. In ***World War II*** the term was applied to the German defensive line established along its western frontier, from the Netherlands to Switzerland. It largely corresponded to the Maginot Line which France constructed along its eastern frontier. The Siegfried Line succeeded in slowing down the offensive of the Allies in World War II. In 1945 British and Canadian troops broke through the northern part of the river Rhine at Milingers.

Singapore (Sanskrit 'Singa pura', city of the lion) country in SE Asia, off the tip of the Malay Peninsula.

Sharpeville *Aftermath of the Sharpeville riots after the South African police opened fire on anti-apartheid demonstrators.*

history Singapore was leased as a trading post in 1819 from the sultan of Johore by the British East India Company. It passed to the crown in 1858.

During World War II, Singapore functioned as a vital British military base in the Far East. Designed to be invulnerable to naval attack, it was invaded by land and occupied by Japan Feb 1942–Sept 1945. Singapore became a separate British crown colony in 1946 and fully self-governing, with Lee Kuan Yew as prime minister, from 1959. It joined the Federation of ◊Malaysia in 1963 but seceded in 1965, alleging discrimination against the federation's Chinese members. A new independent republic of Singapore was thus formed in Sept 1965, which remained within the ◊Commonwealth.

the republic The new republic's internal political affairs were dominated by Prime Minister Lee Kuan Yew's People's Action Party, which gained a monopoly of all parliamentary seats in the elections between 1968 and 1980. Under Lee's stewardship, Singapore has developed rapidly as a commercial and financial entrepot and as a centre for new export industries. Today its inhabitants enjoy the highest standard of living in Asia outside Japan and Brunei. During the early 1980s, as the pace of economic growth briefly slowed, opposition to the Lee regime began to surface. In the Dec 1984 election two opposition deputies won parliamentary seats for the first time. Lee took a firm line against dissent: J B Jeyaretnam, the Workers' Party leader, was conveniently found guilty of perjury in Nov 1986 and deprived of his parliamentary seat. Support for the PAP held steady, at 62%, in the Sept 1988 election and the opposition won only one seat. Plans were unveiled to create a new position of elected executive president. In Nov 1990 Lee resigned, handing over to his deputy, Goh Chok Tong, but remaining a senior member of the cabinet. Singapore allied itself closely with the USA 1965–74. Since the mid-1970s, however, it has pursued a neutralist foreign policy and improved its relations with China. It is a member of ◊ASEAN.

single party state another name for ◊one party state.

Sinn Féin ('We ourselves') Irish nationalist party founded by Arthur Griffith (1872–1922) in 1905; in 1917 Eamon de Valera became president and reorganized it. It is the political wing of the ◊Irish Republican Army, and is similarly split between comparative moderates and extremists. In 1985 it gained representation in 17 out of 26 district councils in Northern Ireland.

Sino-Japanese Wars wars waged by Japan against China to expand to the mainland.

First Sino-Japanese War 1894–95. Under

the treaty of Shimonoseki, Japan secured the 'independence' of Korea, cession of Taiwan and the nearby Pescadores Islands, and the Liaodong peninsula (for a naval base). France, Germany, and Russia pressured Japan into returning the last-named, which Russia occupied 1896 to establish Port Arthur (now Lüda); this led to the Russo-Japanese War 1904–05.

Second Sino-Japanese War 1931–45.

1931–32 The Japanese occupied Manchuria, which they formed into the puppet state of Manchukuo. They also attacked Shanghai, and moved into NE China.

1937 Chinese leaders Chiang Kai-shek and Mao Zedong allied to fight the Japanese; war was renewed as the Japanese overran NE China and seized Shanghai and Nanjing.

1938 Japanese capture of Wuhan and Guangzhou was followed by the transfer of the Chinese capital to Chongqing; a period of stalemate followed.

1941 Japanese attack on the USA (see ◊Pearl Harbor) led to the extension of lend-lease aid to China and US entry into war against Japan and its allies.

1944 A Japanese offensive threatened Chongqing.

1945 The Chinese received the Japanese surrender at Nanjing in Sept, after the Allies had concluded World War II.

Sino-Soviet split period of strained relations between the two major communist powers, China and the USSR during the early 1960s, thus dividing the communist world. The tension was based partly on differences in ideology but also involved rivalry for leadership and old territorial border claims. The Chinese Communists also criticized the USSR for supplying aircraft to India and for withdrawing technical and military aid to China in 1960. The USSR supported India in its border warfare with China 1961–62.

Six Day War another name for the third ◊Arab-Israeli War.

Smith Ian Douglas 1919– . Rhodesian politician. He was a founder of the Rhodesian Front 1962 and prime minister 1964–79. In 1965 he made a unilateral declaration of Rhodesia's independence and, despite United Nations sanctions, maintained his regime with tenacity. In 1979 he was succeeded as prime minister by Bishop Abel Muzorewa, when the country was renamed Zimbabwe. He was suspended from the Zimbabwe parliament in April 1987 and resigned in May as head of the white opposition party.

Smuts Jan Christian 1870–1950. South African politician and soldier; prime minister 1919–24 and 1939–48. He supported the Allies in both world wars and was a member of the British imperial war cabinet 1917–18.

During the Second South African War 1899–1902 Smuts commanded the Boer forces in his native Cape Colony. He subsequently worked for reconciliation between the Boers and the British and on the establishment of the Union of South Africa, he became minister of the interior 1910–12 and defence minister 1910–20. During World War I he commanded the South African forces in E Africa 1916–17. He was prime minister 1919–24 and minister of justice 1933–39; on the outbreak of World War II he succeeded General Hertzog as premier 1939–48. He was made a field marshal in 1941; and received the Order of Merit in 1947. Although more of an internationalist than his contemporaries, Smuts was a segregationalist, voting in favour of legislation that took away black rights and land ownership.

social democracy political ideology or belief in the gradual evolution of a democratic ◊socialism within existing political structures. The earliest was the German *Sozialdemokratische Partei* (SPD), today one of the two major German parties, created in 1875 from August Bebel's earlier German Social Democratic Workers' Party, itself founded 1869. Parties along the lines of the German model were founded in the last two decades of the 19th century in a number of countries including Austria, Belgium, Holland, Hungary, Poland, and Russia. The British Labour Party is in the social democratic tradition.

Social Democratic Party (SDP) British centrist political party formed 1981 by members of Parliament who resigned from the Labour Party.The SDP founders, known as the Gang of Four, were Roy Jenkins (its first leader), David Owen (leader from 1983), Shirley Williams, and William Rodgers. The 1983 and 1987 general elections were fought in alliance with the Liberal Party as the ***Liberal/SDP Alliance*** with limited electoral success (1983, six seats, 11.6% of the vote; 1987, five seats, 9.8% of the vote). A merger of the two parties was voted for by the SDP 1987, and the new party became the Social and Liberal Democrats, leaving a rump SDP that folded 1990.

socialism movement aiming at the establishment of a classless society through the substitution of common for private ownership of the means of production, distribution and exchange. The term is used both to cover all movements with this aim, such as communism and anarchism, and more narrowly for evolutionary socialism or democracy. In general the tendency since 1917 has been for a clear distinction, if not opposition, to exist between parties governed by Marx's revolutionary, 'scientific' socialism and the gradualist, reforming approach of the British Labour Party and Western European Social Democratic Party.

In the later 19th century socialist parties arose in most European countries; for example, in Britain the ◊Independent Labour Party. This period, when in Russia the Bolsheviks were reviving, witnessed a reaction against Marxism. This was typified by the Fabian Society in Britain and the German Revisionists, which appealed to popular nationalism and solved economic problems by similar means of state control of the economy, but in the general interests of private capital.

The late 19th and early 20th centuries saw a division between those who reacted against Marxism leading to social-democratic parties and those who emphasised the original revolutionary significance of Marx's teachings. Weakened by these divisions, the second International (founded in 1889) collapsed in 1914, right-wing socialists in all countries supporting participation in World War I while the left opposed it. The Russian Revolution removed socialism from the sphere of theory to that of practice, and was followed in 1919 by the foundation of the Third International, advocating a popular front against Hitler, which completed the division between right and left. This lack of unity, in spite of the temporary successes of the popular fronts in France and Spain in 1936–38, facilitated the rise of fascism and National Socialism (◊Nazism).

After World War II socialist and communist parties tended to formal union in Eastern Europe, although the rigid communist control that ensued was later modified in some respects in, for example, Poland, Romania, and Yugoslavia. Subsequent tendencies to broaden communism were suppressed in Hungary (1956) and Czechoslovakia (1968). In 1989, however, revolutionary change throughout Eastern Europe ended this rigid control. In Western Europe a communist takeover of the Portuguese revolution failed 1975–76, and elsewhere, as in France under ◊Mitterrand, attempts at socialist-communist cooperation petered out. Most countries in W Europe have a strong socialist party, for example, in Germany the Social Democratic Party and in Britain the ◊Labour Party.

social security state provision of financial aid to alleviate poverty. The term 'social security' was first applied officially in the USA, in the Social Security Act 1935. It was first used officially in Britain 1944, and following the Beveridge Report 1942 a series of acts was passed from 1945 to widen the scope of social security. Basic entitlements of those paying National Insurance contributions in Britain include an old-age pension, unemployment benefit, widow's pension, and payment during a period of sickness in one's working life. Other benefits include family credit, child benefit, and attendance allowance for those looking after sick or disabled people. Entitlements under National Insurance, such as unemployment benefit, are paid at flat rates regardless of need; other benefits, such as income support, are 'means-tested', that is, claimants' income must be below a certain level. Most payments, with the exception of unemployment benefit, are made by the Department of Social Security (DSS).

The concept of such payments developed in the later 19th century in Europe. In the 1880s Germany introduced compulsory accident and sickness insurance, and old-age pensions. Britain introduced noncontributory old-age pensions from 1909; and compulsory health and unemployment insurance from 1911. The US social-security legislation was passed to enable the federal government to cope with the effects of the Depression of 1929.

Solidarity (Polish ***Solidarność***) the national confederation of independent trade unions in Poland, formed under the leadership of Lech ◊Wałesa Sept 1980. An illegal organization from 1981 to 1989, it now heads the Polish government and divisions have emerged in the leadership.

Solidarity emerged from a summer of industrial disputes caused by the Polish government's attempts to raise food prices. The strikers created a trade-union movement independent of the Communist Party, and protracted negotiations with the government led to recognition of Solidarity in exchange for an acceptance of the leading role of the Communist Party in Poland. Continuing unrest and divisions in Solidarity's leadership led to the declaration of martial law in Dec 1981; the union was banned and its leaders were arrested. Wałesa was released Dec 1982, and Solidarity continued to function as an underground organization. It was legalized again April 1989 following a further wave of strikes under its direction and round-table talks with the governmemt. In the elections of June 1989 it won almost every seat open to it, and became the senior partner in a 'grand coalition' government formed Sept 1989 with Tadeusz Mazowiecki as prime minister.

Solidarity's achievements inspired the successful 'people power' movements in other E European countries during 1989, as well as the formation of more independent labour unions in the USSR.

Rural Solidarity and a political wing, the Citizens' Committee of Solidarity, were formed May 1989. Mazowiecki was the editor of the union newspaper, Solidarity Weekly.

Solzhenitsyn Alexander (Isayevich) 1918– . Soviet novelist, a US citizen from 1974. After military service, he was in prison and exile 1945–57 for anti-Stalinist comments. Much of his writing is semi-autobiographical and highly critical of the system, including *One Day in the Life of Ivan Denisovich* 1962 which deals with the labour camps under Stalin, and *The Gulag Archipelago* 1973, an exposé of the whole Soviet labour camp network. This led to his expulsion from the USSR 1974.

He was awarded a Nobel prize in 1970. He has adopted a Christian position, and his criticism of Western materialism is also stringent.

Somme, Battle of the Allied offensive in World War I July–Nov 1916 at Beaumont-Hamel-Chaulnes, on the river Somme in N France, during which severe losses were suffered by both sides. It was planned by the Marshal of France Joseph Joffre, and commander-in-chief Douglas Haig; the Allies lost over 600,000 men and advanced 32 km/20 mi. It was the first battle in which tanks were used. The German offensive around St Quentin Mar–Apr 1918, in which they regained the territory, is sometimes called the Second Battle of the Somme.

South Africa country on the southern tip of Africa, bounded N by Namibia, Botswana, and Zimbabwe and NE by Swaziland and Mozambique.

government The 1984 constitution is based on racial discrimination. The legislature and government are dominated by the descendants of Europeans, termed Whites in the context of ◊apartheid. There is only conditional participation in government for non-Whites, in the form of Coloureds, or persons of mixed European and African descent, and Asians. Black Africans are completely unrepresented at national level.

history The area was originally inhabited by Bushmen and Hottentots. Bantus, including Sotho, Swazi, Xhosa, and Zulu, settled there before the 17th century. The Dutch East India Company founded Cape Town 1652 as a port of call on the way to the Indies. Occupied by Britain, Cape Town and the hinterland were purchased by Britain 1814. Britons also settled in Natal 1824. In 1836 some 10,000 Dutch, wishing to escape from British rule, set out north on the Great Trek and founded the republic of Transvaal and the Orange Free State.

Boer war The discovery of diamonds at Kimberley, Cape Colony, 1867, and of gold in Transvaal 1886, attracted prospectors, who came in conflict with the Dutch farmers, the Boers. Britain attempted to occupy Transvaal 1877–81 but withdrew after a severe defeat at Majuba. Denial of citizenship rights to the migrant miners (*uitlanders*) in Transvaal, and the imperialist ambitions of Cecil Rhodes and others, led to the Jameson Raid from Mafeking into Transvaal in an attempt to overthrow the government, and the Boer War 1899–1902, won by Britain.

Union of South Africa In 1910 the Union of South Africa was formed, comprising the provinces of Cape of Good Hope, Natal, Orange Free State, and Transvaal. A Boer rebellion on the outbreak of World War I was speedily crushed by Jan Smuts. South Africa occupied German SW Africa (see ◊Namibia). Between the wars the union was alternately governed by the republican nationalists under Hertzog and the South African Party under Smuts, who supported the ◊Commonwealth connection. Hertzog wanted South Africa to be neutral in World War II, but Smuts took over as premier, and South African troops fought with the Allies.

apartheid introduced The National Party (NP) came to power 1948 and has ruled South Africa ever since. Its leader, Daniel Malan, initiated the policy of apartheid, attempting to justify it as 'separate but equal' development. In fact, all but the White minority are denied a voice in the nation's affairs. In the 1950s the ◊African National Congress (ANC) led a campaign of civil disobedience until it and other similar movements were, in 1960, declared illegal, and in 1964 the ANC leader Nelson Mandela was sentenced to life imprisonment for alleged sabotage. He became a central symbol of Black opposition to the apartheid regime remaining in prison until 1990.

'homelands' established Malan was succeeded 1958 by Hendrik ◊Verwoerd, who withdrew from the Commonwealth rather than abandon apartheid, and the Union became the Republic of South Africa 1961. Verwoerd was assassinated 1966, but his successor, B J ◊Vorster, pursued the same policy. Pass laws restricting the movement of Blacks within the country had been introduced, causing international outrage, and ten 'homelands' (Bantustans; see ◊Black National State) were established to contain particular ethnic groups. By the 1980s thousands of the apartheid regime's opponents had been imprisoned without trial and more than 3,000,000 people had been forcibly resettled in Black townships. International condemnation of police brutality followed the news of the death in detention of the Black community leader Steve Biko 1977. Despite all this, the NP continued to increase its majority at each election, until the Sept 1989 election, when its majority was greatly reduced.

constitutional reform In 1978 Vorster resigned and was succeeded by Pieter W Botha. He embarked on constitutional reform to involve Coloureds and Asians, but not Blacks, in the governmental process. This led to a clash within the NP, and in March 1982 Dr Adries Treurnicht, leader of the hardline (*verkrampte*) wing, and 15 other extremists were expelled. They later formed a new party, the Conservative Party of South Africa (CPSA). Botha's proposals were approved by 66% of the voters in an all-White referendum and came into effect Sept 1984. In 1985 a number of apartheid laws were amended or repealed, including the ban on sexual relations or marriage between people of different races and the ban on mixed racial membership of political parties, but the underlying inequalities in the system remained and dissatisfaction of the Black community grew. In the 1986 cabinet of 21, including Botha, there were 19 Whites, 1 Coloured, and 1 Indian.

state of emergency In May 1986 South Africa attacked what it claimed to be guerrilla strongholds in Botswana, Zambia, and Zimbabwe. The exiled ANC leader Oliver Tambo was receiving increasing moral support in meetings with politicians throughout the world, and Winnie ◊Mandela, during her husband's continuing imprisonment, was 'banned' repeatedly for condemning the system publicly. Non-violent resistance was advocated by Bishop Desmond Tutu, the ◊Inkatha movement, and others. A state of emergency was declared June 1986, a few days before the tenth anniversary of the first ◊Soweto uprising, marked by a strike in which millions of Blacks participated. Serious rioting broke out in the townships and was met with police violence, causing hundreds of deaths. Between 1980 and 1990 1,070 people were judicially executed.

sanctions imposed Abroad, calls for economic ◊sanctions against South Africa grew during 1985 and 1986. At the Heads of Commonwealth conference 1985 the Eminent Persons' Group (EPG) of Commonwealth politicians was conceived to investigate the likelihood of change in South Africa without sanctions. In July 1986 the EPG reported that there were no signs of genuine liberalization. Reluctantly, Britain's prime minister, Margaret Thatcher, agreed to limited measures. Some Commonwealth countries, notably Australia and Canada, took additional independent action. The US Congress eventually forced President Reagan to move in the same direction. Between 1988 and 1990 economic sanctions cost the South African treasury more than $4 billion in lost revenue. The decisions by individual multinational companies to close down their South African operations may, in the long term, have the greatest effect.

Namibia At the end of 1988 South Africa signed a peace agreement with Angola and Cuba, which included the acceptance of Namibia's independence, and in 1989, under UN supervision, free elections took place there. In Feb 1989 state president Botha suffered a stroke that forced him to give up the NP leadership and later the presidency. He was succeeded in both roles by F W ◊de Klerk, who promised major constitutional reforms. Meanwhile the non-racialist Democratic Party was launched, advocating universal adult suffrage, and made significant progress in the Sept 1989 Whites-only assembly elections. Despite de Klerk's release of the veteran ANC activist, Walter Sisulu, and some of his colleagues, Oct 1989, the new president's promises of political reform were treated with scepticism by the opposition, until he announced the lifting of the ban on the ANC, followed, on 11 Feb 1990, by the release of Nelson Mandela. In Sept President de Klerk declared membership of the National Party open to all races. In Dec ANC president Oliver Tambo returned triumphantly and in Jan 1991 a meeting between Mandela and Zulu leader Chief Buthelezi was arranged.

abandonment of apartheid announced In Feb 1991 President de Klerk announced the intended repeal of all remaining apartheid laws. With growing opposition from the extreme right-wing activists, the abandonment of apartheid and the establishment of a fully democratic political system will require considerable skill from both de Klerk and Mandela.

soviet (Russian 'council') originally a strike committee elected by Russian workers in the 1905 revolution; in 1917 these were set up by peasants, soldiers, and factory workers. The soviets sent delegates to the All-Russian Congress of Soviets to represent their opinions to a future government. They were later taken over by the ◊Bolsheviks.

Soviet Jew a member of the Jewish ethnic minority in the USSR. The ◊Jewish Autonomous Region was created for them.

Soweto (*So*uth *We*st *To*wnship) racially segregated urban settlement in South Africa, SW of Johannesburg; population (1983) 915,872.

It has experienced civil unrest because of the ◊apartheid regime.

It began as a shanty town in the 1930s and is now the largest black city in South Africa, but until 1976 its population could have status only as temporary residents, serving as a workforce for Johannesburg. There were serious riots in June 1976, sparked by a ruling that Afrikaans be used in African schools there. Reforms followed, but riots flared up again in 1985 and have continued into the 1990s.

space probe any instrumented object sent beyond Earth to collect data from other parts of the solar system and from deep space. The first probe was the Soviet *Lunik 1*, which flew past the Moon 1959. Other probes include *Giotto*, the Moon probes, and the Mariner, Pioneer, Viking, and Voyager series.

Space Shuttle reusable US crewed spacecraft, first launched 12 Apr 1981. It was developed by NASA to reduce the cost of using space for commercial, scientific, and defence purposes. After leaving its payload in space, the rocket can be flown back to Earth like any conventional airplane, and is then available for reuse.

Four orbiters were built. One of them, *Challenger* was destroyed in a mid-air explosion just over a minute into its tenth launch 28 Jan 1986, killing all seven crew members. At the end of the 1980s, an average of $375 million had been spent on each Space Shuttle mission.

Spain country in SW Europe, on the Iberian Peninsula between the Atlantic and the Mediterranean, bounded N by France and W by Portugal.

government The 1978 constitution puts a hereditary monarch as formal head of state. The monarch appoints a prime minister, called president of government, and a council of ministers, all responsible to the national assembly, *las Cortes Generales*. The *Cortes* consists of two chambers: the Chamber of Deputies, and the Senate. Deputies are elected by universal suffrage through a system of proportional representation.

Spain has developed a regional self-government whereby each of the 50 provinces has its own council (*Diputación Provincial*) and civil governor. The devolution process was extended 1979 when 17 autonomous communities were approved, each with a parliament elected for a four-year term.

history Republicanism, socialism, and anarchism grew after 1900; Primo de Rivera's dictatorship 1923–30 failed to preserve the monarchy under Alfonso XIII, and in 1931 a republic was established. In 1936 the Popular Front, a centre-left alliance, took office and introduced agrarian and other reforms that aroused opposition. A military rebellion led by General Francisco ◊Franco resulted in the Spanish ◊Civil War 1936–39. Franco, who was supported by the German Nazis and Italian Fascists, won the war, establishing a military dictatorship.

democratic government In 1947 Franco allowed the revival of a legislature with limited powers and announced that after his death the monarchy would be restored, naming Prince Juan Carlos de Bourbon, as his successor. Franco died 1975, and King Juan Carlos became head of state. There followed a slow but steady progress to democratic government, with the new constitution endorsed by referendum 1978.

regional demands Spain faced two main internal problems, the demands for independence by regional extremists and the possibility of a right-wing military coup. The aims of the ruling Democratic Centre Party (UCD), led by Adolfo Suárez, included a devolution of power to the regions (Basque, Catalonia, and eventually Andalucia), entry into NATO, and membership of the European Community. In 1981 Suárez suddenly resigned and was succeeded by his deputy, Calvo Sotelo. He was immediately confronted with an attempted army coup in Madrid, while at the same time the military commander of Valencia declared a state of emergency there and sent tanks out on the streets. Both uprisings failed, and the two leaders were tried and imprisoned. Sotelo's decision to take Spain into NATO was widely criticized, and, after defections from the party, he was forced to call a general election Oct 1982. The result was a sweeping victory for the Socialist Workers Party (PSOE), led by Felipe Gonzalez.

Basque separatist campaign The Basque separatist organization, ETA, had stepped up its campaign for independence with widespread terrorist activity, spreading in 1985 to the Mediterranean holiday resorts and threatening Spain's lucrative tourist industry.

Gonzalez's administration The PSOE had fought the election on a policy of taking Spain out of NATO and carrying out extensive nationalization. Once in office, however, Gonzalez showed himself to be a pragmatist. His nationalization programme was highly selective, and he left the decision on NATO to a referendum. In Jan 1986 Spain became a full member of the European Community, and in March the referendum showed popular support for remaining in NATO. In the July 1986 election the PSOE won 184 seats in the Chamber of Deputies, and Gonzalez returned for another term as prime minister. In Nov 1988 Spain, with Portugal, became a member of the Western European Union (WEU). In the Nov 1989 general election PSOE won only 50% of the seats in the National Assembly but retained power under prime minister Gonzales.

Spanish Civil War 1936–39. See ◊Civil War, Spanish.

Spartacist member of a group of left-wing radicals in Germany at the end of World War I, founders of the ***Spartacus League***, which became the German Communist party in Dec 1918. The league participated in the Berlin workers' revolt of Jan 1919, which was suppressed by the Freikorps on the orders of the socialist government. The agitation ended with the murder of Spartacist leaders Karl Liebknecht and Rosa ◊Luxemburg. The movement took its name from Spartacus, who led the slave uprising in Rome in the 1st century BC.

Special Areas Acts Acts of Parliament 1936, and 1937, aimed at dealing with unemployment in some regions of Britain. These areas, which were designated as 'special areas', attracted government assistance in the form of loans and subsidies to generate new employment. Other measures included setting up industrial and trading estates which could be leased at subsidized rates. The Acts were an early example of regional aid.

Sputnik (Russian 'fellow traveller') a series of ten Soviet Earth-orbiting satellites. *Sputnik 1* was the first artificial ◊satellite, launched 4 Oct 1957. It weighed 84 kg/185 lb and carried only a simple radio transmitter which allowed scientists to track it as it orbited Earth. It burned up in the atmosphere 92 days later. *Sputnik 2*, launched 3 Nov 1957, weighed about 500 kg/1,100 lb including the dog Laika, the first living creature in space. Unfortunately, there was no way to return the dog to Earth, and it died in space. *Sputnik 3* was launched 15 May 1958 and weighed about 1,300 kg/2,900 lb.

Sri Lanka island in the Indian Ocean, off the southeast coast of India.

history Ceylon was ceded to Britain 1802 and became a crown colony. In 1931, universal suffrage was introduced for an elected legislature and executive council in which power was shared with the British, and in Feb 1948 independence was achieved.

dominion status Between 1948 and 1972, Sri Lanka remained a dominion within the British Commonwealth with a titular governor-general. The United National Party (UNP), led consecutively by Don and Dudley Senanayake, held power until 1956, when the radical Socialist and more narrowly Sinhalese Sri Lanka Freedom Party (SLFP), led by Solomon Bandaranaike, gained electoral victory and established Sinhalese rather than English as the official language. This precipitated Tamil riots, culminating in the prime minister's assassination 1959. Bandaranaike's widow, Sirimavo, became prime minister and held office until 1977, except for UNP interludes 1960 and 1965–70. She implemented a radical economic programme of nationalization and land reform, a pro-Sinhalese educational and employment policy, and an independent ◊nonaligned defence policy.

Tamil separatist movement In 1972 the Senate upper chamber was abolished and the republic declared. The new national name Sri Lanka 'Resplendent Island' was adopted. Economic conditions deteriorated, spawning a serious wave of strikes 1976, while Tamil complaints of discrimination bred a separatist movement calling for the creation of an independent Tamil state (Eelam) in the N and E. The Tamil United Liberation Front (TULF) coalition was formed 1976 to campaign for this goal and emerged as the second-largest party in parliament from the elections July 1977, led by Junius Jayawardene. The new government remodelled the 1972 constitution and introduced a new freer-market economic programme. The guerrilla activities of the Liberation Tigers of Tamil Eelam (LTTE) in the north and east provoked the frequent imposition of a state of emergency. In 1982 Jayawardene was re- elected president, and the life of parliament was prolonged by referendum.

civil war The violence escalated 1983, causing the deaths of over 400 people, mainly Tamils in the Jaffna area. This prompted legislation outlawing separatist organizations, including the TULF. The near civil war has cost thousands of lives and blighted the country's economy.

the Colombo Accord All-party talks with Indian mediation repeatedly failed to solve the Tamil dispute, but in July 1987, amid violent protest riots, President Jayawardene and the Indian prime minister Rajiv ◊Gandhi signed a peace pact. It proposed to make Tamil and English official languages, create a semi-autonomous homeland for the Tamils in the north and east, recognize the Tigers (once disarmed) as their representatives, and hold a referendum 1988. To police this agreement, a 7,000-strong Indian Peace Keeping Force (IPKF) was despatched to the Tiger-controlled Jaffna area. The Tamil Tigers put down their weapons and agreed to talks with the Sri Lankan government April 1989. This employment of Indian troops provoked protest riots among the Sinhala community who viewed the July 1987 Colombo Accord as a 'sell out' to Tamil interests.

reconciliation attempts Prime minister Ranasinghe Premadasa stood for the governing party in the presidential election of Dec 1989 and defeated Sirimavo Bandaranaike. Finance minister Dingri Banda Wijetunge was appointed prime minister and proceeded, with Premadasa, to work for national reconciliation. Negotiations were held with Tiger leaders in June 1989 and in Sept 1989 agreement was reached with India that the IPKF would be withdrawn by April 1990. Despite these moves the civil war, with its two fronts in the north and south, continued, with the death toll exeeding 1,000 a month. Among those assassinated during 1989 was Appapillai Amirthalingam, the leader of the TULF, and Rohana Wijeweera, who had led the JVP since its formation in 1967. Sri Lanka remains a member of the Commonwealth and ◊non-aligned movement and joined the South Asian Association for Regional Cooperation 1985. India withdrew its troops from Sri Lanka in March 1990.

SS Nazi elite corps (German *Schutz-Staffel* 'protective squadron') established 1925. Under Himmler its 500,000 membership included the full-time ***Waffen-SS*** (armed SS), which fought in World War II, and spare-time members. The SS performed state police duties and was brutal in its treatment of the Jews and others in the concentration camps and occupied territories. It was condemned at the Nuremberg Trials of war criminals.

stagflation economic condition (experienced in Europe in the 1970s) in which rapid inflation is accompanied by stagnating, even declining, output and by increasing unemployment. Its cause is often sharp increases in costs of raw materials and/or labour.

Stakhanov Aleksei 1906–1977. Soviet miner who exceeded production norms; he gave his name to the ***Stakhanovite*** movement of the 1930s, when workers were offered incentives to simplify and reorganize work processes in order to increase production.

Stalin Joseph. Adopted name (Russian 'steel') of Joseph Vissarionovich Djugashvili 1879–1953. Soviet politician. A member of the October Revolution Committee 1917, Stalin became general secretary of the Communist Party 1922. After ◊Lenin's death 1924, Stalin sought to create 'socialism in one country' and clashed with ◊Trotsky, who denied the possibility of socialism inside Russia until revolution had occurred in W Europe. Stalin won this ideological struggle by 1927, and a series of five-year plans was launched to collectivize industry and agriculture from 1928. All opposition was eliminated in the Great Purge 1936–38. During World War II, Stalin intervened in the military direction of the campaigns against Nazi Germany. His role was denounced after his death by Khrushchev and other members of the Soviet regime.

Born in Georgia, the son of a shoemaker, he was educated for the priesthood but was expelled from his seminary for Marxist propaganda. He became a member of the Social Democratic Party 1898, and joined Lenin and the Bolsheviks 1903. He was repeatedly exiled to Siberia 1903–13. He then became a member of the Communist Party's ◊Politburo, and sat on the October Revolution committee. Stalin rapidly consolidated a powerful following (including Molotov); in 1921 he became commissar for nationalities in the Soviet government, responsible for the decree granting equal rights to all peoples of the Russian Empire, and was appointed general secretary of the Communist Party 1922. As dictator in the 1930s, he disposed of all real and imagined enemies.

He met Churchill and Roosevelt at Tehran 1943 and at Yalta 1945, and took part in the Potsdam conference. After the war, Stalin maintained an autocratic rule.

Stalingrad former name (1925–61) of the Soviet city of Volgograd.

Star Wars popular term for the ◊Strategic Defence Initiative announced by US president Reagan in 1983.

Stauffenberg Claus von 1907–1944. German colonel in World War II who, in a conspiracy to assassinate Hitler, planted a bomb in the dictator's headquarters conference room in the Wolfs Lair at Rastenburg, East Prussia, 20 July 1944. Hitler was merely injured, and Stauffenberg and 200 others were later executed by the Nazi regime.

Stopes Marie (Carmichael) 1880–1958. Scottish birth-control campaigner. With her husband Humphrey Roe (1878–1949), she founded a London birth-control clinic 1921. The Well Woman Centre in Marie Stopes House, London, commemorates her work. She wrote plays and verse as well as the best-selling manual *Married Love* 1918.

Strategic Arms Limitation Talks (SALT) a series of US-Soviet discussions aimed at reducing the rate of nuclear-arms build-up. The talks, delayed by the Soviet invasion of Czechoslovakia 1968, began in 1969 between the US President Lyndon Johnson and the Soviet leader Brezhnev. Neither the SALT I accord (effective 1972–77) nor SALT II called for reductions in nuclear weaponry, merely a limit on the expansion of these forces. SALT II was mainly negotiated by US President Ford before 1976 and signed by Soviet leader Brezhnev and President Carter in Vienna in 1979. It was never fully ratified because of the Soviet occupation of Afghanistan, although the terms of the accord were respected by both sides until President ◊Reagan exceeded its limitations during his second term 1985–89. SALT talks were superseded by START (Strategic Arms Reduction Talks) negotiations under Reagan, and the first significant reductions have begun under Soviet President Gorbachev.

US-Soviet summits

1969 SALT talks began in Helsinki
1972 Nixon and Brezhnev signed SALT I accord
1973 Brezhnev met Nixon in Washington DC
1974 (June) Nixon met Brezhnev in Moscow
1974 (Nov) Ford met Brezhnev in Vladivostok
1975 Ford and Brezhnev attend 35-nation meeting in Helsinki
1979 Carter and Brezhnev signed SALT II accord in Vienna
1983 Strategic Arms Reduction Talks (START) in Geneva
1986 Reagan and Gorbachev met in Reykjavik
1987 Intermediate Nuclear Forces treaty signed in Washington DC
1989 Cuts on short-range missiles in Europe proposed conditional on reduction of conventional forces

strategic bombing bombing of enemy territory with the aim of disrupting its economy and destroying morale. During World War II strategic bombing of cities was extensively used by both the Axis and the Allied powers. Rotterdam in the Netherlands, Warsaw in Poland, Dresden in Germany, and London all experienced heavy bombardment.

Strategic Defense Initiative (SDI) also called ***Star Wars***. An attempt by the USA to develop a defence system against incoming nuclear missiles, based in part outside the Earth's atmosphere. It was announced by President Reagan Mar 1983, and the research had by 1990 cost over $16.5 billion. In 1988, the joint Chiefs of Staff announced that they expected to be able to intercept no more than 30% of incoming missiles.

The essence of the SDI is to attack enemy missiles at several different stages of their trajectory, using advanced laser and particle-beam technology, thus increasing the chances of disabling them. Israel, Japan, and the UK are among the nations assisting in SDI research and development. In 1987 Gorbachev acknowledged that the USSR was developing a similar defence system.

Stresa Front summit meeting 11–14 Apr 1935 between the prime ministers of Britain, France, and Italy (Ramsay MacDonald, Pierre Flandin, and Benito Mussolini) with the aim of forming a common front against Germany. This followed Adolf Hitler's announcement that Germany would not be bound by the limitations imposed upon its armaments by the Versailles Treaty of June 1919. The 'front' soon broke up: in Oct 1935 Italy was severely criticized for launching an Abyssinian War 1935–36 to establish an East African Italian empire, and on 2 Nov 1936 Benito Mussolini proclaimed the Rome–Berlin Axis, which brought Germany and Italy into close collaboration 1936–45.

Stresemann Gustav 1878–1929. German politician, chancellor in 1923 and foreign minister 1923–29 of the ◊Weimar Republic. During World War I he was a strong nationalist but his views became more moderate under the Weimar Republic. His achievements included reducing the amount of war reparations paid by Germany after the Treaty of Versailles 1919; negotiating the Locarno Treaties 1925; and Germany's admission to the League of Nations. He shared the 1926 Nobel Peace Prize with Aristide Briand.

submarine underwater warship. A naval submarine, or submersible torpedo boat, was launched by France 1888. The conventional submarine of World War I was driven by diesel engine on the surface and by battery-powered electric motors underwater. In both world wars submarines played a vital role.

In 1954 the USA launched the first nuclear-powered submarine, the *Nautilus*. The US nuclear submarine *Ohio*, in service from 1981, carries 24 Trident missiles, each with 12 independently targetable nuclear warheads.

Three Vanguard-class Trident missile-carrying submarines, which when armed will each wield more firepower than was used in the whole of World War II, are being built in the 1990s in the UK.

Sudan country in NE Africa, S of Egypt, with a Red Sea coast; it is the largest country in Africa.

history The region was jointly administered as an Anglo-Egyptian condominium from 1899. The Sudan, as it was called, achieved independence as a republic 1956. Two years later a coup ousted the civil administration, and a military government was set up, which in 1964 was itself overthrown and civilian rule was reinstated. Five years later the army returned in a coup led by Col Gaafar Mohammed Nimeri. All political bodies were abolished, the Revolutionary Command Council (RCC) set up, and the country's name changed to the Democratic Republic of Sudan. Close links were soon established with Egypt, and in 1970 an agreement in principle was reached for eventual union. In 1972 this should have become, with the addition of Syria, the Federation of Arab Republics, but internal opposition blocked both developments. In 1971 a new constitution was adopted, Nimeri confirmed as president, and the Sudanese Socialist Union (SSU) declared to be the only party.

regional problems The most serious problem confronting Nimeri was open aggression between the Muslim north and the chiefly Christian south, which had started as long ago as 1955. At a conference in Addis Ababa 1972 he granted the three southern provinces a considerable degree of autonomy, but fighting continued. Nimeri had come to power in a left-wing revolution but soon turned to the West, and the USA, for support. In 1983 he was re-elected for a third term, but his regional problems persisted. By sending more troops south against the Sudan People's Liberation Army he alienated the north and then caused considerable resentment in the south by replacing the penal code with strict Islamic law. His economic policies contributed to the widespread unrest.

bloodless coup In March 1985 a general strike was provoked by a sharp devaluation of the Sudanese pound and an increase in bread prices. General Swar al-Dahab, took over in a bloodless coup. He set up a transitional military council and held elections for a legislative assembly Apr 1986, contested by more than 40 parties. A coalition government was formed, with Ahmed Ali El-Mirghani (DUP) as president of the Supreme Council and Oxford-educated Sadiq al-Mahdi (NNUP) as prime minister. Strikes and shortages persisted, with inflation running at about 100% and the highest national debt in Africa, and in July 1987 a state of emergency was declared. In Oct 1987 the prime minister announced the break-up of the government of national unity and the formation of a new coalition. In Dec 1988 the signing of a peace agreement with the Sudan People's Liberation Movement (SPLM), led by John Garang, threatened to split the coalition government and eventually led to a military takeover, by General Ahmed el-Bashir, in July 1989. El-Bashir established a 15-man revolutionary council with himself as head of state and government. Bashir's government announced that its first priority was to end the six-year war between the Muslim north and the Christian and Animist south.

Sudetenland mountainous region of N Czechoslovakia, annexed by Germany under the ◊Munich Agreement 1938; returned to Czechoslovakia 1945.

Suez Crisis military confrontation Oct–Dec 1956 following the nationalization of the Suez Canal by President Nasser of Egypt. In an attempt to reassert international control of the canal, Israel launched an attack, after which British and French troops landed. Widespread international censure (Soviet protest, US non-support, and considerable domestic opposition) forced the withdrawal of British and French troops. The crisis resulted in the resignation of British prime minister Eden. There were allegations of collusion between Israel, France, and Britain.

suffragette or ***suffragist*** a woman fighting for the right to vote. In the UK, women's suffrage bills were repeatedly introduced and defeated in Parliament between 1886 and 1911, and a militant campaign was launched 1906 by Emmeline ◊Pankhurst and her

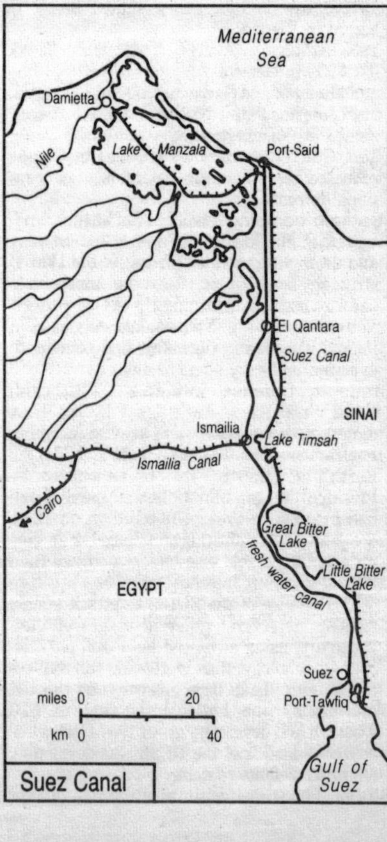

Suez Canal

Suharto *General Suharto, president of Indonesia.*

daughters. In 1918 women were granted limited franchise; in 1928 it was extended to all women over 21. In the USA the 19th amendment to the constitution 1920 gave women the vote in federal and state elections.

Suffragettes (the term was coined by a *Daily Mail* reporter) chained themselves to railings, heckled political meetings, refused to pay taxes, and in 1913 bombed the home of Lloyd George, then chancellor of the Exchequer. One woman, Emily Davison, was killed in her attempt to stop the king's horse at the Derby in 1913. Many suffragettes were imprisoned and were force-fed when they went on hunger strike; under the notorious 'Cat and Mouse Act' of 1913 they could be repeatedly released to regain their health and then rearrested. The struggle was called off on the outbreak of World War I.

Suharto Raden 1921– . Indonesian politician and general. He ousted Sukarno to become president in 1967. He ended confrontation with Malaysia, invaded East Timor in 1975, and reached a cooperation agreement with Papua New Guinea 1979. His authoritarian rule has met domestic opposition from the left. He was re-elected in 1973, 1978, 1983, and 1988.

Sukarno Achmed 1901–1970. Indonesian nationalist, president 1945–67. During World War II he cooperated in the local administration set up by the Japanese, replacing Dutch rule. After the war he became the first president of the new Indonesian republic, becoming president-for-life in 1966; he was ousted by ◊Suharto.

Sunni a member of the larger of the two main sects of ◊Islam, with about 680 million adherents. Sunni Muslims believe that the first four caliphs were all legitimate successors of the prophet Muhammad, and that guidance on belief and life should come from the Koran and the Hadith (the teachings of Muhammed), and from the Shari'a (religious law) not from a human authority or spiritual leader. Imams in Sunni Islam are educated lay teachers of the faith and prayer leaders.

Sun Yat-sen or ***Sun Zhong Shan*** 1867–1925. Chinese revolutionary leader and statesman, founder of the ◊Guomindang (Nationalist party) 1894, and provisional president of the Republic of China 1912 after playing a vital part in deposing the emperor. He was president of a breakaway government from 1921.

Sun Yat-sen was the son of a Christian farmer. From 1894–1905 he led the 'Save China League' while in exile. He returned to China during the 1911 revolution that overthrew the Manchu dynasty and was provisional president of the republic in 1912. In an effort to bring unity to China, he soon resigned in favour of the military leader Yuan Shih-k'ai. As a result of Yuan's increasingly dictatorial methods, Sun established an independent republic in S China based in Canton 1921. He was criticized for lack of organizational ability, but his 'three people's principles' of nationalism, democracy, and social reform are accepted by both the Nationalists and the Chinese Communists.

superpower term used to describe the USA and the USSR from the end of World War II 1945, when they emerged as significantly stronger than all other countries.

SWAPO (***South West Africa People's Organization***) organization formed 1959 in South West Africa (now ◊Namibia) to oppose South African rule. SWAPO guerrillas, led by Sam Nujoma, began attacking with support from Angola. In 1966 SWAPO was recognized by the United Nations as the legitimate government of Namibia, and won the first independent election 1989.

Sweden country in N Europe on the Baltic Sea, bounded W by Norway and NE by Finland.

history Sweden has a long tradition of neutrality (remaining neutral during both world wars) and political stability, and a highly developed social welfare system. The office of ombudsman is a Swedish invention, and Sweden was one of the first countries to adopt a system of open government.

constitutional reform The Social Democratic Labour Party (SAP) was continuously in power 1951–76, usually in coalition. In 1969 the leadership of the party changed hands, and Olof Palme became prime minister. He carried out two major reforms of the constitution, reducing the chambers in parliament from two to one 1971 and 1975 removing the last of the monarch's constitutional powers.

In 1976 the general election was fought on the issue of the level of taxation needed to fund the welfare system, and Palme was defeated. Thorbjorn Fälldin, leader of the Centre Party, formed a centre-right coalition government. The Fälldin administration fell 1978 over its wish to follow a non-nuclear energy policy, and it was replaced by a minority Liberal government led by Ola Ullsten. Fälldin returned 1979, heading another coalition, and pursued a limited nuclear-energy programme. Fälldin remained in power until 1982, when the Social Democrats, with Olof Palme, returned with a minority government. Palme was soon faced with deterioriating relations with the USSR, arising from suspected violation of Swedish territorial waters by Soviet submarines. The situation had improved substantially by 1985. After the general election in that year, Palme's party had 159 *Riksdag* seats, and he was able to continue with Communist support. The Moderate Party won. In Feb 1986, Olof Palme was murdered. Palme's deputy, Ingvar Carlsson, took over as prime minister and leader of the SAP. In the Sept 1988 general election Carlsson and the SAP were re-elected with a reduced majority. The Green Party won enough votes to gain representation in the *Riksdag*, the first new party to gain a seat in 70 years. In Feb 1990, with mounting opposition to its economic policies, the government resigned, leaving Carlsson as a caretaker prime minister. In Dec the *Riksdag* supported the government's decision to apply for EC membership.

Switzerland landlocked country in W Europe, bounded N by West Germany, E by Austria, S by Italy, and W by France.

government Switzerland is a federation of 20 cantons and six half-cantons (canton is the name for a political division, derived from Old French). The constitution dates from 1874 and provides for a two-chamber federal assembly, consisting of the National Council and the Council of States. The National Council is elected by universal suffrage, through a system of proportional representation. The Council of States has 46 members, each canton electing two representatives and each half-canton one.

The federal government is in the hands of the Federal Council, each heading a specific federal department. The federal assembly also appoints one member to act as federal head of state and head of government for a year.

history Switzerland, for centuries a neutral country, has been the base for many international organizations and the host of many international peace conferences. A referendum 1986 rejected the advice of the government and came out overwhelmingly against membership of the United Nations. Its domestic politics have been characterized by coalition governments and a stability that has enabled it to become one of the world's richest countries (per person).

Of several political parties, the most significant are the Radical Democratic Party, the Social Democratic Party, the Christian Democratic Party, the People's Party, and the Liberal Party. Women were not allowed to vote in federal elections until 1971. The first female cabinet minister was appointed 1984. After the Oct 1987 election, the four-party coalition continued in power, although there was a significant increase in the number of seats held by the Green Party. In 1989, a referendum found widespread dissatisfaction with the citizen army and military service requirements.

syndicalism (French *syndicat* 'trade union') political movement that rejected parliamentary activity in favour of direct action, culminating in a revolutionary general strike to secure worker ownership and control of industry. The idea acquired its more violent aspects in France from the philosopher Georges Sorel's work, such as *Reflections on Violence* 1908, and also reached the USA. After 1918 syndicalism was absorbed in communism, although it continued to have an independent existence in Spain until the late 1930s.

Syria country in W Asia, on the Mediterranean, bounded N by Turkey, E by Iraq, S by Jordan, and SW by Israel and Lebanon.

history Syria was part of the ◊Ottoman Empire 1516–1918. It was occupied by British and French troops 1918–19 and in 1920 placed under French mandate. Syria became independent in 1946 and three years later came under military rule.

military coup In 1958 Syria merged with Egypt to become the United Arab Republic (UAR), but after an army coup in 1961 Syria seceded, and the independent Syrian Arab Republic was established. In 1963 a government was formed, mainly from members of the Arab Socialist Renaissance (Ba'ath) Party, but three years later the army removed it. In 1970 the moderate wing of the Ba'ath Party, led by Lt-Gen Hafez al-Assad, secured power in a bloodless coup, and in the following year Assad was elected president. Since then

President Assad has remained in office without any serious challenges to his leadership.

Middle East affairs Externally Syria has played a leading role in Middle East affairs. In the Six Day War 1967 it lost territory to Israel, and after the Yom Kippur War 1973 Israel formally annexed the Golan Heights, which had previously been part of Syria. During 1976 Assad increasingly intervened in the civil war in Lebanon, eventually committing some 50,000 troops to the operations. Relations between Syria and Egypt cooled after President Sadat's Israel peace initiative 1977 and the subsequent ◊Camp David agreements. Assad has consistently opposed US-sponsored peace moves in Lebanon, arguing that they infringed upon Lebanese sovereignty. He has also questioned Yasser Arafat's leadership of the ◊Palestine Liberation Organization (PLO) and supported opposition to him. In 1984 President Assad and the Lebanese president Amin Gemayel approved plans for a government of national unity in Lebanon, which would give equal representation to Muslims and Christians, and secured the reluctant agreement of Nabih Berri of the Shi'ite Amal Militia and Walid Joumblatt, leader of the Druse. Fighting still continued, and Assad's credibility suffered, but in 1985 his authority proved sufficient to secure the release of 39 US hostages from an aircraft hijacked by the extremist Shi'ite group Hezbollah (Party of God). In Nov 1986 Britain broke off diplomatic relations after claiming to have proof of Syrian involvement in international terrorism, when a Syrian citizen attempted to blow up an Israeli plane at Heathrow, London. Syria has been leaning to the west, its policies in Lebanon in direct conflict with Iran's dream of an Islamic republic, and its crumbling economy has been promised Arab aid if Damascus switches allegiance. In June 1987, following a private visit by former US president Jimmy ◊Carter, Syria's relations with the USA began to improve, and efforts were made to arrange the release of Western hostages in Lebanon. In Nov 1990 full diplomatic relations with Britain were resumed.

T

Taff Vale case 1901 legal decision that threatened the existence of trade unions in Britain. Reaction to the decision resulted in increasing the strength of the Labour Party and support for the trade-union movement.

The case was heard before the House of Lords as a result of claims for damages made by the Taff Vale Railway Company against the Amalgamated Society of Railway Servants after an official strike. The union was found responsible for the actions of its members and ordered to pay compensation of £23,000. The legal implications of the case were recognized by trade unionists, who argued that the costs of strike action would be prohibitive and that the judgement was a deliberate attempt to weaken the ◊trade unions. Immunity against similar claims was introduced by the ◊Trade Disputes Act passed by Harry Campbell Bannerman's Liberal government on election in 1906.

Taft William Howard 1857–1930. 27th president of the USA 1909–13, a Republican. He was secretary of war 1904–08 in Theodore Roosevelt's administration. As president his conservatism provoked Roosevelt to stand against him in the 1912 election. Taft served as chief justice of the Supreme Court 1921–30, in which role he supported a minimum wage.

His first interest was the judiciary, although he accepted a post as governor of the Philippines and took responsibility for the construction of the ◊Panama Canal. His single term as president was characterized by struggles against progressives, although he prosecuted more trusts than had his predecessor.

Taft-Hartley Act, 1947 US Act prohibiting sympathy strikes and strikes by government employees. It was sponsored by Robert Taft (1889–1953), US Republican senator from 1939 and a candidate for the presidential nomination 1940, 1944, 1948, and 1952. He was the son of President William Taft.

Taiwan country in SE Asia, officially the Republic of China, occupying the island of Taiwan between the E China Sea and the S China Sea.

history Taiwan was annexed by the Manchu dynasty 1683. It was ceded to Japan under the terms of the Treaty of Shimonoseki after the 1895 Sino-Japanese war and not regained by China until the Japanese surrender Aug 1945.

Chinese nationalist government In Dec 1949 Taiwan became the refuge for the Chinese Nationalist government forces of ◊Chiang Kai-shek after their defeat by the Communist troops of ◊Mao Zedong. Chiang and his Nationalist followers, though only a 15% minority, dominated the island and maintained an army of 600,000 in the hope of reconquering the mainland, over which they still claimed sovereignty. They continued to be recognized by the USA as the legitimate government of China, and occupied China's United Nations and Security Council seats until Oct 1971 when they were expelled and replaced by the People's Republic.

economic growth Taiwan was protected by US naval forces during the Korean War 1950–53 and signed a mutual defence treaty with the USA 1954. Benefiting from such security, the country enjoyed a period of rapid economic growth during the 1950s and 1960s, emerging as an export-oriented, newly industrialized country. Political power during these years was concentrated in the hands of the Kuomintang and the armed forces led by President Chiang Kai-shek, with martial law imposed and opposition activity outlawed. During the 1970s the Taiwanese government was forced to adjust to rapid external changes as the USA adopted a new policy of détente towards Communist China. In Jan 1979 this culminated in the full normalization of Sino-US relations, the severing of Taiwanese-US diplomatic contacts, and the annulment of the USA's 1954 security pact. Other Western nations followed suit in ending diplomatic relations with Taiwan during the 1970s and early 1980s.

democratization and 'Taiwanization' Chiang Kai-shek died April 1975 and his son Chiang Ching-kuo became party chair and, from 1978, state president. A programme of gradual democratization and 'Taiwanization' was adopted, with elections being held for 'vacated seats' within the National Assembly and Legislative Yuan, and native Taiwanese being more rapidly inducted into the Kuomintang. In the Dec 1986 elections a formal opposition party, the Democratic Progressive Party (DPP), led by Chiang Peng-chien, was tolerated and captured 22% of the vote to the Kuomintang's 69%. In July 1987 martial law was lifted and replaced with a national-security law under which demonstrations and the formation of opposition parties were legalized, so long as they forswore communism and supported Taiwanese independence. Press restrictions were also lifted.

reform President Chiang was succeeded on his death by Lee Teng-hui, a Taiwan-born Christian. The new president, who headed the party's modernizing technocrat wing, accelerated the pace of reform. Many 'old guard' figures were retired during 1988–89 and a plan for phasing out by 1992, through voluntary retirement, up to 200 mainland constituencies and replacing them with Taiwanese deputies was approved. In the Dec 1989 Legislative Yuan elections, the first to be freely held on the island, the Kuomintang's vote share fell to 59% and the DPP increased its number of seats. By the end of 1991 the remaining 'old guard' will have retired.

Tanganyika African National Union (TANU), a moderate socialist national party organized by Tanzanian politician Julius ◊Nyerere in the 1950s. TANU won electoral successes in 1958 and 1960, ensuring that Nyerere was recognized as prime minister on 1 May 1961, when Tanganyika prepared for independence from Britain.

tank armoured fighting vehicle that runs on tracks and is fitted with weaponry capable of destroying life and property and defeating other tanks. The term was originally a code name for the first effective tracked and armoured fighting vehicle, invented by the British soldier and scholar Ernest Swinton, and used in the battle of the Somme 1916.

Tannenberg, Battle of battle 26–30 August 1914, named after a village which was part of East Prussia and is now in N Poland. The Russian army under General Rennenkampf and General Samsonov penetrated East Prussia at the beginning of World War I. German General von Hindenburg routed the Russians, and captured over 100,000 prisoners. The scale of the defeat made the launch of another Russian invasion into German territory impossible during World War I.

Tanzania country in E Africa, on the Indian Ocean, bounded N by Uganda and Kenya; S by Mozambique, Malawi, and Zambia; and W by Zaïre, Burundi, and Rwanda.

history Zanzibar was under Portuguese control during the 16th–17th centuries. In 1822 it was united with the nearby island of Pemba. It was a British protectorate 1890–1963, when it became an independent sultanate; an uprising followed, and the sultan was overthrown 1964.

independence Tanganyika was a German colony 1884–1914, until conquered by Britain during World War I; it was a British League of Nations mandate 1920–46 and came under United Nations (UN) trusteeship 1946–62. It achieved full independence, within the ◊Commonwealth, in 1961, with Julius ◊Nyerere as prime minister. He gave up the post some six weeks after independence to devote himself to the development of the ◊Tanganyika African National Union (TANU), but in Dec 1962, when Tanganyika became a republic, he returned to become the nation's first president.

Republic of Tanzania formed Tanzania was founded by the union of Tanganyika and Zanzibar in April 1964. Nyerere became president of the new United Republic of Tanzania and dominated the nation's politics for the next 20 years, being re-elected in 1965, 1970, 1975, and 1980. He established himself as a Christian Socialist and in the Arusha Declaration of 1967 he committed himself to building a Socialist state for the millions of poor peasants through a series of village cooperatives (*ujamas*). Nyerere became one of Africa's most respected politicians. His achievements have included the best public health service on the African continent, according to UN officials, and a universal primary school system.

foreign policy The East African Community (EAC) of Tanzania, Kenya, and Uganda, formed in 1967, broke up in 1977, and relations between Tanzania and the more capitalistic Kenya became uneasy. In 1979 Nyerere sent troops to support the Uganda National Liberation Front in its bid to overthrow President Idi Amin. This enhanced Nyerere's reputation but damaged his country's economy. Tanzania also supported the liberation movements in Mozambique and Rhodesia. In 1977 TANU and the Afro-Shirazi Party of Zanzibar merged to become the Revolutionary Party of Tanzania (CCM), and this was made the only legal political organization. Nyerere retired from the presidency at the end of 1985 but remained as CCM chair. The president of Zanzibar, Ali Hassan Mwinyi, was adopted as the sole presidential candidate by the CCM congress in Dec 1985. In May 1990 Julius Nyerere announced his retirement as party chair and in Aug 1990 he was replaced by President Mwinji.

tariff tax on imports or exports from a country. Tariffs have generally been used by governments to protect home industries from lower-priced foreign goods, and have been opposed by supporters of free trade. For a tariff to be successful, it must not provoke retaliatory tariffs from other countries. Organizations such as the European Community, EFTA, and the General Agreement on Tariffs and Trade (GATT) 1948 have worked towards mutual lowering of tariffs between countries.

Tariff Reform League organization set up in 1903 as a vehicle for the ideas of the Liberal politician Joseph Chamberlain on protective tariffs. It aimed to unify the British Empire by promoting imperial preference in trade.

This policy was unacceptable to dominion governments as it would constrict their economic policies and put taxation on to foodstuffs imported into Britain. Consequently, the league's objective became the introduction of protection for British goods against competition from Germany and the USA.

technology the practical application of science in everyday life. The growth of technology began with the Industrial Revolution in the second half of the 18th century with the invention of the steam engine. The introduction of electricity as a power source and of the internal combustion engine (leading to the motorcar and aircraft) in the early 20th century transformed everyday life in the industrialized countries. The pace of technological development escalated in the middle and late 20th century with the introduction of electronics, nuclear power, computers, robots, and space ◊satellites. Areas of current development include information technology (the use of computers to store, retrieve, and manipulate information by using systems such as teletext and videotext), medical technology (organ transplants and tomography), military technology (such as the US ◊Strategic Defense Initiative), energy (solar energy and tidal power stations), communications (the cellphone and optical fibres), and entertainment (many developments in television and video).

Tehran Conference conference held 1943 in Tehran, Iran, the first meeting of World War II Allied leaders Winston Churchill, F D Roosevelt, and Josef Stalin. The chief subject discussed was coordination of Allied strategy in W and E Europe.

telecommunications communications over a distance, generally by electronic means. Long-distance voice communication was pioneered 1876 by Alexander Graham Bell, when he invented the telephone as a result of Faraday's discovery of electromagnetism. Today it is possible to communicate with most countries by telephone cable, or by satellite or microwave link, with over 100,000 simultaneous conversations and several television channels being carried by the latest satellites. Integrated-services digital network (ISDN) is a system that transmits voice and image data on a single transmission line by changing them into digital signals, making videophones and high-quality fax possible; the world's first large-scale centre of ISDN began operating in Japan 1988. The chief method of relaying long-distance calls on land is microwave radio transmission.

The forerunner of the present telecommunications age was the electric telegraph. As a result of Heinrich Hertz's discoveries using electromagnetic waves, Guglielmo Marconi pioneered a 'wireless' telegraph, ancestor of the ◊radio. He established wireless communication between England and France 1899 and across the Atlantic 1901. The modern telegraph uses teleprinters to send coded messages along telecommunications lines. Telegraphs are keyboard-operated machines that transmit a code. The receiving teleprinter automatically prints the received message.

The first public telegraph line was laid between Paddington and Slough 1843. In 1980 the Post Office opened its first System X (all-electronic, digital) telephone exchange in London, a method already adopted in North America. In Britain, Goonhilly and Madley are the main Earth stations for satellite transmissions.

television (TV) reproduction at a distance by radio waves of visual images.

history In 1908 Campbell-Swinton pointed out that cathode-ray tubes would best effect transmission and reception. Mechanical devices were used at the first practical demonstration of television, given by John L Baird in London 27 Jan 1926, and cathode-ray tubes were used experimentally in the UK from 1934.

The world's first public television service was started from the BBC station at Alexandra Palace in N London, 2 Nov 1936. In 1990 in the UK, the average viewing time per person was 25.5 hours each week.

Teng Hsiao-ping alternative spelling of ◊Deng Xiaoping, Chinese politician.

Tennessee Valley Authority (TVA) US government corporation founded 1933 to develop the Tennessee river basin (an area of some 104,000 sq km/40,000 sq mi) by building hydroelectric power stations, producing and distributing fertilizers, and similar activities. The TVA was one of President F D Roosevelt's ◊New Deal measures, promoting economic growth by government investment.

Its two major functions were to control the destructive flooding that had long plagued the valley and to provide employment in a seven-state area hard hit by the ◊Depression. There were 32 major dams incorporated into a massive river-control system that also provided electric power for a wide region. Today about half of TVA's electrical output is devoted to defence installations surrounding the generating plants. The TVA has undertaken reforestation projects and agricultural research.

terrorism systematic violence in the furtherance of political aims, often by small ◊guerrilla groups, such as the Fatah Revolutionary Council led by Abu Nidal, a splinter group that split from the Palestine Liberation Organization in 1973.

Test Ban Treaty international agreement signed by the USA, the USSR, and the UK 5 Aug 1963 contracting to test nuclear weapons only underground (banning testing in the atmosphere, underwater, and outer space). In the following two years 90 other nations signed the treaty, the only major nonsignatories being France and China, which continued underwater and ground-level tests.

Tet Offensive in the Vietnam War, a prolonged attack mounted by Vietcong and North Vietnamese troops against Saigon (now Ho Chi Minh City) and in more than 100 cities in South Vietnam, beginning 30 Jan 1968. Some 84,000 Communist troops took part in the offensive, with 32,000 being killed by mid-Feb. The fighting in Saigon was especially fierce, and in Hue, which the Communists controlled for almost a month, 3,000 civilians were executed. The US Marine base at Khe San was besieged for almost three months, and although the Communists were finally repulsed with heavy losses, the USA later abandoned the base. The Tet Offensive proved the continued strength of the Communists and embarassed US military leaders. Although Communist losses were heavy, the Tet Offensive proved a major propaganda victory for the Communists.

Thailand country in SE Asia on the Gulf of Siam, bounded E by Laos and Cambodia, S by Malaysia, and W by Myanmar (Burma).

history Anglo-French diplomatic agreements of 1896 and 1904 established Siam as a neutral buffer kingdom between British Burma and French Indochina. After World War I, a movement for national renaissance developed, which culminated in a coup against the absolute monarch King Prajadhipok and the establishment instead of a constitutional monarchy and an elected, representative system of government 1932. The name of Muang Thai ('Land of the Free') was adopted 1939. Thailand was occupied by Japan 1941–44. The government collaborated, but there was a guerrilla resistance movement. A period of instability followed the Japanese withdrawal, King Ananda Mahidol was assassinated 1946, and the army assumed power in a coup 1947 led by Field Marshal Pibul Songgram.

military junta rule The army retained control during the next two decades, with the leader of the military junta periodically changed by a series of bloodless coups: Field Marshal Pibul Songgram 1947–57, Field Marshal Sarit Thanarat 1958–63, and General Thanom Kittikachorn 1964–73. The monarch, King Bhumibol Adulyadej, was only a figurehead, and experiments with elected assemblies were undertaken 1957–58 and 1968–71. During this era of junta rule, Thailand allied itself with the USA and encountered serious Communist guerrilla insurgency along its borders with ◊Laos, ◊Cambodia, and ◊Malaysia. Despite achievements in the economic sphere, the junta was overthrown by violent student riots in Oct 1973. A democratic constitution was adopted a year later, and free elections were held in 1975 and 1976. A series of coalition governments lacked stability, and the military assumed power again 1976–77. The army supreme commander, General Kriangsak Chomanan, held power 1977–80 and brought in a new constitution in Dec 1978. This established a mixed civilian and military form of government under the monarch's direction. Having deposed Kriangsak in Oct 1980, General Prem Tinsulanonda (1920–) formally relinquished his army office and headed the civilian coalition governments that were formed after the parliamentary elections of April 1983 and July 1986. Attempted coups in April 1983 and Sept 1985 were crushed by Prime Minister Prem, who ruled in a cautious apolitical manner and retained the confidence of the army leadership and the public. The country achieved a rapid rate of economic growth, emerging as an export-oriented newly industrializing country. Following the general election of July 1988, a six-party coalition was formed. The conservative Chatichai Choonhavan took over as premier. He proceeded to pursue a growth-oriented policy course similar to his predecessor's.

foreign policy The continuing civil war in Cambodia and Laos, which has resulted in the flight of more than 500,000 refugees to Thailand since 1975, has provided justification for continued quasi-military rule and the maintenance of martial law. Thailand has drawn closer to its ◊ASEAN allies, who jointly support the Cambodian guerrilla resistance to the Vietnamese-imposed government, and its relations with China have thawed. Thailand has recently been drawn more deeply into the Cambodian civil war, with the shelling July 1989 of a refugee camp in Thailand.

Thatcher *Margaret Thatcher, the first prime minister to be re-elected for a third term of office since Lord Liverpool.*

Thatcher Margaret Hilda (born Roberts) 1925– . British Conservative politician, prime minister 1979–1990. She was education minister 1970–74, and Conservative party leader from 1975. In 1982 she sent British troops to recapture the Falkland Islands from Argentina. She confronted trade union power during the miners' strike 1984-85, sold off majority stakes in many public utilities to the private sector, and reduced the influence of local government through such measures as the abolition of metropolitan councils, the control of expenditure through 'rate-capping', and the introduction of the community charge or poll tax from 1989. In 1990 splits in the cabinet over the issues of Europe and consensus government forced her resignation. An astute Parliamentary tactician, she tolerated little disagreement, either from the opposition or from within her own party.

Born in Grantham, Margaret Thatcher was the daughter of a grocer, and studied chemistry at Oxford, before becoming a barrister. As minister for education 1970–74 she faced criticism for abolishing free milk for schoolchildren over eight. She was nonetheless an unexpected victor in the 1975 leadership election when she defeated Edward Heath. As prime minister she sharply reduced public spending to bring down inflation, but at the cost of generating a recession: manufacturing output fell by a fifth, and unemployment rose to over three million. Her popularity revived after the Falklands War.

Her second term of office was marked by the miners' strike 1984-85, which ended in defeat for the miners and indicated a shifted balance of power away from the unions. In 1984 she narrowly avoided injury from an IRA bomb which exploded during the Conservative party conference in October. Her election victory in 1987 made her the first prime minister in 160 years to be elected for a third term, but she became increasingly isolated by her autocratic, aloof stance, which allowed little time for Cabinet debate. In 1986 defence minister Michael Heseltine resigned after supporting a European-led plan for the rescue of the Westland helicopter company. In 1989 Nigel Lawson resigned as chancellor when she publicly supported her financial advisor, Alan Walters, against him. The introduction of the Poll Tax 1989 in Scotland, 1990 in England and Wales was widely unpopular. Finally, Geoffrey Howe resigned as home secretary in Nov 1990 over her public denial of an earlier cabinet consensus over the single European currency. Mrs Thatcher was the most influential peace-time Conservative prime minister this century. She claimed to have 'rolled back the frontiers of the state' by reducing income tax rates, selling off council houses, and allowing for greater individual choice in areas such as education. However, such initiatives often resulted paradoxically in greater central government control. She left the opposition Labour party in disarray, and forced it to a fundamental review of its policies, in order to regain credibility. Her vindictiveness against the left was revealed in her crusade against local councils, which she pursued at the cost of a concern for social equality.

Third Reich (Third Empire) term used by the Nazis to describe Germany during the years of Hitler's dictatorship after 1933. The idea of the Third Reich was based on the existence of two previous German empires, the medieval Holy Roman Empire and the second empire 1871–1918. The term was coined by the German writer Moeller van den Bruck (1876–1925) in the 1920s.

Third Republic the system of government established in France 1870–1946. It was characterized by a series of scandals and crises, such as the Dreyfus Case 1894–99 and the Stavisky affair 1933. The Republic survived World War I, and the interwar years were more stable, despite the multiplicity of political parties, and short-lived governments (there were 44 successive governments between 1918 and 1944). The weakness of the political system led to popular demonstrations by both left wing and right wing extremists, but it was the shock of military defeat in the German invasion 1940 and the subsequent pro-German Vichy regime that precipitated the fall of the Third Republic. In 1944 France was liberated by Allied forces and Charles de Gaulle established a provisional government that gave way to the Fourth Republic 1946.

Third World the world's hundred poorest countries, as defined by the World Bank, as measured by their income per head of population; they are concentrated in Asia, Africa, and Central America. They are divided into low-income countries, including China and India, and middle-income countries, such as Nigeria, Indonesia, and Brazil. The Third World has 75% of the world's population but consumes only 20% of its resources.

Problems associated with poor countries include high population growth and mortality rates, poor educational and health facilities, heavy dependence on agriculture and commodities for which prices and demand fluctuate, high levels of underemployment and, in some cases, political instability. Third World countries account for over 75% of all arms imports. The economic performance of these countries in recent years has been mixed, with sub-Saharan Africa remaining in serious difficulties and others, in Asia, making significant progress. Failure by many countries to meet their enormous debt obligations has led to more stringent terms being imposed on loans by industrialized countries, as well as rescheduling (deferring payment).

Tiananmen Square (Chinese 'Square of Heavenly Peace') paved open space in central Beijing (Peking), China, the largest public square in the world (area 0.4 sq km/0.14 sq mi). On 3–4 June 1989 over 1,000 unarmed protesters were killed by government troops in a massacre that crushed China's emerging pro-democracy movement.

Hundreds of thousands of demonstrators had occupied the square from early May, calling for political reform and the resignation of the Communist leadership. They were led by students, 3,000 of whom staged a hunger strike in the square. The massacre that followed was sanctioned by the old guard of leaders, including Deng Xiaoping.

Tiananmen Square *The 'Goddess of Democracy' made a brief, symbolic appearance in the square during the student demonstrations of 1989. The statue was destroyed in the massacre that followed.*

Tibet autonomous region of SW China (Pinyin form ***Xizang***), area 1,221,600 sq km/471,538 sq mi; population (1986) 2,030,000.

history Tibet was an independent kingdom from the 5th century AD. It came under nominal Chinese rule about 1700. Independence was regained after a revolt 1912. China regained control 1951 when the historic ruler and religious leader, the Dalai Lama, was driven from the country and the monks (who formed 25% of the population) were forced out of the monasteries. Between 1951 and 1959 the Chinese People's Liberation Army (PLA) controlled Tibet, although the Dalai Lama returned as nominal spiritual and temporal head of state.

Tibetan uprising In 1959 a Tibetan uprising spread from bordering regions to Lhasa and was supported by the Tibet local government. The rebellion was suppressed by the PLA, prompting the Dalai Lama and 9,000 Tibetans to flee to India. The Chinese proceeded to dissolve the Tibet local government, abolish serfdom, collectivize agriculture, and suppress Lamaism (a form of Mahāyāna Buddhism). In 1965 Tibet became an autonomous region of China. Chinese rule continued to be resented, however, and the economy languished.

Chinese rule relaxed From 1979, the leadership in Beijing adopted a more liberal and pragmatic policy towards Tibet. Traditional agriculture, livestock, and trading practices were restored (under the 1980 slogan 'relax, relax, and relax again'), a number of older political leaders and rebels were rehabilitated or pardoned, and the promotion of local Tibetan cadres was encouraged. In addition, a somewhat more tolerant attitude towards Lamaism has been adopted (temples damaged during the 1965–68 Cultural Revolution are being repaired) and attempts, thus far unsuccessful, have been made to persuade the Dalai Lama to return from exile.

independence movement suppressed Pro-independence demonstrations erupted in Lhasa in Sept–Oct 1987, repeatedly throughout 1988, and in Mar 1989 when they were forcibly suppressed by Chinese troops. In May and Oct 1988 peacefully demonstrating monks and civilians were shot by police. In 1989 many anti-China demonstrators were shot and all foreigners were expelled. These clashes exhibit the continuing strength of nationalist feeling. The country is of immense strategic importance to China, being the site of 50,000–100,000 troops and a major nuclear missile base at Nagchuka.

Tirpitz Alfred von 1849–1930. German admiral. As secretary for the navy 1897–1916, he built up the Germany navy to match the British one. The German Navy Law 1898 marked the beginning of German naval expansion, ostensibly to protect Germany's colonies and overseas trade. In 1906, Tirpitz decided to build battle ships to rival the British ◊Dreadnoughts. He retired 1916 because of Kaiser Wilhelm's unwillingness to make full use of German sea-power, in particular, opposition to his policy of unrestricted submarine warfare in World War I.

Tito adopted name of Josip Broz 1892–1980. Yugoslav soldier and communist politician, in power from 1945. In World War II he organized the National Liberation Army to carry on guerrilla warfare against the German invasion 1941, and was created marshal 1943. As prime minister 1946–53 and president from 1953, he followed a foreign policy of 'positive neutralism'.

Born in Croatia, Tito served in the Austrian army during World War I, was captured by the Russians, and fought in the Red Army during the civil wars. Returning to Yugoslavia 1923, he became prominent as a communist and during World War II as partisan leader against the Nazis. In 1943 he established a provisional government and gained Allied recognition, and with Soviet help proclaimed the federal republic 1945. As prime minister, he settled the Yugoslav minorities question on a federal basis, and in 1953 took the newly created post of president (for life from 1974). In 1948, he was criticized by the USSR and other communist countries, for his successful system of decentralized profit-sharing workers' councils, and became a leader of the ◊nonaligned movement.

Togo country in W Africa, bounded W by Ghana, E by Benin, and N by Burkina Faso.

government The 1979 constitution created a one-party, socialist republic based on the Assembly of the Togolese People (RPT). The president, elected by universal suffrage, is head of state and head of government, appointing and presiding over a council of ministers. He is also president of RPT.

There is a single-chamber legislature, the National Assembly, elected by universal suffrage from a list of RPT nominees and serving for five years. There is an illegal opposition party, the Togolese Movement for Democracy, which is based in Paris.

history Togoland was a German protectorate 1885–1914, when it was captured by Anglo-French forces. It was divided between Britain and France in 1922 under a League of Nations mandate and continued under United Nations trusteeship from 1946. In 1956 British Togoland voted for integration with Ghana, where it became Volta region 1957.

the republic French Togoland voted to become an autonomous republic within the French union. The new Togolese republic achieved internal self-government in 1956 and full independence in 1960. Sylvanus Olympio, leader of the United Togolese (UT) party, became president in an unopposed election in April 1961. In 1963 Olympio was killed in a military coup and his brother-in-law Nicolas Grunitzky, who had gone into exile, was recalled to become president.

gradual democratization In 1967 Grunitzky was, in turn, deposed in a bloodless military coup, led by Lt-Gen Etienne Gnassingbé Eyadéma. The new constitution was suspended; Eyadéma assumed the presidency and banned all political activity. Six years later he founded a new party, the socialist, nationalist RPT, and declared it the only legal political organization. Between 1967 and 1977 there were several attempts to overthrow him but by 1979 Eyadéma felt sufficiently secure to propose a new coalition and embark on a policy of gradual democratization. An attempt to overthrow him in Oct 1986, by mercenaries from Burkina Faso and Ghana, was easily thwarted.

Tōgō Heihachirō 1846–1934. Japanese admiral who commanded the fleet at the battle of Tsushima 1905, when Japan defeated the Russians and effectively ended the Russo-Japanese War of 1904–05.

Tōjō Hideki 1884–1948. Japanese general and premier 1941–44 during World War II. Promoted to chief of staff of Japan's Guangdong army in Manchuria 1937, he served as minister for war 1940–41. He was held responsible for defeats in the Pacific 1944 and forced to resign. After Japan's defeat, he was hanged as a war criminal.

totalitarianism government control of all activities within a country, overtly political or otherwise, as in fascist or communist dictatorships. Examples of totalitarian regimes are Italy under Benito ◊Mussolini 1922-45; Germany under Adolf ◊Hitler 1933-45; the USSR under Joseph ◊Stalin from 1930s until his death in 1953; more recently Romania under Nicolae ◊Ceauşescu 1974–89.

total war a war which combines widespread blanket destruction of armed forces, civilians, and property, with heavy civilian involvement so that the distinction between forces and civilians is blurred. British, Soviet, and German civilians in World War II experienced total war in the form of air raids, food shortages and restrictions on their personal freedom, and were expected to take heavy responsiblity for civil defence. Civilians in other parts of Europe and the Far East suffered similarly.

Trade Disputes Act 1906 UK Act of Parliament 1906 which protected trade unions against claims by their employers for damages resulting from trade disputes. The Act reversed the ◊Taff Vale judgement 1901 which made trade unions liable for their members' actions.

Trades Union Congress (TUC) voluntary organization of trade unions, founded in the UK 1868, in which delegates of affiliated unions meet annually to consider matters affecting their members. In 1988 there were some 100 affiliated unions, with an aggregate membership of about 11 million.

trade union organization of employed workers formed to undertake collective bargaining with employers and to try to achieve improved working conditions for its members. Attitudes of government to unions and of unions to management vary greatly from country to country. Probably the most effective trade-union system is that of Sweden, and the most internationally known is the Polish Solidarity.

history Five centuries of repressive legislation in Britain culminated in the passing of the Combination Laws 1799 and 1800 which made unions illegal. The repeal of these 1824–25 enabled organizations of workers to engage in collective bargaining, although still subject to legal restrictions and with no legal protection for their funds until the enactment of a series of Trade Union Acts 1871–76. In 1868, 34 delegates representing 118,000 trade unionists met at a 'congress' in Manchester; the Trades Union Congress (TUC) gradually became accepted as the central organization for trade unions. Under the Trade Union Act of 1871 unions became full legal organizations and union funds were protected from dishonest officials. Successive acts of Parliament enabled the unions to broaden their field of action, for example the Trade Disputes Act of 1906 protected the unions against claims for damages by their employers (see ◊Taff Vale Judgement); and the 1913 Trade Union Act allowed the unions to raise a political levy (see ◊Osborne Judgement).

The Trades Union Congress was for many years representative mainly of unions of skilled workers, but in the 1890s the organization of unskilled labour spread rapidly. Industrial Unionism (the organization of all workers in one industry or trade) began about this time, but characteristic of the so-called New Unionism at the time of the 1889 dock strike was the rise of general labour unions (for example, the Dock Workers and General Labourers in the gas industry).

During World War I the leading trade unions cooperated with the employers and the government, and by 1918 were stronger than ever before with a membership of eight million. In 1926, following a protracted series of disputes in the coal industry, the TUC called a general strike in support of the miners; this collapsed and after nine days it was called off, leaving the miners' union to continue the strike alone for a further six months. Under the Trade Disputes and Trade Union Act of 1927 general strikes or strikes called in sympathy with other workers were made illegal. During World War II a number of trade union leaders served in the coalition government and membership of trade unions had again risen to eight million by 1944. The restrictive 1927 Act was repealed under the Labour government in 1946.

The postwar period was marked by increased unionism among white-collar workers. From the 1960s onwards there were confrontations between the government and the trade unions, and unofficial or 'wildcat' strikes set public opinion against the trade union movement. The Labour governments' (1964–70) attempts to introduce legislative reform of the unions was strongly opposed and eventually abandoned in 1969. The Conservative government's Industrial Relations Act 1971 (including registration of trade unions, legal enforcement of collective agreements, compulsory 'cooling-off' periods, and strike ballots) was repealed by the succeeding Labour government 1974, and voluntary wage restraint attempted under a social contract. The Employment Protection Act 1975 and the Trade Union Act 1976 increased the involvement of the government in industrial relations. An Advisory Conciliation and Arbitration Service (ACAS) was set up 1975 to arbitrate in industrial disputes.

The Thatcher government, in the Employment Acts of 1980 and 1982, restricted the closed shop, picketing, secondary action against anyone other than the employer in dispute, immunity of trade unions in respect of unlawful activity by their officials, and the definition of a trade dispute, which must be between workers and employers, not between workers. The Trade Union Act 1984 made it compulsory to have secret ballots for elections and before strikes. Picketing was limited to the establishment at which strikes were taking place. The Employment Act 1988 contains further provisions regulating union affairs, including: further requirements for ballots; rights for members not to be unfairly disciplined (for example, for failing to support a strike); and prohibiting the use of union funds to indemnify union officers fined for contempt of court or other offences.

trench warfare hostilities conducted from defensive long, narrow, deeply dug trenches, which were extensively used on the ◊Western Front in World War I. Trenches were commonly used from the advent of mechanized war until increased mobility provided by the aeroplane and the motor car enabled attacking armies to avoid such large-scale, immobile forms of defence.

Triad secret society, founded in China as a Buddhist cult AD 36. It became known as the Triad because the triangle played a significant part in the initiation ceremony. Today it is reputed to be involved in organized crime (drugs, gambling, prostitution) among overseas Chinese. Its headquarters are alleged to be in Hong Kong.

Triple Alliance pact from 1882 between Germany, Austria-Hungary, and Italy to offset the power of Russia and France. It was last renewed 1912, but during World War I Italy's initial neutrality gradually changed and it denounced the alliance 1915. The term also refers to other alliances: 1788 – Britain, Prussia, and Holland; 1795 – Britain, Russia, and Austria.

Triple Entente alliance of Britain, France, and Russia 1907–17. In 1911 this became a military alliance and formed the basis of the Allied powers in World War I against the Central Powers, Germany and Austria-Hungary.

The failure of the alliance system to create a stable balance of power, coupled with widespread horror of the carnage created by World War I, led to attempts to create international cooperation with the League of Nations.

Trotsky Leon. Adopted name of Lev Davidovitch Bronstein 1879–1940. Russian revolutionary. He joined the ◊Bolshevik party and took a leading part in the seizure of power 1917 and raising the Red Army that fought the Civil War 1918–20. In the struggle for power that followed ◊Lenin's death 1924, ◊Stalin defeated Trotsky, and this and other differences with the Communist Party led to his exile 1929. He settled in Mexico, where he was assassinated with an ice pick at Stalin's instigation. Trotsky believed in world revolution and in permanent revolution, and was an uncompromising, if liberal, idealist.

Trotsky became a Marxist in the 1890s and was imprisoned and exiled for opposition to the tsarist regime. He lived in W Europe from 1902 until the 1905 revolution, when he was again imprisoned but escaped to live in exile until 1917. Although as a young man Trotsky admired Lenin, when he worked with him organizing the revolution of 1917, he objected to Lenin's dictatorial ways. He was second in command until Lenin's death. Trotsky's later works are critical of the Soviet regime; for example, *The Revolution Betrayed* 1937. His greatest work is his magisterial *History of the*

Trotsky *Leon Trotsky in 1917, the year of the Russian Revolution.*

Russian Revolution 1932–33. Official Soviet recognition of responsibility for his assassination through the secret service came in 1989.

Trudeau Pierre (Elliott) 1919– . Canadian Liberal politician. He was prime minister 1968–79 and 1980–84. In 1980 his work helped to defeat the Québec independence movement in a referendum. He repatriated the constitution from Britain 1982, but by 1984 had so lost support that he resigned.

Truman Harry S 1884–1972. 33rd president of the USA 1945–53, a Democrat. In Jan 1945 he became vice president to Franklin D Roosevelt, and president when Roosevelt died in Apr that year. He used the atom bomb against Japan, launched the Marshall Plan to restore W Europe's economy, and nurtured the ◊European Community and NATO (including the rearmament of West Germany).

Born in Lamar, Missouri, he ran a clothing store that was bankrupted by the Great Depression. He became a senator 1934, was selected as Roosevelt's last vice president, and in 1948 was elected for a second term in a surprise victory over Thomas Dewey (1902–1971), the governor of New York. At home, he had difficulty converting the economy back to peacetime conditions, and failed to prevent the witch-hunts on suspected communists (see Joe ◊McCarthy). In Korea, he intervened when the South was invaded, but sacked General ◊MacArthur when the general's policy threatened to start World War III. Truman's decision not to enter Chinese territory, betrayed by the double agent Kim Philby, led to China's entry into the war. Truman had a sign on his desk that said: 'The buck stops here.'

Truman *Harry Truman was US president during the Allied victory in World War II and US involvement in the Korean War.*

Truman Doctrine US president Harry Truman's 1947 dictum that the USA would 'support free peoples who are resisting attempted subjugation by armed minorities or by outside pressures'. It was used to justify sending aid to Greece following World War II and sending US troops abroad; for example, to Korea.

tsarist rule system of political government in Russia. It was adopted by Ivan IV in 1547 and meant to express the highest form of domination, similar to that of the Holy Roman emperor in western Europe. Tsarist rule lasted until the abdication in 1917 and execution in 1918 of Tsar Nicholas II.

Tunisia country in N Africa, on the Mediterranean, bounded SE by Libya and W by Algeria.

history Tunisia became a French protectorate 1881. The Socialist Destourien Party (PSD), founded 1934 by Habib Bourguiba, led Tunisia's campaign for independence from France. The country achieved internal self-government 1955 and full independence 1956, with Bourguiba as prime minister. A year later the monarchy was abolished, and Tunisia became a republic, with Bourguiba as president. A new constitution was adopted 1959, and the first national assembly elected. Between 1963 and 1981 PSD was the only legally recognized party, but since then others have been allowed. In Nov 1986 PSD won all the assembly seats, while other parties boycotted the elections.

Middle East affairs President Bourguiba followed a distinctive foreign policy, establishing links with the Western powers, including the USA, but joining other Arab states in condemning the US-inspired Egypt–Israel treaty. He allowed the Palestine Liberation Organization (PLO) to use Tunis as its headquarters, and this led to an Israeli attack 1985 that strained relations with the USA. Diplomatic links with Libya were severed 1985. Bourguiba's firm and paternalistic rule, and his long period in Tunisian politics, made him a national legend. However, in Nov 1987 he was deposed and replaced by Zine al-Abidine Ben Ali. In July 1988, a number of significant constitutional changes were announced, presaging a move to more pluralist politics, but in the April 1989 elections the ruling RDC won all 141 assembly seats.

Turkey country between the Black Sea and

the Mediterranean, bounded E by the USSR and Iran, S by Iraq and Syria.
history The Bulgarian uprising of 1876 led to a war between Turkey and Russia, and by the Treaty of Berlin 1878 Turkey lost Bulgaria, Bosnia, and Herzegovina. A militant nationalist group, the Young Turks, secured the grant of a constitution 1908; Italy took advantage of the ensuing crisis to seize Tripoli in 1911–12, while the Balkan states in 1912–13 expelled the Turks from Albania and Macedonia. Turkey entered World War I on the German side 1914, only to lose Syria, Arabia, Mesopotamia, and its nominal suzerainty in Egypt.
independent republic The Greek occupation of Izmir 1919 provoked the establishment of a nationalist congress with Mustafa Kemal (◊Atatürk) as president. Having defeated Italian and French forces, he expelled the Greeks 1922. Peace was concluded 1923 with the Treaty of ◊Lausanne, and Turkey was proclaimed an independent republic with Kemal as its first president. He introduced a policy of westernization and a new legal code. He died 1938, but his People's Party remained in power.
military rule Turkey's first free elections were held 1950 and won by the Democratic Party (DP), led by Celal Bayar and Adnan Menderes. Bayar became president and Menderes prime minister. In 1960, after a military coup, President Bayar was imprisoned and Menderes executed. A new constitution was adopted 1961 and civilian rule restored, but with the leader of the coup, General Cemal Gursel, as president. There followed a series of civilian governments, led mainly by the veteran politician Ismet Inonu until 1965, when the Justice Party (JP), led by Suleyman Demirel, came to power. Prompted by strikes and student unrest, the army forced Demirel to resign 1971, and for the next two years the country came under military rule again.
effective partition of Cyprus A civilian government was restored 1973, a coalition led by Bulent Ecevit. The following year Turkey sent troops to Cyprus to protect the Turkish-Cypriot community, resulting in the effective partition of the island. Ecevit's government fell when he refused to annex N Cyprus, and in 1975 Suleyman Demirel returned at the head of a right-wing coalition. Faced with a deteriorating economy he had lost his working majority by 1979 and resigned.

In Sept 1980 the army stepped in and set up a national security council, with Bulent Ulusu as prime minister. Martial law was imposed, political activity suspended, and a harsh regime established. Strong international pressure was put on Turkey to return to a more democratic system of government, and in May 1983 political parties were allowed to operate again. The old parties reformed under new names and in Nov three of them contested the assembly elections: the conservative Motherland Party (ANAP), the Nationalist Democracy Party (MDP), and the Populist Party (SDHP). ANAP won its leader, Turgut Ozal, became prime minister. Since 1984 there has been guerrilla fighting in Kurdistan, and a separatist Kurdish Workers' Party (PKK) is active.
foreign policy After World War II Turkey felt itself threatened by the USSR and joined a number of military alliances, including NATO 1952 and the Baghdad Pact 1955, which became the Central Treaty Organization 1959 and was dissolved 1979. Turkey strengthened Western links and by 1987 was making overtures to the European Community. Turkey has long been criticized for the harshness of its penal system and its violations of human rights. Its application for membership of the European Community was refused 1989 and is not eligible for reconsideration until the mid-1990s.

Tutu Desmond (Mpilo) 1931– . South African priest, Anglican archbishop of Cape Town and general secretary of the South African Council of Churches 1979–84. One of the leading figures in the struggle against apartheid in the Republic of South Africa, he received the 1984 Nobel Peace Prize.

U

U-2 Incident a US military reconnaissance aeroplane, Lockheed U-2 (used in secret flights over the USSR from 1956 to photograph military installations) was shot down over the USSR 1960. The pilot, Gary Powers, was captured and imprisoned. He was exchanged for a US-held Soviet agent two years later.

The U-2 incident led to the cancellation of a proposed meeting in Moscow between President Eisenhower and Soviet leader Khrushchev, precipitating a greatly increased Soviet arms spending in the 1960s and 1970s. U-2 flights in 1962 revealed the construction of Soviet missile bases in Cuba.

U-boat (German *Unterseeboot* 'undersea boat') German submarine. The term was used in both world wars. Of the 178 German submarines lost in World War I, at least 48 were destroyed by mines.

In World War II, 785 German U-boats were sunk of which 288 were destroyed by aircraft at sea, and 246 by the weapons of surface ships. Many hundreds of U-boats were destroyed in the Battle of the Atlantic.

UDI acronym for ◊***u***nilateral ***d***eclaration of ***i***ndependence.

Uganda landlocked country in E Africa, bounded N by Sudan, E by Kenya, S by Tanzania and Rwanda, and W by Zaïre.

history Uganda was a British protectorate 1894–1962. Uganda became an independent member of the ◊Commonwealth in 1962, with Dr Milton Obote, leader of the Uganda People's Congress (UPC), as prime minister. In 1963 it was proclaimed a federal republic; King Mutesa II became president, ruling through a cabinet. King Mutesa was deposed in a coup 1966, and Obote became executive president. One of his first acts was to end the federal status. After an attempt to assassinate him in 1969 Obote banned all opposition and established what was effectively a one-party state.

the Amin regime In 1971 Obote was overthrown in an army coup led by Maj-Gen Idi Amin Dada, who suspended the constitution and all political activity and took legislative and executive powers into his own hands. Obote fled to Tanzania. Amin proceeded to wage what he called an 'economic war' against foreign domination, resulting in the mass expulsion of Asians, many of whom settled in Britain. In 1976 Amin claimed that large tracts of Kenya historically belonged to Uganda. Relations with Kenya became strained, and diplomatic links with Britain were severed. During the next two years the Amin regime carried out a widespread campaign against any likely opposition, resulting in thousands of deaths and imprisonments.

military coups In 1978, when Amin annexed the Kagera area of Tanzania, near the Uganda border, the Tanzanian president, Julius Nyerere, sent troops to support the Uganda National Liberation Army (UNLA), which had been formed to fight Amin. Within five months Tanzanian troops had entered the Uganda capital, Kampala, forcing Amin into exile. A provisional government, drawn from a cross-section of exiled groups, was set up, with Dr Yusuf Lule as president. A military commission made arrangements for national elections, which were won by the UPC, and Milton Obote came back to power.

Obote's government was soon under pressure from a range of exiled groups operating outside the country and guerrilla forces inside, and he was only kept in office by the presence of Tanzanian troops. When they were withdrawn in June 1982 a major offensive was launched against the Obote government by the National Resistance Movement (NRM) and the National Resistance Army (NRA), led by Dr Lule and Yoweri Museveni. Obote was ousted in July in a coup led by Brig Tito Okello. Obote fled to political asylum in Zambia.

national reconciliation Museveni was sworn in as president 1986 and announced a policy of national reconciliation, promising a return to normal parliamentary government within three to five years. He formed a cabinet in which most of Uganda's political parties were represented, including the NRM, which is the political wing of the NRA, the Democratic Party, the Conservative Party, the UPC, and the Uganda Freedom Movement.

Ulbricht Walter 1893–1973. East German communist politician, in power 1960–71. He

Ulbricht *East German politician Walter Ulbricht (front row, third from right).*

lived in exile in the USSR during Hitler's rule 1933–45. A Stalinist, he became first secretary of the Socialist Unity Party in East Germany 1950 and (as chair of the Council of State from 1960) was instrumental in the building of the Berlin Wall 1961. He established East Germany's economy and recognition outside the Eastern European bloc.

Ulster former kingdom in Northern Ireland, annexed by England 1461, from Jacobean times a centre of English, and later Scottish, settlement on land confiscated from its owners; divided 1921 into Northern Ireland (counties Antrim, Armagh, Down, Fermanagh, Londonderry, and Tyrone) and the Republic of Ireland (counties Cavan, Donegal, and Monaghan).

unemployment lack of paid employment. Unemployment is generally subdivided into ***frictional unemployment***, the inevitable temporary unemployment of those moving from one job to another; ***cyclical unemployment***, caused by a downswing in the business cycle; ***seasonal unemployment***, in an area where there is high demand only during holiday periods, for example; and ***structural unemployment***, where changing technology or other long-term change in the economy results in large numbers without work. Periods of widespread unemployment in Europe and the USA in the 20th century include 1929–1930s, and the years since the mid-1970s.

In Britain, for at least 150 years before 1939, the supply of labour always exceeded demand except in wartime, and economic crises accompanied by mass unemployment were recurrent from 1785. The percentage of unemployed in trade unions averaged 6% during 1883–1913 and 14.2% (of those covered by the old Unemployment Insurance Acts) 1921–38. World War II and the rebuilding and expansion which followed meant shortage of labour rather than unemployment in the Western world, and in Britain in the 1950s the unemployment rate fell to 1.5%. Fluctuation in employment returned in the 1960s, and in the recession of the mid-1970s to 1980s was a worldwide problem. In Britain deflationary economic measures tended to exacerbate the trend, and in the mid-1980s the rate had risen to 14% (although the basis on which it is calculated has in recent years been changed several times and many commentators argue that the real rate is higher).

Most present-day governments attempt to prevent some or all of the various forms of unemployment. The ideas of John Maynard Keynes influenced British government unemployment policies during the 1950s and 1960s. The existence of a clear link between unemployment and inflation (that high unemployment can be dealt with by governments only at the cost of higher inflation) is now disputed.

UNESCO ***United Nations Educational, Scientific, and Cultural Organization*** agency of the UN, established 1946, with its headquarters in Paris. The USA, contributor of 25% of its budget, withdrew 1984 on grounds of its overpoliticization and mismanagement, and Britain followed 1985.

Unilateral Declaration of Independence (UDI) declaration made by Ian Smith of the Rhodesian Front government 11 Nov 1965. He unilaterally declared Rhodesia an independent state, to resist sharing power with the black African majority. It was a move condemned by the United Nations and by the UK who imposed sanctions (trade restrictions and an oil embargo). With the support of the United Nations, Britain imposed a naval blockade that was countered by the South African government breaking sanctions. Negotiations between British prime minister Harold Wilson and Smith foundered. It was not until April 1980 that the Republic of ◊Zimbabwe was proclaimed.

unilateralism in politics, support for ***unilateral nuclear disarmament***: scrapping a country's nuclear weapons without waiting for other countries to agree to do so at the same time.

In the UK this principle was Labour Party policy in the 1980s but was abandoned 1989.

Union of Soviet Socialist Republics (USSR) country in N Asia and E Europe, stretching from the Baltic Sea and the Black Sea to the Arctic and Pacific oceans.

government Under the 1977 constitution, amended in 1989, the USSR is a federal state comprising 15 constituent union republics. Each union republic, theoretically, has the right of secession and has its own constitution, legislature, and government (Council of Ministers) that is responsible for local administration. A number of union republics in turn include autonomous republics and regions. The central (federal) government is solely responsible for defence, foreign policy, foreign trade, communications, and heavy industries. In other spheres the scope for initiative by union and autonomous-republic governments is restricted by the centrally planned nature of the Soviet economy and the constant scrutiny of the Communist Party.

The highest organ of the Moscow-based central government is the Congress of the USSR People's Deputies (CUPD). It functions as a constitutional assembly rather than as a legislature, deciding key constitutional, political and socioeconomic questions. It elects, at its outset, a state president, vice president, prime minister, who is chair of the council of ministers (the body that has charge of the USSR's day-to-day executive administration), and the chair of the Supreme Court. The state president has responsibility for directing defence and foreign policy and for guiding the drafting of legislation. The state president presides over the Supreme Soviet's presidium.

Lower-level elected soviets operate at the village, town, regional, and republic levels. However, the dominating force in the country is the Communist Party of the Soviet Union (CPSU), the only currently permitted political party in the USSR which forms a second and parallel form of government that dominates the state tier. It is set up like a pyramid with at its base over 400,000 primary party branches in factories and villages. The CPSU's highest authority is its Party Congress. Congress ratifies party programmes and elects a Central Committee to assume authority over the party between congresses.

The Central Committee meets twice a year and elects the Politburo of normally eleven full members and seven candidates and the specialist twelve-member administrative Secretariat. The Politburo is the most powerful political body in the USSR. It meets fortnightly as an executive cabinet, controls and determines the policy of the CPSU, and sets out the medium- and long-term goals for the nation. Its members select from their ranks the party leader, or general secretary (since Mar 1985 Mikhail Gorbachev), who presides over the Secretariat and serves in practice as the leader of the Soviet Union.

history For early twentieth century history, see ◊Russian Revolution, 1905 and ◊Russian Revolution. The Union of Soviet Socialist Republics was formed 1922, and a constitution adopted 1923. Lenin, who had led the new regime, died 1924, and an internal party controversy broke out between Stalin and Trotsky over the future of socialism and the necessity of world revolution.

Stalin's socialism Trotsky was expelled 1927, and Stalin's policy of socialism in one country adopted. During the first two five-year plans 1928–39, heavy and light industries were developed, and agriculture collectivized. The country was transformed as industry grew at an annual (official) rate of 16% with, as a consequence, the size of the manual workforce quadrupling and the urban population doubling. However, the social cost was enormous, with millions dying in the Ukraine and Kazakhstan famine of 1932–34, as well as in the political purges and liquidations launched during the 1920s and 1930s. Leading party figures, including Nikolai Bukharin, Lev Kamenev, and Grigory Zinoviev were victims of these 'show trial' purges. In the process, the Soviet political system was deformed, as inner-party democracy gave way to autocracy based around a Stalinist personality cult.

From 1933 the USSR put forward a policy of collective resistance to aggression. In 1939 it concluded a nonaggression pact with Germany, and Poland was invaded and divided between them. The USSR invaded Finland 1939 but signed a brief peace 1940. For events 1941–45, see ◊World War II. 25 million Russians perished during this 'Great Patriotic War'.

cold war During the immediate postwar years the USSR concentrated on consolidating its empire in Eastern Europe and on providing indirect support to anti-colonial movements in the Far East. Relations with the West, particularly the USA, sharply deteriorated. On the death of Stalin in March 1953 a collective leadership, including Nikita Khrushchev (CPSU first or general secretary 1953–64), Georgi Malenkov (prime minister 1953–55), Nikolai Bulganin (prime minister 1955–58), Vyacheslav Molotov (foreign minister 1953–56), and Lazar Kaganovich, assumed power. They introduced a new legal code that regularized the political system. Strong differences emerged within the collective leadership over future political and economic reform, and a fierce succession struggle developed.

Khrushchev's 'liberalization' policy Khrushchev emerged dominant from this contest and combined the posts of prime minister and party first secretary. At the 1961 Party Congress, Khrushchev introduced a new party programme for rapid agricultural, industrial, and technological development to enable the USSR to move ahead of the USA in economic terms by 1980 and attain full Communism. He launched a 'virgin lands' cultivation campaign in Kazakhstan, increased rural incentives and decentralized industrial management through the creation of new regional economic councils (*sovnarkhozy*). In addition, Khrushchev introduced radical new party rule changes, sanctioned a cultural thaw, and enunciated the principle of 'peaceful coexistence' with the West to divert resources from the defence sector. These reforms enjoyed initial success; having exploded its first hydrogen bomb 1953 and launched a space satellite (*Sputnik I*) 1957, the USSR emerged as a serious technological rival to the USA. But Khrushchev's liberalization policy and his denunciation of the errors and crimes of the Stalin era at the Feb 1956 Party Congress had serious repercussions among the USSR's satellites – a nationalist revolt in Hungary and a breach in relations with Yugoslavia and China – while his administrative reforms were fiercely opposed by senior party and state officials. After a series of poor harvests in overcropped Kazakhstan and the ◊Cuban missile crisis 1962, these opponents succeeded in ousting Khrushchev Oct 1964.

A new and conservative collective leadership, based around the figures of Leonid Brezhnev (CPSU general secretary 1964–82), Alexei Kosygin (prime minister 1964–80), Nikolai Podgorny (state president 1965–77), and Mikhail Suslov (ideology secretary 1964–82), assumed power and immediately abandoned Khrushchev's *sovnarkhozy* and party reforms and reimposed strict censorship in the cultural sphere. Priority was now given to the expansion and modernization of the Soviet armed forces. This, coupled with the Warsaw Pact invasion of Czechoslovakia 1968, resulted in a renewal of the ◊cold war 1964–70.

the Brezhnev doctrine During the later 1960s, Leonid Brezhnev slowly emerged as the dominant figure. He governed in a cautious and consensual manner and brought into the Politburo leaders from all the significant centres of power. Brezhnev introduced a series of minor economic reforms and gave new priority to agricultural and consumer-goods production. He oversaw the framing of a new constitution 1977 where the limits for internal dissent were clearly set out and the 'Brezhnev doctrine' was also declared 1968, establishing the power of the Soviet Union to intervene to preserve Socialism in E Europe as it did in Czechoslovakia.

détente era Brezhnev, who became the new state president May 1977, emerged as an international figure during the 1970s, frequently meeting Western leaders during a new era of détente. The landmarks of this period were the Salt-1 and Salt-2 Soviet-US arms-limitation agreements of 1972 and 1979 (see ◊Strategic Arms Limitation Talks) and the Helsinki Accord 1975, which brought Western recognition of the postwar division of Eastern Europe. Another cultural thaw resulted in the emergence of a vocal dissident movement. The political and military influence of the USSR was extended into Africa with the establishment of new Communist governments in Mozambique 1974, Angola and Ethiopia 1975, and South Yemen 1978. The détente era was brought to an end by the Soviet invasion of Afghanistan Dec 1979 and the Polish crisis 1980–81, when unrest led to the imposition of martial law, banning of trade unions and curfews. The final years of the Brezhnev administration were ones of hardening policy, mounting corruption, and economic stagnation.

Yuri Andropov, the former KGB chief, was elected CPSU leader on Brezhnev's death Nov 1982 and began energetically to introduce a series of radical economic reforms aimed at streamlining and decentralizing the planning system and inculcating greater labour discipline. Andropov also launched a major campaign directed against corrupt and complacent party and state bureaucrats. These measures had a perceptible impact on the Soviet economy during 1983, but when Andropov died Feb 1984 he was succeeded by the cautious and elderly Brezhnev supporter, Konstantin Chernenko. Chernenko held power as a stopgap leader for 13 months, his sole initiative being a renewed search for détente with the USA that was rejected by the hardline Reagan administration.

Gorbachev's 'market socialism' On Chernenko's death March 1985, power was transferred to Mikhail Gorbachev, who introduced a number of reforms. He began to free farmers and factory managers from bureaucratic interference and to increase material incentives in a 'market Socialist' manner. He restructured the party and state bureaucracies and replaced cautious Brezhnevites with ambitious new technocrats. Gorbachev made explicit his renunciation of the 'Brezhnev doctrine' 1989.

These changes were not lost on the opposition leaders in the Baltic republics or on Communist deputies in the newly assertive

Soviet Parliament. Lithuania declared that it would permit free elections, then the Lithuanian Communist party declared its independence from Moscow. By Jan 1990, Gorbachev was faced with growing calls for secession from the Soviet Union, and he had been forced to reconsider his earlier opposition to a multiparty system in the Soviet Union itself. He also was forced to declare a state of emergency and dispatch thousands of troops to quell near civil warfare between Armenians and Azerbaijanis who were fighting each other for religious and territorial reasons, as well as the Soviet forces sent to suppress the violence.

détente initiative Working with the foreign secretary, Edvard Shevardnadze, Gorbachev made skilful use of the foreign media to put the case against space weapons and nuclear testing. He met US President Ronald Reagan at Geneva and Reykjavik Nov 1985 and Oct 1986, and, at the Washington summit in Dec 1987, he concluded a treaty designed to eliminate medium-range Intermediate Nuclear Forces (INF) from European soil. This treaty was formally ratified at the Moscow summit of May–June 1988. As part of the new détente initiative, the USSR also effected a full withdrawal of its troops from Afghanistan in Feb 1989 and made broad cutbacks in the size of its conventional forces during 1989–90.

glasnost and perestroika Gorbachev pressed for an acceleration of his domestic, economic, and political programme of restructuring (*perestroika*) from 1987, but faced growing opposition both from conservatives grouped around Yegor Ligachev and radicals led by Boris Yeltsin. Gorbachev's *glasnost* ('openness') policy helped fan growing nationalist demands for secession among the republics of the Baltic and Transcaucasia. To add momentum to the reform process, Gorbachev convened, in June 1988, a special All-Union Party Conference, the first since 1941. At this meeting a radical constitutional overhaul was approved. A new 'super-legislature', the CUPD, was created, from which a full-time working parliament was subsequently to be elected, headed by a state president with increased powers. The members of this CUPD were to be chosen in competition with one another. The authority of the local soviets was enhanced and their structures made more democratic, while, in the economic sphere, it was agreed to re-introduce private leasehold farming, reform the price system and allow part-time private enterprise in the service and small-scale industry sectors.

socialist pluralism The June 1988 reforms constituted the most fundamental re-ordering of the Soviet policy since the 'Stalinist departure' of 1928, entailing the creation of a new type of 'socialist democracy', as well as a new mixed, private–public economic system. In the CUPD elections of March–April 1989, public opposition to conservative *apparatchiks* was made apparent. In May 1989, the CUPD elected Gorbachev as its chair, and thus as state president. During 1989 this movement towards 'socialist pluralism' was furthered by Gorbachev's abandonment of the ◊Brezhnev doctrine and his sanctioning of the establishment of non-communist and 'reform communist' governments elsewhere in Eastern Europe. This led to the ruling regimes of Poland, Czechoslovakia, and Romania being overthrown in a wave of 'people's power'. Responding to these developments in Feb 1990, the CPSU Central Committee agreed to create a new directly elected state executive presidency on US and French models. In March 1990 the Soviet parliament authorized private ownership of the means of production, forbidden since the NED during the 1920s. Further, constitutional amendments made in 1990 supported the right of self-determination, including secession of republics, and ended the CPSU's monopoly of power. The Gorbachev reform programme showed signs of running out of control during 1989–90 for two reasons. One was the effect of the growing nationalist tensions, which in April 1989 and Jan 1990 had prompted the dispatch of troops to the Caucasus region, first to break up demonstrations in Tbilisi, Georgia, and then to attempt to quell a civil war that had broken out between Armenia and Azerbaijan over the disputed enclave of Nagorno-Karabakh. The other problem was the mounting popular discontent over the failure of *perestroika* to improve living standards. In their Dec 1989 summit meeting at Malta, Gorbachev and US president George Bush were able to declare an end to the Cold War, which opened the possibility of most-favoured nation trading status with the USA, membership in the GATT, and an influx of Western investment. A Gorbachev trip to Canada and the USA followed in May–June 1990.

United Kingdom (UK) country in NW Europe off the coast of France, consisting of England, Scotland, Wales, and Northern Ireland.

government The UK is a constitutional monarchy with parliamentary government. There is no written constitution. Cabinet government, which is at the heart of the system, is founded on rigid convention, and the relationship between the monarch as head of state and the prime minister as head of government is similarly based. Parliament is sovereign, in that it is free to make and unmake any laws that it chooses, and the government is subject to the laws that Parliament makes. Parliament has two legislative and debating chambers, the ◊House of Lords and the ◊House of Commons.

history The domestic issues after 1900 were social reform and home rule for Ireland; the Labour Party emerged from an alliance of trade unions and small Socialist bodies 1900; the ◊suffragettes were active until ◊World War I. After the war a wave of strikes culminated in the general strike 1926; three years later a world economic crisis precipitated the Depression that marked the 1930s and brought to power a coalition government 1931.

the Depression The 1930s were dominated by unemployment, which reached almost 3 million in 1933, and the approach of ◊World War II. The death of George V Jan 1936 brought Edward VIII to the throne, closely followed by the ◊abdication crisis precipitated by his desire to marry US divorcee Wallis Simpson. In Dec 1936, Edward VIII abdicated, and George VI came to the throne.

World War II In 1939 the Germans invaded Poland, and Britain entered World War II by declaring war on Germany. In 1940 Winston Churchill became prime minister, leader of the Conservative Party, and head of a coalition government. The country sustained intensive bombardment in the 'Battle of Britain' July–Oct 1940, and the 'blitz' of night bombing which affected London and Coventry particularly. Following the defeat of Germany 1945, the Labour Party, led by Clement Attlee, gained power.

reform and renewal The problem of rebuilding the war-damaged economy was greatly helped, as in other W European countries, by support from the USA through the ◊Marshall Plan. Between 1945 and 1951 the Labour government carried out an ambitious programme of public ownership and investment and laid the foundations of a national health service and welfare state. During the same period the dismemberment of the British Empire, restyled the British ◊Commonwealth, was begun, a process that continued into the 1980s.

Suez Canal crisis In 1951 the Conservative Party was returned to power, under Winston Churchill who handed over to the foreign secretary, Anthony Eden in 1956. Eden found himself confronted by the takeover of the Suez Canal by the president of Egypt, Gamal Nasser. Eden's perception of the threat posed by Nasser was not shared by everyone, even within the Conservative Party. The British invasion of Egypt, in conjunction with France and Israel, brought widespread criticism and was abandoned in the face of pressure from the USA and the United Nations. Eden resigned, on the grounds of ill health, and the Conservatives chose Harold Macmillan as their new leader and prime minister.

By the early 1960s, the economy had improved, living standards had risen, and Prime Minister Harold Macmillan was known as 'Supermac'. However, the UK's economic performance was not as successful as that of many of its competitors, such as West Germany and Japan. The Labour Party won the general election 1964, and its leader, Harold Wilson, became prime minister. The election had been fought on the issue of the economy. Wilson created the Department of Economic Affairs (DEA) to challenge the short-term conservatism of the Treasury, and brought in a leading trade unionist to head a new Department of Technology, which was disbanded 1969. An ambitious plan for the reform of industrial relations was dropped in the face of trade-union opposition.

Heath's 'counter-revolution' In 1970 the Conservatives returned to power under Edward Heath. He, too, saw institutional change as one way of achieving industrial reform and created two new central departments (Trade and Industry, Environment). He attempted to change the climate of industrial relations through a long and complicated Industrial Relations Bill. He saw entry into the EC as the competition that industry needed, and membership was negotiated 1972.

national miners' strike Heath's 'counter-revolution', as he saw it, was frustrated by the trade unions, and the sharp rise in oil prices 1973 forced a U-turn in economic policy. The introduction of a statutory incomes policy precipitated a national miners' strike in the winter of 1973–74 and Heath decided to challenge the unions by holding an early general election 1974. The result was a hung Parliament. Heath tried briefly to form a coalition with the Liberals and, when this failed, resigned.

Wilson's 'social contract' Harold Wilson returned to the premiership, taking over a damaged economy. He jointly agreed a 'social contract' with the trade unions: the government pledged itself to redress the imbalance between management and unions created by the Heath industrial-relations legislation, and the unions promised to cooperate in a voluntary industrial and incomes policy. Wilson met criticism from a growing left-wing movement within his party, impatient for radical change. In March 1976 Wilson retired in midterm.

the 'Lib-Lab Pact' Wilson was succeeded by James Callaghan. In 1977, to shore up his slender parliamentary majority, Callaghan entered into an agreement with the new leader of the Liberal Party, David Steel. Under the 'Lib-Lab Pact' Labour pursued moderate, nonconfrontational policies in consultation with the Liberals, who, in turn, voted with the government, and the economy improved dramatically. The Lib-Lab Pact had effectively finished by the autumn of 1978, and soon the social contract with the unions began to disintegrate. Widespread and damaging strikes in the public sector badly affected essential services during what became known as the 'winter of discontent'. At the end of March 1979 Callaghan lost a vote of confidence in the House of Commons and was forced into a general election.

The Conservatives returned to power under the UK's first female prime minister, Margaret Thatcher. She inherited a number of inflationary public-sector pay awards that together with a budget that doubled the rate of value added tax, resulted in a sharp rise in prices and interest rates. The Conservatives were pledged to reduce inflation and did so by mainly monetarist policies, which caused the number of unemployed to rise from 1.3 million to 2 million in the first year. In foreign affairs Zimbabwe became independent 1980 after many years, and without the bloodshed many had feared.

creation of the SDP Meanwhile, changes were taking place in the other parties. Callaghan resigned the leadership of the Labour Party 1980 and was replaced by the left-winger Michael Foot. In 1981 three Labour shadow cabinet members, David Owen, Shirley Williams, and William Rodgers, with the former deputy leader Roy Jenkins (collectively dubbed the 'Gang of Four'), broke away to form a new centrist group, the ◊Social Democratic Party (SDP). The new party made an early impression, winning a series of by-elections within months of its creation. From 1983 to 1988 the Liberals and the SDP were linked in an electoral pact, the Alliance. They advocated the introduction of a system of proportional representation.

Unemployment continued to rise, passing the 3 million mark in Jan 1982. The general election 1983 was fought with the euphoria of the Falklands Islands victory still in the air and the Labour Party, under Foot, divided and unconvincing. The Conservatives had a landslide victory. The next three years were marked by rising unemployment and growing dissent: a bitter and protracted miners' strike; increasing violence in Northern Ireland; an attempted assassination of leading members of the Conservative Party during their annual conference; and riots in inner-city areas of London, Bristol, and Liverpool. The government was further embarrassed by its own prosecutions under the Official Secrets Act and the resignations of two prominent cabinet ministers. With the short-term profits from North Sea oil and an ambitious privatization programme, the inflation rate continued to fall.

party leadership changes Leadership changes took place by 1987 in two of the other parties. Michael Foot was replaced by his Welsh protégé, Neil Kinnock; Roy Jenkins was replaced by David Owen as SDP leader, to be succeeded in turn by Robert MacLennan Sept 1987, when the SDP and Liberal parties voted to initiate talks towards a merger. Despite high unemployment and Thatcher's increasingly authoritarian style of government, the Conservatives were re-elected June 1987. The merger of the Liberal and Social Democratic parties was an acrimonious affair, with the SDP, led by David Owen, refusing to join the merged party and operating as a rival group. Paddy Ashdown emerged as the leader of the new party. In a cabinet reshuffle July 1989, Geoffrey Howe was replaced as foreign secretary by John Major. In Oct 1989 the chancellor of the Exchequer, Nigel Lawson, resigned because of disagreements with the prime minister, and Major replaced him. Douglas Hurd took over the foreign office. In Dec 1989 Mrs Thatcher won the party leadership election. The government was widely criticized for its decision forcibly to repatriate Vietnamese 'boat people' and for the perceived over-liberality of its decision to give UK right of abode to the families of 50,000 'key' Hong Kong citizens, after the transfer of the colony to China in 1997.

In Sept 1990 the House of Commons was recalled for an emergency debate that endorsed the government's military activities in the Gulf. In Oct, shortly before the Conservative annual conference, the government announced that it was joining the European Exchange Rate Mechanism (ERM). In Nov the deputy prime minister, Geoffrey Howe, resigned. After a dramatic resignation speech by Howe, strongly critical of Mrs Thatcher, Michael Heseltine announced his candidacy for the leadership of the Conservative Party. In the subsequent leadership election, Thatcher resigned and John Major was voted in. His handling of the Gulf War Jan 15–Feb 28 1991, with his subsequent proposal for a 'safe haven' for the Kurdish refugees, was an immediate test of his leadership capabilities.

United Nations (UN) association of states (successor to the ◊League of Nations) for international peace, security, and cooperation, with its headquarters in New York. Its charter was drawn up at the San Francisco Conference 1945, based on proposals drafted at the Dumbarton Oaks conference. The original intention was that the UN's Security Council would preserve the wartime alliance of the USA, USSR, and Britain (with France and China also permanent members) in order to maintain the peace. This never happened because of the outbreak of the Cold War, but the UN has played a role in many other areas such as refugees, development assistance, disaster relief, and cultural cooperation.

Members contribute financially according to their resources, an apportionment being made by the General Assembly, with the addition of voluntary contributions from some governments to the funds of the UN. These finance the programme of assistance carried out by the UN intergovernmental agencies, the ***United Nations Children's Fund*** (UNICEF), the UN refugee organizations, and the ***United Nations Special Fund*** for developing countries. There are six official working languages: English, French, Russian, Spanish, Chinese, and Arabic.

The influence in the UN, originally with the Allied states of World War II, is now more widely spread. Although part of the value of the UN lies in recognition of member states as sovereign and equal, the rapid increase in membership of minor – in some cases minute – states was causing concern by 1980 (154 members) as lessening the weight of voting decisions. Taiwan, formerly a permanent member of the Security Council, was expelled 1971 on the admission of China. The UN also suffers from a lack of adequate and independent funds and forces, the latter having been employed with varying success, for example, in Korea, Cyprus, and Sinai, and the intrusion of the Cold War which divided members into adherents of the East or West and the uncommitted. However, since becoming UN secretary general in 1982, Javier Pérez de Cuellar has been responsible for several successful peace initiatives, including the ending of the Iran–Iraq war and the withdrawal of South African and Cuban troops from Angola, paving the way for the independence of Namibia. He has also initiated talks between Greek and Turkish leaders in Cyprus. UN forces were successfully deployed in routing Iraqi troops from Kuwait in the Gulf War.

The UN comprises: ***General Assembly*** one member from each of 159 member states who meet annually; decisions on major issues require a two-thirds majority, while on minor ones a simple majority suffices; ***Security Council*** five permanent members (China, France, UK, USA, USSR, which exercise a veto in that their support is requisite for all decisions), plus ten others which hold office on a rotating basis. It may undertake investigations into disputes and make recommendations to the parties concerned and may call on all members to take economic or military measures to enforce its decisions; ***Economic and Social Council*** 54 members elected for three years, one-third retiring in rotation. It initiates studies of international economic, social, cultural, educational, health, and related matters, and may make recommendations to the General Assembly. It operates largely through specialized commissions of international experts on economics, transport and communications, human rights, status of women, and so on.

United States of America (USA) country in North America, extending from the Atlantic to the Pacific oceans, bounded N by Canada and S by Mexico, and including the outlying states of Alaska and Hawaii.

government The USA is a federal republic comprising 50 states and the District of Columbia. Under the 1787 constitution, which has had 26 amendments, the constituent states are reserved considerable powers of self-government. The federal government concentrated originally on military and foreign affairs and the coordination of interstate concerns, leaving legislation in other spheres to the states, each with its own constitution, elected legislature, governor, supreme court, and local taxation powers.

The executive, legislative, and judicial branches of the federal government are deliberately separate from each other, working in a system of checks and balances. At the head of the executive branch is an elected president. The president serves as head of state, of the armed forces, and the federal civil service. He or she is restricted to a maximum of two terms and, once elected, cannot be removed except through impeachment and subsequent conviction by Congress. The president works with a personally selected cabinet team, subject to the Senate's approval.

The second branch of government, Congress, the federal legislature, comprises two houses, the 100-member Senate and the 435-member House of Representatives. Senators serve six-year terms, and there are two from each state regardless of size and population. The Senate is the more powerful chamber of Congress, since its approval is required for key federal appointments and for the ratification of foreign treaties. Proposed legislation, to become law (an Act of Congress), requires the approval of both houses of Congress.

The third branch of government, the judiciary, headed by the Supreme Court, interprets the written US Constitution to ensure that a correct balance is maintained between federal and state institutions and the executive and legislature and to uphold the Constitution, especially the civil rights in the first ten (the Bill of Rights) and later amendments. The Supreme Court comprises nine judges appointed by the president with the Senate's approval, who serve life terms and can only be removed by impeachment.

Two broad political parties, divided regionally and ideologically, dominate US politics: the ◊Democrats and the ◊Republicans. Both parties have a relatively weak national organization and seldom vote as a block in Congress. Party organization is centred instead at the state and local levels.

history Native Americans (or American Indians) are thought to have entered North America 60,000–35,000 BC. The Spanish first settled in Florida 1565. The first permanent English settlement was at Jamestown, Virginia, 1607. The Civil War 1861–65 put an end to slavery but left ill feeling between north and south. It stimulated additional industrial development in the N, as well as the construction of roads and railways, which continued until the end of that century. Involvement in international affairs increased with the Spanish– American War 1898, which involved the USA in Cuba and the Philippines. Hawaii ceded itself to the USA 1898. Panama Canal Zone rights were leased 1903. Under President Woodrow Wilson, the USA entered ◊World War I in 1917; it was not a party to the Treaty of Versailles but made peace by separate treaties 1921. A period of isolationism followed. The country's economic, industrial, and agricultural expansion was brought to a halt by the stock-market crash 1929, which marked the start of the ◊Depression. President Franklin Roosevelt's ◊New Deal 1933 tackled but did not solve the problem, and only ◊World War II brought full employment. The USA did not declare war until Japan attacked ◊Pearl Harbor on Honolulu Dec 1941.

the Truman doctrine The USA, having emerged from the war as a superpower, remained internationalist during the prosperity of the postwar era. Under the presidency of Harry S Truman (Democrat) a doctrine of intervention in support of endangered 'free peoples' and of containing the spread of communism was devised by Secretaries of State George Marshall and Dean Acheson. This led to the USA's safeguarding of Greece and Nationalist Taiwan 1949 and its participation in the ◊Korean War 1950–53. The USA, in addition, created new global and regional bodies designed to maintain the peace – the United Nations (UN, 1945), the Organization of American States (OAS, 1948), the North Atlantic Treaty Organization (NATO, 1949), the South-East Asia Treaty Organization (SEATO, 1954) – and launched the Marshall Plan to begin strengthening the capitalist economies of its allies while standing off similar strategies of the USSR-dominated Eastern Bloc. This began the ◊Cold War. Domestically, President Truman sought to introduce liberal reforms designed at extending civil and welfare rights under the slogan 'a fair deal'. These measures were blocked by a combination of Southern Democrats and Republicans in Congress. Truman's foreign policy was criticized as being 'soft on communism' between 1950 and 1952, as a wave of anti-Soviet hysteria, spearheaded by Senator Joseph McCarthy, swept the nation. This rightward shift in the public mood brought Republican victory in the congressional and presidential elections 1952, with popular military commander General Dwight D Eisenhower becoming president. He was re-elected by an increased margin Nov 1956.

the Eisenhower era Working with Secretary of State John Foster Dulles, Eisenhower adhered to the Truman–Acheson doctrine of 'containment', while at home he pursued a policy of 'progressive conservatism' designed to encourage business enterprise. The Eisenhower era was one of growth, involving the migration of southern blacks to the northern industrial cities and rapid expansion in the educational sector. In the southern states, where racial discrimination was openly practised, a new civil rights movement developed under the leadership of Dr Martin Luther King, Jr. Promising a 'New Frontier' programme of social reform, John F Kennedy (Democrat) won the presidential election Nov 1960 and emerged as an active supporter of civil rights and space exploration and an opponent of communism abroad (see ◊Bay of Pigs). He was assassinated Nov 1963.

It was left to his vice president and successor, Lyndon B Johnson, to oversee the passage of additional reforms, called the 'Great Society' by Johnson. These measures, which included the Equal Opportunities, Voting Rights, Housing, and Medicare acts, guaranteed blacks their civil rights and extended the reach and responsibilities of the federal government. They were buttressed by the judicial rulings of the Supreme Court, led by Chief Justice Earl Warren. Abroad, President Johnson escalated US involvement in the ◊Vietnam War (1964–73), which polarized public opinion and deeply divided the Democratic Party into 'hawks and doves'.

Johnson declined to run for re-election Nov 1968, and his vice president, Hubert Humphrey, was defeated by Republican Richard Nixon. Working with National Security Adviser Henry ◊Kissinger, Nixon escalated the Vietnam conflict by invading neighbouring Cambodia (leading to the Kent State University demonstration and shootings) before he began a gradual disengagement, launching a policy of ◊détente that brought an improvement in relations with the Soviet Union (see ◊Strategic Arms Limitation Talks) and a visit to Communist China 1973.

Watergate Nixon, faced with a divided opposition led by the liberal George McGovern, had gained re-election by an overwhelming margin Nov 1972, but during the campaign, Nixon's staff had broken into the Democratic Party's ◊Watergate headquarters. When this and the attempts at cover-up came to light, the scandal forced the resignation of the president Aug 1974, just short of impeachment. Watergate shook the US public's confidence in the Washington establishment. Gerald Ford, who had been vice president only since Dec 1973, pardoned Nixon and kept the services of Kissinger and the policy of détente when he became president. He faced a hostile, Democrat-dominated Congress that introduced legislation curbing the unauthorized power of the presidency, attemping to mend fences both at home and abroad. He also had to deal with the economic recession and increased OPEC oil prices that began under Nixon 1973. Ford ran in the presidential election Nov 1976, but was defeated by political outsider and Democrat Jimmy Carter, who promised open and honest government. Carter was a fiscal conservative but social liberal, who sought to extend welfare provision through greater administrative efficiency. He substantially ended the fuel crisis through enforced conservation in the energy bills 1978 and 1980.

Carter's foreign policy In foreign relations President Carter emphasized human rights. In the Middle East, he moved close to a peace settlement 1978–79 (the Camp David Agreements) and in Jan 1979 the USA's diplomatic relations with Communist China were fully normalized. The Carter presidency was however brought down by two foreign-policy crises 1979–80: the fall of the shah of Iran and the Soviet invasion of Afghanistan. The president's leadership style, military economies, and moralistic foreign policy were blamed for weakening US influence abroad. There was a swell of anti-communist feeling and mounting support for a new policy of rearmament and selective interventionism. President Carter responded to this new mood by enunciating the hawkish Carter Doctrine 1980 and supporting a new arms-development programme, but his popularity plunged during 1980 as economic recession gripped the country and US embassy staff members were held hostage by Shi'ite Muslim fundamentalists in Tehran.

the Reagan administration The Republican Ronald Reagan was elected Nov 1980, when the Democrats also lost control of the Senate. The new president had risen to prominence as an effective, television-skilled campaigner. He purported to believe in a return to traditional Christian and family values and promoted a domestic policy of supply-side economics, decentralization and deregulation. The early years of the Reagan presidency witnessed substantial reductions in taxation, with cutbacks in federal welfare programmes that created serious hardships as economic recession gripped the nation. Reagan rejected détente and spoke of the USSR as an 'evil empire' that needed to be checked by a military build-up and a readiness to employ force. This led to a sharp deterioration in Soviet-US relations, ushering in a new cold war during the Polish crisis 1981. He was re-elected on a wave of optimistic patriotism Nov 1984. A radical tax-cutting bill passed in Congress, and in 1986 a large budget and trade deficit developed (as a spending economy was developed to control Congress). At home and overseas the president faced mounting public opposition to his interventions in Central America. The new Soviet leader Mikhail ◊Gorbachev pressed unsuccessfully for arms reduction during superpower summits at Geneva (Nov 1985) and Reykjavik (Oct 1986), but a further summit Dec 1987, with an agreement to scrap intermediate-range nuclear missiles, appeared to promise a new détente.

Irangate In Nov 1986 the Republican party lost control of the Senate in the midterm elections, just before the disclosure of a scandal concerning US arms sales to Iran in return for hostages held in Beirut, with the profits illegally diverted to help the Nicaraguan Contra (anti-communist) guerrillas. The Irangate scandal, where members of the government and senior Whitehouse staff were involved in the secret sales of American arms to Iran, while the US government was publicly calling for a worldwide ban on sending arms there, briefly dented public confidence in the administration and forced the dismissal and resignation of key cabinet members, including national security adviser John Poindexter, in Nov 1986, and chief of staff Donald Regan, in Feb 1987. During the last two years of his presidency, a more consensual Reagan was on view and, helped by his Dec 1987 arms reduction deal, he left office with much of his popular affection resto.ed. Reagan's popularity transferred itself to vice president George Bush who, despite selecting the inexperienced Dan Quayle as his running-mate and despite opposition charges that he had been indirectly involved in the Irangate proceedings, defeated the Democrat's candidate Michael Dukakis in the presidential election of Nov 1988, after one of the most scurrilous campaigns on record.

Bush came to power, after six years of growth, at a time of economic uncertainty. Reagan's tax-cutting policy had led to mounting Federal trade and budget deficits which had served to turn the US into a debtor nation for the first time in its history and had precipitated a Wall Street share crash in Oct 1987. Retrenchment was thus needed and this became concentrated, during 1989–90, in the military sphere, being helped by continuing Soviet moves towards both conventional and nuclear forces reduction. Domestically, Bush set as the goal for his presidency to work to create a 'kinder, gentler nation', and unveiled a number of initiatives in the areas of education, drugs control and the environment designed to deal with problems that had surfaced during the Reagan years. (In 1990, almost 500,000 children were suffering from malnutrition and at least 100,000 were homeless.) With his overthrowing of the corrupt Panamanian leader, General Manuel Noriega in Dec 1989, Bush had established his presidency.

the Gulf War The USA responded to Iraq's unprovoked invasion and annexation of Kuwait on 2 Aug 1990 by coordinating, in the United Nations, the passage of a series of resolutions demanding Iraq's unconditional withdrawal and imposing comprehensive economic sanctions. By late Nov the USA had sent more than 230,000 troops and support personnel to Saudi Arabia to form the core of a 400,000-strong Western and Arab 'desert shield' with the object of defending the Saudi frontier and, if necessary, dislodging Iraq from Kuwait. The 'Desert Storm' mission was successfully performed 15 Jan–Feb 28 1991, when US troops, as part of the United Nations forces, expelled Iraqi forces from Kuwait, with minimal losses to the Allies. Bush was however, initially reluctant to help the Kurdish refugees in the rebellion and brutal repression by Saddam's forces which followed the aftermath of the Gulf War.

untouchable or ***harijan*** a member of the lowest Indian caste, formerly forbidden to be touched by members of the other castes. Contact with the untouchables was regarded as defiling for members of higher castes. Mohandas Gandhi undertook his first 'fast to the death' 1932 during his civil disobedience campaign in an effort to alter the government's attitude and public perception towards the untouchables. The use of the term, and the social restrictions which accompanied it, was declared illegal in the constitution adopted by the Constituent Assembly of India 1949 and of Pakistan 1953.

urbanization the process by which the proportion of a population living in or around towns and cities increases through migration as the agricultural population decreases. The growth of urban concentrations in the US and Europe is a relatively recent phenomenon, dating back only about 150 years to the beginnings of the Industrial Revolution (although the world's first cities were built more than 5,000 years ago.)

Urbanization has had a major effect on the social structures of industrial societies, affecting not only where people live but how they live, and urban sociology has emerged as a distinct area of study.

Uruguay country in South America, on the Atlantic, bounded N by Brazil and W by Argentina.

history Uruguay was declared independent 1828, although not recognized by its neighbours until 1853. From 1951 to 1966 there was a collective leadership called 'collegiate government', and then a new constitution was adopted and a single president elected, the Blanco candidate, Jorge Pacheco Areco. His presidency was marked by high inflation, labour unrest, and growing guerrilla activity by the Tupamaros.

political repression In 1972 Pacheco was replaced by the Colorado candidate, Juan Maria Bordaberry Arocena. Within a year the Tupamaros had been crushed, and all other left-wing groups banned. Bordaberry now headed a repressive regime, under which the normal democratic institutions had been dissolved. In 1976, he refused any movement towards constitutional government, was deposed by the army, and Dr Aparicio Méndez Manfredini was made president. Despite promises to return to democratic government, the severe repression continued, and political opponents were imprisoned.

the 'Programme of National Accord' In 1981 the deteriorating economy made the army anxious to return to constitutional government, and a retired general, Gregorio Alvarez Armellino, was appointed president for an interim period. By 1984 anti-government activity had reached a crisis point, and eventually all the main political leaders signed an agreement for a 'Programme of National Accord'. The 1966 constitution, with some modifications, was restored, and in 1985 a general election was held. The Colorado Party won a narrow majority, and Dr Julio Maria Sanguinetti, became president. The army stepped down, and by 1986 Sanguinetti was presiding over a government of national accord. In the Nov 1989 elections Luis Lacalle Herrera (PN), was narrowly elected president, with 37% of the vote compared with 30% for his PC opponent.

USSR abbreviation for the ◊***Union of Soviet Socialist Republics.***

U Thant 1909–1974. Burmese diplomat, secretary general of the United Nations 1962–71. He helped to resolve the US-Soviet crisis over the Soviet installation of missiles in Cuba (see ◊Cuban Missile Crisis), and he made the controversial decision to withdraw the UN peacekeeping force from the Egypt–Israel border 1967 (see ◊Arab–Israeli Wars).

V

Vatican City State sovereign area in central Rome, Italy.

government The pope, elected for life by the Sacred College of Cardinals, is absolute head of state. He appoints a pontifical commission to administer the state's affairs on his behalf and under his direction.

history The pope has traditionally been based in Rome, where the Vatican has been a papal residence since 1377. The Vatican City State came into being through the Lateran Treaty of 1929, under which Italy recognized the sovereignty of the pope over the city of the Vatican. The 1947 Italian constitution reaffirmed the Lateran Treaty, and under its terms, Roman Catholicism became the state religion in Italy, enjoying special privileges. This remained so until under a new 1984 Concordat (ratified 1985) Catholicism ceased to be the state religion.

Vatican Councils Roman Catholic ecumenical councils called by Pope Pius IX 1869 (which met 1870) and by Pope John XXIII 1959 (which met 1962–63). These councils deliberated over major elements of church policy.

Venezuela country in northern South America, on the Caribbean Sea, bounded E by Guyana, S by Brazil, and W by Colombia.

history Venezuela became independent from Spain 1830. After a long history of dictatorial rule, it adopted a new constitution 1961, and three years later Rómulo Betancourt became the first president to serve a full term of office. He was succeeded by Dr Raúl Leoni 1964 and by Dr Rafael Caldera Rodríguez 1969. The latter did much to bring economic and political stability, although underground abductions and assassinations still occurred. In 1974 Carlos Andrés Rodríguez, of the Democratic Action Party (AD), became president, and stability increased. In 1979 Dr Luis Herrera, leader of the Social Christian Party (COPEI), was elected.

austerity policies Against a background of growing economic problems, the 1983 general election resulted in the election of Dr Jaime Lusinchi as president and a win for the Democratic Action Party (AD) in Congress. President Lusinchi's austere economic policies were unpopular, and he tried to conclude a social pact between the government, trade unions, and business. He reached an agreement with the government's creditor bankers for a rescheduling of Venezuela's large public debt. In 1988 Venezuela suspended payment on its foreign debt, which had grown due to a drop in oil prices since the 1970s. In Feb 1989, newly elected president Carlos Andrés Pérez instituted price increases and other austerity measures designed to satisfy loan terms imposed by the International Monetary Fund. Riots followed in which at least 300 people were killed. In May a general strike was declared to protest against the austerity programme. Elections held in Dec were boycotted by the main opposition groups.

Verdun fortress town in NE France on the river Meuse, site of one of the most terrible battles during World War I 21 Feb–16 Dec 1916. The battle was fought between French and German forces for strategic control of Verdun. Despite very high casualties the French withstood the onslaught, although to relieve some of the pressure, the British and French launched a counter-offensive on the ◊Somme. German losses in the battle were some 350,000, and French casualties about 400,000.

Versailles, Treaty of peace treaty after World War I between the Allies and Germany, signed 28 June 1919. It established the League of Nations. Germany surrendered Alsace-Lorraine to France, and large areas in the east to Poland, and made smaller cessions to Czechoslovakia, Lithuania, Belgium, and Denmark. The Rhineland was demilitarized, German rearmament was restricted, and Germany agreed to pay reparations for war damage. The treaty was never ratified by the USA, which made a separate peace with Germany and Austria 1921.

Verwoerd Hendrik (Frensch) 1901–1966. South African right-wing Nationalist Party politician, prime minister 1958–66. As minister of native affairs 1950–58, he was the chief promoter of apartheid legislation (segregation by race). He made the country a republic 1961. He was assassinated in the House of Assembly by a parliamentary messenger, Dimitri Tsafendas.

Vichy government in World War II, the right-wing government of unoccupied France after the country's defeat by the Germans in June 1940, named after the spa town of Vichy, France, where the national assembly was based under Prime Minister Henri Pétain until the liberation 1944. ***Vichy France*** was that part of France not occupied by German troops until Nov 1942. Authoritarian and collaborationist, the Vichy regime cooperated with the Germans even after they had moved to the unoccupied zone in Nov 1942.

Vietcong ('Vietnamese Communists') in the Vietnam War 1954–75, the members of the National Front for the Liberation of South Vietnam, founded 1960, who fought the South Vietnamese and US forces. The name was coined by the South Vietnamese government to differentiate these Communist guerrillas from the Vietminh.

Vietminh the Vietnam Independence League, founded 1941 to oppose the Japanese occupation of Indochina and later directed against the French colonial power. The Vietminh were instrumental in achieving Vietnamese independence through military victory at Dien Bien Phu 1954.

Vietnam country in SE Asia, on the South China Sea, bounded N by China and W by Cambodia and Laos.

history Vietnam was at times nominally subject to China. France conquered Vietnam between 1858–1884, and it joined Cambodia, Laos, and Annam as the French colonial possessions of Indochina. French Indochina was occupied by Japan 1940–45. ◊Ho Chi Minh, who had built up the ◊Vietminh (Independence) League, overthrew the Japanese-supported regime of Bao Dai Sept 1945. French attempts to regain control and restore Bao Dai led to bitter fighting 1946–54, and final defeat of the French at Dien Bien Phu.

Vietnam War At the 1954 Geneva Conference the country was divided along the 17th parallel of latitude into Communist North Vietnam, led by Ho Chi Minh, with its capital at Hanoi, and pro- Western South Vietnam, led by Ngo Dinh Diem (the former premier to Bao Dai), with its capital at Saigon. Within South Vietnam, the Communist guerrilla National Liberation Front, or Vietcong, gained strength, being supplied with military aid by North Vietnam and China.

the Tonkin Gulf incident The USA gave strong backing to the incumbent government in South Vietnam. Following the Aug 1964 Tonkin Gulf incident, where two US destroyers reported that they had been fired on by North Vietnamese torpedo boats, the USA became actively embroiled in the ◊Vietnam War. The years 1964–68 witnessed an escalation in US military involvement to 500,000 troops. From 1969, however, as a result of mounting casualties and domestic opposition, the USA gradually began to withdraw its forces and sue for peace. A ceasefire agreement was negotiated Jan 1973 but was breached by the North Vietnamese, who proceeded to move south, surrounding and capturing Saigon (which was renamed Ho Chi Minh City) April 1975.

socialist republic The Socialist Republic of Vietnam was proclaimed July 1976, and a programme to integrate the south was launched. The new republic encountered considerable problems. The economy was in ruins, two decades of war having claimed the lives of more than two million, maimed four million, left more than half the population homeless and resulted in the destruction of 70% of the country's industrial capacity. In addition, the new Communist administration faced opposition from the intelligentsia and from rural groups, who refused to cooperate in the drive to collectivize southern agriculture. In Dec 1978 Vietnam was at war again, toppling the pro-Chinese Khmer Rouge government in Kampuchea (now Cambodia) led by Pol Pot and installing a puppet administration led by Heng Samrin. A year later, in response to accusations of maltreatment of ethnic Chinese living in Vietnam, China mounted a brief, but largely unsuccessful, punitive invasion of North Vietnam Feb–March 1979. These actions, coupled with the contemporary campaigns against private businesses in the south, induced the flight of about 700,000 Chinese and middle-class Vietnamese from the country 1978–79, often by sea (the 'boat people'). Economic and diplomatic relations with China were severed as Vietnam became closer to the Soviet Union, being admitted into ◊Comecon June 1978.

economic reform Despite considerable economic aid from the Eastern bloc, Vietnam did not reach its planned growth targets 1976–85. This forced policy adjustments, extending incentives and decentralizing decision-taking, 1979 and 1985. Further economic liberalization followed the death of Le Duan (1907–86), effective leader since 1969, and the retirement at the Dec 1986 Communist Party Congress of other prominent 'old guard' leaders, including Prime Minister Pham Van Dong and President Truong Chinh. Under the pragmatic lead of Nguyen Van Linh, a 'renovation' programme was launched. The private marketing of agricultural produce and formation of private businesses were now permitted, agricultural cooperatives were partially dismantled (farmers were given 15-year land leases instead), foreign 'joint venture' inward-investment was encouraged and more than 10,000 political prisoners were released. Economic reform proved most successful in the south. In general, however, the country faced a severe economic crisis from 1988, with inflation, famine conditions in rural areas, and rising urban unemployment inducing a further flight of 'boat people' refugees during 1989–90, predominantly to Hong Kong. In Dec 1989, the British colony of ◊Hong Kong began the forced repatriation of some Vietnamese refugees, many of whom had fled economic conditions in the north. Earlier in the year, Vietnam announced the final withdrawal of its troops from Cambodia. Vietnam ranks as the third-largest communist power in the world, exerting control over Laos and Cambodia (where Vietnamese troops were based until 1990). Border disputes with China and guerrilla resistance in Cambodia force the diversion of a third of the gross national product to defence.

Vietnam War 1954–75. War between communist North Vietnam and US-backed South Vietnam. 200,000 South Vietnamese soldiers, one million North Vietnamese soldiers, and 500,000 civilians were killed. 56,555 US soldiers were killed 1961–75, a fifth of them by their own troops. The war destroyed 50% of the country's forest cover and 20% of agricultural land. Cambodia, a neutral neighbour, was bombed by the US 1969–75, with one million killed or wounded.

Although US forces were never militarily defeated, Vietnam was considered a most humiliating political defeat for the US.

1954 Under the Geneva Convention the former French colony of Indochina was divided into the separate states of North Vietnam and South Vietnam. Within South Vietnam the communist Vietcong, supported by North Vietnam and China, attempted to seize power. The USA provided military aid to the South Vietnamese government.

1964 The Tonkin Gulf Incident.

1967 Several large-scale invasion attempts by North Vietnam were defeated by local and US forces.

1968 My Lai massacre in which US troops killed all the civilian inhabitants of My Lai village.

1969 US bombing incursions into Cambodia began, without endorsement from Congress for this widening of the war.

1973 The unpopularity of the war within the USA led to the start of US withdrawal. A peace treaty was signed between North Vietnam and South Vietnam.

1975 South Vietnam was invaded by North Vietnam in Mar.

1976 South Vietnam was annexed by North Vietnam and the two countries were renamed the Socialist Republic of Vietnam.

Vimy Ridge spur of the ridge of Nôtre Dame de Lorette, 8 km/5 mi NE of Arras, France. A German defensive position, it was taken in World War I by Canadian troops under Gerneral Byng during the battle of Arras, Apr 1917. Its capture helped safeguard Arras and Amiens in the subsequent offensive by the Germans in 1918, at the cost of 11,285 lives.

Vorster Balthazar Johannes 1915–1983. South African Nationalist politician, prime minister 1966–78, and president 1978–79. During his premiership some elements of apartheid were allowed to lapse, and attempts were made to improve relations with the outside world. He resigned the presidency because of a financial scandal.

Vyshinsky Andrei 1883–1954. Soviet politician. As commissar for justice, he acted as prosecutor at Stalin's treason trials 1936–38. He was foreign minister 1949–53 and often represented the USSR at the United Nations.

W

Waldheim Kurt 1918– . Austrian politician and diplomat, president from 1986. He was secretary general of the United Nations 1972–81, having been Austria's representative there 1964–68 and 1970–71. He was elected president of Austria despite revelations that during World War II he had been an intelligence officer in an army unit responsible for transporting Jews to death camps.

Wałesa Lech 1943– . Polish trade-union leader and president of Poland from 1990, founder of ◊Solidarity (Solidarność) in 1980, an organization, independent of the Communist Party, which forced substantial political and economic concessions from the Polish government 1980–81 until being outlawed. Nobel Peace Prize 1983.

Wałesa, as an electrician at the Lenin shipyard at Gdańsk, became a trade-union organizer. A series of strikes led by Wałesa, a devout Catholic, drew wide public support. In Dec 1981 Solidarity was outlawed and Wałesa arrested, following the imposition of martial law by the Polish leader General Jaruzelski. Wałesa was released in 1982.

After leading a further series of strikes during 1988, he negotiated an agreement with the Jaruzelski government in Apr 1989 under the terms of which Solidarity once more became legal and a new, semi-pluralist 'socialist democracy' was established. The coalition government elected in Sept 1989 was dominated by Solidarity.

Waldheim Austrian chancellor Kurt Waldheim, elected in 1986 despite his wartime service with the German army in Yugoslavia. He was secretary general of the United Nations 1972–81.

Wall Street crash a period of postwar economic depression in the USA following an artificial boom 1927–29 fed by speculation, led to panic selling on the New York Stock Exchange. On 24 Oct 1929 13 million shares changed hands, with further heavy selling on 28 Oct and the disposal of 16 million shares on 29 Oct. Many shareholders were ruined, banks and businesses failed, and unemployment rose to approximately 17 million.

The repercussions of the Depression, experienced throughout the USA, were also felt in Europe, worsened by the reduction of US loans. A world economic crisis followed the crash, bringing an era of depression and unemployment.

war communism the first emergency phase of communist policy introduced by the ◊Bolshevik government 1918, to ensure an effective war effort against Germany. Tight controls were imposed on industry and agriculture in an effort to maintain supplies; factories came under government control; workers were directed to where they were needed; and food was rationed. Despite such directives, millions of workers left the towns and industrial areas for the countryside, and production slumped. The revolutionary policy of the socialization of all means of production and the centralized planning of the economy, together with the effects of the civil war and the Allied blockade, led to the virtual collapse of the economic system by 1921. Faced with a severe crisis, the Communist Party adopted the ◊New Economic Policy.

war crime offence (such as murder of a civilian or a prisoner of war) that contravenes the internationally accepted laws governing

Wall Street crash *Bewildered crowds in Wall Street after the stock market crash of 1929.*

the conduct of wars, particularly The Hague Convention 1907 and the Geneva Convention 1949. A key principle of the law relating to such crimes is that obedience to the orders of a superior is no defence.

War crimes became a major issue in the aftermath of World War II. The United Nations War Crimes Commission was set up in 1943 to investigate German atrocities against Allied nationals. Leading Nazis were tried in ◊Nuremberg 1945–46. High-ranking Japanese defendants were tried in Tokyo before the International Military Tribunal, and others by the legal section of the Allied supreme command. In subsequent years the hunt for Nazis who escaped justice has continued, led notably by Simon Wiesenthal (1909–), who tracked down Adolf Eichmann in 1960. Perhaps the last major Nazi war criminal to be brought to justice was Klaus Barbie, tried in France 1987 for crimes committed while he was commandant at Lyons.

war debts the debts owed to the USA by the Allied Powers (including France, Italy, Russia, and the UK) during and immediately after World War I.

Warsaw (Polish ***Warszawa***) capital of Poland, on the river Vistula. It was taken by the Germans 27 Sept 1939, and 250,000 Poles were killed during two months of street fighting that started 1 Aug 1944. It was finally liberated 17 Jan 1945. The old city was virtually destroyed in World War II but has been reconstructed.

Warsaw Pact or ***Eastern European Mutual Assistance Pact*** defensive military alliance established 14 May 1955 between the USSR and E European communist states as a response to the admission of West Germany into NATO.

The Warsaw Pact countries included Albania (until 1968), Bulgaria, Czechoslovakia, East Germany, Hungary, Poland, Romania, and the USSR. Theoretically, the Pact was a treaty of friendship, cooperation, and mutual assistance. In practice, it was designed as a prop for Soviet strategy, to control other members of the alliance.

Warsaw Uprising an unsuccessful attempt by the Polish Home Army to regain control of Warsaw 1 Aug–2 Oct 1944, from the occupying German forces during World War II. Under the command of General Komorowski, the uprising was initially successful. However, the poorly armed Poles could not possibly defeat the Germans without Russian aid: the Poles in Warsaw made no effort to coordinate their actions with the Russians. The Russians under Marshal Rokossovsky gave little assistance: only in mid-September did they drop supplies and mount an attack. Stalin refused to allow British and US planes to land on Soviet airfields in order to relieve Warsaw, although some attempt was made by the Allies to fly in arms and supplies. Many Poles were convinced that the Russians had deliberately refused to intervene so that the eventual communist takeover of Poland would be simpler. The uprising cost the Polish Army about 15,000, in addition to thousands of civilian casualties, to the Germans 10,000 casualties.

Wasp or WASP abbreviation for ***White Anglo-Saxon Protestant***, it usually refers to a middle-class American White Protestant descended from N European settlers. They are often considered to be part of the most dominant, privileged and influential group in US society.

Watergate US political scandal, named after the building in Washington DC that housed the Democrats' campaign headquarters in the 1972 presidential election. Five men, hired by the Republican Committee to Re-elect the President (CREEP), were caught after breaking in to the Watergate with complex electronic surveillance equipment. Over the next two years, investigations by the media and a Senate committee revealed that the White House was implicated in the break-in, and that there was a 'slush fund', used to finance unethical activities. In Aug 1974, President Richard ◊Nixon was forced by the Supreme Court to surrender to Congress tape recordings of conversations he had held with administration officials, and these indicated his complicity in a cover-up. Nixon resigned rather than face virtually certain impeachment for obstruction of justice and other crimes, the only US president to have left office through resignation.

Weimar Republic the constitutional republic in Germany 1919–33, which was crippled by the election of antidemocratic parties to the ◊Reichstag (parliament), and then subverted by the Nazi leader Hitler after his appointment as chancellor in 1933. It took its name from the city where in Feb 1919 a constituent assembly met to draw up a democratic constitution.

Weizmann Chaim 1874–1952. Zionist leader, the first president of Israel (1948–52), and chemist. Born in Russia, he became a naturalized British subject, and as director of the Admiralty laboratories 1916–19 discovered a process for manufacturing acetone, a solvent. He conducted the negotiations leading up to the Balfour Declaration, by which Britain declared its support for an independent Jewish state. He became head of the Hebrew University in Jerusalem, then in 1948 became the first president of the new republic of Israel.

welfare state political system under which the state (rather than the individual or a private sector) has responsibility for the welfare of its citizens. Services such as unemployment and sickness benefits, family allowances and incomes supplements, pensions, medical care, and education may be provided and financed through state insurance schemes and taxation. For example, Germany under Chancellor Otto von Bismarck introduced a national insurance system in the 1880s. In Britain David Lloyd George, as chancellor, introduced a National Insurance Act in 1911. The Labour government 1945–50 (influenced by economist William Beveridge's report of 1942) set up a comprehensive welfare system, including the National Health Service.

Wells H(erbert) G(eorge) 1866–1946. English writer of 'scientific romances' such as *The Time Machine* 1895 and *The War of the Worlds* 1898. His later novels had an anti-establishment, anti-conventional humour remarkable in its day, for example *Kipps* 1905 and *Tono-Bungay* 1909. His many other books include *Outline of History* 1920 and *The Shape of Things to Come* 1933, a number of his prophecies from which have since been fulfilled. He also wrote many short stories.

West Bank area (5,879 sq km/2,270 sq mi) on the W bank of the river Jordan; population (1988) 866,000. The West Bank was taken by the Jordanian army 1948 at the end of the Arab- Israeli war that followed the creation of the state of Israel; and was captured by Israel during the Six Day War 5–10 June 1967. The continuing Israeli occupation and settlement of the area has created tensions with the Arab population.

In 1988 King Hussein announced that Jordan was cutting 'legal and administrative ties' with the West Bank, leaving responsibility for Arabs in the region to the ◊Palestine Liberation Organization (which was already the de facto position).

Western Front battle zone between Germany, and its enemies France and Britain in World War I, extending along lines of trenches from Nieuport on the Belgian coast through Ypres, Arras, Albert, Soissons, Rheims to Verdun, constructed by both Germany and the Allies.

For over three years neither side advanced far from their defensive positions. During the period of trench warfare there were a number of significant changes. Poison gas was used by Germany at Ypres, Belgium in April 1915 and tanks were employed by Britain on the Somme river, in Sept 1916. A German spring offensive in 1918 enabled the troops to reach the Marne river. By summer the Allies were advancing all along the front and the Germans were driven back into Belgium.

West Germany see ◊Germany, West.

West Pakistan a province of ◊Pakistan.

White counter-revolutionary, especially during the Russian civil wars 1917–21. Originally the term described the party opposing the French Revolution, when the royalists used the white lily of the French monarchy as their badge.

Wilhelm II 1859–1941. Emperor of Germany and King of Prussia 1888–1918, the son of Frederick III and Victoria, daughter of Queen Victoria of Britain. In 1890 he forced Chancellor Bismarck to resign and began to direct foreign policy himself, which proved disastrous. He encouraged warlike policies and built up the German navy. In 1914 he first approved Austria's ultimatum to Serbia and then, when he realized war was inevitable, tried in vain to prevent it. In 1918 he fled to Holland, after Germany's defeat and his abdication.

Wilkinson (Cecily) Ellen 1891–1947. Journalist and Labour politician. She was an early member of the Independent Labour Party and an active campaigner for women's suffrage. As a member of Parliament for Jarrow in 1936, she led the ◊Jarrow Crusade, a march of 200 unemployed shipyard workers from Jarrow to London.

Wilson (James) Harold, Baron Wilson of Rievaulx 1916– . British Labour politician, party leader from 1963, prime minister 1964–70 and 1974–76. His premiership was dominated by the issue of UK admission to membership of the European Community, the social contract (unofficial agreement with the trade unions), and economic difficulties.

Wilson, born in Huddersfield, West Yorkshire, was president of the Board of Trade 1947–51 (when he resigned because of social service cuts). In 1963 he succeeded Gaitskell as Labour leader and became prime minister the following year, increasing his majority in 1966. He formed a minority government in Feb 1974 and achieved a majority of three in Oct 1974. He resigned in 1976 and was succeeded by James Callaghan. He was knighted in 1976 and created Baron Wilson of Rievaulx 1983.

Wilson (Thomas) Woodrow 1856–1924. The 28th president of the USA 1913–21, a Democrat. He kept the USA out of World War I until 1917, and in Jan 1918 issued his 'Fourteen Points' as a basis for a just peace settlement. At the peace conference in Paris he secured the inclusion of the ◊League of Nations in individual peace treaties, but these were not ratified by Congress, so the USA did not join the League. Nobel Prize for Peace in 1919.

Wilson *US president Woodrow Wilson, who took the USA into World War I. He created the basis for a peace settlement and the League of Nations.*

Wilson, born in Virginia, became president of Princeton University in 1902. In 1910 he became governor of New Jersey. Elected president in 1912 against Theodore Roosevelt and Taft, he initiated anti-trust legislation and secured valuable social reforms in his progressive 'New Freedom' programme. He strove to keep the USA neutral during World War I but the German U-boat campaign forced him to declare war in 1917. In 1919 he suffered a stroke from which he never fully recovered.

Women's Land Army organization founded 1916 for the recruitment of women to work on farms during World War I. At its peak in Sept 1918 it had 16,000 members. It re-formed June 1939, before the outbreak of World War II. Many 'Land Girls' joined up to help the war effort and by Aug 1943, 87,000 were employed in farm work.

women's movement the campaign for the rights of women, including social, political, and economic equality with men. Early European campaigners of the 17th–19th centuries fought for women's right to own property, to have access to higher education, and to vote (see ◊suffragette). Once women's suffrage was achieved in the 20th century, the emphasis of the movement shifted to the goals of equal social and economic opportunities for women, including employment. A continuing area of concern in industrialized countries is the contradiction between the now generally accepted principle of equality and the demonstrable inequalities that remain between the sexes in state policies and in everyday life.

Pioneer 19th-century feminists, considered radical for their belief in the equality of the sexes, include Mary Wollstonecraft and Emmeline Pankhurst in the UK, and Susan B Anthony and Elizabeth Cady Stanton in the USA.

The women's movement gained worldwide impetus after World War II with such theorists as Simone de Beauvoir, Betty Friedan, Kate Millett, Gloria Steinem, and Germaine Greer, and the founding of the National Organization of Women (NOW) in New York 1966. From the late 1960s the radical and militant wing of the movement argued that women were oppressed by the male-dominated social structure as a whole, which they saw as pervaded by sexism, despite legal concessions towards equality of the sexes.

In the UK since 1975 discrimination against women in employment, education, housing, and provision of goods, facilities, and services to the public has been illegal under the Sex Discrimination and Equal Pay Acts. The economic value of women's unpaid work has been estimated at £2 trillion annually.

1882 Married Women's Property Act gave wives legal control over their own earned income.

1883 Contagious Diseases Acts were repealed.

1885 Age of consent was raised to 16.

1887 National Union of Women's Suffrage Societies became a nationwide group under Millicent Fawcett.

1903 Women's Social and Political Union was founded by Emmeline and Christabel Pankhurst.

1905–10 Militant campaigns split WSPU. Sylvia Pankhurst formed East London Women's Federation.

1918 Parliament (Qualification of Women) Act gave the vote to women householders over 30.

1923 Wives were given equal rights to sue for divorce on the grounds of adultery.

1925 Guardianship of Infants Act gave women equal rights to the guardianship of their children.

1928 The 'Flapper' Vote: all women over 21 were given the vote.

1937 Matrimonial Causes Act gave new grounds for divorce including desertion for three years and cruelty.

1944 Butler Education Act introduced free secondary education for all.

1946 Royal commission on equal pay was formed.

1948 Cambridge University allowed women candidates to be awarded degrees.

1960 Legal aid became available for divorce cases.

1967 Abortion Law Reform Act made abortion legal under medical supervision and within certain criteria.

1969 Divorce reform was introduced that reduced the time a petitioner needed to wait before applying for a divorce.

1973 Matrimonial Causes Act provided legislation to enable financial provision to be granted on divorce.

1975 Sex Discrimination and Equal Pay Acts. National and Scottish Women's Aid Federations were formed.

1976 Domestic Violence and Matrimonial Proceedings Act. Sexual Offences (Amendment) Act attempted to limit a man's defence of consent in rape cases.

1977 Phasing out of employed married women's option to stay partially out of the National Insurance system. Women qualified for their own pensions.

1980 Social Security Act allowed a married woman to claim Supplementary Benefit and Family Income Supplement if she was the main wage earner.

1983 Government forced to amend the 1975 Equal Pay Act to conform to EC directives.

1984 Matrimonial and Family Proceedings Act made it less likely for a woman to be granted maintenance on divorce. It also reduced the number of years a petitioner must wait before applying for a divorce to one year.

1986 Granting of invalid care allowance was successfully challenged in the European Court of Justice. Sex Discrimination Act (Amendment) allowed women to retire at the same age as men, and lifted legal restrictions preventing women from working night shifts in manufacturing industries. Firms with less than five employees were no longer exempt from the act.

1990 Legal limit for abortion reduced to 24 weeks.

1991 Rape within marriage became a prosecution offence within the UK.

women's services the organized military use of women on a large scale, a 20th-century development. First, women replaced men in factories, on farms, and in noncombat tasks during wartime; they are now found in combat units in many countries, including the USA, Cuba, the UK, the USSR, and Israel.

In Britain there are separate corps for all three services: ***Women's Royal Army Corps*** (WRAC) created 1949 to take over the functions of the Auxiliary Territorial Service, established 1938 – its World War I equivalent was the Women's Army Auxiliary Corps (WAAC); ***Women's Royal Naval Service*** (WRNS) 1917–19 and 1939 onwards, allowed in combat roles on surface ships from 1990; and the ***Women's Royal Air Force*** (WRAF) established 1918 but known 1939–48 as the Women's Auxiliary Air Force (WAAF). There are also nursing services: Queen Alexandra's Royal Army Nursing Corps (QARANC) and Naval Nursing Service, and for the RAF Princess Mary's Nursing Service.

Women's Social and Political Union, The (WSPU) British political movement founded 1903 by Emmeline ◊Pankhurst to organize a militant crusade for female suffrage.

In 1909, faced with government indifference, the WSPU embarked on a campaign of window smashing, painting slashing, telephone wire cutting, and arson of public buildings. This civil disobedience had little result and was overtaken by the outbreak of World War I. In Nov 1917, the WSPU became the ***Women's Party*** led by Christabel Pankhurst.

World War I 1914–1918. War between the Central European Powers (Germany, Austria–Hungary, and allies) on one side and the Triple Entente (Britain and the British Empire, France, and Russia) and their allies, including the USA (which entered 1917), on the other side. An estimated 10 million lives were lost and twice that number were wounded.

outbreak On 28 June the heir to the Austrian throne was assassinated in Sarajevo, Serbia; on 28 July Austria declared war on Serbia; as Russia mobilized, Germany declared war on Russia and France, taking a short cut in the west by invading Belgium; on 4 Aug Britain declared war on Germany.

1914 Western Front The German advance reached within a few miles of Paris, but an Allied counter-attack at Marne drove them back to the Aisne River; the opposing lines then settled into trench warfare.

Eastern Front The German commander Hindenburg halted the Russian advance through the Ukraine and across Austria-Hungary at the Battle of Tannenberg in E Prussia.

Africa On 16 Sept all Germany's African colonies were in Allied hands.

Middle East On 1 Nov Turkey entered the war on the side of the Central Powers and soon attacked Russia in the Caucasus Mountains.

1915 Western Front Several offensives on both sides resulted in insignificant gains. At Ypres, Belgium, the Germans used poison gas for the first time.

Eastern Front The German field marshals Mackensen and Hindenburg drove back the Russians and took Poland.

Middle East British attacks against Turkey in Mesopotamia (Iraq), the Dardanelles, and at Gallipoli were all unsuccessful.

Italy declared war on Austria; Bulgaria joined the Central Powers.

war at sea Germany declared all-out U-boat war, but the sinking of the British ocean liner *Lusitania* (with Americans among the 1,198 lost) led to demands that the USA enter the war.

1916 Western Front German attack at Verdun was countered by the Allies on the Somme, where tanks were used for the first time.

Eastern Front Romania joined the Allies but was soon overrun by Germany.

Middle East Kut-al-Imara, Iraq, was taken from the British by the Turks.

war at sea The Battle of Jutland between England and Germany which, although indecisive, put a stop to further German naval participation in the war.

1917 The USA entered the war in Apr. The UK launched the third battle at Ypres and by Nov had taken Passchendaele.

1918 Eastern Front On 3 Mar Soviet Russia signed the Treaty of Brest-Litovsk with Germany, ending Russian participation in the war (the Russian Revolution 1917 led into their civil war 1918–21).

Western Front Germany began a final offensive. In Apr the Allies appointed the French marshal Foch supreme commander, but by June (when the first US troops went into battle) the Allies had lost all gains since 1915, and the Germans were on the Marne. The battle at Amiens marked the launch of the victorious Allied offensive.

Italy At Vittorio Veneto the British and Italians finally defeated the Austrians.

German capitulation began with naval mutinies at Kiel, followed by uprisings in the major cities. Kaiser Wilhelm II abdicated, and on 11 Nov the armistice was signed.

1919 18 June, peace treaty of Versailles. (The USA signed a separate peace accord with Germany and Austria 1921.)

World War II 1939–1945. War between Germany, Italy, and Japan (the Axis powers) on one side, and Britain, the Commonwealth, France, the USA, the USSR, and China (the

***World War II** The liberation of Paris by the Allies in June 1944; General de Gaulle leads jubilant Parisians down the Champs-Elysées.*

Allied powers) on the other. An estimated 55 million lives were lost, 20 million of them citizens of the USSR.

1939 Sept German invasion of Poland; Britain and France declared war on Germany; the USSR invaded Poland; fall of Warsaw (Poland divided between Germany and USSR).

Nov The USSR invaded Finland.

1940 Mar Soviet peace treaty with Finland.

Apr Germany occupied Denmark, Norway, the Netherlands, Belgium, and Luxembourg.

May Germany outflanked the defensive French Maginot Line.

May–June Evacuation of 337,131 Allied troops from Dunkirk, France, across the Channel to England.

June Italy declared war on Britain and France; the Germans entered Paris; the French prime minister Pétain signed an armistice with Germany and moved the seat of government to Vichy.

July–Oct Battle of Britain between British and German air forces.

Sept Japanese invasion of French ◊Indochina.

Oct Abortive Italian invasion of Greece.

1941 Apr Germany occupied Greece and Yugoslavia.

June Germany invaded the USSR; Finland declared war on the USSR.

July The Germans entered Smolensk, USSR.

Dec The Germans within 40 km/25 mi of Moscow, with Leningrad under siege. First Soviet counter-offensive. Japan bombed Pearl Harbor, Hawaii, and declared war on the USA and Britain. Germany and Italy declared war on the USA.

1942 Jan Japanese conquest of the Philippines.

June Naval battle of Midway, the turning point of the Pacific War.

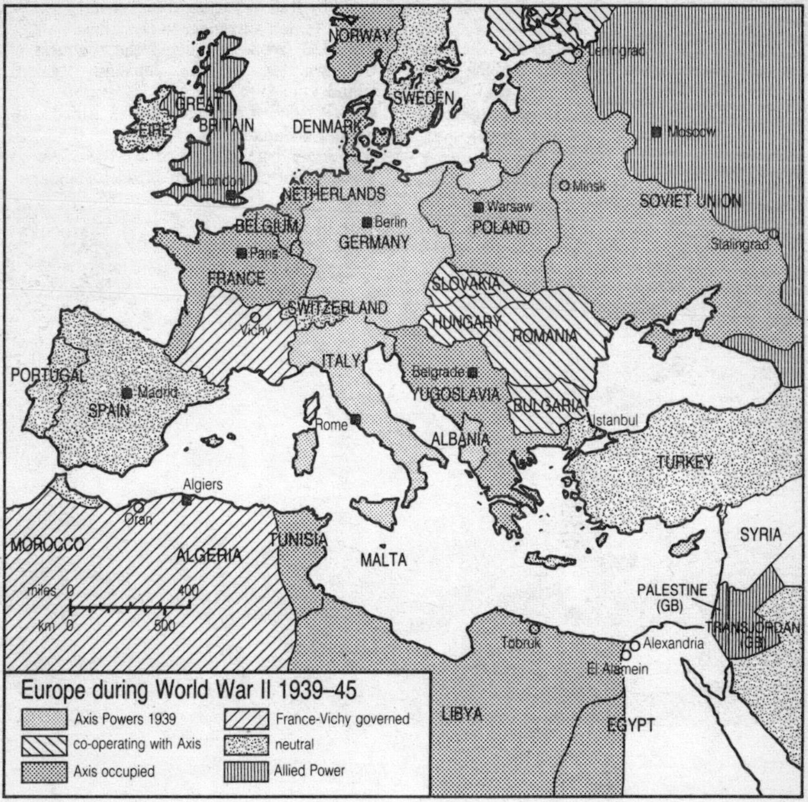

Aug German attack on Stalingrad (now Volgograd), USSR.

Oct–Nov Battle of El Alamein in N Africa, turn of the tide for the Western Allies.

Nov Soviet counter-offensive on Stalingrad.

1943 Jan Casablanca Conference issued Allied demand of unconditional surrender; the Germans retreated from Stalingrad.

Mar The USSR drove the Germans back to the river Donetz.

May End of Axis resistance in N Africa.

July A coup by King Victor Emmanuel and Marshal Badoglio forced Mussolini to resign.

Aug Beginning of campaign against the Japanese in Burma (now Myanmar); US Marines landed on Guadalcanal, Solomon Islands.

Sept Italy surrendered to Allies; Mussolini rescued by Germans who set up Republican Fascist government in northern Italy; Allied landings at Salerno; the USSR retook Smolensk.

Oct Italy declared war on Germany.

Nov US Navy defeated the Japanese in Battle of Guadalcanal.

Nov–Dec Allied leaders met at Tehran Conference.

1944 Jan Allied landing in Nazi-occupied Italy: Battle of Anzio.

Mar End of German U-boat campaign in the Atlantic.

May Fall of Monte Cassino, S Italy.

6 June D-day: Allied landings in Nazi-occupied and heavily defended Normandy.

July Bomb plot of German generals against Hitler failed.

Aug Romania joined Allies.

Sept Battle of Arnhem on the Rhine; Soviet armistice with Finland.

Oct The Yugoslav guerrilla leader Tito and Soviets entered Belgrade.

Dec German counter-offensive, Battle of the Bulge.
1945 Feb The Soviets reached the German border; Yalta conference; Allied bombing campaign over Germany (Dresden destroyed); US reconquest of the Philippines completed; the Americans landed on Iwo Jima, S of Japan.
Apr Hitler committed suicide; Mussolini captured by Italian partisans and shot.
May German surrender to the Allies.
June US troops completed the conquest of Okinawa (one of the Japanese Ryukyu Islands).
July Potsdam Conference issued Allied ultimatum to Japan.
Aug Atom. bombs dropped by the USA on Hiroshima and Nagasaki; Japan surrendered.

Y

Yahya Khan Agha Muhammad 1917–1980. Pakistani president 1969–71. His mishandling of the Bangladesh separatist issue led to civil war, and he was forced to resign.

Yahya Khan fought with the British army in the Middle East during World War II, escaping German capture in Italy. Later, as Pakistan's chief of army general staff, he supported General Ayub Khan's 1958 coup and in 1969 became military ruler. Following defeat by India in 1971, he resigned and was under house arrest 1972–75.

Yalta Conference in 1945, a meeting at which the Allied leaders Winston Churchill (UK), F D Roosevelt (USA), and Josef Stalin (USSR) completed plans for the defeat of Germany in World War II and the foundation of the United Nations. It took place in Yalta, a Soviet holiday resort in the Crimea.

Yeltsin Boris Nikolayevich 1931– . Soviet 'reform' communist politician, president of the Russian Republic from 1990. He was Moscow party chief 1985–87, when he was dismissed after criticizing the slow pace of political and economic reform. He was re-elected in Mar 1989 with a 89% share of the vote, defeating an 'official Communist Party' candidate, and was elected to the Supreme Soviet in May 1989. He supported the Baltic states in their calls for greater independence and has demanded increasingly more radical economic reform.

Yeltsin began his career in the construction industry. He joined the Communist Party of the Soviet Union (CPSU) in 1961 and became district party leader in Sverdlovsk 1976. Brought to Moscow by Mikhail Gorbachev and Nikolai Ryzhkov in 1985, he was appointed secretary for construction and then, in Dec 1985, Moscow party chief.

A blunt-talking, hands-on reformer, Yeltsin was demoted to the post of first deputy chair of the State Construction Committee in Nov 1987. This was seen as a blow to Gorbachev's ◊perestroika initiative and a victory for the conservatives grouped around Yegor Ligachev. In 1990 he renounced his CPSU membership and was elected president of the Russian Republic, the largest republic of the USSR. Having criticized the slow pace of economic reform effected by the Gorbachev–Ryzhkov team and advocated greater autonomy (economic and political sovereignty) for the constituent republics within a federal USSR, Yeltsin prompted the Russian parliament in June 1990 to pass a decree giving the republic's laws precedence over those passed by the Soviet parliament.

Yemen two countries (North Yemen and South Yemen) between which union was agreed 1989. Unification was proclaimed in May 1990, with a 30-month period of implementation. The capital of the new Republic of Yemen will be Sana'i. A democratic system of government is promised; a presidential council will oversee the process of unification; the president is Lt-General Ali Abdullah Saleh.

Yom Kippur War the suprise attack 1973 ***October War*** caused by the Arab advance on Israel; see ◊Arab-Israeli Wars. It is named after the Jewish holiday on which it began, the holiest day of the Jewish year.

Young Plan scheme to reschedule German payments of war reparations in 1929 devised by US entrepreneur Owen D Young, a businessman appointed by President Hoover. It revised the Dawes Plan 1924. The Young Plan reduced German indebtedness by approximately 70% and scheduled its payments over a longer period lasting until 1988. The first instalment was paid in 1930, but the world depression which followed led to President Hoover's moratorium in 1932, and in 1933 Hitler suspended all reparations debts.

Young Turks reformist movement of young army officers in the Ottoman Empire founded 1889. The movement was instrumental in the constitutional changes of 1908 and the abdication of Sultan Abdul-Hamid II 1909. It gained prestige during the Balkan Wars 1912–13 and encouraged Turkish links with the German empire. Its influence diminished after 1918. The term is now used for a member of any radical or rebellious faction within a party or organization.

Ypres (Flemish ***Ieper***) Belgian town in W Flanders, 40 km/25 mi S of Ostend, a site of three major battles 1914–1917 fought in World War I. In Oct–Nov 1914 the Germans launched an assault on British defensive positions and captured the Messines Ridge, but failed to take Ypres. In April–May 1915, the Germans launched a renewed attack using poison gas and chlorine (the first recorded use in war), in an unsuccessful attempt to break the British line. In July–Nov 1917 (known also as ◊Passchendaele), an allied offensive, including British, Canadian, and Australian troops, was launched under British commander-in-chief Douglas Haig, in an attempt to capture ports on the Belgian coast held by Germans. The long and bitter battle, fought in appalling conditions of driving rain and waterlogged ground, achieved an advance of only 8 km/5 mi of territory that was of no strategic significance. The allied attack cost over 300,000 casualties.

Yugoslavia country in SE Europe, on the Adriatic Sea, bounded W by Italy, N by Austria and Hungary, E by Romania and Bulgaria, and S by Greece and Albania.

history Anti-Ottoman uprisings secured Serbia a measure of autonomy from the early 19th century and full independence from 1878, and the new kingdom proceeded to enlarge its territory, at Turkey and Bulgaria's expense, during the Balkan Wars of 1912–13. However, not until the collapse of the Austro-Hungarian empire at the end of World War I were Croatia and Slovenia liberated from foreign control. A new 'Kingdom of the Serbs, Croats and Slovenes' was formed in Dec 1918, with the Serbian Peter Karageorgevic at its helm, to which Montenegro acceded following its people's deposition of its own ruler, King Nicholas.

Peter I died 1921 and was succeeded by his son Alexander, who renamed the country Yugoslavia ('nation of the South Slavs') and established a military dictatorship 1929. He was assassinated Oct 1934. Alexander's young son Peter II succeeded, and a regency under the latter's uncle Paul (1893–1976) was set up that came under increasing influence from Germany and Italy. The regency was briefly overthrown by pro-Allied groups March 1941, precipitating a successful invasion by German troops. Peter II fled, while two guerrilla groups – the pro-royalist, Serbian-based Chetniks, led by General Draza Mihailovič, and the Communist partisans, led by Josip Broz (Marshal ◊Tito) – engaged in resistance activities.

the Yugoslav Federal Republic Tito established a provisional government at liberated Jajce in Bosnia and Herzegovina Nov 1943 and proclaimed the Yugoslav Federal Republic Nov 1945 after the expulsion, with Soviet help, of the remaining German forces. Elections were held, a Communist constitution on the Soviet model was introduced. Tito broke with Stalin 1948 and, with the constitutional law of 1953, adopted a more liberal and decentralized form of communism centred around workers' self-management and the support of private farming. Tito became the dominating force in Yugoslavia and held the newly created post of president from 1953 until his death May 1980.

regional discontent In foreign affairs, the country sought to maintain a balance between East and West and played a leading role in the creation of the ◊nonaligned movement 1961. Domestically, the nation experienced continuing regional discontent, in particular in Croatia where a violent separatist movement gained ground in the 1970s. To deal with these problems, Tito encouraged further decentralization and devolution of power to the constituent republics. A system of collective leadership and the regular rotation of office posts was introduced to prevent the creation of regional cliques. This collective leadership has held power since Tito's death. However, the problems of regionalist unrest have grown worse since 1980, notably in Kosovo and Bosnia, where Albanian and Islamic nationalism respectively are strong.

economic austerity This regionalist discontent has been fanned by a general decline in living standards since 1980, caused by mounting foreign debt, a spiralling inflation rate, which reached 700% in 1989. From 1987 to 1988 the federal government under the leadership of prime minister Branko Mikulic, a Bosnian, instituted a 'market socialist' programme of prices and wages decontrol and the greater encouragement of the private sector and foreign 'inward investment'. The short term consequence of this restructuring programme was a period of increased economic austerity and a rise in the unemployment rate to 15%. Following a wave of strikes and mounting internal disorder, Mikulic was replaced as prime minister in Jan 1989 by Ante Marković, a reformist Croatian. The unity of the ruling Communist party began to crumble between 1988 and 1990 as both personal and ideologically based feuds developed between the leaders of its republican branches.

Serbian autonomy threatened In the republic of Serbia a new multi-party constitution was approved July 1990 and came into force Sept. It effectively stripped Kosovo and Vojvodina of their autonomy. In late July the Serbian Assembly voted to dissolve the Kosovo Assembly. The Albanians of Kosovo reacted defiantly by calling a general strike on 3 Sept and by convening an underground parliament that proclaimed a new, unrecognized, constitution for the autonomous province. In multi-party elections held in Serbia in Dec, Slobodan Milosević was elected president and his Serbian Socialist Party achieved an assembly majority. In July 1990 the Slovenian Assembly issued a proclamation of full republican sovereignty and in Sept moved towards confrontation with the federal army by proclaiming control of its own defence.

Croatian assertion of autonomy In Croatia, ethnic tension between the majority Croat and minority Serb populations increased following the election April–May 1990 of a right-wing Croat nationalist government led by Franje Tudman. The new republic assembly approved constitutional changes that removed the word 'socialist' from its official title, and entailed assertion of regional autonomy. Fearing a resurgence of the ethnic persecution that had characterized the years of Croat extremist administration following World War II, Serbian community leaders organized the holding, in Aug, of unofficial referenda on the issue of cultural autonomy. In the same month there was an anti-Croat uprising in the Serb-dominated town of Knin. In Bosnia-Herzegovina there was mounting Muslim versus Serb inter-ethnic violence.

Concerned at the rising tide of ethnic conflict and political disintegration, Prime Minister Marković founded the Alliance of Reform Forces in July 1990 with the aim of preserving Yugoslav unity within a pluralist federation.

Z

zaibatsu Japanese 'financial clique', industrial conglomerate.

The old, family-owned Japanese *zaibatsu* had been involved in the military build up preceding World War II, and were in 1945, after the country's defeat, broken up by the authorities of the US occupation. Similar conglomerates soon formed in the course of Japan's industrial revival. By the late 1980s there were six *zaibatsu* with 650-member companies between them, employing 6% of the country's workforce and controlling more than 2% of the world economy.

Zaïre country in central Africa.

history Leopold II of Belgium established the Congo Free State under his personal rule 1885. Local resistance was suppressed, and the inhabitants were exploited. When the atrocious treatment of local labour was made public, Belgium annexed the country as a colony, the Belgian Congo, 1908. and conditions were marginally improved.

independence Zaïre was given full independence in June 1960 as the Republic of the Congo. The new state was intended to be governed centrally from Leopoldville by President Joseph Kasavubu and Prime Minister Patrice Lumumba, but Moise Tshombe immediately declared the rich mining province of Katanga independent under his leadership. a period of political instability and civil war followed 1960–65, during which United Nations forces intervened in 1961 and 1964.

the 'second republic' The army, under Mobutu, established a 'second republic' in Nov 1965. A new constitution was adopted 1967, Tshombe died in captivity 1969, and 1970 Mobutu was elected president. The following year the country became the Republic of Zaïre, and 1972 the Popular Movement of the Revolution (MPR) was declared the only legal political party.

political stability Mobutu, re-elected 1977, carried out a large number of political and constitutional reforms. He gradually improved the structure of public administration and brought stability to what had once seemed an ungovernable country, although he faced two revolts in Katanga province. The first in March 1977 was put down with the support of Moroccan forces airlifted to Zaïre by France. The second in May 1978 was repulsed by French and Belgian paratroopers. both invasions were instigated by the Congolese National Liberation Front, operating from bases in Angola. However, the harshness of some of his policies brought international condemnation and 1983 he offered amnesty to all political exiles. Marshal Mobutu was re-elected 1984 for a third term. Towards the end of 1988 a potentially dangerous, and not fully explained rift with Belgium was narrowly averted. In Jan 1991, 19 political parties were approved to fight the 1992 multi-party elections.

Zambia landlocked country in central Africa.

history As Northern Rhodesia the country became a British protectorate 1924, together with the former kingdom of Barotseland (now Western Province), taken under British protection at the request of its ruler 1890. From 1953 the country, with Southern Rhodesia (now Zimbabwe) and Nyasaland (now Malawi), was part of the Federation of Rhodesia and Nyasaland, dissolved 1963. Northern Rhodesia became an independent republic 1964, within the Commonwealth, with Dr Kenneth Kaunda leader of the United Indepence Party (UNIP), as its first president. Between 1964 and 1972, when it was declared a one-party state, Zambia was troubled with frequent outbreaks of violence because of disputes within the governing party and conflicts between the country's more than 70 tribes.

Zambia was economically dependent on neighbouring white-ruled Rhodesia but tolerated liberation groups operating on the border, and relations between the two countries deteriorated. The border was closed 1973, and 1976 Kaunda declared his support for the Patriotic Front, led by Robert Mugabe and Joshua Nkomo, which was fighting the white regime in Rhodesia. In 1980 there was an unsuccessful coup against the president, allegedly promoted by South Africa. Despite his imposition of strict economic policies, Kaunda was re-elected 1983. In 1985 he was appointed to succeed President Nyerere of Tanzania as chair of the Black African Front Line States. In Oct 1988 he was re-elected, unopposed, for a sixth consecutive term. In Sept 1990 President Kaunda announced that, without a referendum, a multi-party system would be introduced by Oct 1991.

Zanzibar island region of Tanzania, area 1,658 sq km/640 sq mi.
history Settled by Arab traders in the 7th century, it became a sultanate. Britain and Germany divided Zanzibar's mainland territories between them and, under the Treaty of Zanzibar 1890, it came under British protection until 1963. In Dec 1963 it became an independent member of the Commonwealth. In Jan 1964 the last sultan was exiled and a republic proclaimed. It merged with Tanganyika as Tanzania Apr 1964.

Zhao Ziyang 1918–. Chinese politician, prime minister from 1980, and secretary of the Chinese Communist Party (CCP) 1987–89. His reforms included self-management and incentives for workers and factories. He lost his secretaryship and other posts after the ◊Tiananmen Square massacre in Beijing June 1989.

Zhao, son of a wealthy landlord from Henan province, joined the Communist Youth League 1932 and worked underground as a CCP official during the liberation war 1937–49. He rose to prominence in the party in Guangdong from 1951. As a supporter of the reforms of Liu Shaoqi, he was dismissed during the 1966–69 ◊Cultural Revolution, paraded through Canton in a dunce's cap, and sent to Inner Mongolia.

He was rehabilitated by Zhou Enlai 1973 and sent to China's largest province, Sichuan, as first party secretary 1975. Here he introduced radical and successful market-oriented rural reforms. Deng Xiaoping had him inducted into the Politburo 1977. After six months as vice premier, Zhao was appointed prime minister 1980 and assumed, in addition, the post of CCP general secretary Jan 1987. His economic reforms were criticized for causing inflation, and his liberal views of the pro-democracy demonstrations that culminated in the student occupation of Tiananmen Square led to his downfall.

Zhou Enlai or ***Chou En-lai*** 1898–1976. Chinese politician. Zhou, a member of the Chinese Communist Party (CCP) from the 1920s, was prime minister 1949–76 and foreign minister 1949–58. He was a moderate Maoist and weathered the Cultural Revolution. He played a key role in foreign affairs.

Born into a declining mandarin gentry family near Shanghai, Zhou studied in Japan and Paris, where he became a founder member of the overseas branch of the CCP. He adhered to the Moscow line of urban-based revolution in China, organizing communist cells in Shanghai and an abortive uprising in Nanchang 1927. In 1935 Zhou supported the election of Mao Zedong as CCP leader and remained a loyal ally during the next 40 years. He served as liaison officer 1937–46 between the CCP and Chiang Kai-shek's nationalist Guomindang government. In 1949 he became prime minister, an office he held until his death Jan 1976.

Zhou, a moderator between the opposing camps of Liu Shaoqi and Mao Zedong, restored orderly progress after the ◊Great Leap Forward (1958–60) and the ◊Cultural Revolution (1966–69), and was the architect of the Four Modernizations programme in 1975. Abroad, Zhou sought to foster Third World unity at the Bandung Conference 1955, averted an outright border confrontation with the USSR by negotiation with Prime Minister Alexei Kosygin 1969, and was the principal advocate of détente with the USA during the early 1970s.

Zhukov Georgi Konstantinovich 1896–1974. Marshal of the USSR in World War II and minister of defence 1955–57. As chief of staff from 1941, he defended Moscow 1941, counterattacked at Stalingrad in 1942, organized the relief of Leningrad 1943, and led the offensive from the Ukraine Mar 1944 which ended in the fall of Berlin. He subsequently commanded the Soviet occupation forces in Germany.

Zhukov joined the Bolsheviks and the Red Army 1918 and led a cavalry regiment in the Civil War 1918–20. His army defeated the Japanese forces in Mongolia 1939. At the end of World War II, he headed the Allied delegation that received the German surrender. Under the Khrushchev regime he was denounced 1957 for obstructing party work and encouraging a Zhukov cult, but was restored 1965.

Zimbabwe landlocked country in central Africa.
history Mashonaland and Matabeleland, together with what is now Zambia, were granted to the British South Africa Company 1889, and the whole was named Rhodesia 1895 in honour of Cecil Rhodes. King Lobengula of Matabeleland accepted British protection 1888 but rebelled 1893; he was defeated, but 1896 after the Jameson Raid in the Transvaal by British troops seeking to overthrow the Boer government, Matabele once more unsuccessfully tried to regain their independence. The portion of the area south of the Zambezi River, then known as Southern Rhodesia, became self-governing 1923 and a member of the Federation of Rhodesia and Nyasaland 1953.

African nationalists were campaigning for full democracy, and the African National Congress (ANC), which had been present since 1934, was reconvened 1957 under the leadership of Joshua Nkomo. It was banned 1959, and Nkomo went into exile to become leader of the National Democratic Party (NDP), which had been formed by some ANC members. When the NDP was banned, 1961, Nkomo created the Zimbabwe African People's Union (ZAPU); this was banned 1962. In 1963 a splinter group developed from ZAPU, the Zimbabwe African National Union (ZANU), led by the Rev Ndabaningi Sithole, with Robert Mugabe as its secretary general.

unilateral declaration of independence After the dissolution of the Federation of Rhodesia and Nyasaland 1963 the leader of the Rhodesian Front party (RF), Winston Field, became the first prime minister of Rhodesia. The RF was a group of white politicians committed to maintaining racial segregation. In Apr 1964 Field resigned and was replaced by Ian ◊Smith, who rejected terms for independence proposed by Britain that required clear progress towards majority rule. Four months later ZANU was banned, and Nkomo and Mugabe imprisoned. In Nov 1965, after further British attempts to negotiate a formula for independence, Smith annulled the 1961 constitution and unilaterally announced Rhodesia's independence. Britain broke off diplomatic and trading links and the United Nations initiated economic sanctions, but these were bypassed by many multinational companies.

In 1969 Rhodesia declared itself a republic and adopted a new constitution, with white majority representation in a two-chamber legislature. Armed South African police at times supported the Smith regime against ZAPU and ZANU guerrillas. A conference in Geneva 1975 was attended by deputations from the British government, the Smith regime, and the African nationalists, represented by Bishop Abel Muzorewa, president of the African National Council, which had been formed 1971 to oppose the earlier independence arrangements, and Robert Mugabe and Joshua Nkomo, who had been released from detention and had jointly formed the Patriotic Front.

At the beginning of 1979 Smith produced a new 'majority rule' constitution, which contained an inbuilt protection for the white minority but which he had managed to get Muzorewa to accept. In June 1979 Bishop Muzorewa was pronounced prime minister of what was to be called Zimbabwe Rhodesia. The new constitution was denounced by Mugabe and Nkomo as another attempt by Smith to perpetuate the white domination, and they continued to lead the Zimbabwe African National Liberation Army from bases in neighbouring Mozambique.

In Aug 1979 the new British prime minister, Margaret ◊Thatcher, under the influence of her foreign secretary, Lord Carrington, and President Kenneth Kaunda of Zambia, agreed to the holding of a constitutional conference in London at which all shades of political opinion in Rhodesia would be represented. The conference, in Sept 1979, resulted in what became known as the Lancaster House Agreement and paved the way for full independence. A member of the British cabinet, Lord Christopher Soames, was sent to Rhodesia as governor-general to arrange a timetable for independence. Economic and trade sanctions were lifted. A small Commonwealth Monitoring Force supervised the disarming of the thousands of guerrilla fighters who brought their weapons and ammunition from all parts of the country.

independence A new constitution was adopted, and elections were held under independent supervision, in Feb 1980. They resulted in a decisive win for Robert Mugabe's ZANU-PF party. The new state of Zimbabwe became fully independent in April 1980, with the Rev Canaan Banana as president and Robert Mugabe as prime minister. During the next few years a rift developed between Mugabe and Nkomo and between ZANU-PF and ZAPU supporters. Nkomo was accused of trying to undermine Mugabe's administration and was dismissed from the cabinet. Fearing for his safety, he spent some months in the UK. ZAPU was opposed to the 1984 proposal by ZANU-PF for the eventual creation of a one-party Socialist state.

Mugabe's party increased its majority in the 1985 elections and early in 1986 he announced that the separate seats for the whites in the Assembly would be abolished within a year. Relations between the two parties and the two leaders eventually improved and by 1986 discussions of a merger were under way. In Dec 1989 a draft constitution was created that renounced Marxism-Leninism as the state ideology and created a one-party state, fusing the governing party and opposition groups. A new opposition group headed by Edgar Tekere, was launched earlier in the year, with the intention to challenge the ZANU-PF in 1990 elections. Tekere announced that his Zimbabwe Unity movement would advocate capitalism and multiparty democracy.

Zinoviev 1883–1936. Russian politician. A prominent Bolshevik, he returned to Russia in 1917 with Lenin and played a leading part in the Russian Revolution. As head of the Communist International 1919 (a coordinating body established by labour and socialist organizations), his name was attached to a forgery, the ***Zinoviev letter***, inciting Britain's communists to rise, which helped to topple the Labour government in 1924. As one of the 'Old Bolsheviks', he was seen by Stalin as a threat. He was accused of complicity in the murder of the Bolshevik leader Sergei Kirov 1934, and shot.

Zionism a Jewish political movement for the establishment of Jewish homeland in Palestine, the 'promised land' of the Bible, with its capital Jerusalem, the 'city of Zion'.

1896 As a response to European ◊anti-Semitism, Theodor Herzl published his *Jewish State*, outlining a scheme for setting up an autonomous Jewish commonwealth under Ottoman Turkish suzerainty.

1897 The World Zionist Congress was established in Basel, Switzerland, with Herzl as its first president.

1917 The ◊Balfour Declaration was secured from Britain by Chaim Weizmann. It promised the Jews a homeland in Palestine.

1940–48 Jewish settlement in the British mandate of Palestine led to armed conflict between militant Zionists and both Palestinian Arabs and the British.

1947 In Nov the United Nations divided Palestine into Jewish and Arab states, with Jerusalem as an international city.

1948 The Jews in Palestine proclaimed the state of Israel on 14 May, but the Arab states rejected both the partition of Palestine and the existence of Israel. The armies of Iraq, Syria, Lebanon, Trans-Jordan, Saudi Arabia, Yemen, and Egypt attacked Israel but were defeated.

1975 The General Assembly of the UN condemned Zionism as 'a form of racism and racial discrimination'; among those voting against the resolution were the USA and the members of the European Community.

1982 ◊PLO base in Lebanon was destroyed by Israeli invasion.

THE HUTCHINSON PAPERBACK ENCYCLOPEDIA

With more than 17,000 entries and over 750 tables, charts, maps and diagrams, of *The Hutchinson Paperback Encyclopedia* is the most comprehensive, up-to-date, and easy-to-use paperback encyclopedia on the market. With 50% more entries and double the number of illustrations of its nearest competitor, it is also unrivalled value for money. Derived from the authoritative *Hutchinson Encyclopedia* database, it is ideal for school and college students.

THE HUTCHINSON PAPERBACK DICTIONARY OF BIOGRAPHY

The most famous and infamous names in history, sport, the arts, current affairs and science are covered in this remarkably comprehensive dictionary. Here are Arafat and Aristotle; Beethoven, Botham, and Bush; Winston Churchill, John Cleese and Marie Curie; Angela Davis, Bette Davis, and Miles Davis; Henry VIII and Vaclav Havel; Christine Keeler and Colonel Khaddhafi; Stephen Spielberg and Alan Sugar; Lech Walesa, Oscar Wilde, and thousands more. Up to date and authoritative, this compact volume is also illustrated with over 250 photographs.